Much is Taken,
Much Remains

Much is Taken, Much Remains

Canadian Issues in Environmental Conservation

by

Rorke Bryan

Department of Geography
University of Alberta

Duxbury Press
North Scituate, Mass.

Duxbury Press
A Division of Wadsworth Publishing Company, Inc.

ISBN-087872-042-1
L. C. Cat. Card No. 72-85270
Printed in the United States of America

1 2 3 4 5 6 7 8 9 10---76 75 74 73

Dedication:
To Karin and Feargus who, with their
generation, will inherit our mistakes.

Contents

Preface   xiii
List of Figures   xv
List of Plates   xvii

Part 1
INTRODUCTION

1. The Canadian Environment   3

Part 2
POLLUTION AND DEVELOPMENT
IN THE CANADIAN ENVIRONMENT

2. A Theoretical Approach to Pollution   19

Definitions of Pollution   19
Approaches to Pollution Control   20
    Dilution   20
    Control of growth   22
    Unacceptability of the dilution approach   24
    Recycling   25
Pollution Issues in Canada   26

3. Sewage and Its Effects on Waterways   27

The Effects of Sewage Pollution   27
    Pathogenic contamination   27
    Organic pollution   28
    Eutrophication   29

Sewage Treatment   32
Sewage Systems   34
Financing Sewage Treatment   35

4. **Industrial Water Pollution**   37

The Pulp and Paper Industry   38
Pulping technology   39
Effluents and pollution   41
Pollution control   43
Mercury Contamination   45
Forms and health effects   45
History of mercury contamination   46
Mercury uses and sources in Canada   49
Mercury contamination in Canada   50
Effects of mercury contamination   54
  Public health   54
  Economic repercussions   56
Conclusion   56

5. **Insecticides**   61

Insecticides   63
Organochlorine insecticides   63
  Organochlorine residues   64
    Residues in soils, air, and water   64
    Residues in plants   65
    Residues and their effects on fish and other wildlife   66
    Residues and their effects on human beings   67
    The future of organochlorine insecticides   73
    Government action   74
Organophosphorus insecticides   76
Carbamate insecticides   78
Alternative methods of insect control   79
Herbicides   80
Herbicide classification   80
Herbicide use   81
Environmental effects of herbicide use   82
Conclusion   85

6. **Oil Pollution and Arctic Development**   93

Oil Pollution in Canada   93
Arctic Oil Discoveries   95
Environmental effects of oil exploration   96
Environmental effects of drilling and oil well operation   98

Transportation of oil from the Arctic 99
 Surface tankers 99
 Submarine tankers 105
 Pipelines 106
Arctic Development 111
Conclusion to Part Two 113

Part 3
TRANSFER AND EXPORT
OF CANADIAN WATER

7. **Water Transfer and the Canadian Water Resource** 121

The Canadian Water Resource 123
 Canadian river basins 123
 Measurement of streamflow 125
 Estimation of streamflow 126
 The available water resource 126
 Canadian water use 127
Water Transfer within Canada 128
 The PRIME project 129
 The Saskatchewan-Nelson Basin Board 131
Potential Benefits of Water Transfer in Canada 132
 Irrigation 132
 Pollution abatement 134
 Additional benefits 134

8. **Water Supply in the United States** 137

Water Demand for Irrigation 138
 Salinization 139
 Future requirements 140
 Increasing efficiency of irrigation water use 140
General Water Demand in Deficit Areas 141
 Water demand in the southwestern states 142
 Potential sources of water supply for southern California 144
  Water diversion and supply within California 144
  Water sources outside California 145
Alternative Means of Water Supply Supplementation 145
 Cloud Seeding 146
 Desalination 146
Cost of Water Supplies 146
Government Policy and Growth in Water Demand 148

9. Proposals for Water Export from Canada   151

The North American Water and Power Alliance   152
The Kuiper Diversion Scheme   158
The Central North America Water Project   160
The Western States Water Augmentation Concept   162
The Magnum Diversion Scheme   164
The GRAND Canal   165
Other Proposals   167

10. Potential Effects of Water Export in Canada   169

Financial and Political Effects   170
Ecological Effects   172
Flooding of wildlife habitats   172
Reduction in streamflow   173
Drying of marshes and lakes   175
Creation of lakes of fluctuating level   179
Economic and Social Effects   189
Conclusion fo Part Three   181

Part 4
THE STATUS AND CONSERVATION
OF WILDLIFE IN CANADA

11. The Use of Wildlife in Canada   187

Attitudes Toward Wildlife   187
Wildlife as a Resource   189
Use of the Wildlife Resource   191
Wildlife as a primary food source   191
The fur trade   193
Historical development   193
The role of the beaver   195
Fur conservation   196
Recreational hunting of wildlife   199
Nonconsumptive uses of wildlife   203

12. The Decline of Wildlife in Canada   206

The Effect of Hunting Pressure   206
Reduction of Habitat   209
Predator Control   212

13. Some Threatened Species in Canada and Their Conservation   217

The Barren-Ground Caribou   218

The Polar Bear 220
The Musk-Ox 224
The Grizzly Bear 228
Wildlife Management and Conservation 232
The legal background 233
Administrative structure 234
Research on Wildlife 235
Conclusion to Part Four 235

Part 5
NATIONAL PARKS IN CANADA

14. **The Origins and Development of the National Park System** 243

The National Park Concept 243
The Development of National Parks in Canada 247
Development of a Canadian National Park Policy 251

15. **Problems and Conflicts in the National Parks** 258

Visitation to National Parks 258
The Impact of Increasing Visitation on Roads and Accommodation 263
The Impact of Visitor Activity in National Parks 266
Visitors and Park Wildlife 268
Wildlife Management in National Parks 271
Leases and Concessions in National Parks 273

16. **Toward a Comprehensive Canadian National Park System** 276

Inadequate Area 277
Restriction of entry to national parks 278
Uneven use of park areas 279
Incompatibility of Park Functions 281
Attempts to Reconcile Activities in National Parks 282
Provisional master plans 282
A diversified national park system 286
Wilderness parks 287
Recreation parks 289
Inventory for Park Development 292
Conclusion to Part Five 293

Part 6
CONCLUSION

17. **Conclusion** 297

Preface

Only a rash man would set himself up as an expert on all aspects of the environment crisis. Certainly I do not claim to be fully conversant with all aspects of environmental degradation, even in this country, and I therefore make no apology for limiting the range of topics discussed in this book. I believe that all the issues examined are important, but undoubtedly many which are just as critical have been omitted. The issues and principles discussed do provide a reasonable cross-section of the types of environmental problems which Canadians now face.

Many books dealing with environmental conservation have recently appeared in North America, but the emphasis in this book is slightly different, as it does not deal exclusively or almost exclusively with pollution. In Canada, as in the rest of the world, pollution is an extremely serious problem, and about one third of the book is devoted to some aspects of pollution. Indeed, pollution may well threaten the future of human life, and under these circumstances I have considerable faith in the determination of the human race to survive and to put its house in order.

I have rather less faith in the character of our brave new pollution-free world. Will it be a world encased in concrete in which wild things have no place? Will it be a world in which all rivers are dammed, diverted, and piped to serve the purposes of man? Will it be a world devoid of wildlife because we were not sufficiently interested and prescient to make a place for wildlife in our society? If this is the world for which we must defeat pollution, perhaps the goal is not worth the effort. I certainly want no part of a world in which poisoning of the body is replaced by poisoning of the spirit. To me the forms of environmental degradation and change which produce such a world are as serious and pervasive as environmental pollution.

Conservation has come to mean many things since the beginning of the twentieth century, when it first became identified with the environment through the influence of men such as Gifford Pinchot, Teddy Roosevelt, and John Muir. A society that practises environmental conservation is one that makes a conscious effort to manage its environment so that it will remain habitable and desirable for as long as man survives. It is not a wilderness preserve in which resources remain untouched, but it is a society in which some areas are preserved. Essentially it is a carefully planned and managed society in which space has been allowed for the needs and activities of all people and species. Above all it is a society which has seen itself in perspective in the pattern of human existence and which has planned not just for the present generation but for future generations as well.

Canada is a good place about which to write a book on environmental problems, for the environment is still basically intact. The country has a comprehensive range of problems but vast areas have still hardly been touched. Some species of wildlife have been extinguished, but many remain. We have civilised and urbanised much of our land, but at least our last wilderness was not lumbered before the birth of Christ, as in England. Although much is taken, there is still much to save, and we have the knowledge, the ability, and the financial resources to save it. If we can overcome the environmental problems in Canada, perhaps some of our remedies can be applied to other countries. If we cannot surmount our problems, then I feel that there is little hope for the maintenance of environmental quality in less well endowed lands.

Many people directly or indirectly helped write this book. I am grateful to all these people, who are too numerous to name individually. I am particularly grateful to Dr. Ken Hare, of the University of Toronto; Dr. Andrew Macpherson, of the Canadian Wildlife Service; and to my colleague Dr. Arleigh Laycock all of whom commented constructively on the manuscript or contributed useful ideas. Any errors of fact or opinion are, however, my sole responsibility.

Permission for the use of photographs and figures is gratefully acknowledged, and the assistance of the Oxford University Press in granting permission to quote from the work of Aldo Leopold is also acknowledged.

The book could not have been written without the assistance of the highly competent technical staff of the Department of Geography at the University of Alberta. Geoff Lester designed and drafted the maps and figures with the help of Stephanie Kucharyshyn and Inge Huemmert. Jack Chesterman and Arne Breitkreuz carried out the photographic reproduction. Joan McLeod, Judi Senio, Kathy Harrish, and Irene Huk cooperated in typing the manuscript. I am grateful to all these people.

Finally, I would like to thank my wife, Ingrid, for her constant encouragement and assistance, without which the book would not have been written.

List of Figures

4.1.   Major industrial sources of mercury.

5.1.   Herbicide treatment in Manitoba, Saskatchewan, Alberta and British Columbia.

5.2.   2,4-D and MCPA use in Alberta.

6.1.   Voyages of the *S.S. Manhattan* in the Canadian Arctic, 1969 and 1970.

6.2.   Proposed pipeline routes from Alaska and the Canadian Arctic.

7.1.   Major drainage basins of Canada.

7.2.   Water management proposals for Alberta made under the Prairie Rivers Improvement and Management Evaluation.

7.3.   Water management proposals for the Prairie Provinces made by the Saskatchewan-Nelson Basin Board.

8.1.   Major existing and proposed water management projects in the south-western United States.

9.1.   Water management projects proposed by the North American Water and Power Alliance.

9.2.   Water management and diversion proposals in the Kuiper scheme.

9.3.   Water management and diversion proposals in the Central North America Water Project.

9.4.   Water management and diversion proposals in the Western States Water Augumentation Concept.

9.5.   Water management and diversion proposals in the Magnum scheme.

9.6.   Water management and diversion proposals in the G.R.A.N.D. Canal scheme.

10.1.   The Peace-Athabasca Delta, Northern Alberta.

10.2.   Seasonal flow reversal in the outlet channels of the Peace-Athabasca Delta.

11.1.   Selected fur trading posts and the location of Rupert's Land in 1859.

11.2.   Fluctuations in beaver and muskrat returns of the Hudson's Bay Company.

11.3.   Relative values of annual pelt production for leading fur producers.

11.4. Annual values of hunting and angling license sales.

12.1. Payments under the wolf and bear bounty schemes in Nova Scotia and Ontario.

13.1. Ranges of the Barren Ground Caribou.

13.2. Distribution and major denning areas of Polar Bears.

13.3. Range areas of Muskoxen.

13.4. Changes in the range areas of Grizzly Bears.

14.1. Existing and proposed national parks in Canada.

15.1. Visitation to Canadian national parks, I.

15.2. Visitation to Canadian national parks, II.

16.1. Provisional master plan for kootenay National Park.

List of Plates

I.   Waterton Lakes National Park.

II.   Imperial Oil rig at Atkinson Point, Northwest Territories.

III.   W.A.C. Bennett Dam and Lake Willesden, British Columbia.

IV.   Polar Bear.

V.   Cameron Lake, Waterton Lakes National Park.

Part 1

Introduction

Chapter 1

The Canadian
Environment

The human environment may appear to be a concise, easily comprehended concept, but anyone who has studied environmental problems will
know that in reality the environment is both complex and nebulous. Its elusive
quality caused one delegate to the United Nations Conference on the Human
Environment in Stockholm to describe attempts to define it as "like trying to
swim in tapioca."[1] Avoiding for the moment the pitfalls of rigorous definition, for practical purposes the environment can be regarded as the complex
blend of physical, biological, and human elements which interweave to form a
backdrop for our lives.

The environment affects us physically and mentally and can strongly
influence our behaviour patterns. In turn, our reactions to the environment can
alter it, so that its character depends on our environmental perception. In this
sense it is incorrect to speak of one human environment, for actually each
person creates a separate environment. The individual's perceived environment
may closely approximate the actual physical, biological, or social situation or
it may be widely removed. The size of this perceptual gap can be of great practical importance, because action on environmental problems is initiated by
response to the perceived environment rather than by actuality. Gilbert White
has said, "At the heart of managing a natural resource is the manager's per-

ception of that resource and the alternatives open to him in dealing with it."
[2] Development of this tenet indicates that all action in response to environmental problems is bounded by constraints. Some of these constraints are physical realities: is it physically possible to control the leakage of oil from a
sunken tanker or to construct a pipeline across permafrost that will not cause
severe erosion? Others are social: it is technically possible for every community
in Canada to have a tertiary system of sewage treatment, but to finance this
would cause an unacceptable reduction of other services, such as schools, hos-
pitals, and social assistance. Control of severe river pollution by pulp mill
effluent might require closure of the mill, but this action could be restricted
by the unemployment, labour troubles, and social unrest which could result.
Most countries are also affected by political or international constraints: how
will a given environmental action affect one nation's relations with another? If
Canada should extend her territorial waters to two hundred miles from the
Canadian coast the shipping and fishing fleets of many countries would be affected; how would these countries react, and what retaliatory measures might
be attempted? If Canada places a national boycott on Atlantic salmon caught
by Danish fishermen, could Denmark respond by forbidding flight over Greenland by Canadian airliners?

These few examples indicate the complexity of the actual constraints
which limit environmental action. To these must be added an almost infinite
range of perceptual constraints that depend on imponderables such as human
emotions and communication difficulties. It does not matter whether or not
Denmark would forbid flight over Greenland; if Canadian authorities believe
that Denmark would, this belief rather than the actual situation will influence
action.

Decisions on environmental policies are partly the product of
perceived problems, but how is individual perception translated into communal
action? A rigorous examination of decision-making processes is beyond the
scope of this book, but some of the problems can be suggested. In a democracy
policy decisions and actions should reflect the opinions and desires of the
majority of the population. In the past, however, environmental matters have
not been of sufficient public interest to be included in political platforms, and
the individual has had little opportunity to express preferences on environmental policies. This seems to be changing in Canada and elsewhere, but the
electoral system will never be able to encompass more than a broad review of
environmental policies. In the absence of electoral direction, how is an environmental minister to chart a policy? The finance minister can normally
assume that the majority of the population will be in favour of such measures
as reduction of income tax, but the environmental minister can assume no such
uniformity of opinion; everyone's concept of the ideal environment is unique.

In the absence of referenda, public preference on environmental
policies may be estimated in several ways. First, the minister can respond to
briefs submitted to his department. The weakness of this system is that only

particularly well-informed or interested individuals or groups will respond, and so the preferences expressed may reflect the opinions of only a very small proportion of the population. The same objection also applies to the second method, the holding of public hearings. These may be somewhat more effective, for they will normally be well publicised, but they still tend to attract only those who feel strongly for or against a policy. A further problem is that public hearings can only handle a relatively small number of briefs; if each individual demanded his rights to express a viewpoint the hearing would be interminable. This problem has already been experienced in Canada, notably in connection with public hearings on the plans to develop a recreational village at Lake Louise in Banff National Park. The third means of assessing public preference is to assume that news media reflect public opinion. To some extent this is true, but even the most enlightened and objective editorial policy will tend to reflect the individual preferences of editors and correspondents. In any case, news media are probably more important as moulders than as reflectors of public opinion.

It is now necessary to look more closely at the Canadian situation. In the preface I suggested that Canada could be used to develop guidelines for environmental conservation policies in other countries, which implies that the problems in Canada are similar to those in other countries. In a broad sense this is true—there is no environmental problem found here that is not found in some other country. At the same time, Canada has a remarkably complete range of problems, and reaction to them is bounded by a unique set of constraints. Before discussing some of Canada's problems in detail, we should examine briefly the major constraints which limit environmental conservation in Canada.

The first, and the simplest, constraint is the physical character of the country. Mankind has sufficiently technological sophistication so that few physical problems present major technical difficulty, but the solution may be unacceptably expensive. Among Canadian physical problems two—climate and size—far outweigh all the rest. Size is important primarily in relation to Canada's small population, for it means that the per capita cost of providing such basic services as roads, railways, and telephone communications is high. As a result, the density of such services is comparatively low, which tends to impede the planned, orderly development of natural resources. The effects of climate vary from the problem of melting permafrost, which impedes the construction of buildings and pipelines in the Arctic and subarctic, to heavy sea ice, which hinders marine transportation in the Arctic and along the east coast. It encompasses the problems of too much snow in Roger's Pass and Fraser Canyon and too little rainfall in a dry area of the southern prairies known as Palliser's Triangle. Canada's climate is a variable constraint to environmental action, but the net effect is to make man's activities more difficult, more dangerous, and more expensive—and sometimes completely unfeasible.

The second major constraint to environmental management is the manner in which Canadians view their environment. Is it regarded as something desirable to be maintained intact or simply as a source of resources and wealth. The formation of attitudes is complex and only partially understood, and any attempt to generalise about national attitudes is fraught with pitfalls and begs contradiction. In addition, many actions are constrained not so much by present attitudes as those which existed in past centuries.

We have little direct evidence of the way in which early Canadians viewed their environment, but the way in which they managed it may be some guide. Before European settlement, which followed Cartier's voyage to the Gulf of St. Lawrence in 1513, man had made very little impact on the Canadian environment. The inhabitants were simply hunters and gatherers who were impeded by a lack of firearms and metal implements; only the Iroquois practiced agriculture, and only the Kwakiut in British Columbia used copper implements. Whether through preference or necessity, the life style that had evolved was closely attuned to the natural environment; in the absence of European settlement this life style would probably have persisted for a long time.

European settlement was motivated by the potential wealth of natural resources, in particular, fur resources. It is doubtful if permanent settlement was an objective except insofar as it was necessary for the fur trade or to support colonial territorial claims. The history of the fur trade in Canada, which spans the complete recent history of the country, is a case study in destructive exploitation of a natural resource. As the beaver were trapped out around the Gulf of St. Lawrence, the fur traders penetrated westward in search of new sources of furs. West of the Ottawa valley there was no attempt to establish any permanent community beyond the immediate needs of the fur trade, which resulted in the establishment of small fortified trading posts whose sole function was to facilitate the movement of furs to the east. By the end of the ninteenth century the intense rivalry between the Hudson's Bay Company and the Quebec-based Northwest Company together with the short-sighted destruction of beaver in eastern areas, had driven exploration westward as far as the Rockies. There was still wealth to be gained from the fur trade, but the days of great prosperity were ending, and the dominance of the Canadian economy by the fur trade was almost over.

There is no indication that the fur traders perceived any practical value in Canada beyond the fur supply, although passages in their journals indicate some appreciation of other qualities of the environment. After a visit in 1787, Sir Alexander Mackenzie described the Peace River country of Alberta as "the most beautiful scenery I ever beheld." Despite such appreciation, the fur trade cast Canada in its role as resource supplier to other countries—a role it has filled throughout most of its history and still largely fills today.

After the end of the nineteenth century the fur trade was replaced by the developing lumber trade, which rose in response to the needs of Nelson's navy. The lumber industry was based on a "mining," rather than a "harvesting" approach to forests and was essentially a shifting pattern of exploitation centred on temporary lumber camps. More than a century passed before sustained-yield forestry practises, which could provide a basis for permanent settlement, gained widespread acceptance. Although the economic base of the country was broadened by the development of lumbering, Canada's fundamental role was unchanged—the country remained a resource supplier to other countries, and very little secondary industry was generated. The Industrial Revolution and the explosive population growth, which were already changing the face of Europe and which gave rise to the massive transatlantic migrations of the nineteenth century, passed Canada by, and at confederation Canada was still an under-populated country with a simple infrastructure. The population had risen from an estimated 100,000 when Cartier arrived to only about 3.5 million by 1867, and 90 percent lived in the eastern provinces.[4]

For the first three hundred fifty years after European settlement the role of Canada was a straightforward one of resource supplier. It was a comparatively simple role, made even simpler by a population that was derived from a few main sources. At Confederation 60 percent of the population were of British origin, many of whom had descended from Loyalists of the American War of Independence. Thirty percent were of French origin, 6 percent hailed from elsewhere in Europe, and the remainder were indigenous Indians, Eskimos, and Métis who numbered approximately 123,000.[5]

After Confederation the economy and the population diversified swiftly. Actually the turning point was probably 1859, when the monopoly of the Hudson's Bay Company over Rupert's Land came to an end. This vast area was now open to settlement and, where feasible, to agricultural development.

The government had started to lay the foundations for such development even before the termination of the monopoly—Captain John Palliser's journey across the western provinces was primarily an agricultural reconnaissance—and the Macdonald government embarked on the development of western Canada as a definite policy to cement Canadian unity. The keystone of this policy was construction of the Canadian Pacific Railway, completed in 1885, which opened the way for settlers and homesteaders to move into the western provinces. At first the movement was slow and settlement was concentrated within ten miles of the tracks, but by the early part of the twentieth century it had become a flood, and between 1900 and 1910, 73 million acres of farmland were taken up on the prairies. Although there was some diversity, agricultural development largely centred on wheat, assisted by the development of early-ripening Marquis grain to reduce frost hazard. The prairies seemed an ideal breadbasket, and soon wheat was contributing substantially to the flow of Canadian raw materials to Europe and the eastern United States. In their enthusiasm some settlers overstepped the bounds of environmental prudence in ploughing up the prairies; in an almost literal sense they "reaped the whirlwind" in the dust bowl, drought, and depression of the 1930s.

Earlier settlers in Canada had been primarily of British or French origin, but the flood of immigrants who moved into the newly opened prairies came from Germany, Poland, Scandinavia, the Ukraine, Holland, Galicia, and

Italy. Some melded rapidly into the existing Canadian population; others retained their cultural identity for a long time. They brought new cultures and new attitudes to the Canadian environment, but more important, they came with their families to settle and to build a country which would not merely be a resource supplier. The days of dominance by the fur trader and the lumberjack were ending.

The building of the Canadian Pacific Railway also triggered the development of metallic mining, which would be of even greater economic importance than agriculture. As the railway was pushed through Ontario, the rich copper and nickel ores of Sudbury were unearthed in 1883, followed by cobalt and silver at Cobalt in 1904. These discoveries triggered extensive mineral exploration in the Canadian Shield during the interwar years, but the tremendous expansion of the Canadian mining industry has been mainly a post–Second World War phenomenon. Sudbury is still the core of this immensely wealthy industry, but extensive ore bodies have also been located elsewhere on the Shield, notably the iron deposits of Schefferville and Gagnon in Quebec, and Labrador City and Lac Allard in Labrador, the lead and zinc deposits at Pine Point in the Northwest Territories, and the uranium deposits of Elliott Lake, Ontario, and Uranium City, Saskatchewan. To these were added the wealthy metallic ores of British Columbia and the Yukon Territory.

Agriculture and mining by themselves would have generated substantial population growth at the end of the nineteenth and beginning of the twentieth century, but they were aided by the development of pulp and paper industries, which diversified forest-based activities. The bulk of the production of this industry did and still does go abroad, but major secondary industries are being added to the lumbering industries, further reducing Canada's simple role of resource supplier.

Another major element in the development of the Canadian economy was merely foreshadowed in the nineteenth century. The date of first oil production in Canada is not entirely certain, but it was sometime around 1852, at Enniskillen Township, Ontario.[6] The first drilling for oil in 1858 at Oil Springs, Ontario, was soon followed by commercial development for kerosene, and by the early 1860s ten refineries were operating there. The Oil Springs field is still in production. The first real oil rush occurred, in Alberta, at Turner Valley, where oil was discovered in 1909. Production eventually rose to 27,000 barrels per day, but the potential of the field was largely wasted by faulty extraction, and production is now negligible. The value of oil and natural gas reserves wasted is estimated at more than $1 billion.

Turner Valley created some stir, as did the discovery of oil at Norman Wells, in the Northwest Territories, in 1920, but the dramatic development of the oil industry and to wait until 1948, when a major producing field was brought in at Leduc, Alberta. This triggered an oil rush which resulted in the discovery of a number of Albertan oil fields, such as Swan Hills and Rainbow-Zama Lakes, and which in a decade transformed Alberta from one of the poorer provinces in Canada to one of the wealthiest. The tempo in Alberta has now slowed, overshadowed by the promise of wealthy oil and gas reserves in the Canadian Arctic, where oil was found at Atkinson Point near Tuktoyaktuk in 1970, and off the east coast, where oil was struck on Sable Island in 1971.

The development and diversification of the Canadian economy which followed Confederation provided the basis for a rapid increase in population from 3.5 million in 1867 to over 20 million at the last census (1970). This growth rate is not excessive compared with that of many developing countries, but it does represent an increase by a factor of six. Despite the overall increase large periodic fluctuations in the growth pattern have occurred, resulting primarily from the high emigration rate (mainly to the United States). Although 9 million immigrants have arrived during the century since Confederation, nearly 7 million people have emigrated. Only since 1900 has a net positive migration been recorded, and during periods such as the 1930s it shrank to almost nothing. The largest part of the growth has resulted from natural increase.

Discussion of the environmental attitudes of the rapidly increasing population of the late nineteenth and early twentieth centuries is inevitably speculative. Whether the people were of Eruopean or of native Canadian origin, their attitudes must have been strongly influenced by the succession of resource discoveries and developments. To immigrants from overcrowded Europe in particular, Canada must have appeared as an infinitely spacious and abundant land, rich in timber, wildlife, grazing and mineral resources. To add gilt to the already bright picture came the Cariboo gold rush of the 1860s and the Klondike gold rush of 1898. Natural resources must have appeared inexhaustible in an atmosphere similar to that prevailing in the United States two generations earlier, when settlers moved westward onto the plains.

By the late 1880s the frontier had all but disappeared in the United States, and concern was already developing about resource scarcity, which stimulated the development of the first conservation movement. Some ripples of this concern must have reached Canada, yet because the westward expansion was much later in Canada, concern must have seemed somewhat irrelevant. Not until the drought, wind erosion, and abandoned farms of the 1930s did the environment really begin to show signs of stress, and doubts about the doctrine of resource abundance became commonplace. By then a new frontier had appeared as the bush pilots wrote a unique page of aviation history in the north, and again the potential for development expanded, reinforced after the Second World War by oil and metallic mineral resources, rekindling faith in resource abundance.

Resources were abundant and may have appeared even more so, but their use by the pioneers was barred by environmental barriers. The winter cold and the summer draughts were savage, many of the rivers—protected by waterfalls and formidable gorges like Fraser Canyon—were hard to navigate, and the forest were impenetrable and stocked with apparently dangerous mammals. Although the resource wealth was immense, the barriers to its exploitation were awe inspiring, and this carved a second facet in the environmental attitudes of the growing population: nature was not pleasant, friendly, and desirable; it was hostile and savage, something to be tamed, conquered, or thrust aside. As in the United States, the preservationist ideals of men like John Muir were slow to take root.

The pioneer attitude to the environment, expressed through belief in resource abundance and hostility to nature, was the inevitable product of the pattern of Canadian development and is still widespread in the country today, for much of the population grew up in proximity to the frontier, and many others are first-generation immigrants. This attitude appears to have dwindled, particularly during the last few years, but it is still a powerful constraint on environmental action.

Another constraint on environmental conservation also originated in the pattern of Canadian development. Exploitation of fur resources was profitable, at least in earlier years, but it required considerable capital from abroad, which initially came from France and then almost completely from Britain. The real need for foreign investment in Canada emerged after Confederation, however, when the minute population was faced with the cost of such projects as transcontinental railways, which were essential to the development of the country. Again the capital was dominantly British, but later, as the emphasis in resource development shifted to oil and metallic minerals, American capital became increasingly prominent: total foreign investment increased from $1.25 million in 1900 to over $32 billion in 1965, but the American share has risen from $250 million to $23.3 billion.[7]

At the time of writing foreign investment is a controversial, emotional issue in Canada. The controversy rests on two basic issues: is such a heavy involvement of foreign capital necessary to the Canadian economy, and is such a strong American influence in investment capital harmful to Canada? Foreign investment was essential to the economy of the country and the development of resources in the past, and some feel that this is still true. Others believe that Canadian funds are now adequate to support development, at least to a much greater degree than at present, and to support their contention they point to the extent of Canadian investment in the United States. Validation of either viewpoint is difficult, but Canadian industry is certainly dominated by foreign capital to a degree unparalleled among developed countries.

It is widely believed that much resource development carried out with the aid of foreign capital is on terms which are disadvantageous to Canada. There is no clear evidence to suggest that foreign-financed industries cause greater environmental damage than Canadian-financed firms, but inevitably there is a suspicion that their managers may show less concern for protection of our environment. This could be counteracted by vigorous and vigilant government environmental protection agencies, but they might be constrained by social repercussions. Foreign capital pervades many sectors of the economy but is perhaps most obvious in areas of sparse settlement or unemployment, where it is often critical to the viability of whole communities. In this situation the governments of such areas are not well placed to insist on strict environmental controls, and protection of environmental quality will therefore depend largely on the interest of the federal government and the steps it takes to control foreign investment.

Foreign investment could have deleterious effects on the Canadian environment, and there is no doubt that in some cases it does conflict with the development of Canadian resources in the broad interests of Canadian society. Obviously the prime objective for foreign investors is a healthy profit, preferably to be derived reasonably quickly. The principle of resource conservation—the setting aside of short-term benefits in favour of prolongation of use—is totally opposed to this objective. In other words, to extract a resource as quickly as possible is the foreign investor's main concern, but the needs of Canadian society might be better served by a more prolonged extraction, which would provide a stable source of employment. By and large resource extraction industries in Canada have failed to produce much stable employment; both the oil and mining industries are notorious for generating a "boom-and bust" pattern of settlement.

The country offers many examples of the rapid rise and fall of towns based on the extraction of nonrenewable natural resources. Two of the most dramatic are Dawson City, in the Yukon Territory, and Elliot Lake, Ontario. Different factors were involved in their decline. In 1897–98 Dawson City grew as a result of the Klondike gold rush until its population was over 25,000. It was the only town of significant size which has ever existed in Canada's north. The gold reserves of the Klondike were rich and could have supported a stable mining population (although not one of 25,000) for many years, but exploitation was too rapid. Production was increased, and the placer deposits were worked by large mechanical dredges until production finally became submarginal and was abandoned in 1966. The population of Dawson has dwindled to around 800, and a number of smaller surrounding settlements have disappeared. The wealthy Klondike, which could have supported a stable, thriving community, now supports a handful of people who survive on tourism and welfare. One can speculate, but not demonstrate, that the gold dredges would still be in operation if the Yukon Consolidated Gold Corporation had been owned by Canadian rather than by predominantly South African interests.

Elliot Lake, an area that contains 93 percent of the Canadian reserves of uranium, developed as a mining community in the early 1950s. Development was based on the United States market for uranium, which declined greatly at the end of the 1950s, causing the population to dwindle and the community to become virtually a ghost town. The case of Elliot Lake emphasises one of the great weaknesses of the Canadian economy: some 60 percent of Canadian mineral production is exported in raw form. This contributes to Canada's favourable trade balance but also makes much of Canadian industry excessively dependent on the vagaries of international markets, which places many settlements in a precarious situation. A few of the mining settlements, such as Yellowknife and Schefferville, have developed other functions as administrative and communications centres. For other settlements the only hope for a stable future is the development of secondary industry. If this major challenge can be met, it offers one of the best hopes for the maintenance of environmental quality in these areas, because a permanent population will hopefully be more concerned with environmental quality than most temporary ones.

The manner in which Canadians view their environment, the role as resource supplier which Canada has seemed destined to fill, and the degree to which investment is dominated by foreign capital are all powerful social constraints on the action Canadian governments can take to solve environmental problems. At least as important is the governmental and legal framework within which such action must be taken. Environmental deterioration is so far-reaching and complex at present that there is a general agreement that it can be handled effectively only by action at a national or international level. Canada is at considerable disadvantage, because its political system vests a high degree of autonomy in provincial governments. Under the provisions of the British North America Act of 1867, a provincial government is responsible for the management and sale of public lands belonging to the province and the timber on these lands. Provincial governments also have control over the development of mineral resources and all aspects of wildlife; federal control is retained only in Indian reserves and within national park boundaries. Under the British North America Act, the federal government has full jurisdiction over marine and inland fisheries, although jurisdiction over fresh-water fisheries has been delegated to provincial authorities in Ontario, Manitoba, Saskatchewan, Alberta, and British Columbia. In most provinces this distribution of jurisdiction has existed since 1867 or since the creation of the province, but Manitoba, Saskatchewan, and Alberta did not obtain control over Crown lands within their borders until 1930. In the Yukon and Northwest territories the federal government still retains control over Crown lands and resources, although control of wildlife resources has been ceded to the territorial governments.

The federal government is the only body which could initiate the integrated, far-reaching action necessary for effective environmental conservation, particularly as it would concern national economic policy and would possibly involve constitutional reform. But because so much authority is vested in provincial authorities, it is difficult for the federal government to initiate such action. In many situations the federal government no longer retains the authority to act without provincial concurrence, which is not always a problem, but there are occasions when local provincial interests should be subjugated to national or international interests. In these circumstances provincial concurrence is not always forthcoming. As a case in point, federal attempts to expand the Canadian national park system at an adequate rate have been largely frustrated by a lack of support from provincial governments. In some areas of environmental concern, such as the protection of navigable waterways, federal authority overrides that of provincial governments, but the federal government is reluctant to force its will upon uncooperative provinces for the spectre of separatism is never far away in this fragile confederation.

The government system of delegated authority does have many disadvantages, but it might be impossible to organise a viable, strongly centralised government in such a large and diverse country. It can also be argued that the decentralised system of government allows more rapid response to crises than the monolithic bureaucracy of a federal government. Theoretically this may be so, but in practise any advantage is probably more than offset by the fact that provincial governments are frequently more amenable to local pressures than to national or international needs.

The disadvantages of decentralised government are apparent in environmental problems at a national level, but many problems of local importance are appropriately dealt with at a provincial or municipal level. This applies to sewage treatment and disposal, for example, which is normally organised and financed locally, although funds from federal sources may be involved. At the same time, it is clear from the example of Montreal, which treats only 8.4 percent of its sewage output, that municipal governments cannot always be relied upon to take appropriate action.

A strongly centralised federal government is desirable in dealing with internal environmental problems, but it becomes essential in attempting to coordinate efforts at an international level. Most environmental problems do not confine themselves conveniently within national or provincial boundaries. It is futile for any government to attempt to control such problems as air pollution or the pollution of boundary waters without the cooperation of neighbouring nations. There would be little advantage, for example, in preventing Canadian industries from dumping untreated wastes into the Great Lakes if their American counterparts were free to continue to do so. Cooperation exists between the United States and Canada in some areas, such as the Great Lakes, which are being examined by the International Joint Commission. In other areas of concern, such as marine pollution by oil spillage and jurisdiction over the waters of the continental shelf, virtually no cooperation has yet been achieved. Even where cooperation is significant, generation of effective legislation and action is difficult because of contrasting political systems.

Problems like the pollution of the Great Lakes are obviously matters of concern to both countries, and the interests of both countries would be served by finding joint solutions but there are problems where the interests of the countries appear to be in conflict. This has become apparent particularly with regard to such questions as the export of water from Canada to the United States and the damming of international rivers for hydroelectric power development. Such actions benefit the regions receiving the water at considerable cost to the exporting regions. The costs are assessed and in theory are compensated by rental or lump sum payments. In practise the assessment is often erroneous, considering only losses which are easily assessed in financial terms, such as flooding of marketable timber, to the exclusion of potentially more important losses, such as the destruction of recreation land or wildlife, which are less easily quantified. This assessment is particularly important because it is often determined by a provincial government that concentrates on local costs and benefits rather than on national interests.

The authority of provincial governments in such matters has been appreciably curtailed by the International River Improvements Act of 1955, which requires Canadian federal permission for construction on international rivers, although the effectiveness of such joint legislation is considerably impaired by the existence of previous agreements. In the Skagit valley, British Columbia, for example, the authority to flood by raising the Ross Dam in Washington is based on an International Joint Commission authorization of 1942, nullifying the effect of the 1955 act. This project was supported by the former British Columbian government, although it is questionable whether the negotiated compensation bears any real relationship to the costs involved.

The Skagit valley question, like many joint problems before it, raised objections based on Canadian nationalism. This is unfortunate, for the real issues become obscured behind a fog of outdated chauvinism. The problem is not a question of who is stealing whose water, but whether or not the benefits conferred by water transfer outweigh the cost of environmental damage. It is irrelevant whether or not the water crosses a political boundary. If the costs of damage outweigh the benefits, all people are eventually losers.

Development of effective international legislation to deal with environmental problems is of prime importance, but the power of any national government to influence or accelerate the passage of such legislation is limited. Canada has shown a willingness to move beyond the bounds of international agreement in asserting territorial control over Arctic waters in an attempt to develop effective control over environmental deterioration. The potential for similar initative in other Canadian-American problems is limited, however, and the exercise of such initiative would probably be undesirable. As a result, any rapid advances in legislative control over environmental problems will probably affect matters of primarily Canadian concern.

A large volume of legislation concerned with aspects of environmental deterioration exists in Canada and has for many years. The Canada Shipping Act, the National Parks Act, the Pest Control Products Act, and the Fisheries Act, among many others, contain passages relevant to environmental control. Despite such legislation, effective control has been lacking in the past. Legislation has not been sufficiently strong, it has not been designed specifically for the maintenance of environmental quality, and in application it has suffered from division of responsibility between federal and provincial agencies. Probably the most effective obstacle to environmental control has been the fragmentation of authority between enforcement agencies.

Since the beginning of 1970 some progress has been made toward solving some of the problems in legislation and its enforcement. On June 26, 1970, three important bills were assented—the Canada Water Act, the Arctic Waters Pollution Prevention Act, and the Northern Inland Waters Act. Together these vested significant powers of water pollution control in the federal government, not only within Canada but also in the Arctic, extending to 100 miles from the coast. The Clean Air Act was passed in the 1971 session of Parliament, giving similar powers of control over air pollution. Perhaps the most promising action, however, was the creation of a Department of the Environment and Renewable Resources, which takes over all the pollution control functions of existing agencies, with "a mandate for protection of the biosphere."[8] This department should reduce the problem of fragmentation of authority in the federal government, but the division of responsibility between federal and provincial governments remains. Until this is clarified, either by court action or constitutional reform, the prospect of effective action in environmental matters is not encouraging. In addition, however powerful legislation may appear on paper, it cannot be effective unless it is backed by the enthusiasm and authority of the administering governments, and this support may be more difficult to obtain than legislation.

Perhaps the most important criticism and limitation of existing and proposed legislation is that it has been drawn up under duress in response to crises, in attempt to promote remedial action. Action thus determined tends to become piecemeal. Like most countries, what Canada lacks is a comprehensive philosophy of the type of life and environment desired for the future. Until such a philosophy founded on reliable information and rational consideration of alternatives is developed as a basis for legislative and administrative action, the maintenance or restoration of a tolerable environment will not be realised. Apart from the fundamental problem of world overpopulation, the development of such a philosophy is the most important task facing environmental conservationists.

References

1. Anon., "Whole earth conference," *Time*, 22 May, 1972, 55.

2. G. F. White, "Formation and Role of Public Attitudes," in *Environmental Quality in a Growing Economy*, edited by H. Jarrett, pp. 105–128 (Baltimore: The Johns Hopkins Press, 1966).

3. B. Hitchon, "Early Natural History Explorations," in *Alberta, a Natural History*, edited by W. G. Hardy, pp. 295–301 (Edmonton: Hurtig, 1967).

4. T. R. Weir, "The People," in *Canada, A Geographical Interpretation*, edited by J. Warkentin, pp. 137–176 (Toronto: Methuen Publications, 1968).

5. T. R. Weir, *op. cit.*

6. E. Gray, *The Great Canadian Oil Patch* (Toronto: Maclean-Hunter Limited, 1970).

7. Dominion Bureau of Statistics, *Canada Year Book* (Ottawa: Queen's Printer, 1969).

8. *Speech from the Throne*, opening the Third Session of the 28th Parliament, 1970.

Part 2

Pollution and Development in the Canadian Environment

The Imperial Oil Limited discovery rig at Atkinson Point, Northwest Territories, where oil was discovered in January, 1970.

Chapter 2

A Theoretical Approach to Pollution

Saturation coverage in the news media in recent years has probably ensured that few people in North America are unaware of the existence of environmental pollution. Because coverage has varied in quality and at times has been of questionable reliability, even people who have studied the subject carefully have garbled ideas about the problem. Virtually everyone agrees that polution is bad, but probably no two people have exactly the same idea of what pollution means, how it is caused, the type of damage it produces, and the importance of this in comparison with the costs of pollution control. This confusion is a reflection both of the number of ways in which our environment is being polluted and of newspaper and magazine articles containing half truths, incomplete statements, and exaggerations. Before discussing detailed examples of pollution in Canada it is therefore necessary to outline some of the problems and principles involved in the subject. Most of these are applicable to other countries.

Definitions of Pollution

Agreement on exact definitions, causes, and effects of pollution may not seem important, but it becomes so if coherent pollution control is to be instituted, particularly if the definition is to be incorporated into legislation and used as the basis for legal action. Essentially pollution is the accumulation of any product of man's activity in places or in quantities in which it is not wanted. The term should cover some intentional acts, such as pesticide use, but it is frequently confined to waste products. These are of immense variety and may be deposited in the air, in rivers and lakes, in oceans, on land, or underground. One definition which has been used as the basis for legal action on water pollution is "the addition of something to water which changes its natural qualities."[1] This definition is simple and clear with regard to the act of pollution, but it is difficult to apply because of variations in natural water quality, the inventory of which is rudimentary. Even if we had complete knowledge of natural water quality variations the definition would probably be regarded as an unrealistic ideal. There can be few people who believe that in the near future we will see rivers leaving industrial areas in a state of "natural" purity, however desirable this might be.

     A more realistic working definition of pollution is the accumulation of waste products to such a degree that they constitute an annoyance or a hazard to health. This is similar to the definition used in the present Canada Water Act, in which pollution is regarded as the addition of "waste" to a waterway, waste being defined as "any substance which, if added to any waters, would degrade or alter . . . those waters to an extent that is detrimental to their use by man, or by any animal, fish, or plant that is useful to man." These definitions are more realistic, although still difficult to apply. Using the Canada Water Act definition, it is necessary to clarify exactly what is meant by "use." For example, is a person whose garden overlooks a river using it simply by looking at it, or must use be a direct, measurable action? The "detrimental effects" also need further clarification. In many cases these may not become apparent for years. Does the definition of pollution apply only to immediate effects, or can it be applied without a time limit? If the latter, is the polluter allowed to continue pollution pending the development of evidence of detrimental effects, or must he prove that such effects will not occur before he commences or continues operations? Some of these problems are peculiar to water, but most general principles apply to all forms of pollution.

Approaches to Pollution Control

Dilution

     The dilution philosophy is that pollution is acceptable as long as it is diluted sufficiently. The problem then is to define not pollution but "sufficient dilution." Two approaches may be followed, neither of which is very satisfactory. In the first, pollution severity is judged by impairment of use. If waste products accumulate to a level at which they interfere with other uses of the environment they become unacceptable. This is the approach used in the Canada Water Act, and some of the problems have already been outlined.

The second approach is to establish definite tolerance levels for specific pollutants that cannot be exceeded without impairment of health. This approach is realistic if the identity of the waste product is known and if its effects on health have been comprehensively studied, but this is rarely the case, for thousands of new compounds are introduced every year. When released these may interact with one another or with other elements, such as sunlight, to produce a variety of unknown secondary compounds. Comprehensive study of the effects on health is not possible, and adequate instrumentation for monitoring concentrations is rarely available.

In theory it might appear simple to keep pollution within tolerance levels if they can be established, but in fact it is extremely difficult and will eventually require the reevaluation of social philosophies. The first principle of pollution control must be the recognition that our physical environment is finite and therefore has a definite fixed capacity to dilute or absorb pollution. If the pollution load is allowed to rise above this capacity, it cannot be diluted to specified levels. The second principle is that the total amount of pollution produced in a given area is a function of the area's population. Obviously this is an oversimplification, for the individual is only one source of pollution, but in general the number of factories, motorcars, aircraft, and coal mines is related to the population and will increase if the population increases.

At an early stage in a society's development pollution is not generally a problem. Because the population is small the environment has an adequate capacity to asborb and dilute pollutants, even if they are completely untreated. High pollutant concentrations occur only locally at pollution sources, before dilution take place. As development continues the population increases, and the total production of waste material rises, although the per capita production of waste will probably increase as well, because the developing society becomes more complex and sophisticated. Eventually waste production will equal the dilution capacity of the environment. Subsequent events may follow one of three patterns. In the first, no action is taken, population continues to increase, and waste production continues to expand until the environment becomes loaded with waste products far above its dilution capacity. The result is critical pollution which becomes progressively worse as the population continues to grow.

In the second pattern, when the production of waste material reaches the dilution capacity level of the environment, wastes are treated to reduce their quantity and to make them easier to dilute in order to keep pollution within specified limits. As the population continues to rise, larger and larger proportions of the total waste production must be treated, at progressively greater expense. Eventually one of two things may happen: the cost of increased waste treatment may become so expensive that the society can no longer afford to keep pace and ceases treatment of new wastes, or some of the pollutants may be so powerful or lethal that technology is no longer sufficiently advanced to ensure adequate treatment. In either case the second pattern eventually leads to abandonment of levels originally specified, and an increasingly severe pollution problem develops as the population continues to rise. In the ultimate stage of both these patterns the environment becomes so polluted that it is no longer tolerable or healthy.

The third pattern differs: population growth in the society ceases when the total pollution production reaches the dilution capacity of the environment. If any further growth of population occurs, the excess must move to areas which have not yet reached their capacity. When no such areas remain, no further population growth may take place. This pattern, which admittedly has been simplified almost to absurdity, would ensure that pollution could be kept within the specified limits. It is probable that it cannot be followed, for the world is not divided into a series of independent cells with separate pollution production, and population is more or less free to migrate between areas in response to many factors other than pollution. Furthermore, the increased industrial production to meet the needs of population growth in one area may take place in a second area, so that the relationship between population increase and pollution growth is indirect. A more recent realisation is that some forms of pollution spread so rapidly that they cannot be contained within one small area of the world. Also, some pollutants, such as the products of certain nuclear reactions, are so virulent or persistent that the environment of the whole world may be inadequate to dilute them to safe levels.

If development follows either of the first two patterns the end product will be a global environment which is intolerable and unhealthy. By stating this I do not intend to predict instant global disaster but simply to show the logical end point of current developments. Virtually every society in the world is operating on one of these two patterns. Simpler societies and those in less densely populated areas operate on the first pattern. More complex societies and those in areas of dense population concentration operate on the second. The first pattern, if followed to its conclusion, will lead inevitably to the destruction of the world environment. The second will avoid doing so only if population growth is halted before pollution control becomes too expensive or technologically impossible. The third pattern requires the halting of population growth at a much lower level.

Control of Growth

If we continue to follow the philosophy that pollution is simply a matter of dilution, we can survive as a species only if we halt population growth. This is essential on grounds other than pollution. The demand for resources already exceeds the available supply. More than half the population of the world is either undernourished and/or malnourished, and perhaps as much as one-eighth the population is actually starving. Even if food could be produced to feed this population adequately, which is uncertain, material resources which would be sufficient to bring the material standard of living in underdeveloped countries up to the level of North America and Western Europe do not exist. It has been calculated that the resources of the world are adequate to support only a population of one billion at such a level.[2] Cessation of population growth is essential to avoid the destruction of man by starvation—it is the most fundamental and urgent problem of mankind today. It is also essential, if slightly less urgent, for pollution control.

Cessation of growth will require a major change in social philosophy, because the belief that growth is beneficial is one of the most fundamental tenets of mankind. Many religions include in their dogma the instructions to their followers to multiply so that they may prosper, which partly explains the considerable reluctance of religious groups to support family planning and birth control programmes. In most aspects Western society is based on a belief in growth. A man is unhappy if his salary does not increase every year, and industrial management is dissatisfied if production remains static. A sales manager who only maintains sales at a steady level will not survive long in competitive marketing. A city of stable population is regarded as a stagnant, unprogressive community. Hence the enthusiasm with which chambers of commerce gloat over increasing municipal populations and the horror with which they regard suggestions that the size of their cities should be limited. Societies everywhere operate on the fallacious assumption that to stand still is to move backward.

This fundamental belief in the benefits of growth makes any hope for eventual extensive pollution control rather sanguine. Perhaps the ultimate insanity, however, is that the increase in demand associated with population growth is not sufficient to satisfy the craving for growth. Industry has found it necessary to stimulate an increasing per capita demand by a variety of advertising devices. Built-in obsolescence and annual model changes are established practises, although the motor industry is now reevaluating its approach. The food products industry, also caught up in the rush to grow, must increase per capita consumption to ensure that production can continue to rise. A person can only consume a limited amount without becoming obese or otherwise unhealthy, so the rise in production must be based on non-nutritious foods guaranteed to have no effect other than boosting the sales performance of the manufacturer. The net result of the growth tactic is to increase our per capita rate of resource use at a phenomenal rate at a time when the resources of the world are already inadequate. It also ensures that per capita use of resources in the complex societies of developed countries is much higher than that in the simpler societies of underdeveloped countries. It has been estimated that consumption of raw materials in the United States is about 30 percent of the total world consumption, although its population is only about 6 percent of the world total. It need hardly be pointed out that production of waste is proportional to consumption of raw materials, so that the per capita production of

pollution in the United States and other developed countries is also dispropor-
tionately high.

Unacceptability of the dilution approach

If pollution control by dilution is to be successful, the growth of
waste production must be halted. The growth philosophy is so deeply engrained
in society that it is not easy to believe that this will occur. It therefore appears
that efforts to control pollution will fail. At present most pollution control
efforts concentrate on curing the symptoms rather than treating the disease. As
long as this situation exists, dilution cannot produce adequate pollution control.

In addition to its ineffectiveness, dilution has been widely rejected
as an ultimate solution for other reasons. Even if the population is small and
the absolute capacity of the environment is not exceeded, dilution does not
occur instantaneously; extremely high pollution concentrations will occur at
the point of waste input. In many towns and cities waste production already
greatly exceeds the dilution capacity of the environment. To institute effective
pollution control would require extensive relocation of industries and population, which is certainly beyond the capability of society. Even if population
growth were halted instantly, dilution could not produce effective control
in areas of high population concentration.

Also, the belief is growing that dilution is unacceptable on social
grounds. The environment of a country is the common property of the people
of that country; in effect it is a resource which no industry or settlement has
the right to use destructively for its own advantage. An industry that dumps
untreated waste material into a river benefits directly by keeping its production costs at a lower level than a competing industry that treats its waste.

It is also unacceptable because we now realise that although dilution
may occur locally, the waste product simply moves elsewhere and eventually
accumulates. This is best shown by the use of rivers for waste dilution and
transport: the river itself may not suffer from waste accumulation, but the lake
or ocean into which the river discharges has a limited capacity to take up waste.
The capacity for *biodegradable* waste is high, because it can be broken down by
bacterial action to harmless end products but many pollutants, such as radioactive waste, DDT, metallic garbage, and nerve gas, are not biodegradable and
therefore will accumulate until they reach damaging levels. Some are so potent
that they require vast dilution for safety; one ton of radioactive waste may
require dilution with 1.7 million cubic miles of ocean water to reach a safe
level.[3] Pollutants may be responsible for extensive destruction of lake or
marine life, destroying a potential food source and possibly rendering water
bodies sterile. Accumulation of toxic chemical compounds such as DDT might
eventually destroy phytoplankton in the oceans, which is responsible for a
large part of the world's oxygen supply. The potential for serious oceanic pol-

lution along the coast of Canada has already been demonstrated by fish kills in Placentia Bay, Newfoundland, in late 1968 and early 1969, caused by phosphorus dumped by the ERCO plant at Long Harbour.

Recycling

Waste material which is diluted and sometimes transported away is the end point of the use of raw materials, many of which are already in short supply. It has been estimated, for example, that recoverable world supplies of platinum, silver, gold, tin, zinc, lead, uranium, and copper will be expended by the year 2000 if current rates of use continue;[4] known reserves of mercury will be expended by about 1980 at current use rates. We cannot afford to throw away the waste products of our society, because many of them contain usable supplies of scarce resources. This waste is serious when it involves resources used in manufacturing; it can become catastrophic when resources essential to life, such as phosphates, are discarded. It is imperative that usable materials be removed from wastes and used again; a complete change in our ideas of what constitutes waste is needed. As the director of the Science Council of Canada, P. McTaggart Cowan, has said, pollution is merely unrealised profit. Few waste products cannot be reused, although not all are as valuable as the metals mentioned. For example, newspapers can be used to make excelsior, garbage can be compounded to form building blocks, fly ash from power stations can be turned into brick, and sewage sludge can be used as fertilizer. Sometimes reuse is inconvenient or uneconomical, but in the long run it is inevitable if we wish to continue present life patterns.

Continued reuse of materials is termed *recycling,* a fundamental process in nature. Man is the only organism that does not recycle waste products to ensure a constant supply of essential raw materials. The merits for resource conservation are obvious. Although at the moment it may be more expensive to recycle materials than to locate new sources, this situation will not continue indefinitely. Recycling is already extensively employed in some industries, notably the iron and steel industry, where scrap metal has been used for many years. It is ideal from a pollution control viewpoint, for few wastes are produced to pollute the environment. If each industry could purify water used to 100 percent purity, for example, the water could be reused indefinitely without difficulty. A municipality that carried out 100 percent purification of sewage waste could reuse the same water over and over again, eliminating the need for augmentation of supplies. It would be extremely optimistic to suggest that our entire society could be converted to recycling in the near future. In some cases our technology is not yet sufficiently advanced to recycle all wastes. It should be our objective, however, and it could be feasible within fifty or a hundred years if we start now. The institution of large-scale recycling will obviously require initiative and imagination from governments at all levels and substantial expenditure, but it is the only rational long-term solution to the problems of resource scarcity and environmental pollution.

Pollution Issues in Canada

The problems of environmental pollution which currently afflict Canada are no different and perhaps no more serious than those in other countries, and in some instances they simply represent the extension of a global problem. Canada is perhaps a little unusual, however, because it is encountering such a wide range of pollution problems at the same time. In the densely settled eastern parts of the country, like areas of dense urban settlement in the United States and Europe, it is suffering from extensive water and air pollution. Pollution from pulp mills is spread throughout the country, as is the problem of inadequately treated municipal and domestic wastes. Wealthy oil reserves have been matched by the pollution associated with extraction and transport. The lengthy and tortuous coastline has suffered from marine oil pollution, rendered particularly problematic by cold offshore waters.

The list of Canada's pollution problems could be extended almost indefinitely, but the point has been made. Our problems are not unique, but we have a representative selection. It is significant that pollution problems in Canada are reaching a crucial point at this particular stage in our cultural and technological development. Perhaps for the first time most people are in a position to appreciate at least some of the possible repercussions of pollution, and this appreciation comes at a time when we have an extensive technical capacity to control pollution. Our situation differs from that in Western Europe, for there most pollution problems arose when little was known about the subject. We have to control pollution, and unlike many countries, we probably have sufficient funds to do so.

It is not possible within the limited space available to discuss all aspects of the Canadian pollution problem in detail. Readers who desire a broader and more general treatment of Canadian pollution problems are referred to two recently published books which are entirely devoted to this subject.[5] [6]

References

1. Coulson and Forbes, *The Law of Waters and Land Drainage,* ed. S. R. Hobday, Sixth Edition (London: Sweet and Maxwell, 1952).

2. H. R. Hulett, "Optimum World Population," *Bioscience* 20 (3) (1970): 160–161.

3. L. Klein, *River Pollution* (New York: Academic Press, 1959).

4. P. E. Cloud, "Realities of Mineral Distribution," *Texas Quarterly* 11 (1968): 103–126.

5. F. Morgan, *Pollution – Canada's Critical Challenge,* volume 4 in the series: *Shaping Canada's Environment,* general ed. J. Forrester (Toronto: Ryerson Press/Maclean-Hunter, Ltd., 1970).

6. D. A. Chant, *Pollution Probe* (Toronto: New Press, 1970).

Chapter 3

Sewage and Its Effects on Waterways

Domestic sewage is probably the most ubiquitous pollutant in Canada, although others are of greater local importance. Sewage varies considerably, but in general it is a combination of liquid and solid wastes, including laundry water, food remains, bath water, faecal material, and street washings. Most urban communities collect sewage for disposal, usually by means of a subsurface pipe network. Disposal is almost universally by deposition into rivers, lakes, or the sea, which in theory dilute the sewage to acceptable levels and which may transport it away. Severe sewage pollution occurs where the dilution capacity of the water body is exceeded and can be prevented only by strict limitation of settlement along watercourses or by adequate treatment of sewage prior to release into them.

The Effects of Sewage Pollution

Pathogenic contamination

Sewage pollution is aesthetically unpleasant, but a much more critical problem is the hazard it presents to health. Faecal material contains a variety of microorganisms, most of which are harmless, but some, *pathogens,* are responsible for diseases such as typhoid, paratyphoid, and cholera. If dilution is inadequate, sewage pollution can present a grave threat to public health. Pathogenic organisms are not always present in sewage, and it is therefore difficult to test sewage dilution by monitoring pathogen content. The common approach is to monitor the content of *Escherichia coli,* an intestinal bacterium abundant in faecal material. If it is present in water only in small quantities there is little risk of contamination by pathogens, most of which are relatively short-lived. Its presence in large quantities does not necessarily indicate an immediate health danger, but it does show that sewage dilution is inadequate and that pathogenic contamination could occur.

The monitoring of *E. coli* concentration is referred to as the *coliform count,* which can be determined by a number of different techniques that differ in accuracy. The coliform count has been criticised because it measures only intestinal bacteria and does not necessarily indicate the presence of other pathogens. Opinion about what constitutes a tolerable coliform count for various water uses also varies. Despite these disadvantages the technique has indicated that many Canadian waterways are seriously contaminated and cannot be used safely for such purposes as bathing and drinking. Polluted areas range from the beaches of the Okanagan in British Columbia to the shellfish beds of the Maritimes. In the Okanagan coliform counts up to 1,609 per 100 cubic centimetres of water have been measured off bathing beaches (the provincial standard for bathing water is 240 per 100 cubic centimetres). In Nova Scotia and Prince Edward Island clam fishing has been restricted by contamination, which could be damaging because shellfish are frequently eaten uncooked.

Organic pollution

Pathogenic contamination of waterways due to inadequate sewage treatment is undoubtedly the most dangerous aspect of sewage pollution. Aesthetically and in terms of uses to which the waterway can be put, the organic load of sewage is also a troublesome pollutant. Rivers and lakes can break down organic material by bacterial action to produce stable, harmless end-products, a process of aerobic decay and self-purification that occurs in the presence of adequate supplies of oxygen. If the oxygen supply is inadequate, breakdown is by an anaerobic process, producing different end products, such as a number of sulphur compounds, many of which are unpleasant and some of which are dangerous.

If the amount of organic material passing into the stream is not too large, absorption of oxygen at the water surface will ensure a supply adequate for aerobic breakdown and to meet the needs of aquatic flora and fauna. If the amount of material rises too high, the oxygen supply will become deficient and anaerobic decay will start. The effects are seen first in the decay of fish populations. In general, desirable sport fish such as salmon and trout require moderately high concentrations of dissolved oxygen. As the oxygen supply dwindles these fish are replaced by suckers and catfish, which can tolerate low oxygen contents. These in turn are replaced by organisms requiring even less oxygen, until eventually the complete aquatic fauna declines.

The degree of pollution by organic debris is assessed by measuring the BOD, or *biochemical oxygen demand,* which is the amount of oxygen absorbed by a sample of water during a five-day period under controlled conditions. The higher the BOD rises the more seriously polluted the water is and the more imparied the waterway's power of self-purification is. In Canada high BODs arise from many sources, particularly from sewage pollution and from debris dumped by the pulp industry.

Eutrophication

Although organic debris dumped into lakes and streams is the chief cause of deoxygenation, reduction can also be caused by the oxygen demands of aquatic vegetation. In a geological sense all lakes are temporary water bodies that in time are eliminated by silting and by colonisation with vegetation. The rate at which rooted aquatic vegetation invades a lake is extremely variable, depending on such factors as the depth of water, the temperature, sunlight, and most of all, on the availability of plant nutrients, of which nitrates and phosphates are most commonly in short supply.

Lakes generally fall into two categories. Those which are low in nutrients, almost devoid of plant life, and generally have a high oxygen content and clear water are *oligotrophic* lakes. Lakes which have an abundance of plant life, low oxygen content, and usually murky water are *eutrophic* lakes. Intervening stages are referred to as *mesotrophic* lakes. Most lakes are oligotrophic immediately after formation but change into eutrophic lakes as they silt up, as nutrients become available, and as plants appear. The rate at which the change takes place varies immensely. If the lake is deep and rock-floored, like many lakes in the Rockes, the progression from ologotrophic to eutrophic is very slow. There is little soil on the lake floor for plants to root in, and nutrients become available only over a long period of time as rock is eroded. If the lake is in a shallow depression over fine-grained glacial or alluvial deposits, like most of the pothole lakes of the prairies, vegetation can root quickly and usually finds a ready supply of nutrients. Such lakes are eutrophic almost from birth.

Whether a lake is oligotrophic is important for man's use. An oligotrophic lake, with its clear, deep water and oxygen-loving game fish, is ideal for recreation, particularly as rock erosion frequently produces sandy beaches. The eutrophic lake is murky, weed-choked, and populated by coarse fish. Aquatic vegetation may build up to such a level that it completely covers beaches with an accumulation of rotting organic matter, and it may even obstruct boating. Anaerobic conditions in the lower waters of the lake lead to the creation of unsavory sulphurous bottom sludge. In this condition the lake is of little use for any of man's activities and may actually become partly toxic due to the development of blue-green algae, which cause gastroenteritis.

Eutrophication of lakes is a natural process that proceeds regardless of man, but it can be greatly accelerated by man's activities; a process that may take thousands of years under natural conditions can occur within a few years. The mechanisms of eutrophication and its acceleration are complex and are not entirely understood, but the general cause appears to be the addition of plant nutrients to lake waters in large quantities, stimulating plant growth formerly retarded by nutrient deficiency. Thermal pollution has also been blamed. Considerable controversy has arisen about whether the most important nutrient added is carbon, phosphorus, or nitrogen,[1] [2] [3] but the majority of opinions appear to favour phosphorus. All three nutrients come from a variety of sources, particularly from untreated or partially treated sewage. All are normal components of organic debris, but the "normal" load of phosphates is greatly supplemented by detergent effluent. It has been suggested, for example, the 40 percent of all the phosphates entering Lake Erie, which suffers from advanced eutrophication, come from detergents.[4] The remainder come from human and animal wastes, from vegetal matter, and from chemical fertilizers and industrial wastes.

Detergents date from the early 1940s, when it was discovered that the addition of sodium tripolyphosphate to synthetic soaplike compounds greatly increased their cleaning power, and their use has since become widespread. Detergents differ widely in composition, but the bulk of the material is always composed of a *builder,* which has usually been sodium tripolyphosphate, and a *surfactant,* a foam producing agent. These two components produce different problems. For many years the most common surfactant was alkyl benzene sulphonate, a nonbiodegradable material that passes normal sewage treatment, resulting in a foam pollution problem in receiving waters. Since 1966 this has been replaced in all Canadian detergents by the biodegradable surfactant linear alkylate sulphonate. This change affected only the foam pollution problem and not the biodegradability of the remainder of the material, which may reach 80 percent of the total. The sodium tripolyphosphate content of the remainder varies considerably. It used to range up to nearly 60 percent, but federal action reduced it to a maximum of 20 percent as of August 1, 1970.[5] Federal activity has been somewhat misdirected in concentrating on the phosphate content of the detergent rather than on the laundry effluent, which may depend on both the washing instructions and the degree to which they are followed as well as on the initial phosphate content.

The Canadian government's move to reduce the phosphate content of detergents to 20 percent in 1970 and to zero by 1972 was controversial and was not followed by the United States. This effectively nullified the effect of the Canadian move, at least in the boundary waters of Lake Erie, Lake Superior, and Lake Ontario, where the worst eutrophication has occurred.[6] [7] The U. S. refusal to ban or to reduce phosphates was based on a lack of evidence supporting the role of phosphates in promoting algal growth and on the absence of a safe replacement.

Several chemicals have been tested as possible replacements for sodium tripolyphosphate, the most promising of which is sodium nitriloacetate (NTA). This has been tested for a number of years in Sweden without apparent ill effects, although it does contain small quantities of nitrates. A persistent worry that NTA could eventually prove to have harmful side effects (nitrates can cause a disease called methaemoglobanemia, which if often fatal to infants) was reinforced when work by the United States Public Health Service showed that NTA in combination with small quantities of heavy metals such as cadmium and mercury could produce foetal abnormalities in rats and mice. Because NTA is a chelating agent, it may be able to dissolve and mobilise these metals from lake sediments.[8] Another potential problem is that on breakdown NTA could produce nitrosamines which are carcinogenic in very low dosages. Because of these possibilities the U. S. government banned NTA from detergents in December 1970.

Further complications were added to the controversy in early 1971, when the results of research by American oceanographers indicated that the major factor contributing to excessive algal growth on the eastern coast of the United States was nitrogen rather than phosphorus.[9] Replacement of sodium tripolyphosphate by NTA could aggravate rather than ease the eutrophication situation. These observations help to confirm growing opinion that the problem is much more complicated than originally suspected and that it results from a variety of nutrients acting in conjunction with other environmental factors.

The action of the Canadian federal government has been criticised by those who do not believe that phosphates are the chief cause of eutrophication on the grounds that it victimises an industry without adequate proof of pollution. Such criticism is justified, although it is perhaps more properly directed to the scientific community than to the government. Another interesting point is also raised: the criticism assumes that the government should prove more clearly that phosphates are a pollutant. There are those who feel, however, that industry should prove that its product is not a pollutant before production is permitted. Regardless of the legal merits of these viewpoints, there is further cause for criticising the Canadian ban: phosphates come from many sources, and banning phosphates in detergents will remove only one source. Lake Erie will continue to receive 60 percent of its present phosphate load, which should still be adequate to cause rapid eutrophication, particularly if phosphorus is only one of the important nutrients. Therefore, the appropriate measure is not to ban phosphates in detergents alone but to ensure that all sewage passing into waterways is treated to remove phosphates before release. This precaution would reduce phosphate pollution to a low level.

At least as important as the pollution aspect is the fact that phosphorus is essential to organic life; it is involved in genetic transmission and in cellular energy use. Phosphorus is found in all living organisms as part of a cycle. In terrestrial animals it is lost by excretion and passes into the soil, to be eventually incorporated into vegetation and thus returned to the animal. Little phosphorus is lost from the cycle, although local deficits and surpluses may appear, and the supply of phosphorus that is essential for life is maintained. Phosphorus is also found in phosphate rock, in the guano deposits of marine birds, and in fossil bone beds, but none of these sources is extensive. Because man does not recycle waste materials and because mined phosphates are used for industrial purposes, a large amount of phosphorus finds its way via drainage networks to the sea, where it is lost for practical human use. We cannot waste this essential resource without eventually endangering the existence of terrestrial life. Phosphates should be removed from sewage and recycled by being incorporated in fertilizers, although such removal would involve treatment of sewage effluent to a much higher degree than is performed at present.

Sewage Treatment

Treatment of domestic sewage in Canada varies immensely. The simplest approach, as practised, for example, in Richmond, British Columbia, is simply to leave the sewage untreated in open drainage ditches. Fortunately not many communities follow this example, although many individual dwellings in rural areas have no sewage collection or treatment, and many other individual dwellings are served by septic tanks, in which sewage is collected and anaerobically decomposed. The effluent is filtered off through a tile field, and the sludge accumulates, to be pumped out periodically. The system works quite well if it is efficiently maintained and if the absorptive capacity of the soil is not exceeded, but will not work well in shallow soil or in soil which allows rapid drainage of water, which might result in contamination of ground water. Major pollution problems are not caused by individual dwellings, although recreational lakes surrounded by extensive cabin development may be open to contamination. This problem has appeared in British Columbia and Manitoba and on the western coast of the Bruce Peninsula in Ontario, stimulating the OWRC (Ontario Water Resources Commission) to seek a ban on septic tanks.

Many communities collect sewage in an underground system before releasing it without treatment at one point into a water body, trusting to the dilution capacity of the receiving waters. The simplest form of sewage treatment for communities is the *settling lagoon*. Sewage is collected in an open lagoon for the variable time period, during which bacterial decay and oxidation reduce much of the sewage to stable end products. Algae growing in the lagoon incorporate nutrients and minerals, and pathogens complete their lifespan. Once or several times per year the lagoon is flushed out into a river or lake. The system works quite well under the right conditions of sunlight, wind, and temperature, but is becomes rather ineffective during the winter, when freezing prevents oxygenation and bacterial action. Also, serious pollution of receiving waters may occur during flushing, particularly if bottom sludge is washed out. The lagoons are unsightly, often malodorous, and they occupy a lot of land, averaging ten acres per thousand people. The lagoon system is a rudimentary form of treatment and is satisfactory only for small communities, but it is infinitely better than no treatment at all.

The next step up from lagoon treatment is *primary* treatment in sewage disposal works, which is designed to remove solid materials. Sewage is first screened to remove garbage and grit, then it passes to a shredder where paper is chopped, and then into settling tanks, where it is retained for sedimentation. The bottom sludge is removed, and grease and scum are skimmed off the surface, after which the effluent is chlorinated to kill bacteria and released. The sludge and scum are commonly either used as land fill (usually referred to as "sanitary" land fill) or incinerated.

Primary treatment may be followed by the more advanced *secondary* treatment, in which organic material is also removed, by using either *activated sludge* or a *trickling filter.* The activated sludge method involves decomposition of organic material by aerobic bacteria in *aeration tanks,* which generates a sludge that is removed in settling tanks. Part is returned to the aeration tanks; the remainder is disposed of as in primary treatment. The trickling filter system involves slow percolation of effluent through beds of gravel or crushed rock; aerobic decomposition takes place by bacteria coating the rocks. This method is rather less efficient than the activated sludge method and is passing out of use. In either case the effluent is chlorinated and released. In this condition about 90 percent of the solid material and 75 to 90 percent of the BOD has been removed, compared with 60 percent of the solids removed by primary treatment. The effluent, however, still retains most of its nitrate and phosphate content. To remove this it is necessary to pass the effluent on for *tertiary* treatment, which is considerably more complicated and is still at an experimental stage. In the system used at Lake Tahoe, California, phosphates are removed by a "flash mix" with lime, which produces flocculation and settling. [10] The lime sludge is collected and incinerated; reclaimed lime is recycled in the process. The effluent still contains nitrogen, mostly in the form of ammonia, which is removed in a stripping tower by forced aeration. The effluent finally passes through an electrolyte and activated carbon before release.

Sewage treatment in Canada is disgraceful for a country that is among the richest in the world and that boasts a high standard of living. No Canadian community carries out tertiary treatment and many perform no treatment at all. It has been estimated that only about 75 percent of the urban population is served by a sewerage system, and in many cases the system includes only collection, not treatment. In British Columbia in 1967, 90 out of 130 communities were sewered, but only 53 treated the sewage, and only 40 practised secondary treatment.[11] In Saskatchewan only 286 out of 491 communities were sewered. In 5 of these primary or secondary treatment was practised; the remaining 281 had lagoon treatment.[12] In Quebec only 125 communities out of 1,700 had sewage treatment.[13] Despite rapid progress in extending sewage treatment facilities, there is immense scope for improvement. The situation in some major Canadian cities is particularly bad. Halifax, Quebec City, Hull, and St. John's, with a combined population of over 366,000, carry out absolutely no sewage treatment. Montreal, with a population of close to 2.5 million, dumps 91.6 percent of its sewage untreated into the St. Lawrence. In British Columbia, Victoria practises secondary treatment of 1.1 percent of its sewage but releases the remainder into the Strait of Juan de Fuca without treatment, contributing to a high rate of infectious hepatitis in the area. Vancouver carries out primary treatment of only 41 percent of its sewage, while Saint John and Saskatoon treat 0.3 percent and 7 percent respectively. Winnipeg treats all its sewage, but only by settling lagoon. Even Ottawa carries out only primary treatment. This story of untreated sewage polluting Canadian waterways is even more intolerable when one realises that the 100 percent treatment carried out in cities like Toronto is purely theoretical due to inadequate sewerage systems.

Sewerage Systems

Sewerage systems follow a number of different patterns but fall into two general categories. The traditional system has involved the collection of domestic sewage and street runoff after rainstorms into one network; more recent systems usually separate the two collections. The separate system is advantageous because the maximum flow of sewage can be predicted and the capacity of the sewerage system planned accordingly. A combined system may have to receive unpredictably high flows after severe storms. It is obviously impossible to build a system capable of handling the highest flow which could occur, so a series of *storm overflows* are usually incorporated. These come into operation when a specified flow is exceeded, passing untreated effluent directly to the drainage network. The threshold flow is usually calculated as a multiple of the minimum, or *dry-weather flow* (DWF). In Britain, for example, storm overflows operate at six times the DWF.

This situation is satisfactory only if such flows occur infrequently, so accurate forecasting becomes essential. In practise such forecasting is difficult, particularly because the increasing asphalt cover of drainage basins in urban areas drastically alters storm runoff patterns. Forecasting problems make it difficult to design an adequate combined system which precludes occasional severe pollution. As a result, in Britain the concentration of pollutants in some streams may reach eighty times the tolerable level after severe rainstorms. This difficulty is obviously accentuated where there is a big seasonal difference in rainfall or where much flow comes at one season as a result of melting snow. The only satisfactory answer is the use of separate sewerage and storm networks. Most new systems follow this pattern, but a large backlog of dual systems still exists in older communities, where flows sometimes increase fiftyfold during storms.[14] The separation of systems in these communities will be very expensive. In Toronto, for example, the cost of providing separate systems is estimated at more than $330 million. Even where a dual system exists some treatment of street washoff is desirable, because in addition to garbage and dust street washoff usually contains a variety of traffic waste, particularly hydrocarbons.

Financing Sewage Treatment

As suggested, satisfactory control of water pollution by sewage in Canada requires tertiary treatment, at least in urban communities. The present situation precludes any real hope for satisfactory control in the near future, although some Okanagan communities are installing tertiary treatment facilities. The chief problem is the inability of communities to raise adequate funds. Even adequate collection of sewage is expensive, without the added cost of treatment. The major treatment expense is the capital cost of establishing a sewage disposal work, which varies considerably with the size of works and the type and flow of sewage to be handled. For a city of 100,000 people a primary treatment plant would cost somewhere between $1.3 million and $5 million; a secondary treatment plant would cost $2.5 million to $12 million. Only a guess at the potential cost of a tertiary plant can be made, but the Lake Tahoe operation suggests a capital cost of at least $25 million, of which 25 percent would be spent on phosphate removal alone. In addition to the capital cost, annual operating costs for a city of 100,000 would range from $75,000 to $345,000 for primary treatment and from $115,000 to $395,000 for secondary treatment.

Very few communities have adequate resources or borrowing capability for the capital expenditure involved. If the country as a whole is to work seriously toward abatement of water pollution, adequate federal funds must be made available. All construction of sewage treatment works is eligible for a 66 percent loan from the Central Mortgage and Housing Corporation, but in practise the available funds are rarely adequate to cover demands. Unless this situation changes it is difficult to foresee early radical improvement in the water pollution situation. The latest plans for Montreal will not lead to elimination of untreated sewage until 1985. As Montreal has been under court order to eliminate untreated sewage since 1930, this progress is not very impressive. In short, what is required for adequate control of water pollution is a major reassessment of priorities on the part of government at all levels. The necessary legislation exists in the form of Canada Water Act, but this is useless unless it is enforced.

References

1. R. F. Legge and D. Dingeldein, "We Hung Phosphates without a Fair Trial," *Canadian Research and Development* 3 Mar.–Apr. (1970): 19–42.

2. J. R. Vallentyne, "Phosphorus and the Control of Eutrophication," *Canadian Research and Development* 3 May–June (1970): 36–49.

3. R. F. Legge, "Phosphates and the Swedish View," *Canadian Research and Development* 3 July–August (1970): 42–44.

4. International Lake Erie and Lake Ontario–St. Lawrence River Pollution Boards, "Pollution of Lake Erie, Lake Ontario and the International Section of the St. Lawrence River," vol. 1, Report to the International Joint Commission (1969).

5. P. D. Goulden, W. J. Traversy and G. Kerr, "Detergents, Phosphates and Water Pollution," *Inland Waters Branch Technical Bulletin* (1970): 22.

6. D. A. Okum, "Managing the Great Lakes Water Resource," *Journal of the Water Pollution Control Federation* 41 (1969): 1859–1862.

7. A. M. Beeton, "Eutrophication of the St. Lawrence Great Lakes," *Limnology and Oceanography* 10 (1965): 240–254.

8. S. S. Epstein, "NTA," *Environment* (7) (1970): 2–11.

9. J. Ryther and W. Dunstan, "Nitrogen, Phosphorus and Eutrophication in the Coastal Marine Environment," *Science* 171 (3975) (1971): 1008–1013.

10. E. J. Middlebrooks, E. A. Pearson, M. Tunzi, A. Adinarayana, P. H. McGauhey and G. A. Rohlich, "Eutrophication of Surface Water–Lake Tahoe," *Journal of the Water Pollution Control Federation* 43 (1971): 242–251.

11. C. J. Keenan, "A Review of the Progress in Water Pollution Abatement in British Columbia." Background papers for the *National Conference on Pollution and Our Environment,* Vol. 2 (Ottawa: Queen's Printer, 1967).

12. M. H. Prescott, B. Boyson and R. C. Landine, "A Review of the Progress in Water Pollution Abatement in Saskatchewan." Background papers for the *National Conference on Pollution and Our Environment,* Vol. 2 (Ottawa: Queen's Printer, 1967).

13. M. R. Desjardins, "Brief on Efforts in the Province of Quebec to Eliminate or Control Pollution of Water." Background papers for the *National Conference on Pollution and Our Environment,* Vol. 2 (Ottawa: Queen's Printer, 1967).

14. D. S. Caverly, L. M. Tobias and B. C. Palmer, "Work of the Provincial Government (Ontario) toward the Control of Water Pollution." Background papers for the *National Conference on Pollution and Our Environment,* Vol. 2 (Ottawa: Queen's Printer 1967).

Chapter 4

Industrial Water Pollution

Domestic sewage does not vary much in composition from region to region and the development of standardised treatment which can be applied almost anywhere has therefore been relatively easy. Industrial wastes are much more difficult to handle. Every industry turns out different waste products, so that it is difficult to standardise treatment procedures. Waste material is frequently nonbiodegradable and may be lethal to aquatic life or may render water sterile. Some wastes are toxic in minute quantities and require immense dilution, particularly heavy metals such as arsenic, produced in effluent from a variety of metallic industries and tolerable only at a dilution of 0.5 ppm (parts per million). Other materials such as radioactive wastes or some acids and alkalis may be dangerous to workers or damaging to equipment. Whether or not industrial wastes should be moved to sewage treatment plants for treatment is still being discussed. There are some advantages to this policy—for example, it makes possible the full use of skilled labour and allows scale economies in equipment purchase and operation costs. However, the disadvantages tend to outweigh the advantages.

One obvious disadvantage is the necessity for the sewage plant to install equipment that is more complex and expensive than the equipment normally required for domestic sewage. This problem is compounded by the need to install equipment to handle a wide variety of wastes. It is not appropriate that the community should bear the cost of this additional equipment, although it might choose to contribute as an incentive to industrial location. Such an incentive is the recent $3.2 million contribution by the Alberta government to the costs of pollution control at the Grande Prairie pulp mill. The varying costs of treating wastes from different industries can also be accommodated by graded sewer service charges. Transport of waste to the treatment plant might cause damage to sewerage or dangerous overspills from storm overflows. Transport of wastes to the plant might also involve a reduction of flow in rivers for considerable distances. The riparian proprietors (those who own land along river banks and who are legally assumed to have some rights to the water in the river) of river water tend to object to losing part of their water, even if it is highly polluted. As a result of these disadvantages, it is now generally agreed that industrial wastes should be treated at their points of origin. This may be discouragingly expensive for small industries, and they might also encounter a scarcity of trained personnel, but both these problems can be overcome by adequate planning, particularly of industrial location policy, in most cases. We should point out here that most industries, regardless of size, practice no treatment at all, discharging untreated wastes directly into receiving streams and trusting to the stream's dilution capacity.

It is not possible to discuss industrial water pollution in general because of the great variety of industries, wastes, and treatment procedures, so I have chosen two examples from the wide range of industrial pollution problems in Canada. Both exemplify in different ways the difficulties of pollution control. The pulp and paper industry is a pollution source which is of immense economic and social importance in Canada, and attempts to completely control pollution by this industry at an early date might produce extensive social disruption. The second example, mercury contamination, is only partially of industrial origin. It is included because it is one of the most puzzling and potentially damaging forms of pollution in Canada.

The Pulp and Paper Industry

The pulp and paper industry has been the leading manufacturing industry in Canada for many years, contributing about 2 percent of the gross national product and 16 percent of the exports. In 1966, 134 paper and pulp mills were in operation, owned by sixty odd companies, but recent figures indicate a rapid increase in the number of mills. In 1966 the total production of pulp was 15,958,000 tons. The major producing provinces are Quebec, Ontario, and British Columbia, but operations are active in all provinces except Prince Edward Island. The industry is therefore not only the most important but also the most widespread in the country.

The pulp industry has two vital raw material requirements: timber and water of good quality. Water must be low in calcium and magnesium, turbidity, colour, and dissolved gases or the quality of paper will be adversely affected. An extremely high, though variable, quantity of water is also necessary. Amounts required vary from 10,000 gallons per ton of pulp for mills that make single products such as groundwood pulp to 100,000 gallons per ton for integrated mills that produce several grades of pulp and paper.

Because of the high water demands pulp mills are usually constructed in mountain or forest areas, where water and timber supplies are abundant and of high quality. The market for pulp and paper also exerts an attraction, so that some pulp factories locate close to the market despite polluted water sources. However, the bulk of pulp and paper mills are located at some distance from centres of major settlement, which means that they are far from urban waste disposal plants and must rely on the dilution capacity of neighbouring streams or lakes for waste removal. Dilution may eventually be satisfactory, but because high inputs of waste occur, severe local pollution may precede adequate dilution. The water pollution problem associated with pulp mills is serious, and the industry is also frequently associated with conspicuous air pollution that produces a characteristic smell of rotting cabbages.

Pulp mill pollution has an immense aesthetic impact, not only because the waste is unsightly and malodorous but also because many pulp mills are juxtaposed with magnificent mountain and forest scenery. Pollution is offensive in an urban environment, but we accept some pollution as an inevitable part of urban like, and this decline in expectations of environmental quality has progressed to the point that most of us do not recognize the existence of "mild" pollution. The presence of magnificent unspoiled country close to many pulp mills provides a standard of environmental quality that dramatizes our loss. One of the worse examples of such decline is the North Western Pulp and Power mill at Hinton, Alberta, which produces a foul-smelling haze through which visitors must pass to reach Jasper National Park.

Pulping technology

The production of paper today almost inevitably involves the production of pulp from reduced timber, but the first paper mill in Canada used linen and cotton rags. Paper was handmade in a factory which opened at St. Andrews, eastern Quebec, in 1805. Gradually machines took over from hand production, and in 1838 a process was developed in Nova Scotia by which spruce was pulped mechanically for use as a raw material. This *groundwood,* or *mechanical,* pulping technique soon became widespread and dominated the industry for many years, and despite the subsequent introduction of more sophisticated processes it is still important, particularly as a producer of newsprint. Seventy-two groundwood mills in Canada still supply 80 to 85 percent of the requirements of the Canadian newsprint industry. The basic process has not changed much since 1838, although technical improvements, such as the replacement of natural sandstone grinders by artificial silicon carbide pulpstones, have been introduced. The process involves grinding whole timber or chips into a slurry with water, then passing the slurry through a series of centrifugal screens to separate the pulp from course fibres, knots, and dirt.

Groundwood monopolised the Canadian industry until 1865, when the first chemical pulp mill was set up at Windsor Mills, Quebec. This was a *soda* pulp mill, in which timber was reduced by an alkaline process developed in England in 1854. The pulp was produced by "cooking" timber with a liquor of sodium hydroxide and sodium carbonate. Because sodium hydroxide is expensive, the process involves partial recovery of chemicals from the spent cooking liquor by evaporation and incineration. A less expensive version of the alkaline process was subsequently developed, in which sodium carbonate was replaced by sodium sulphite. This process, known as the *kraft* process, produces a *sulphate* pulp. The first kraft mill in Canada opened at East Angus, Quebec, in 1907. In the kraft process, timber is steam heated under pressure with the cooking liquor, or "white" liquor. After pulping, the spent cooking liquor, or "black" liquor, is burned, and the residue is dissolved to give "green" liquor, which is treated with lime and converted back to "white" liquor for reuse. After separation, the pulp is screened and bleached to produce a very strong, though rather dark, paper. One of the disadvantages of the kraft process is that the paper is difficult to bleach properly and on bleaching loses much of its strength.

Shortly after the introduction of soda pulping, an acidic process was developed. The principles of this *sulphite* process were discovered in the United States in 1857, but it was not perfected until 1872 in Sweden. The first sulphite mill in Canada was opened at Sheet Harbour, Nova Scotia, in 1885. The process involves treatment of timber with a cooking liquor of sulphurous acid and calcium bisulphite at temperatures above 135 degrees C. The spent cooking liquor, or "red" liquor, is discharged as waste. Between 1885 and the 1930s most chemical pulp was produced by the sulphite process. Although the pulp is relatively weak compared with kraft pulp, it can be bleached much more easily. In the past, however, it could be produced only from timber of relatively low resin content, such aa spruce, fir, and hemlock. The alkaline cooking liquor used in the kraft process, on the other hand, could penetrate resinous timber, such as pine, as well. The growth of kraft pulping at the expense of sulphite pulping in the 1930s was due both to advances in bleaching techniques, which extended the utility of kraft paper, and to the development of paper packaging, which demands strong brown paper. Recent changes in the sulphite process, such as the replacement of the calcium base by a magnesium base, allow the use of a wider range of timber and some recovery of chemicals from the spent cooking liquor, but the vast majority of chemical pulp mills use the kraft process.

In British Columbia, for example, nineteen of the twenty-one chemical pulp mills used the kraft process in 1966.

Effluents and pollution

This brief discussion of pulping processes indicates that pulp and and paper technology is heterogeneous and produces a variety of effluents. In general, the polluting effect of these effluents includes deoxygenation of receiving waters by organic wastes, toxicity, encouragement of nuisance organism growth, effects of suspended solids, tainting of fish, and the avoidance of nonlethal wastes by fish.[1] The most important contributors of organic waste are the sulphite pulp mills, because the spent liquor is not recovered. The waste organic matter derived from sulphite pulping is twenty times more than that from kraft pulping,[2] and most of it comes from the spent sulphite liquor, which has a five-day BOD of up to 35,000 ppm.[3]

The effects of organic waste from the pulp industry are identical to those of sewage wastes. If dilution is adequate, the ability of the stream to purify itself will not be impaired. If the receiving water body is too small, oxygen depletion will inhibit aquatic life. Research on the oxygen requirements of fish has shown a wide variation.[4] The requirement depends on such habitat factors as water temperature and velocity of stream flow,[5] but it also varies with species. Because cold water game fish like salmon, trout, and char have the highest requirements, even relatively mild deoxygenation can seriously effect recreational and commercial fishing.

The daily BOD output of a sulphite mill is equivalent to a town of nearly 4 million people. The five-day BOD output is about 600,000 pounds, which would require dilution with 180 million gallons of water to meet minimal standards. Many inland receiving waters simply are not large enough to dilute the waste of mills situated beside them, and narrow coastal bays may also become deoxygenated. Because much less organic waste is released from kraft mills, deoxygenation is also much lower, but the black liquor used in kraft pulping is extremely toxic, and its effects are increased by even mild reduction of dissolved oxygen.

The distinction between toxicity and deoxygenation is technically significant, although fish probably do not appreciate the distinction between asphyxiation and poisoning. Spent sulphite liquor appears to be relatively non-toxic, although it has a high five-day BOD and also reduces the ability of fish to withstand low oxygen contents. It also tends to have a rather high acidity, around pH=3 (pH is a measure of acidity on a fourteen point scale; pH=7 is neutral), which is potentially damaging to fish. Kraft mill effluent, on the other hand, is highly toxic if it leaves the mill. The kraft process should be

safe, because it involves recovery of the black liquor, but in practise such recovery is often much less than 100 percent[6] even if accidental release does
not occur. The toxic effects of black liquor even in dilute solution have been
documented by much research, but the exact source of toxicity is not entirely
certain.[7] [8] [9] It was traditionally believed that sulphate soap, methyl
mercaptan, hydrogen sulphide, and sodium sulphide were responsible, but
phenolic substances are also found in the liquor. A new compound called
4-(p-tolyl-)-1-pentanol, with toxicity comparable to that of cyanide, has also
been discovered.

The accumulation of suspended solids can also have serious effects.
These include the waste from debarking before pulping and the course fibres,
knots, and dirt removed by screening after pulping. Although the waste does not
damage fish directly, if the accumulation is sufficient food organisms on the
bottom may be buried. The bulk of the suspended solids are organic and will,
of course, eventually contribute to deoxygenation. The quantities involved
vary from twenty to forty tons per day for kraft and sulphite mills to about
eighty tons per day for groundwood mills. The cumulative effect of such
waste quantities is immense; it is not surprising that the bottom of the Ottawa
River, for example, is blanketed by a thirty-foot thickness of pulp mill debris
in the vicinity of the Eddy pulp mill at Hull, Quebec.

The other effects of pulp mill effluents are minor by comparison.
Spent sulphite liquor in very low dilutions can encourage the growth of nuisance organisms such as *Sphaerotilus natans* (sewage fungus).[10] Avoidance of
nonlethal effluent by fish has been demonstrated for some salmonid fish, which
appear to tolerate quite high levels of pollution by spent sulphite liquor but
much lower levels of kraft mill effluent.[11] The problem of tainting fish by
pulp mill effluents is somewhat difficult to document, due in part to the sub-
jectivity of assessment. Tainting by spent sulphite liquor has been suspected but
not proven, but untreated kraft mill effluent definitely can produce measurable
flavour impairment in salmon exposed for periods of seventy-five to ninety
hours.[12] The mechanism has not been demonstrated, but phenolic substances can reasonably be suspected, as they have been shown to cause tainting
elsewhere.

Most of this discussion has dealt only with the effluent from pulping
operations. In many mills the pulp is bleached as well, so that other chemicals
may be added to the normal effluent. The effect of these agents on aquatic life
has not been widely studied, but there is little doubt that some, such as zinc
hydrosulphite, could prove highly toxic. In general, pollution from bleaching
pulp mills is much more serious than from nonbleaching mills: nonbleaching
kraft, soda, and sulphite mills produce 116, 132, and 176 pounds of organic
chemicals per ton of pulp respectively; bleaching mills produce 149, 92, and
818 pounds per ton.

A serious form of pollutant associated with the pulp and paper
industry are chemicals used as slimicides. Pulp and paper systems offer a fertile

breeding ground for bacteria and fungi, which, if uncontrolled, can cause stain-
ing and deterioration of the paper and damage to machinery. A variety of
substances are used as slimicides, particularly chlorine, organomercurial compounds, and chlorinated phenols. The last two are particularly toxic to aquatic
life if released in effluent. Sodium pentachlorophenol, for example, is toxic in
concentrations as low as 0.2 to 0.3 ppm. It was traditionally believed that the
release of slimicides was only in small, nondamaging quantities, but recent
evidence shows that the problem is much more widespread than suspected.
(This subject is reviewed more thoroughly below.)

 Air pollution is also associated with the pulping industry, particularly
with kraft mills. The pollutants produced are not a proven health hazard, but
the odour of gases, particularly methyl disulphide, methyl sulphide, methyl
mercaptans, and hydrogen sulphide, is unpleasant and is perceptible at levels at
which the concentration of gases cannot be measured.[13] Although odour
occurs wherever pulp mills are located, only in British Columbia is it regarded
seriously as a pollutant. This perhaps reflects the preoccupation of the other
major pulp-producing provinces, Quebec and Ontario, with the more immediately serious problems of urban air pollution. The concern of the previous
British Columbia government was shown by its offer of a $250,000 reward for
the development of an efficient process for controlling odour emission from
pulp mills. The intensity of their concern may be questioned, however, as such
an invention would be worth much more than the reward they offer.

Pollution control

 The pulp and paper industry has shown a high degree of awareness of
the pollution problem for some years, due not so much to public benevolence
as to economic self-interest. Many of the "waste" products lost in pulp mill
effluent are quite valuable; fibre, for example, is worth about $160 per ton.
An economical method of recovery could effect considerable savings in production costs, and thus a large volume of research has been completed on many
aspects of effluent control. With the exception of air pollution, the problem in
the pulp and paper industry is probably economic rather than technologic,
because pollution control equipment is costly—for example, two evaporators
currently under construction in British Columbia for black liquor in kraft mills
will cost $3 million—and the pulp and paper industry claims that it cannot
afford to rapidly reduce pollution.

 The expenditure for control measures which has already taken place
is substantial. In Ontario $32 million was spent between 1960 and 1966 on
solid emission reduction; $28 million was spent on all aspects of pollution in
British Columbia. This investment is considerable, but it is not particularly
impressive compared with the annual production of the industry, which is over
$2 billion. Although considerable progress has been made in some areas—for

example, bark sewering—the overall degree of control is still totally inadequate. So every province in the country but Prince Edward Island, which has no mills, has pollution problems associated with the industry.

Because the industry is economically and socially important, both federal and provincial governments have been reluctant to enforce existing legislation, although this situation is now changing. In Quebec, the leading producer of pulp, the provincial Water Board has turned over the files of twenty-one mills that produce unacceptable pollution to the Justice Department for action, which could include fines, imprisonment, and mill closure. The pulp and paper industry accounts for 19.2 percent of the capital investment in Quebec, which is suffering from chronic unemployment, so it would be unrealistic to expect severe action, but new government attitudes are suggested, at least.

Action similar to that in Quebec is also being prepared in New Brunswick, Nova Scotia, and Newfoundland to ensure that waste is treated at least to some degree before release into drainage networks. In the Maritimes, as in Quebec, chronic unemployment has probably retarded control action. The degree of destruction—for example, in the St. John River, New Brunswick, where the third largest salmon run in North America has been destroyed—has forced action.

In Ontario the Water Resources Commission considers that only ten of forty-two mills have brought their effluent to a satisfactory level. The amount spent in Ontario on pollution control is relatively high, but the effectiveness of enforcement is doubtful. In court action Eddy Forest Products was fined $4,000 for polluting Spanish River, and Domtar Pulp and Paper was fined $1,000 for polluting Lake Superior. In view of the cost of pollution control and the availability of development grants from the government, such fines are not particularly awesome deterrents.

Responsibility for inadequate control of pollution rests with both industry and government, but the problem is even more involved. Most pulp and paper mills in Canada are quite old—many fifty to sixty years old. Obviously the design specifications of such mills do not include provision for processes which have been developed only in the last few years. It might be extremely expensive or physically impossible to convert old mills to new processes so that they can meet present regulations. Mills which cannot be converted should close down in the near future, but instant closure would produce economic disruption and increased unemployment. We cannot expect to solve this pollution problem overnight, and we cannot expect to do it without expense—either in the form of increased prices or taxation to support government subsidies. If we want a clean environment and a reasonable employment level, we must be realistic and be prepared to contribute to the cost. Also, we should demand that all newly constructed mills employ the most advanced control processes available, for the stated expenditure of 4 to 5 percent of capital investment on pollution control has not always been actually spent on effective measures. It will also be necessary to plan mill locations more carefully in relation to the capacity and hydrologic characteristics of receiving waters, because it will be many years before complete recycling is economically feasible.

Mercury Contamination

The discovery in 1968 of high concentrations of mercury in the bottom mud of Lake St. Clair, Ontario, drew attention to a puzzling form of pollution, pinpointed an alarming lack of knowledge about the environmental fate of a notoriously dangerous substance, and generated a well-publicised pollution scare in Canada. Disturbing questions were raised about public health hazards and the efficiency as "public watchdogs" of government agencies.

Environmental pollution by mercury is described as contamination, following a Californian distinction by which contamination is a form of pollution so hazardous that it demands immediate government action. The Lake St. Clair discovery certainly generated such action, thereby sparking a continuing controversy. Some authorities claim that the action was precipitate and criticised research workers for premature release of results; others felt that the restrictions did not go far enough. Despite abundant research results released since 1968, the answers are still not clear.

There is no doubt that mercury is hazardous to health; this has been recognised since at least the fifth century B.C. Mercury has been responsible for illness in many occupationally exposed workers, particularly those in the hatting and chlorine industries,[14] [15] [16] [17] but potential risk to people without occupational exposure had not been widely recognised. Mercury was known to occur in certain industrial effluents, but no transmission to food chains had been discovered and therefore no widespread hazard was expected.

Forms and health effects

The mercury problem is complicated by the variety of forms in which it occurs. Inorganic forms include elemental vapour and mercurous and mercuric salts; organomercurials include salts of phenyl mercury, methoxyethyl mercury, and monoalkyl mercury compounds (methyl and ethyl mercury salts). Exposure to inorganic mercury may be acute or chronic. When it is taken orally only about 2 percent is absorbed into the body. On the other hand, absorption of mercury vapour through the lungs or intestines may reach 75 to 85 percent,[18] much of which is rapidly excreted in urine, although acute exposure may result in high concentrations in the brain, kidneys, and liver.[19] [20] Gastroenteritis, kidney damage, and irritation of lung tissue may follow acute exposure. Concentration in the brain can disrupt the function of the central nervous system, causing violent tremors and psychological disturbances, although these problems are more frequently associated with chronic exposure. The rapid excretion of inorganic mercury ensures that there is little danger of long-term accumulation. Chronic exposure will normally only affect people with occupational exposure.

Organomercurials are less volatile than inorganic mercury, and exposure is mainly to solid or liquid forms. Unlike inorganic mercury, they can be easily absorbed through the intestine in these forms—absorption of methyl mercury may reach 95 percent, compared with 2 percent for inorganic mercury. The fate of organomercurials varies. Both phenyl mercury and methoxyethyl mercuryare rapidly degraded to inorganic forms.[21] Alkyl mercury, particularly methyl mercury, on the other hand, degrades slowly, having a half-life (the time required for concentration of a substance to drop by one-half) of about seventy days.[22] It concentrates in red blood cells and in the brain, where it constitutes 98 percent of the total mercury burden. [23] It can also cross the placental barrier, concentrating in foetal blood to levels appreciably higher than in maternal blood.[24] There is evidence that this "trapping" may protect the mother from some ill effects.[25]

The uses to which organomercurials are put prevents frequent acute exposure. Some cases of acute methoxyethyl mercury poisoning have occurred, resulting (like inorganic mercury) in gastroenteritis and kidney damage. Very few cases of acute phenyl mercury poisoning have been reported, but mild kidney injury can be produced.[26] Chronic exposure to organomercurials is rare, and the rapid metabolism and excretion of methoxyethyl and phenyl mercury prevents accumulation to high levels. The slow degradation and excretion of methyl mercury, on the other hand, poses a serious risk of accumulation to toxic levels, and it is therefore the most dangerous of the mercury compounds. Methyl mercury poisoning produces numbness, paralysis, speech disturbance, impairment of hearing, emotional distrubances, and in extreme cases, death. In children mental retardation, cerebral palsy, and convulsions can occur.[27] In all cases of severe poisoning symptoms are irreversible. Accumulation in the foetus can produce damage to the central nervous system; the brain is particularly vulnerable to damage at the foetal stage.[28] At Minamata, in southwest Kyusku, Japan, approximately 5 percent of the infants born between 1955 and 1959 showed evidence of damage, and evidence of teratogenic (birth-deforming) effects, which may result from the effect of methyl mercury on chromosomes and cell division, was also found.[29]

History of mercury contamination

Although some of the toxic effects of mercury have been known for many years, concern about potential environmental contamination is relatively recent. It has always been assumed that mercuric compounds released in industrial wastes sank to the bottoms of streams and lakes and had no potential contact with man. The first suggestion that this is not the case was at Minamata Bay. Shortly after the Second World War a factory was established there to produce vinyl chloride, acetaldehyde, and sulphuric acid.[30] Methyl mercury chloride was used as a catalyst in the factory and was released in wastes, accumulating in mud on the bottom of the bay. In 1953 neurologic disorders began to appear in inhabitants of the area, who ate fish and shellfish from the bay. By 1956 disease had reached epidemic proportions, and by 1960, 111 cases of mercury poisoning had been recorded.[31] Forty of these had died by 1965, and many of the remainder were permanently disabled. The concentration of methyl mercury chloride in shellfish and fish from the bay was analytically demonstrated, with levels between 27 and 102 parts per million.[32] (The average daily fish intake of inhabitants was 100 to 300 grams of fish.) In 1960 the factory installed waste treatment equipment, and mercury concentrations in fish steadily declined. After 1961 no new cases of "Minamata disease" were recorded, but in 1964 the Agano River in the Nigata Prefecture was contaminated by mercury industrial effluent; 26 people became ill and 5 die.[33]

The mercury problem was also noticed in Sweden at an early stage. Between 1956 and 1963 pheasant and other seed-eating species were poisoned, sometimes lethally, during or after sowing.[34] Mercury concentrations of up to 270 ppm were found in the liver and kidneys, although this decreased to an average value of less than 1 ppm by the shooting season. The source of the contamination was methyl mercury dicyandiamide, used as a fungicide for seed treatment.[35] In 1965 the use of this fungicide was severly restricted, and in 1966 it was banned, although methoxyethyl mercury compounds were allowed instead. This ban reduced mercury use for seed treatment by 68 percent, which greatly reduced mortality among birds, but mercury was still turning up in unusually high concentrations in fish and meat.[36] Extensive research on this problem in the mid-1960s demonstrated that it originated from industrial deposition of mercury in waterways, particularly from chlor-alkali plants and from pulp mills using phenyl mercury compounds as slimicides.[37] This confirmed observations at Minamata and Niigata.

One interesting fact to emerge from the research was that the contaminant was always methyl mercury, regardless of the compounds in the original waste.[38] This supported a suggestion made in connection with the Minamata disaster that metallic mercury can be converted into methyl mercury in waterways. Instead of lying inert in the bottom mud of lakes and streams, it undergoes biological methylation, particularly where the organic content of the water is high or waters are polluted. The mechanism of conversion was demonstrated in 1967 in Sweden. The conversion in waterways is serious because it allows the mercury to become incorporated into food chains.

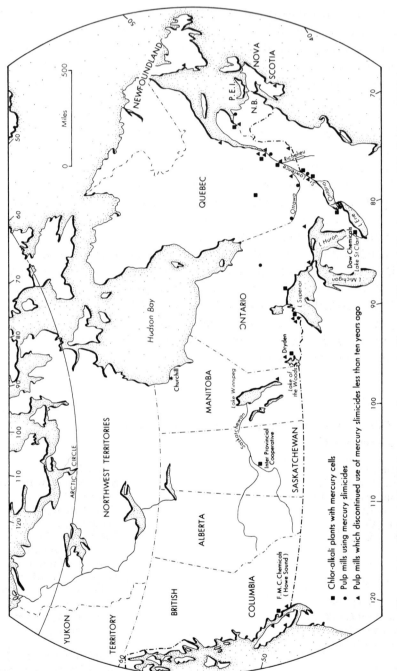

Figure 4.1.   Major industrial sources of mercury. (Source: Fimreite, Environmental Pollution, 1971.)

Mercury uses and sources in Canada

By the mid-1960s it was comparatively common knowledge that use of methyl mercury compounds as fungicides for seed dressing was hazardous. It was also recognised that inorganic mercury in industrial effluents could be transformed into methyl mercury in waterways (although the mechanism was not demonstrated until 1967). Experience in Sweden and Japan indicated potential contamination in any country where chlor-alkali or kraft pulp and paper industries were important or where mercury fungicides were used for seed treatment. It is difficult to understand why research in Canada was not initiated until 1968.

The most important user of mercury in Canada is the chlor-alkali industry. Recently a new process for manufacture of chlorine and caustic soda was developed based on electrolytic use of mercury. The change to this process caused a rapid increase in the Canadian demand for mercury for inventory in chlor-alkali plants which was supplied largely by imports. These reached over $1 million in 1965. Table 4.1 lists the fourteen chlor-alkali plants using mercury cells; the Dow operation at Sarnia includes three units. A chlor-alkali plant that produces 100 tons of chlorine per day requires 75,000 to 150,000 pounds of mercury. Fimreita[39] estimates that Canadian chlor-alkali plants hold about 2 million pounds and require about 200,000 pounds per year to make up for losses in processing. This averages about half a pound per ton of chlorine produced, and most passes out in effluent.

Table 4.1. Chlor-Alkali Plants in Canada That Use Mercury Cells

F. M. C. Chemicals	Squamish, B. C.
Interprovincial Cooperative	Saskatoon, Saskatchewan
Dryden Chemicals Co., Ltd.	Dryden, Ontario
Dow Chemical, Ltd.	Thunder Bay, Ontario
American Can. Co.	Marathon, Ontario
Dow Chemical, Ltd.	Sarnia, Ontario
C. I. L.	Hamilton, Ontario
C. I. L.	Cornwall, Ontario
C. I. L.	Shawnigan, Quebec
C. I. L.	Dalhousie, New Brunswick
Aluminum Co. of Canada	Arvida, Quebec
Standard Chemical Co., Ltd.	Beauharnois, Quebec
Shawnigan Chemicals, Ltd. (Closed about 1968)	Shawnigan, Quebec
Domtar	Lebel-sur-Quevillon, Quebec
Canso Chemicals (Opened 1970)	New Glasgow, Nova Scotia

Source: E. G. Bligh, "Mercury Contamination in Fish" (Paper delivered at the Twentieth Annual Institute for Public Health Inspectors, Winnipeg, October 19–23, 1970).

Mercury has been used for many years in the pulp and paper industry as a slimicide, mainly in an organic form, phenyl mercury acetate. This use has been greatly reduced in Canada in recent years, and in 1969 only nine companies were using mercury slimicides. These totaled about 30,000 pounds, with a phenyl mercury acetate content of 10 percent, most of which remains in the products. Slimicidal use of mercury has now been phased out completely in Canada.

Organomercurials have been widely used in Canada as fungicidal seed dressing for cereals and flax. In some cases they are used in combination with insecticides. The most frequently used fungicides are alkyl compounds, particularly methyl mercury dicyandiamide, although use has declined in recent years; the total use of mercury in seed dressing in 1968 was assessed at just under 20,000 pounds. Some mercury compounds are also used as fungicidal sprays in fruit-growing regions and on potato crops; [40] mercurous chloride, mercuric chloride, and phenyl mercury acetate are also used as turf fungicides.

Several other uses of mercury in Canada are difficult to assess quantitatively. These include medicinal uses in drugs, antibacterials, dental amalgams, and thermometers. A recent estimate suggested that drug preparations sewered from homes in Canada might introduce 4,500 pounds of mercury per year into the environment; broken thermometers could account for another 14,000 pounds.[41] Other uses difficult to assess are in the paint industry and in amalgamation to recover gold and silver. The latter use did amount to about 3,000 pounds per year but is declining. Mercury is also widely used in the electrical industry and as a catalyst in plastic manufacture. One source of mercury contamination which has been largely neglected in the past is fuel burning. No data are available on the mercury content of fuels burned in Canada, but a report on coal mined in Illinois shows a mercury content varying from 0.04 to 0.49 ppm. Some power plants and incinerators in the United States are believed to emit up to 5,300 pounds of mercury per year.[42]

In addition to mercury released into the environment through man's activities, a certain amount of the mercury encountered in the biosphere is of natural origin. Cinnabar deposits occur at several locations in British Columbia, and concentrations of mercury as high as 10 ppm have been found in adjacent soils. Many other metallic ores contain traces of mercury, notably gold, molybdenum, lead, and zinc. Most of the areas where these metals are mined are potential sources of mercury contamination.

Mercury contamination in Canada

The first concrete evidence of mercury contamination in Canada was its discovery in bottom sediment in Lake St. Clair. At approximately the same time, evidence of high concentrations in some game birds in Alberta began to appear. This was followed by a more complete study in 1968 and 1969 that examined seed-eating birds, rodents, and predatory birds in southern Alberta, where the use of methyl mercury dicyandiamide as a fungicide was widespread, and in Saskatchewan, where use was not widespread. Egg samples were also collected. Some residue levels that were recorded are summarised in table 4.2.

Although the concentrations were substantially lower than some of the Swedish findings, they were still considerably higher than natural levels. On the basis of these results, hunting of Hungarian partridge and pheasant was banned in Alberta during the fall of 1969. Although seed treated with mercuric fungicides was theoretically carefully handled and disposed of, in fact considerable spillage and dumping of seed appears to have occurred,[44] and contamination resulted from birds scavenging in the fields. The United States Department of Agriculture banned the use of mercury fungicides because of these results, but the Canadian federal and provicial authorities did not, believing instead in phased withdrawal.[45] In Canada, therefore, these fungicides are still being used despite bans imposed in Sweden as early as 1966. The hunting ban in southern Alberta is believed to have caused revenue losses of about $5 million, which may have influenced its removal in 1970 despite a lack of evidence that contamination no longer existed.

Meanwhile, the discoveries in Lake St. Clair had stimulated investiga-

Table 4.2. Mercury Residues in Tissue of Birds and Rodents in Alberta and Saskatchewan

Species	Alberta (Concentration in ppm) Mean	Range	Saskatchewan (Concentration in ppm) Mean	Range
		(Number of Samples in Parentheses)		
PREDATORS:				
Short-eared owl	6.84(3)	0.42–11.30		
Burrowing owl	3.74	1.23–6.24	0.73(1)	
Prairie falcon	1.26(1)			
Swainson's hawk	0.76(5)	0.23–1.48	0.45(8)	0.22–0.95
SEED-EATERS:				
Ring-necked pheasant	2.84(10)	0.48–5.92	0.55(9)	0.02–4.50
Sharp-tailed grouse	1.12(7)	0.45–2.71	0.20(7)	0.02–1.11
Mallard	0.32(2)	0.22–0.42		
Red-winged blackbird	0.88(1)			
Western meadowlark	0.28(3)	0.77–0.64		
Horned lark	1.57(10)	0.02–10.20	0.45(8)	0.02–0.94
RODENTS:				
Richardson's ground squirrel	1.05(7)	0.02–3.47	0.10(2)	0.08–0.12
White-footed mice			0.23(4)	0.02–0.84

Source: N. Fimreite, R. W. Fyfe, and J. A. Keith, "Mercury Contamination of Canadian Prairie Seed-eaters and Their Avian Predators," *Canadian Field-Naturalist* 84 (1970): 270–76.

tions in many parts of Canada, particularly those close to chlor-alkali plants. In November 1969 mercury was found in fish taken from the Saskatchewan River below the Interprovincial Cooperative chlor-alkali plant as Saskatoon. An extended study of a variety of fish from the North and South Saskatchewan rivers, including goldeye, northern pike, sauger, walleye, and white sucker, showed average mercury concentrations ranging from 0.7 to 9.1 ppm. [46] Subsequent research revealed mercury concentrations up to 1,800 ppm in bottom sludge downstream from the chlor-alkali plant. No fishing ban was instituted in Manitoba at the time of the original discovery, but large quantities of contaminated fish were collected and burned.

Research during following months turned up evidence of contaminated fish in many parts of the country: Howe Sound and Pinchi Lake, British Columbia; the North and South Saskatchewan rivers; Cedar Lake, Lake Winnipeg, the Assiniboine and Red rivers, part of the Nelson River, and the Winnipeg-English-Wabigoon rivers system in Manitoba; Marathon and Thunder Bay in Lake Superior; the St. Clair and Detroit rivers and western Lake Erie; lakes in northeastern Quebec; the St. Lawrence, Ottawa, and Richelieu rivers; and the harbour of Dalhousie, New Brusnwick. Some average mercury concentrations are shown in table 4.3.

Concentrations vary greatly, but some source areas are apparent. The Pinchi Lake contamination is related to the operations of the neighbouring

Table 4.3. Average Concentrations of Mercury in
Fish from Various Locations in Canada

Species	Location	Average Mercury Concentration (ppm)
Lake trout	Pinchi Lake	2.86
Pike	Downstream of Edmonton, Alta.	1.06
Pike	Upstream of Saskatoon, Sask.	0.53
Pike	Downstream of Saskatoon	5.86
Sauger	Downstream of Saskatoon	4.37
Sauger	Lake Winnipeg, Man. (Red River)	0.56
Northern pike	Lake Winnipeg (Hecla Island)	0.57
Walleye	Lake Winnipeg (Sturgeon Bay)	0.39
Northern pike	Cedar Lake, Man.	0.68
Northern pike	Lake Winnipegosis, Man.	0.13
Pike	Thunder Bay, Lake Superior	0.75
Pike	Marathon Harbour, Lake Superior	1.51
Coho salmon	Lake Huron	0.16
Walleye	Lake Huron	1.34
Walleye	Lake Erie	0.41
Perch	Lake St. Clair	1.40
Pike	Ottawa River	0.94–1.83
Pike	St. Lawrence River	0.76–1.85

Source: Bligh, "Mercury Contamination in Fish."

Cominco mercury plant, reopened in 1968 in response to the increasing industrial demand for mercury. High concentrations downstream from Saskatoon reflect the contribution of the chlor-alkali plant there; those in Lake St. Clair are related to chlor-alkali plants in Sarnia, Ontario, and Detroit, Michigan. Average concentrations mask the full extent of contamination, for mercury concentrations vary with the size and age of fish. Individual lake trout from Pinchi Lake, pumpkinseed from the St. Clair River, and walleye from Lake St. Clair contained maximum concentrations of 10.50, 7.09, and 5.01 ppm respectively.

It is not known exactly how much mercury has already been deposited in inland waters, but the quantity appears to be substantial. Contamination of Lake St. Clair and the St. Clair River, for example, was caused by two plants, Wyandotte Chemicals, Ltd., of Detroit, and Dow Chemicals, Ltd., of Sarnia. The Wyandotte plant was dumping between 10 and 20 pounds and the Dow plant about 200 pounds of mercury per day. Dow Chemicals has been using mercury in their chlor-alkali plant at Sarnia since 1949, so the total amount of mercury released in effluent might be as high as 1,500,000 pounds, much of which must still be present in the bottom mud of Lake St. Clair, the St. Clair River, and Lake Erie. Contamination of fish will thus probably continue for many years despite bans on dumping.

Apart altogether from environmental effects, the loss of mercury is also expensive. Mercury currently costs about $7 per pound, so over the twenty-year period of operations Dow Chemicals has lost about $10.5 million worth of mercury. Obviously this is serious from the company's viewpoint, but it becomes alarming when we remember that the total known world supply of mercury is adequate only for another ten years at current use levels.

The widespread contamination of fish in inland waters is alarming, but evidence of contamination in coastal waters and in waters that are remote from industrial sources is even more alarming. It implies a much more comprehensive contamination of the environment than hitherto predicted. Some data are reproduced in table 4.4.

The origins of coastal and marine contamination are difficult to understand. The relationship between contamination at Squamish, British Columbia, and the F.M.C. chlor-alkali plant on Howe Sound seems clear, but the source of mercury in beluga whale in Hudson Bay is uncertain. The issue was further confused when mercury appeared in various deep-sea fish such as swordfish and tuna. It also turned up in a consignment of dogfish from Vancouver destined for the German market. A certain amount of mercury in the marine environment could be accounted for by industrial effluents, but it is difficult to believe that all parts of the oceans are sufficiently contaminated to produce the concentrations encountered. Other possibilities include contributions from the weathering of bedrock; from submarine volcanic eruptions, particularly close to the midoceanic rift zones; from air pollution; and from the weathering of submarine deposits of maganese nodules.

Recognition of natural sources of mercury suggests the possibility that mercury contamination of deep-sea fish may be of natural origin and may present no more hazard now than in the past. This is supported by mercury concentrations in preserved tuna from ninety years ago, which are approximately the same as present levels.[47] On the other hand, studies of museum speciments of birds in Sweden revealed considerable increases in mercury concentration during recent years.[48] Observations in Greenland show a doubling of mercury content in ice since 800 B.C., and most of the increase occurred in the past two decades.[49] One possibility is that this originates in part from the degassing of the earth's upper mantle and lower crust, which are now being exposed by man's activities. In any case, even if mercury concentrations in deep-sea fish have not increased, there is no cause for complacency. These fish are now being used to a greater extent than ever before due to advances in fishing technology. Furthermore, we have no evidence that mercury did not cause extensive mortality or brain damage in the past that was possibly masked by the effects of other diseases or by inadequate medical knowledge.

Effects of mercury contamination

Public health. Despite abundant research in recent years, it is difficult to assess the real danger to health posed by mercury contamination.

Table 4.4. Mercury Contamination in Fish and Mammals in Canadian Coastal Waters

Species	Location	Average Mercury Concentration (ppm)
Crabs	Squamish, B. C.	1.55–13.4
Flounder	Squamish	1.00–1.42
Herring	Squamish	0.14–0.30
Copper rockfish	Port Alberni, B. C.	0.60
Copper rockfish	Nanaimo, B. C.	0.37
Beluga (meat)	Hudson Bay	0.66
Beluga (muktuk)	Hudson Bay	0.18
Beluga (meat)	Hudson Bay	2.69
Sucker	Churchill River (mouth)	0.22
Pike	Churchill River	0.24
Winter flounder	Baie des Chaleurs (Bathurst, N. B.)	1.10
Atlantic tomcod	Baie des Chaleurs (Bathurst)	0.18
Atlantic herring	Baie des Chaleurs (Dalhousie, N. B.)	0.04
Crab	Atlantic coast	0.10
Lobster	Atlantic coast	0.08–0.20
Oyster	Atlantic coast	0.02–0.14

Sources: Bligh, "Mercury Contamination in Fish," and N. Fimreite, W. N. Holdsworth, J. A. Keith, P. A. Pearce, and I. M. Gruchy, "Mercury in Fish and Fish-eating Birds Near Sites of Industrial Contamination in Canada," *Canadian Field-Naturalist* 85 (1971): 211–20.

Studies at the University of Toronto have revealed mercury in a wide variety of foodstuffs, such as bread, cocoa, sage, beef liver, and dill pickles. Some wheat and flour samples contained mercury in concentrations ranging from 0.004 to 0.36 ppm.[50] It does not seem that these residues originate in treatment of seed with methyl mercury dicyandiamide. In tests of nearly 1,400 foods, excluding fish, by the Canadian Food and Drug Directorate, very few concentrations above 0.1 ppm were recorded,[51] and no cases of mercury poisoning attributable to contaminated food have been reported in Canada. On the other hand, the disasters at Minimata and Niigata and the poisoning of the Huckleby family in Alamogordo, New Mexico, show that it can occur.

The difficulty of assessing the hazards stem partly from inadequate knowledge of the concentrations required to produce poisoning symptoms and of the threshold concentration in foodstuffs. The problem is compounded by evidence that individuals have varying tolerances. After reviewing the evidence available at the time, the working group on maximum allowable concentrations of the Permanent Commission and International Association on Occupational Health recommended the following limits:

1. Methyl and ethyl mercury salts: No air concentration is recommended. The mercury level in whole blood should not exceed 10 /μg Hg/100 ml (as total mercury). . . .
2. Mercury vapor: 0.05 mg/cu.m.
3. Inorganic mercury salts and phenyl and methoxy-ethyl salts: 0.10 mg Hg/cu.m.[52]

These limits recognize that inorganic forms of mercury are rapidly excreted and are therefore dangerous only at high dosage levels; that phenyl and methoxy-ethyl mercury degrade rapidly in the body and behave essentially like inorganic mercury; that methyl and ethyl mercury degrade slowly and can therefore accumulate to dangerous levels even if they are originally present only in very small concentrations.

The Canadian Food and Drug Directorate set a working limit of 0.5 ppm for mercury in foodstuffs. The trouble with such threshold limits is that their effectiveness depends on the type of mercury present. Where mercury is rapidly excreted the straightforward limit works well, but in the case of methyl and ethyl mercury it must be accompanied by a dietary limit, because any uniform diet of contaminated food can permit accumulation to high levels. All the illness at Minimata and Niigata occurred in people who lived on a diet composed largely of fish and shellfish. Inhabitants of Dryden, northwestern Ontario, who ate up to five fish meals per day for ten months before testing, were found to have mercury concentrations up to 100 ppm in their hair. In Sweden initial attempts have been made to combine concentrations and dietary information into "allowable daily intakes."[53] The situation is still difficult to assess, for individuals in Niigata have shown poisoning symptoms with blood concentrations as low as 0.6 ppm, whereas Swedish fish-eaters with blood concentrations over 1.0 ppm showed no symptoms. An obvious way around the difficulty is to set the threshold level at zero. Such a stop would have extensive economic repercussions, however, and could cause much unnecessary hardship.

Economic repercussions. Government action resulting from evidence of mercury contamination has already caused some hardship in Canada. It has affected people directly dependent on fishing and, in Alberta, on hunting. Full data are not readily available, but even partial data indicate a considerable loss. Restrictions placed on the sale of fish from Lake Erie have damaged the fishery industry there, one of the largest freshwater fisheries in the world. Although this was already suffering a decline, in 1961, 35.5 million pounds of fish were landed in Canada from Lake Erie, valued at $2.5 million. Landings in the United States reached 19.5 million pounds valued at $1.75 million. The value of landings in Canada from Lake St. Clair was $184,000. These figures apply only to commercial fishing and do not include recreational activity. Fishing bans and restrictions have badly damaged recreational fishing and associated boat rental firms. The extent to which the population as a whole was affected is uncertain, but ultimately thousands of people must have been involved.

Data for other areas are not available, but fishermen in the Atlantic provinces who depend on swordfish were affected, and in Manitoba at least 600 fishermen were put out of work. The government of Manitoba took legal action against Interprovincial Cooperative, Ltd., of Saskatoon for $2 million, which the company claimed caused the subsequent closure of the plant. In Ontario a $25 million suit by the government against Dow Chemicals of Sarnia is still pending.

Conclusion

It is not yet possible to state the extent of the public health hazard in Canada from mercury contamination. Application of the tentative 0.5 ppm threshold limit for foodstuffs has already caused considerable hardship and financial losses of millions of dollars. The absence of reported poisonings suggests that the level is realistic, but this is not yet known. In particular the long-term effects of methyl or ethyl mercury dosage have not been adequately researched.

Some questions raised by the mercury scare are still disturbing. Why was research in Canada not started until 1968 despite abundant evidence of its probability from Japan and Sweden? Some persons claim that this evidence was not freely available because of the obscurity of the journals in which it appeared, but this assertion is not supported by a survey of relevant literature, particularly following the conference on mercury pollution held in Stockholm in early 1966.[54] Even if the claim is true it does not encourage confidence, for one function of government research agencies is to maintain a complete, accurate, and up-to-date survey of foreign research results, especially in the field of public health.

Research workers who released data on mercury contamination to the press have been criticised for premature generation of a public concern. This is controversial, but with the horrible example of the Minamata and Niigata poisonings in mind, it would appear that any researcher who failed to release such data would not be fulfilling a public duty. Certainly much of the information presently available stems from research generated by the scare.

On a broader scale the mercury contamination problem calls into question the whole system of government control of the use of highly toxic chemicals for which no tolerance levels have been established, particularly in the absence of adequate supervision of their disposal. Obviously we can do little about the natural levels of mercury, but the mercury case shows clearly that we cannot assume that any form of pollution is safe until it has been proved harmful; rather, we must assume that all forms of pollution are harmful until they are proved safe. It should be incumbent on any government author- ity, firm, or individual wishing to deposit waste products in the air, soil, or water to demonstrate that no harmful side effects will result.

Perhaps the most frightening aspect of the mercury situation is the suspicion that we may have seen merely the tip of an iceberg. Mercury is only one of a variety of heavy metals released in effluents. All are toxic, many in minute concentrations, and thus all may eventually prove as hazardous as mercury. Recent evidence suggests that cadmium may be the next problem. The Canadian Food and Drug Directorate has found detectable amounts of cadmium in 65 percent of food samples from across the country. Concentra- tions above 0.5 ppm were found in 9 percent of the samples; the highest levels were recorded in vegetables grown in the vicinity of a zinc smelter at Trail, British Columbia. Cadmium residues have also been found in apples sprayed with cadmium chloride,[55] and residues of 1.6 ppm, 0.7ppm, and 0.54 ppm respectively have been detected in lake herring and bloater from Lake Superior and in yellow perch from Lake Erie.[56] The same study has also shown up to 28 ppm of copper in trout from Lake Superior.

As with mercury, there is no definite safe threshold. In Japan 223 cases of degenerative bone disease attributable primarily to cadmium poisoning from mining wastes have been registered since 1962.[57] In the United States close correlation has been found between airborne cadmium and deaths caused by heart disease and high blood pressure. Chronic poisoning resulting in lung and kidney diseases has also been recognized in industrial workers in the United States, Sweden, and Britain.[58] As long ago as 1957 one publication stated that "cadmium has probably more lethal possibilities than any of the other metals."[59]

Space does not permit a full examination of cadmium contamination but it bears a striking similarity to the mercury problem. It seems that research has opened a veritable Pandora's box. Perhaps the sole consolation is that Canadian authorities have been alerted to the potential hazard of heavy metal contamination, and this should stimulate research, monitoring, and perhaps more timely action in the future.

References

1. T. W. Beak, "Water Pollution Problems of the Pulp and Paper Industry," *Pulp and Paper Magazine of Canada* 64 (1) (1963): T-27.

2. V. Kubelka, "Measures Aimed at Reducing Pulping Wastes," *Papir Celulosa* 22(6), 163, abstracted in the *Bulletin of the Institute of Paper Chemistry* 38 (1968): 9333.

3. T. W. Beak, 1963, *op. cit.*

4. M. W. Van Horn, "The Effects of Pulp and Paper Mill Wastes on Aquatic Habitat Requirements." *Pulp and Paper Magazine of Canada* 61(2) (1960): T-67.

5. F. E. J. Fry, "Requirements for the Aquatic Habitat," *Pulp and Paper Magazine of Canada* 61(2) (1960): T-61.

6. T. W. Beak, 1963, *op. cit.*

7. M. F.Fujiya, "Effects of Kraft Pulp Mill Wastes on Fish," *Journal of the Water Pollution Control Federation* 33 (1961): 968-977.

8. D. F. Alderdice and J. R. Brett, "Some Effects of Kraft Mill Effluent on Young Pacific Salmon," *Journal of the Fisheries Research Board of Canada* 14 (1957): 783-795.

9. J. B. Sprague and D. W. McLeese, "Toxicity of Kraft Pulp Mill Effluent for Larval and Adult Lobsters and Juvenile Salmon," *Water Research* 2 (1968): 753.

10. H. R. Amberg and J. F. Cormack, "Factors Affecting Slime Growth in the Lower Columbia River: Evaluation of Some Possible Control Measures," *Pulp and Paper Magazine of Canada* 61(2) (1960): T-70.

11. B. E. Jones, C. E. Warren and C. E. Bond, "Avoidance Reactions of Salmonid Fishes to Pulp Mill Effluents," *Sewage and Industrial Wastes* 28 (11) (1956): 1403-1413.

12. D. L. Shumway, "The Effects of Unbleached Kraft Mill Effluents on Salmon. II. Flavour of Jack Coho Salmon," *National Council of the Paper Indistry for Air and Stream Improvement, Inc.*, New York, Technical Bulletin No. 217. 1968.

13. J. H. Smith, "A Review of the Progress in Air Pollution Abatement in British Columbia." Background papers for the *National Conference on Our Environment*, Vol. 2 (Ottawa: Queen's Printer, 1967).

14. L. Friberg, S. Hammarström and A. Nyström, "Kidney Injury After Chronic Exposure to Inorganic Mercury," *Archives of Industrial Hygiene* 8 (1953): 149-153.

15. P. A. Neal, "A Study of Chronic Mercurialism in Hatters for Cutting Industry," *U. S. Public Health Bulletin* 234 (1937).

16. P. L. Bidstrup, "Chronic Mercury Poisoning in Man Repairing Direct Current Meters," *Lancet* 2 (1951): 856-860.

17. S. Tejning and H. Öhman, "Uptake, Excretion and Retention of Metallic Mercury in Chloralkali Workers," *Proceedings of the 15th International Congress on Occupational Health*, Vienna, 2 (1966): 57.

18. F. Nielsen-Kudsk, "Absorption of Mercury Vapour from the Respiratory Tract in Man," *Acta Pharmacologica* 23 (1965): 250-262.

19. M. Berlin, J. Fazackerly and G. Nordberg, "The Uptake of Mercury in the Brains of

Mammals Exposed to Mercury Vapour and Mercuric Salts," *Archives of Environmental Health* 18 (1969): 719–729.

20. T. Suzuki, "Neurological Symptoms from Concentration of Mercury in the Brain," in *Chemical Fallout*, edited by M. W. Miller and G. G. Berg, pp. 245–257 (Springfield: Charles C. Thomas, 1969.

21. J. C. Gage, "Distribution and Excretion of Methyl and Phenyl Mercury Salts," *British Journal of Industrial Medicine* 21 (1964): 197–201.

22. L. Friberg, "Studies on the Metabolism of Mercuric Chloride and Methyl Mercury Dicyandiamide," *Archives of Industrial Health* 20 (1959): 42–49.

23. T. Norseth and T. Clarkson, "Studies on the Biotransformation of [203]Hg-labeled Methyl-mercurychloride in Rats," *Archives of Environmental Health* 21 (1970): 717–727.

24. T. Suzuki, T. Miyama and H. Katsunuma, "Comparison of Mercury Contents in Maternal Blood, Umbilical Cord Blood and Placental Tissues," *Bulletin of Environmental Contamination and Toxicology* 5 (1970): 501–508.

25. D. J. Clegg, "Embryotoxicity of Mercury Compounds," Paper presented to a special symposium on *Mercury in Man's Environment*, Royal Society of Canada, Ottawa February 1971.

26. L. J. Goldwater, A. C. Ladd, P. G. Berkout and M. B. Jacobs, "Acute Exposure to Phenylmercuric Acetate," *Journal of Occupational Medicina* 6 (1964): 227–228.

27. J. Englesson and A. B. Hernar, "Alkyl Mercury Poisoning," *Acta Paediatrica Scaninavica* 41 (1952): 289–294.

28. F. Berglund and M. Berlin, "Risk of Methylmercury Cumulation in Man and Mammals and Relation Between Body Burden of Methylmercury and Toxic Effects," in *Chemical Fallout* edited by M. W. Miller and G. G. Berg, pp. 258–273 (Springfield: Charles C. Thomas, 1969).

29. S. Skerfving, K. Hansson and J. Lindsten, "Chromosome Breakage in Humans Exposed to Methyl Mercury Through Fish Consumption," *Archives of Environmental Health* 21 (1970): 133–139.

30. K. Irukayama, "The Pollution of Minamata Bay and 'Minamata Disease' " *Journal of the Water Pollution Control Federation Journal* 38 (1966): 384–385.

31. L. T. Kurland, S. N. Faro and H. Siedler, "Minamata Disease: the Outbreak of a Neurologic Disorder in Minamata, Japan, and its Relationship to the Ingestion of Seafood Contaminated by Mercury," *World Neurology* 1(5) (1960): 370–391.

32. F. Berglund and A. Wretlind, "Toxicologic Levels of Mercury in Swedish Fish," *Var Föda* 19 (1) (1967): 9–11.

33. J. Ui, "A Short History of Minamata Disease Research and the Present Situation of Mercury Pollution in Japan," *Norkisk Hygienisk Tidskrift* 50 (1969): 139–146.

34. K. Borg, H. Wanntorp, K. Erne and E. Hanko, "Mercury Poisoning in Swedish Wildlife," *Journal of Applied Ecology* 3 (Supp) (1966): 171.

35. S. Tejning and F Vesterberg, "Alkyl Mercury-treated Seed in Food Grain. Mercury in Tissues and Eggs from Hens Fed with Grain Containing Methylmercury Dicyandiamide," *Poultry Science* 43 (1964): 6–11.

36. A. G. Johnels, T. Westermark, W. Berg, P. I. Persson and B. Sjöstrand, "Pike *(Esox lucius L)* and Some Other Aquatic Organisms in Sweden as Indicators of Mercury Contamination in the Environment," Oikos 18 (1967): 323–324.

37. A. G. Johnels and T. Westermark, "Mercury Contamination of the Environment in Sweden," in *Chemical Fallout*, edited by M. W. Miller and G. G. Berg, pp. 221–244 Springfield: Charles C. Thomas. (1969).

38. A. Jernelov, "Conversion of Mercury Compounds," in *Chemical Fallout*, edited by M. W. and G. G. Berg pp. 68–74, (Springfield: Charles C. Thomas 1969).

39. N. Fimreite, "Mercury Uses in Canada and Their Possible Hazards," *Environmental Pollution* 1 (1970): 119–131.

40. D. K. R. Stewart and R. G. Ross, "Mercury Residues in Apples in Relation to Spray Date Variety and Chemical Composition of Fungicides," *Canadian Journal of Plant Science* 47 (1967): 169–174.

41. N. E. Cooke. Paper presented to the special symposium of *mercury in Man's Environment* Royal Society of Canada Ottawa, Feb. 15 and 16. (1971).

42. Environment Staff, "Mercury in the Air," *Environment* 13 (1971): 24–33.

43. N. Fimreite, R. W. Fyfe and J. A. Keith, "Mercury Contamination of Canadian Prairie Seed-eaters and Their Avian Predators," *The Canadian Field-Naturalist* 84 (1970): 270–276.

44. W. Wishart, "A Mercury Problem in Alberta's Game Birds," *Alberta-Lands-Forests-Parks-Wildlife* 13(2) (1970): 4–9.

45. J. B. Gurba, "The Mercury Situation in Alberta," Paper presented to the *8th Annual Meeting of the Canadian Agricultural Chemicals Association*, Jasper, Alberta, 13th–16th Sept. (1970).

46. G. Wobeser, N. O. Nielsen, R. H. Dunlop and F. M. Atton, "Mercury Concentrations in Tissues of Fish from the Saskatchewan River," *Journal of the Fisheries Research Board of Canada* 27 (1970): 830–835.

47. A. L. Hammond, "Mercury in the Environment: Natural and Human Factors," *Science* 171(3973) (1971): 788–789.

48. W. Berg *et al*. 1966, *op. cit.*

49. H. V. Weiss, M. Koide and E. D. Goldberg, "Mercury in a Greenland Ice Sheet: Evidence of Recent Input by Man," *Science* 174 (1971): 692–694.

50. J. G. Saha, Y. W. Lee, R. D. Tinline, S. H. F. Chinn and H. M. Austenson, "Mercury Residues in Cereal Grains from Seeds on Soil Treated with Organomercury Compounds," *Canadian Journal of Plant Science* 50 (1970): 597–599.

51. E. Somers. Paper presented to the special symposium on *Mercury in Man's Environment*, Royal Society of Canada, Ottawa, Feb. 15 and 16th (1971).

52. "Maximum Allowable Concentrations of Mercury," *Archives of Environmental Health* 19 (1969): 891–905.

53. F. Berglund and M. Berlin, "Human Risk Evaluation for Various Populations in Sweden due to Methylmercury in Fish" in *Chemical Fallout*, edited by M. W. Miller and G. G. Berg, pp. 423–432 (Springfield: Charles C. Thomas, 1969).

54. Swedish Royal Commission on Natural Resources, "The Mercury Problem," symposium concerning mercury in the environment held at Wenner-Gren Centre, Stockholm, Jan. 24–26, (1966), *Oikes*, Supp. 9, 51 pp. (1967).

55. R. G. Ross and D. K. R. Stewart, "Cadmium Residues in Apple Fruit and Foliage Following a Cover Spray of Cadmium Chloride," *Canadian Journal of Plant Science* 49 (1969): 49–52.

56. H. F. Lucas, D. N. Edgington and P. J. Colby, "Concentrations of Trace Elements in Great Lakes Fishes," *Journal of the Fisheries Research Board of Canada* 27 (1970): 677–684.

57. R. Nilsson, "Aspects on the Toxicity of Cadmium and its Compounds," *Ecological Research Committee Bulletin No. 7*, Stockholm: Natural Science Research Council (1970).

58. J. A. Bonnell, "Cadmium Poisoning," *Annals of Occupational Hygiene* 8 (1965): 45.

59. F. C. Christensen and E. C. Olson, "Cadmium Poisoning," *Archives of Industrial Health* 16 (1957): 8–13.

Chapter 5

Pesticides

The problems posed by the discovery of mercury residues in foodstuffs were discussed in the previous chapter. It has been known for some time that residues of a variety of toxic chemicals used as pesticides also occur in many foodstuffs. Both forms of contamination have caused concern for public health, and both are in contravention of Section 4a of the Canadian Food and Drugs Act, which states that "no person shall sell any article of food . . . that has in or upon it any poisonous or harmful substance," although exemption authority within specified tolerance limits is provided in Section 24 of the same act.[1] There are similarities between the mercury and pesticide problems, but the latter is infinitely more complex, because of the wide variety of pesticides in use and because pesticide use has demonstrable beneficial effects.

Pesticides have been in use in the world since at least A.D. 70 and have provided a wide range of benefits to mankind, including the control of insects that damage or destroy agricultural crops, animals, or stored produce; the control of insects that infest standing timber of buildings; and the control of weeds that compete with more valuable vegetation for nutrients and space. By helping to control such pests as the rice weevil, the granary weevil, and the spruce budworm, pesticides have resulted in great savings and considerable increases in agricultural production. Their most impressive results have been the control of the insects that transmit some of mankind's most troublesome diseases, including lice, which are responsible for the spread of typhus; mosquitoes, which can spread malaria, yellow fever, elephantiasis, and encephalitis; and fleas, which spread the plague. Many examples of improvement in public health exist. One of the most dramatic was the successful use of DDT in mosquito control in Ceylon, which resulted in a halved mortality rate within a decade.

Beneficial results have been partially counterbalanced by a number of ill effects, particularly in recent years. As Davignon and her associates state, "Cases of acute poisoning, both accidental and occupational, have been reported for practically every known insecticide, and in practically all of the countries where they are used."[2] Like mercury, many pesticides are toxic in small concentrations. These seldom occur in the natural environment, but the stability and persistence of some pesticides allows them to concentrate to high levels. One of the major problems of many pesticides is that although they are assigned for specific purposes, they are in fact nonspecific in action and can result in extensive nontarget kills either by direct ingestion at toxic levels or by biological concentration.[3]

Ill effects on nontarget wildlife species have generated concern about the possibility that similar effects might occur in humans, who may ingest pesticides directly or through food and drink. In an attempt to avoid such effects, many countries have established tolerance levels for various pesticide residues in foodstuffs. As for mercury, these are based on scanty information; as Goulding points out: "In the present state of knowledge the choice of tolerance levels can be hardly more than the result of guesswork with little basis in toxicology."[4] In particular, knowledge of the potential long-term effects of sublethal dosages is completely inadequate because many compounds have been available only a short time. Another serious gap in knowledge is the possible synergistic interaction of two or more pesticides, which has received very little study. This problem is greatly accentuated by the immense range of chemical compounds in use around the world as pesticides. In the United States, for example, more than 54,000 chemical formulations are registered for pesticide use. In Canada 419 separate ingredients are used as pesticides under approximately 1,000 brand names.[5]

One clear distinction between mercury and pesticide contamination should be made. Mercury is a naturally occurring substance, although not necessarily in all the forms in which it appears in industrial effluents. Most organisms contain small, though measurable, concentrations. This has caused uncertainty about whether high mercury levels in nature are related to man's activities and has raised doubt about the reality of the health hazard involved. Most pesticides in common use are entirely synthetic, and there is no possibility of confusion in identifying their origins in mankind's activities.

Insecticides

Many substances have been used in attempts to control insect infestation. Canadian records show the use of lead arsenate insecticides in the early nineteenth century. Insecticides currently registered include inorganic compounds based on toxic metals such as arsenic or copper, on naturally occurring organic compounds such as nicotine and pyrethrum, and on a wide variety of synthetic compounds, most of which are organochlorine, organophosphorus, or carbamate insecticides. Most problems have arisen with the synthetic compounds.

Organochlorine insecticides

These include a number of well-known insecticides, such as methoxychlor, chlordane, heptachlor, dieldrin, aldrin, endrin, toxaphene, benzene hexachloride, and lindane, DDD (dichloro diphenyl dicholroethane), and the best-known one, DDT (dichlorodiphenyltrichloroethane). They vary in solubility, stability, and toxicity, but all are somewhat similar to DDT, the first organochlorine to be used. DDT was synthesised in 1874 (benzene hexachloride was actually synthesised in 1825, but it was not recognized as a potential insecticide until 1940), but its insecticidal properties were not discovered until 1939. It was used by Allied forces during the Second World War (a closely related insecticide, DFDT, was used by Axis forces). Immediately after the war it came into extensive civilian use, particularly for agriculture.

DDT is classified as a convulsive poison which attacks the insect's central nervous system, producing hyperexcitability, convulsions, paralysis, and death. It is one of the most stable and persistent of all insecticides because it is insoluble in water and very resistant to destruction by light or oxidation. It does break down slowly to DDE, but even if DDT use ceased immediately it would take twenty-five years for a significant amount of the insecticide present in the natural environment to degrade. Its persistence, and cheapness account for its value as an insecticide. It kills insects in very small concentrations, in which it has low toxicity to vertebrates. As a result, few ill effects were initially predicted. Unfortunately, it has an affinity for fatty tissues. When it is ingested in minute amounts it can be stored and concentrated until high levels are reached. This was demonstrated at Clear Lake, California, where western grebes were found to contain DDD and DDT up to 80,000 times the original spray concentration.

Since its commercial introduction in 1945, DDT has been the most widely used of all pesticides. The total quantity used is unknown, but it is at least two million tons.[7] Because of its stability much of this DDT or its metabolite DDE is probably still present in the environment or stored in animal tissue. Residues appear to exist anywhere DDT has been used, and they have appeared in some areas where it has not been used. This was demonstrated by the discovery of residues in the fatty tissue of Adelie penguins, skuas, and Weddell seals in Antarctica.[8] Among these species only the skua wanders an appreciable distance from Antarctica, so it is reasonable to assume that DDT has somehow made its way to this remote continent. In the Arctic Jonkel has reported dieldrin residues of 2.13 ppm and DDT residues of 2.60 ppm in fat samples from polar bears.[9] Although these could be explained by local spraying, they demonstrate the degree to which organochlorine residues now pervade our environment.

The apparently universal occurrence of DDT residues has been attributed to its widespread use, but studies in Sweden have revealed residues in soil more than twice as large as the total amount of the insecticide used in that country during the past twenty years. Much transport of DDT from its original points of application has therefore taken place. The main reason is the drift loss incurred whenever it is applied by spraying, particularly from the air. It has been estimated that on average half the application is blown away, although this depends greatly on wind speed and mode of application.[10] The size of droplets, the stability of atmospheric conditions, and the height of application are also critical. Under unsuitable conditions drift loss may be severe, and minute droplets kept aloft by turbulence could probably travel long distances, even to remote areas such as Antarctica. Another source of contamination may be soil particles coated with insecticide which have been transported by wind erosion. A further possibility is that evaporative loss takes place from falling DDT droplets or by codistillisation as they lie exposed on the surface.[11]

Organochlorine residues. Before we discuss the occurrence of organochlorine residues in the environment, a cautionary note is necessary. Much material has been published on organochlorine residues, but some data are doubtful. Before development of gas-liquid chromatographic techniques, analysis of organochlorine residues was rather inaccurate, and since then it has been complicated by the discovery of the widespread occurrence of polychlorinated biphenyls in the environment.[12] These complex mixtures of compounds, which share most of the chemical properties of DDT and which are easily confused with it,[13] originate as industrial pollutants from paint, plastic, resin, and other industries. The effect of PCB residues in wildfowl appears to be similar to that of DDT,[14] and they have been reported to cause liver injury in rats.

Residues in soils, air, and water. A high proportion of insecticide applications eventually finds its way to the soil, where it remains until broken down or removed by plants or soil fauna or in air or water. It is not surprising that organochlorine residues have been found in soils in many countries. In southwestern Ontario Harris and his associates found mean concentrations of DDT and its metabolites varying from 0.4 to 61.8 ppm, depending on the cover crop.[15] Maximum concentrations, found under orchards, reached 131.1 ppm. In the Atlantic provinces mean concentrations from 1.0 to 2.4 ppm were found, with maximum concentration under root crops reaching 17.1 ppm. [16] In Saskatchewan Saha and his associates found no DDT but did find aldrin, dieldrin, heptachlor, and chlordane.[17] Chopra also found heptachlor residues of 5.60 ppm and 4.90 ppm respectively in Manitoban and Albertan soils.[18] Few studies have been completed on nonagricultural soils, although residues have been found under forest stands in New Brunswick.[19]

The persistence of residues in soil varies greatly, but aldrin, dieldrin, and heptachlor have been found in a British Columbian soil nine years after a single application.[20] The rate of disappearance depends to a large extent on soil texture; heavy soils retain residues longer than sandy soils. Work in Ontario has shown the importance of soil organic matter and microorganisms. Climatic factors are also involved, and high temperatures can increase the removal rate, although rainfall has little effect.

For reasons just mentioned, comparatively little research has been done on residue concentrations in the atmosphere, and most of the available data come from Britain or the United States. In Britain Abbott and associates found concentrations up to 13.0 parts per billion;[21] Tabor found up to 56.1 ppb over eastern cities in the United States.[22] Substantially higher concentrations have been found in rainwater and airborne dust.

Organochlorine insecticides have very low water solubility, but substantial concentrations can occur in water due to insecticides carried on suspended particles. Sources are diverse but include direct spraying and runoff from adjacent soil, sewage, and industrial effluents. Some may also be carried from the atmosphere by rainfall. Although concentrations are usually not large, 908.0 ppb of DDT, 180.0 ppb of benzene hexachloride, and 630.0 ppb of dieldrin have been found.[23] There is evidence that bottom sediments in lakes and rivers may contain much higher concentrations, and passage of lindane, DDE, heptachlor epoxide, aldrin, and dieldrin into groundwater in southern Ontario has been reported.[24] The potential for ill effects from residues in water is higher than is from those in air or soil, for fish can concentrate residues directly from water.

Residues in plants. Because of the potential health hazard from residues in food crops, considerable research on concentrations in plants has been undertaken. The mechanism of uptake is not yet fully understood. Obviously some residues can be taken up by direct deposition on foliage and passage through stoma or possibly through cuticles. Miller and associates[25] have reported DDT and DDD residues up to 5.1 ppm in tomatoes following aerial spraying, and residues up to 11.3 ppm have been found in peaches in Ontario. [26]

Residue uptake can also take place from the soil, but there is no evidence that plants concentrate organochlorines to higher levels than the parent soil. In studies of turnips and wheat grown on contaminated soil in Saskatchewan, concentrations were found to be much higher in the soil than in the plants.[27] This is also true of plants grown from contaminated seed; concentrations of only 0.015 ppm were found in wheat grown from seed with a heptachlor concentration of 543.0 ppm.[28] Plants grown with their roots under water can concentrate residues to levels higher than those in the water.

Residues and their effects on fish and other wildlife. Fish may take up residues from water either directly from water flowing through their bodies or indirectly by feeding on contaminated invertebrate or aquatic vegetation. Residues are accumulated in fatty tissues and are generally not large, although they vary by species and location. On the Atlantic coast of Canada concentrations in trout were found to vary from 0.03 to 0.16 ppm, in mackerel from 0.01 to 2.75 ppm, and in salmon from 8.8 to 30.0 ppm.[29] High concentrations have also been found in Coho salmon from the Great Lakes. In general, residues appear to be higher in freshwater fish, although some comparable concentrations in marine fish have been reported.[30]

Organochlorines in fish can cause direct mortality or impaired reproduction. In Coho salmon mortality is highest among small fish.[31] In New Brunswick the use of aerial DDT sprays to control spruce budworm resulted in severe mortality in Atlantic salmon hatcheries and also affected angling in many rivers. The major effect in rivers was on young fish. After an application of 0.5 pounds of DDT per acre, salmon in their first year were reduced to between 2 and 10 percent of their normal quantity; second and third year fish suffered reductions to 50 to 80 percent respectively.[32] During spraying more than 5,700 tons of DDT was used in the area. Because of the ill effects on salmon, DDT was replaced by phosphamidon, after which angling improved.[33] In British Columbia a similar spraying programme also resulted in high salmon mortality. In four streams 100 percent mortality of young fish was recorded, which in one stream involved 40,000 fish.

Effects on reproduction have been just as disastrous as direct mortality in adult fish. DDT residues tend to become concentrated in the fat of egg yolks, destroying the embryos, which rely on yolks as a food source.[34] Embryo mortality in some lake trout hatcheries has reached 100 percent.

The effects of sublethal dosages of organochlorines on fish have not been extensively studied yet, but some results have been reported. In particular, reduced response to such environmental factors as water temperature and light stimuli have been observed,[35] [36] indicating some impairment of the central nervous system, but the exact significance is not yet known. Any impairment of reaction could certainly lead to a low survival rate.

Although organochlorines have caused damage to fisheries, the potential magnitude of the problem first became apparent through the effects on birds. Several early reports suggested a link between insecticide use and bird mortality, and in 1962 Rachel Carson's *Silent Spring* was a powerful indictment of unrestrained use.[37] In 1963 a British study found residues adequate to cause mortality in a variety of seed-eating birds. Since then organochlorines have been found in many species; 118 in Britain alone have been identified as contaminated.[38]

In general, however, the highest concentrations have been found in raptorial and fish-eating birds. In a study of peregrine falcons in the Northwest Territories, total residue concentrations as high as 368.2 ppm were found in mature breeding birds, compared with 15.8 ppm in immature migrants.[40] The total residue included 37.3 ppm DDT, 284.0 ppm DDE, 39.5 ppm TDE, 3.3 ppm dieldrin, and 4.4 ppm heptachlor epoxide. In the United States concentrations of 127.0 ppm and 227.0 ppm have been recorded in herring gulls [41] and 19.0 ppm in bald eagles.[42] High concentrations in raptorial and fish-eating birds are generally interpreted as a result of progressive concentration up the food chain to the highest levels. Some aspects are not fully understood, and concentration does not always occur to the predicted level, but the basic interpretation appears to be correct.

Organochlorines have been implicated in the population decline of a number of bird species, as a cause both of adult mortality and of interrupted reproduction. The spruce budworm control programme in New Brunswick caused a decline in the woodcock population, partly in combination with the effects of heptachlor application for fire ant control in the woodcock over-wintering grounds in the southern United States. [43] Organochlorines have been associated with a serious population decline of such fish-eating birds as cormorants, gannets, and pelicans.[44] [45] Pelicans have been badly affected, and a population decline has also occurred in gannet rookeries on Bonaventure Island offf the Gaspé Peninsula, Quebec. The gannets examined contained even higher concentrations than peregrine falcons, which are already extinct in eastern Canada and are reduced to a few breeding pairs in the prairies.[46] The decline in peregrine populations has been attributed largely to organochlorine insecticides,[47] although other causes are involved. Only in the Yukon and Northwest territories and in British Columbia are healthy breeding populations of peregrines still found, although they are threatened by insecticides, by poaching for the European bird-hunting market, and in British Columbia by government-licenced capture.[48]

The way in which organochlorines cause mortality in adult birds is not completely understood. Direct ingestion in food and subsequent concentration is obviously most common, and mortality resulting from a contaminated diet has been demonstrated. Interpretation of the results is complicated by the fact that some survivors contain higher concentrations than birds that died, which suggests the possibility that individual susceptibility varies. In addition to direct mortality, long-term effects of sublethal dosages must also be considered. It is believed that residues can cause mental impairment and erratic behaviour, which would obviously affect survival. This is thought to have been the prime cause of the final disappearance of the Sun Life peregrine falcons from Montreal. Another possible result of ingestion is a reduced ability to withstand environmental stress. Residues are stored in fat tissue and may remain for long periods with little ill effect, but if the bird is subjected to starvation or cold stress, fat tissue will be used and mortality will result. This has been demonstrated in woodcocks[49] and, among mammals, in rats.[50] In such cases the exact cause of death may be designated as starvation, cold exposure, or poisoning, but the organochlorine insecticide had caused a reduction in tolerance of environmental stress.

A more severe effect of organochlorines has been interference with reproduction, including toxic accumulation in egg yolks, decrease of chick viability, and interruption of shell formation. High insecticide concentrations have frequently been encountered in eggs, and several studies have reported reduced chick viability.[51] The most extensive information is on the relationship between DDT concentration and the failure of normal eggshell formation. [52] [53] [54] [55] Many examples of extremely thin shells that are too weak to bear the weight of the hatching bird have been reported. In other cases adult birds have pecked through shells and eaten the embryos. Damage to eggs from impact with stones while they are being turned may also be increased. Hickey and Anderson found a correlation between breakage of eggs, reduced hatching, decreases in shell thickness, and the increase in organochlorine use over the previous twenty-five years.[56] However, study of common terns at Chip Lake, Alberta, found no clear relationship between thin shells and DDE concentrations in eggs, which averaged 9 ppm and in one case reached over 100 ppm. [57] Kury also found little apparent relationship between DDE levels and reproductive failure in cormorants.[58] More research on a wider range of species is obviously necessary for clarification. The exact manner in which DDT interferes with shell formation is not known, but a disturbance of calcium metabolism is involved.[59]

Less study has been completed on the occurrence and effects of residues in animals, although some poisoning in small mammals has been reported. Residues in polar bears and Weddell seals have already been mentioned, and DDT, DDE, and rhothane residues have been found in harp seals from the Gulf of St. Lawrence.[60] Data on cencentrations in large mammals have been sparse but have reported from roe deer in the Netherlands and from mule deer and elk in Idaho, Washington, Montana, New Mexico, Colorado, and Wyoming.[61] In no case were ill affects noted. Laboratory experiments with small mammals have indicated some decline in reproductivity and the ability to survive energy loss.[62] Recent research in the United States has shown a relationship between DDT levels and stunted growth in rats and abnormally small foetuses in rabbits. Relatively high embryonic mortality in mammals has been found in ranch mink fed fish from the Miramichi River in New Brusnwick, which was contaminated by DDT from spruce budworm control spraying.[63]

Residues and their effects on human beings. The effects of organochlorines on fish, birds, and animals are serious because wildlife are aesthetically and economically important. The major significance of the research on wildlife, however, is the possibility that ill effects in wildlife may indicate similar effects in human beings. Many problems are involved in attempting to extrapolate from observations on wildlife to possible effects in humans, but the alternative—direct experimentation with humans—is not acceptable.

There is evidence that the ingestion of organochlorine insecticides can be lethal to humans if the dosage is sufficiently large. A number of cases of poisoning after accidental ingestion have been recorded.[64] [65] The main problem is the possibility that sublethal dosages may have long-term ill effects, and because the maximum length of exposure to organochlorines so far is about thirty years, such ill effects may not have become apparent. DDT, at least, is now sufficiently omnipresent to ensure that virtually everybody contains some residue, although the amount varies with occupational and residential exposure, as indicated by table 5.1.

DDT and its metabolite DDE are the most common residues and are present in the largest quantities, as indicated by table 5.2.

Organochlorine residues found in humans may come from sources such as air, water, absorbants and inhalants, and food. An estimated 85 percent of the average total exposure is to DDT and DDE in food,[66] although this varies greatly depending on such factors as the use of cosmetics, in which high concentrations have been found (for example, 8.50 ppm DDT in lipstick). The importance of dietary intake has focused much attention on residues in food-stuffs, and governments in many countries now sample residue contents more or less regularly. In Canada the Food and Drug Directorate regularly samples foodstuffs, ready-cooked foods, and restaurant meals. Such monitoring programmes undoubtedly constitute progress, but major problems still exist. Programmes consist of random spot checks, which are spread rather thinly and which may miss contaminated foods. The checks must be related to a tolerance

Table 5.1. Concentrations of DDT in Human Fat Tissue

Country	Collection Period	Number of Specimens	Concentration (ppm mean)	Range
Canada	1950–60	62	5.3	0–14.3
France	1961	10	5.3	0–17.4
Hungary	1960	48	12.4	
India	1964	86	27.2	2.0–118.0
Israel	1963–64	254	19.2	
Poland	1966–67	72	13.4	2.8–35.4
Britain	1966	53	4.6	1.4–11.0
United States	1955	49	19.9	10.8–54.9
United States	1961–62	130	12.9	2.5–59.6
United States (Alaska)	1960	20	3.0	0–16.0
West Germany	1958–59	60	2.3	0–16.0

Source: J. Robinson, "The Burden of Chlorinated Hydrocarbon Pesticides in Man," *Canadian Medical Association Journal* 100 (1969): 180–91.

level, even if it is only an unofficial rule of thumb used by inspectors. As Goulding[67] points out, such limits do not necessarily relate to proven health hazard. Ingestion to toxic levels depends on dietary habit as well as the residue concentration. For example, a high concentration of DDT in a certain species of fish might pose no threat to a person who eats one fish per year, but it could be dangerous to someone whose diet is composed entirely of fish. It would seem that monitoring programmes should emphasise the study of groups that live on very restricted diets.

Studies have shown considerable variation between foodstuffs, and meat generally has particularly high concentrations. Dairy products have been intensively studied because they could reasonably be expected to contain high concentrations and because of their dietary importance for infants and young children.[68] Residues in dairy products have been widely reported, with DDT, DDE, and DDD the most frequently found.[69] [70] The exact importance of the residues found in milk has not been precisely established. The United States has set a tolerance level of zero, whereas the World Health Organization has suggested a practical limit of 0.005 ppm.[71] Canada has not followed this recommendation and has not set a specific limit, but the Food and Drug Directorate is prepared to ban the shipment or sale of milk or dairy products deemed to be excessively contaminated. In 1965, for example, milk from the Grand Forks area of British Columbia was banned because dieldrin in the butter fat reached a concentration of 0.5 ppm.

Considerable concern has also arisen about residue concentrations in human mothers' milk. In Washington, D.C., DDT levels up to 0.77 ppm were reported as early as 1951 in women free of abnormal exposure.[72] In another study DDT and DDE residues ranging from 0.09 to 0.16 ppm in milk and from 2.9 to 5.3 ppm in the fat fraction were reported.[73] Comparable concentrations have also been found in human milk in parts of Canada. For example, in Alberta sampling between 1966 and 1970 revealed benzene hexachloride, lindane, dieldrin, heptachlor epoxide, DDE, DDD, and DDT; the actual levels have not been released for publication.

Table 5.2. Organochlorine Pesticide Residue in Human Fat Tissue (Toronto 1966)

Pesticide	Number of Samples	Concentration (ppm mean)	Range
DDT	47	1.09	0.28–2.65
DDE	47	2.66	0.6–6.8
Lindane	42	0.07	0.01–0.18
Aldrin	40	0.03	0.01–0.14
DDD	27	0.30	0.01–0.90
Heptachlor epoxide	22	0.09	0.01–0.40

Source: J. R. Brown.

The degree of hazard to human health presented by organochlorine residues in human tissues is not yet known. Cases of poisoning have occurred, but these have resulted from accidental ingestion of large concentrations. No definite causal relationship has yet been demonstrated between health defects and concentrations which commonly occur in humans. The amount necessary to cause immediate ill effects is also still speculation, but it has been stated that DDT administered at a rate of 0.2 g./kg./day will cause mild illness, and 0.5 g./kg./day might be fatal.[74] DDT works through the central nervous system, causing hyperexcitation, generalised tumours, spastic paralysis, and convulsions. The main concern is not about immediate lethal effects from accidental ingestion of high concentrations but the potential long-term effects of small concentrations. As storage of residues is primarily in fat tissue, it seems probable that such ill effects will be manifested in a reduced tolerance of environmental stress, as in fish and birds.

Perhaps the most serious question about the concentration of organochlorines in human tissue is the possibility that they may cause abnormality in foetuses and infants. Some years ago experiments with mice demonstrated transfer of dieldrin and DDT across the placental barrier, and more recently the transfer of DDT and DDE from human mothers to foetuses has also been shown.[75] In the latter study it was suggested that some concentrations of organochlorines probably occur in a fertilized ovum from the beginning of its existence, and concentrations of a variety of organochlorines have been found in foetuses and in newborn infants.[76] In a recent study in Miami the blood of premature babies was found to contain an average of three times as much DDE as that of normal babies, perhaps due to deficient fat reserves in which storage would normally take place.[77] O'Leary and his associates[14] point out that the most serious aspect is that we do not yet know whether small exposures to organochlorines can produce genetic or teratogenic effects, despite the fact that DDT, at least, has been in circulation for thirty years. The possibility of stunted growth has been suggested by research with rats and rabbits, and infertility in females may also be produced. Under these circumstances the significance of organochlorine residues in human milk becomes a disturbing unknown factor. Residue concentrations generally appear to be higher in human milk than in cows' milk, and breast-fed babies will therefore tend to accumulate higher residues than bottle-fed babies. High concentrations may occur in children in some African and Asian countries, where DDT is extensively used and where infants are sometimes breast-fed for several years. It is also possible that the transmission of residues may be greater from mothers with deficient diets. Extensive research into the possible effects of organochlorines on foetuses and infants is of the greatest urgency.

The potential problems in attempting to determine the effects of sublethal dosages of organochlorines on humans are well known. Some experiments involving the feeding of DDT to volunteers have been carried out over a short time period, but in general information is compiled either by attempting to correlate observed residue concentrations with observed effects or by experiments with animals. In the first case it may be difficult to prove a causal relationship because of the variety of environmental stresses to which most human beings are subjected; in the second it is hard to decide the extent to which results from animals apply to human beings. As a result, information about the effects of organochlorine residues on human health is sporadic, largely circumstantial, and frequently conflicting.

Hayes and his associates found no ill effects on the health of any volunteers in their experiment, but the study was extended only over sixteen months.[15] A study of 300 workers employed in the manufacture of aldrin, endrin, and dieldrin over a nine-year period showed no ill effects except some abnormal electroencephalographs.[78] People who died after chronic illness in Arizona showed no abnormally high levels of DDT, DDD, or dieldrin.[79] However, another study revealed unusually high residues in autopsies of people who died from cerebral haemorrhage, hypertension, and cirrhosis of the liver.[80] Apple growers in Quebec, who are exposed to high concentrations, were found to suffer an unusually high incidence of neurologic disorders and leukopenia (abnormal decrease in white corpuscles in the blood). A number of studies have indicated a relationship between benzene hexachloride or its derivative lindane and the occurrence of blood dyscrasias (morbid blood conditions), which in some cases have been fatal.[81][82] Cancer tumour formation in relation to organochlorines has not been demonstrated in humans, but increased occurrence of benign and malignant tumours in the livers of rats and fish has been reported.[83] The addition of aldrin and dieldrin to the diet of mice in a concentration of 10 ppm has also caused tumours.[84] These results do not definitely prove that aldrin and dieldrin are carcinogenic in humans, but they do indicate that this is possible. The reports were regarded as adequate base for classifying the substances as carcinogenic in a report of the United States Department of Health, Education, and Welfare.[85] Among the other results of experiments with animals, DDT, aldrin, and dieldrin have been shown to cause enzyme changes in the liver which affect the concentration of oestrogen in the blood and the level of circulating steroid hormones.[86] In dogs such changes have been observed with a dietary dosage of dieldrin as low as 0.5 ppm. Effects have also been observed in humans who suffered occupational exposure to DDT, endrin, chlordane, and lindane.

In summary, it is not yet possible to determine the extent of the hazard to public health presented by the widespread use of organochlorine insecticides. However, the research results outlined and the proven ill effects on fish and birds leave little doubt that a hazard does exist. Because of the quantities of organochlorines that have been used around the world, any ill effect on health would have widespread repercussions. It is possible that the worst effects may occur only when the insecticide interacts synergistically with another chemical compound, such as carbon tetrachloride. The effects of organochlorines may be limited by the distribution of such synergists, but the possibilities for synergism are endless. Another possibility is that the worst effects may

occur only in abnormally sensitive people. Again this is no cause for complacency, for even if such people represented only 0.001 percent of the population,
some 360,000 people around the world would be affected. Much careful research on these aspects is urgently needed, and in the meantime control
decisions must be taken.

The future of organochlorine insecticides. Decisions on the appropriate approach to the control of organochlorine insecticide use are extremely
difficult. There is the strong likelihood that their use threatens public health
and the certainty that it can cause extensive damage to fish and birds, but it is
undeniable that insecticides have benefited mankind by controlling insect
depredation and disease. These benefits can be obtained by alternative methods,
but in general these are more expensive and in some cases are less effective.
The expense factor is important, because it has been suggested that if DDT were
universally banned, malaria-control programmes in many underdeveloped countries would be abandoned. Expense should not be such a deterrent in developed
countries like Canada and the United States, but it will always be a major
consideration in insect control. Another problem with the use of alternative
insecticides is that their potential effects on health are almost unknown. Our
knowledge of the potential effects of DDT, for example, is inadequate, yet
we know much more about it than about any organophosphate or carbamate
insecticide.

Before examining the reaction of governments in this difficult situation another question must be considered. Organochlorine insecticides have
provided many benefits to mankind, but can these results be maintained in the
future? The problem of resistance appeared at an early stage in the history of
the usage of organochlorine insecticides. The basis of this problem is that in any
insect population a few individuals are resistant to given insecticides due to
some genetic peculiarity. Insecticides may kill off most of the population, but
the few resistant individuals will survive and breed to produce a new population, most of which will inherit resistance. Because of the rapidity with which
insects breed, particularly in hot climates, resistant populations can develop in
a very short time. This situation is often assisted by a dearth of natural predators, which are frequently killed off by the same nonspecific insecticide used
for control of the original pest.

In some subtropical countries DDT resistance appeared in house flies
within two years of the initiation of control programmes. Since then many
insects have developed resistance; a total of 225 species now resist organochlorines in at least one country. Of these, 91 are resistant to DDT and its
relatives, and 135 are resistant to the cyclodiene organochlorines such as
chlordane, dieldrin, and aldrin.[89] Canada has suffered less than many countries from the development of resistance because of low temperatures and
extensive dry areas and because large portions of the country were not treated.
Nevertheless, DDT resistance did appear in the Ottawa Valley before 1956.

In 1960 DDT resistance was also found in the mosquito species *Aedes cantator* at Moncton, New Brunswick, and another mosquito species, *Aedes vexans,* was found to be resistant at Kamloops, British Columbia, in 1961.[88] A number of mosquito species have developed resistance in the United States but not in Canada. Among these is *Culex tarsalis,* in the San Joaquin Valley of California, which transmits encephalitis. In addition to the two mosquito species mentioned and the cabbage looper, in Canada resistance has also appeared in the house fly, and in the mayfly in New Brunswick,[89] and chlordane resistance has appeared in the German cockroach. In New Brunswick resistance in the spruce budworm has been described as incipient.

Once resistance has appeared in a species several courses of action can be taken. Initially some results may be produced by increasing the application rate, which obviously increases the residue problem and ill effects on non-target species. In cases of dieldrin resistance, increase has no effect. Sometimes insects that are resistant to DDT may remain vulnerable to one of the cyclodiene organochlorines, so that application of DDT in conjunction with a cyclodiene pruduces results. In other cases resistance to all organochlorines develops, and further chemical control can be obtained only by using another group of insecticides, usually organophosphates. Resistance to these can also develop; in California *Culex tarsalis* and *Aedes nigromaculus* developed resistance to DDT in 1952, to ethyl parathion in 1961, to methyl parathion in 1963, and to fenthion in 1968. The pattern is one of steady escalation in the cost of control and in the application rates necessary to produce results, until control cannot be maintained without the application of rates posing an immediate hazard to human beings.

The potential for development of resistance is a serious drawback to insecticide use. The early achievement of depredation and disease control encouraged and made possible rapid population growth. In many underdeveloped countries a large proportion of the population depends directly on the continued success of organochlorine insecticides, particularly DDT, for even the meagre standards of living which exist. If these insecticides should fail because of resistance, mortality by famine and disease would be catastrophic. In addition to any hazard the organochlorines pose to health, the continued dependance of a large proportion of the world's population on their success is dangerous because of their proven potential for resistance development. Even if such resistance does not develop, the spectacular increases in agricultural productivity brought about by the "Green Revolution" and use of DDT cannot be maintained indefinitely. Other means of catering to the rapidly expanding population must be found.

Government action. Since the publication of *Silent Spring* the demand for the banning of organochlorine insecticides has been increasing. Because of the confusing complexity of evidence and the multiplicity of purposes for which the insecticides are used, it is not surprising that the response by international and government agencies has been varied. General bans have not been introduced in any country, for organochlorines are not uniformly hazardous, although they share many properties. The most hazardous appear to be DDT, aldrin, dieldrin, lindane, and benzene hexachloride, and action has been directed primarily against these.

In Canada severe restrictions have been placed on the use of some organochlorines. DDT has been banned for use of fifty food crops and is now authorised for use only on twelve. Only in emergencies can it be used for insect control in parks, forests, and outdoor areas. Aldrin and dieldrin have been restricted to soil and seed treatment for a small number of crops and, like heptachlor, cannot be used on crops destined for livestock feed. Dieldrin is still authorised for outdoor control of white-fringed beetles, hornets, bees, wasps, and earwigs. Lindane is authorised for many purposes, such as soil and seed treatment, spraying of livestock and pets, and as an ingredient in mosquito-repellent paints. There are many restrictions on its use, however; it is not permitted in homes, restaurants, or food processing storage areas.

The United States restricted the use of DDT, and two states, Michigan and Arizona, instituted bans. Dieldrin and heptachlor were also severely restricted, and it was recommended that their use should be phased out in favour of chlordane, which has appreciably lower toxicity. Suspension of endrin, aldrin, and lindane was also recommended. In Britain aldrin, dieldrin, and heptachlor had been banned for use in agriculture, horticulture, food storage, and homes since 1964, with a few exceptions. In 1969 virtually all these exceptions were withdrawn, fendrin was banned, and extensive restrictions were placed on DDT.[90] Sweden banned aldrin and dieldrin completely and DDT and lindane for domestic use, all effective January 1, 1970. Other uses of DDT were suspended for a two-year period, except in emergency situations. Denmark banned DDT for general use, effective November 1, 1969; Norway banned all uses of DDT, effective October 1970. Italy also introduced numerous restrictions on DDT, particularly for food crops, in November 1969.

The bans and restrictions introduced represent some progress, but their impact on the global problem is small. The use of organochlorine insecticides still continues in virtually all countries, and in the underdeveloped countries of Africa and Asia this use is on an immense and often excessive scale. In view of the ease with which the insecticides travel around the globe, the restrictions which do exist are largely ineffective. Under these circumstances control procedures in Canada cannot be considered in isolation from those in the rest of the world; international agreement and controls are essential. The difficulties barring concerted action are indicated by the fact that in 1969 UNESCO called for an international ban on DDT, whereas in 1970 the World Health Organization approved an enlarged budget for DDT spraying.

It is not easy to determine what form control action should take. There seem to be strong grounds for a complete ban on DDT, adrin, dieldrin, and lindane in developed countries where effective, though more expensive, alternatives exist, but problems do exist with the alternatives. Organophosphates, for example, have a considerably higher toxicity for mammals than organochlorines. On the other hand, there is less danger of long-term ill effects, because organophosphates decay quickly and will not accumulate to high levels in body tissue. As we have already pointed out, bans in developed countries are only a partial answer, but they would improve conditions locally. To underdeveloped countries the cost of alternative insecticides is prohibitive unless purchase is subsidized by developed countries. In the absence of subsidies it is difficult to see how DDT can be replaced, despite the potential health hazard. A ban without an effective replacement would merely exchange long-term ill effects for immediate widespread famine and disease. It is hard to be optimistic that subsidies will materialise, but unless they do extensive damage may occur in the underdeveloped countries.

Organophosphorus insecticides

The problems which have arisen with organochlorine insecticides have inevitably drawn attention to possible alternatives; commonly these have been organophosphorus compounds. They first appeared in 1854, when tetraethyl pyrophosphate (TEPP) was synthesised, although like DDT, its insecticidal properties were not discovered until the late 1930s. Since then over 100,000 different organophosphorus compounds have been synthesised, of which about forty are commercially successful. Many of these are used in Canada, the most common being malathion, fenthion, phosphamidon, ronnel, abate, diazinon, and fenitrothion. Parathion was used but has been largely phased out.

All organophosphorus insecticides act directly or indirectly as inhibitors of the enzyme cholinesterase. In some cases the insecticide itself is the inhibitor; in others the insecticide is a metabolite formed rapidly in tissue; in the case of parathion, it is an impurity which acts as an inhibitor.[91] Cholinesterase is involved in the action of the nervous system; its inhibition results in tremors, convulsions, paralysis, and death.

Organophosphorus insecticides vary considerably in properties such as metabolism and toxicity. All degrade much more rapidly than organochlorines, although there is considerable variation between short residual compounds such as tetraethyl pyrophosphate and more prolonged residual action compounds like diazinon or fenthion. Rapid degradation is their chief advantage over organochlorines. It means that there is little danger of long-term ill effects because chronic exposure to sublethal dosages cannot result in accumulation of residues to toxic levels. Rapid breakdown has been demonstrated by work with cabbage seedlings in which diazinon residues declined from 2 ppm to less than 0.01 ppm in thirty to forty days.[92] As a result, usually only low concentrations of organophosphorus compounds are found in foodstuffs.

The main disadvantage of the organophosphorus insecticides as a group is that they are highly toxic to mammals. Organochlorines have been involved in a number of fatal accidental poisonings, but many more can be attributed to organophosphorus compounds.[93] Although all organophosphorus insecticides are toxic to mammals, the threshold dosage varies greatly. This is indicated by LD_{50} (lethal dose 50 percent—that dose which will kill half a population) values recorded for oral dosage of rats: TEPP, 1 ppm; phosdrin, 6.1 ppm; parathion, 13 ppm; phosphamidon, 23.5 ppm; fenthion, 215 ppm; trichlorfon, 630 ppm; ronnel, 1,250 ppm; and malathion, 1,375 ppm.[94] More toxic compounds like parathion and phosdrin, which was formerly used in Saskatchewan for grasshopper and cutworm control, have now been phased out in Canada.

Although toxic to mammals, organophosphorus insecticides have greater selective toxicity than organochlorines. For example, the parathion LC_{50} (lethal concentration 50 percent—that concentration which will kill half a population in a given time) for mosquito larvae (*Culex quinquefasciatus*) is 0.0032 ppm, whereas the LD_{50} for rats as measured in the same study is 6 ppm.[95] The malathion LC_{50} for mosquitoes is 0.081 ppm, whereas the LD_{50} for rats may be as high as 1,500 ppm. This selective toxicity makes them potentially valuable, for they can be used at extremely low concentrations for control of target species. At the same time, the rapidity with which they degrade ensures that they will not accumulate to concentrations at which they would endanger mammals. This selective toxicity has made possible the development of highly specific insecticides which can be successfully used in *integrated control programmes,* discussed later.

Despite their greater specificity of action, some nontarget mortality has occurred with organophosphorus insecticides. In New Brunswick replacement of DDT by phosphamidon in spruce budworm control programmes resulted in the death of warblers. A similar result was observed in Quebec following the use of phosphamidon for control of the jack pine sawfly.

Several organophosphorus insecticides appear to have potential as safe replacements for organochlorines in insect control. Compounds of lower toxicity, such as fenthion, ronnel, and malathion, are particularly promising. Caution should accompany wholesale replacement, however, for knowledge about the effects of these compounds is deficient: DDT was also expected to be harmless to most nontarget species. Extensive research is necessary, particularly into the possibility of teratogenic or mutagenic side effects. Studies in Canada have shown that malathion is teratogenic in chicks, and other studies have implicated guthion, parathion, diazinon, and carbophenothion. Transplacental passage of parathion and methyl parathion has been demonstrated in rats and in human beings.[97] Exposure to parathion and methyl parathion has been shown to cause a high incidence of still births in rats. It is not yet known to what extent these results can be applied to humans, but care is needed in the large-scale introduction of organophosphorus insecticides.

Carbamate insecticides

Carbamate insecticides are aromatic carbamic acid esters which were first marketed for insecticidal use in 1958. They have not been widely used in the past but are becoming increasingly common as pressure against organo-chlorine and organophosphorus insecticides mounts. In Canada several are available, including Lannate, zineb, dimethilan, and the most common, carbaryl, or Sevin.

Carbamates are strong inhibitors of cholinesterase and thus resemble the organophosphorus insecticides in action. Poisoning produces violent convulsions and other disorders of the nervous system. They penetrate and act rapidly in insect species and are swiftly metabolized. Miyamoto has reported a carbamate that reached its maximum concentration fifteen minutes after administration and was present only in negligible quantities after four hours. [98] Metabolic breakdown is not yet fully explained, but the number of metabolites is known to vary. The most important, produced by hydrolysis, is 1-naphthol. Metabolites eventually conjugate and in mammals are excreted as sulphates or glucuronides. In plants they persist as glycosides.

Rapid action and metabolism are the chief virtues of carbamates because accumulation in the body tissue of birds and mammals is thereby precluded. Some are highly toxic, but carbaryl has a lower toxicity to birds and mammals than most organophosphorus insecticides.[99] The carbaryl LD_{50} in rats is 540 ppm for oral dosage and more than 4,000 ppm for skin absorption. On the other hand, it is toxic to some species of fish in concentrations as low as 0.7 to 2.0 ppm.[100]

Widespread use of carbamates is so recent that little knowledge of potential problems has accumulated. Resistance to carbaryl has already appeared in some house flies. This can be easily overcome, however, as carbamates display pronounced synergism with a variety of substances, particularly piperonyl butoxide.[101] Poisoning of nontarget species has caused problems. Honeybees appear to be particularly vulnerable, as are some species of shellfish White shrimp have been killed by carbaryl concentrations between 6 and 240 ppb, and 100 percent death of young stages has been produced by concentrations of 10 ppb.[102] Levels of 0.4 to 2.0 ppm have caused reduced hatching and survival in clams and estuarine fish.[103] These effects are accentuated, as both carbaryl and its major metabolite, 1-napthol, are relatively persistent in seawater; carbaryl remains for up to forty days and 1-napthol for up to thirty days. 1-napthol is generally more toxic to fish and shellfish than carbaryl.[104]

No ill effects of carbamate use have yet been demonstrated in human beings, and the main concern is the possibility that teratogenic effects may occur. These have been reported in guinea pigs, dogs, and chickens as a result of carbaryl dosage, and embryo mortality has also been reported in rabbits.

[105] It is not known if these results indicate potential hazard for human beings, but this seems probable.

Alternative methods of insect control

The potential repercussions of insecticidal use of synthetic organic chemicals have not been established beyond doubt, but there are strong grounds for suspecting that they pose a critical threat to public health. Continued use on the present scale is not justifiable unless comprehensive research removes this suspicion. Neither is a return to the situation which existed before the introduction of DDT acceptable. A number of alternatives exist, although some have serious limitations.

A variety of substances other than synthetic organic chemicals can be used as insecticides. Metallic compounds such as lead arsenate have been quite widely used in the past, but they are highly toxic and rather expensive. Several natural organic chemicals exist. Nicotine has been used since the eighteenth century, but it is highly toxic and therefore hazardous. Pyrethrum, produced from a species of chrysanthemum, is an effective insecticide in small concentrations, but it is expensive to produce and consequently has not been widely used in agriculture. It is used as one ingredient in many aerosol sprays, usually in conjunction with piperonyl butoxide. Apart from cost there do not appear to be serious problems, although some ingredients of pyrethrum can cause dermatitis.

The perennial difficulty of obtaining a safe, inexpensive, and effective insecticide has encouraged the investigation of other approaches to control. Much attention is currently being paid to the *"integrated control" approach,* which abandons the unattainable objective of complete elimination of pest species. Instead, control is achieved by habitat management, encouragement of predators, and very limited use of nonpersistent insecticides. Although the concept of insect control by habitat management is a departure from the philosophy of the past twenty-five years, it is not new. In Italy during the 1930s successful control of malaria mosquitoes was achieved in the vicinity of Rome by draining the Pontine Marshes. Among the more hopeful developments in insect control has been the introduction of sterile males into breeding populations. This has been successfully used to eliminate populations of screw-worm in Curaçao and the southeastern United States,[106] the melon fly on the Pacific island of Rota, and the oriental fruit fly in Guam. Undoubtedly the number of species which can be controlled in this way is limited, often by the difficulties of sterilisation (usually carried out by irradiation). There is hope, however, that it will prove to be a valuable and harmless alternative to insecticides.

Herbicides

Some of the doubts concerning the wisdom of current methods of insect control also apply to herbicides—chemicals used to control weeds, which are plants that grow where they are not wanted. Some weeds are objectionable because they are unsightly or a nuisance, and others impair agriculture by reducing crop yields, by poisoning livestock, or by tainting milk. The effects are less obvious than those of insects, but the United States suffers an estimated $4 billion annual loss through weeds of farmland. A more dramatic estimate suggests that in the absence of weed control, corn yields in the United States would drop to 15 percent of their present level.

Herbicide classification

The most extensive use of herbicides is in agriculture, which obviously requires substances that are selective in action and that do not damage valuable plants. Selective herbicides may be applied directly to foliage or through the soil, in which case uptake is through the roots. Soil-acting weed killers are used primarily to control germinating annuals, and they usually persist in the soil for some time. Foliage herbicides are classified as contact weed killers, which scorch foliage, or translocation weed killers, which move about within the plant, interfering with normal growth processes. The history of weed control is long; substances such as ash and salt were used as herbicides for thousands of years. The discovery of more sophisticated chemical weed killers followed the development of modern theories of plant nutrition in the nineteenth century. A variety of inorganic chemical compounds have been used, including copper sulphate, sodium arsenite, ammonium nitrate, sodium tetraborate, sodium chlorate, sulphuric acid, and more recently, Ammonium sulphamate. Most of these substances acted as contact weed killers. In many cases use was limited by the toxicity or corrosivity of the substances, although ammonium sulphamate and the borates have low toxicity to mammals.

The most significant change in control technology was the introduction of organic chemicals. The first was a contact weed killer, 3,5-dinitro-o-cresol (DNOC), introduced in 1932. More important were the phenoxyaliphatic acids, which became available a few years later. These are translocation weed killers, commonly referred to as "hormone weed killers." Chemically they resemble the natural growth-regulating substance indoleacetic acid and act by stimulating growth, resulting in twisted, deformed stems, defoliation, and eventually death. Among these compounds are some of the most widely used herbicides, including 2,4,5-T (2,4,5-trichlorophenoxyacetic acid), 2,4-D (2,4-dichlorophenoxyacetic acid), and MCPA (2-methyl-4-chlorophenoxyacetic acid).

Table 5.3. Total Use of Herbicides in Alberta, Manitoba, and Saskatchewan 1969 and 1970

	1969	*1970*
2, 4-D	5,906,000 lb.	4,240,000 lb.
MCPA	2,472,000 lb.	2,281,000 lb.
TCA	647,000 lb.	588,000 lb.
Dalapon	160,000 lb.	137,000 lb.
Brush Killer (50/50 2, 4-D and 2, 4, 5-T) Dicamba, Bromoxynil, Dichlorprop, etc.	255,211 lb.	200,137 lb.

Source: J. L. Bergsteinson, "Potential Sources of Airborne Pesticides." (Paper presented to the Twelfth Annual Meeting of the Canadian Committee on Agricultural Meteorology, Ottawa, January 26–27, 1971.)

The selective affect of the phenoxyaliphatic acids has been very useful in agriculture and in forest management. In industrial works and on rights-of-way it is frequently desirable that all plant growth be controlled. Non-selective effects can be achieved by using phenoxyaliphatic acids at much higher than normal application rates or by using nonselective herbicides. The triazines, substituted ureas, and substituted uracils have been developed for this purpose. They include such herbicides as simazine, manuron, dalapon, and paraquat, most of which are soil-active herbicides that act by blocking photosynthesis.

Herbicide use

All the herbicides mentioned above and many more are currently in use in Canada; a total of 106 formulations are licenced as herbicides, and an additional 99 are licenced as fungicides.[107] No complete data are available on the type and amount of herbicides in use in each province. The data available indicate that 2,4-D, 2,4-DB, and MCPA are the most frequently used on grain and fodder crops, atrazine (a symmetrical trazine) and amine dinitro are widely used on root crops, and simazine on fruit crops. The most comprehensive information for the prairie provinces, collected by the Canada Weed Committee (Western Section), is summarised in table 5.3.

Figure 5.1. shows the variations in acreage sprayed with herbicides in the prairie provinces between 1953 and 1970; figure 5.2 shows the acreage in Alberta sprayed with 2,4-D and MCPA between 1960 and 1970.

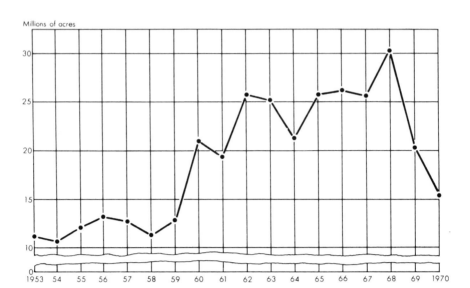

Figure 5.1. Summary of acreage treated with herbicides in Manitoba, Saskatchewan, Alberta and British Columbia, 1953–1970. (Source: Bergsteinsson, 1971.)

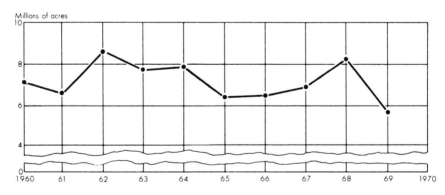

Figure 5.2. Summary of 2, 4–D and MCPA use in Alberta, 1960–1970. (Source: Bergsteinsson, 1971.)

Environmental effects of herbicide use

The high toxicity of some inorganic herbicides has been mentioned. Occasional wildlife mortality and accidental poisoning in humans have occurred. Similar effects are not to be expected from the organic chemical herbicide, because the growth regulation and photosynthesis blocking only affect plants. Obviously weed control has affected some wildlife species which feed on the weeds concerned, but direct mortality has not been recorded. The possibility of residues remaining in the blood or tissue of livestock feeding on treated forage was an obvious matter of concern, but studies indicate that dosage of animals has little effect because excretion is rapid.[108][109] As shown in table 5.4, the mammalian toxicity of the most commonly used herbicides is relatively low.

There have been reports that some herbicides can induce toxic substances in crops or forage plants. Increases in nitrate content has been found in some plants, such as sugar beets, treated with 2,4-D. Excessive nitrate can cause a disease called methaemoglobanemia in infants, and may produce tumours in cattle. The last possibility is being investigated in some Atlantic provinces, where livestock losses have occurred. An increased content of hydrogen cyanide (HCN) in the leaves of wild cherry sprayed with a mixture of 2,4-D and 2,4,5-T has been reported but not confirmed.

Drifting onto nontarget vegetation has been one of the persistent problems of herbicide use. As with insecticides, the amount actually reaching target areas is often low, sometimes dropping to 30 percent. This has resulted from time to time in damage to sensitive unsprayed crops like cotton, grapes, and tomatoes. Improvements in spraying techniques by the use of spray-thickening emulsifiers and careful attention to weather conditions at the time of spraying can greatly reduce drift.

Persistence is a problem which has arisen with soil-active herbicides. Most herbicides break down or disappear rapidly by comparison with organo-chlorine insecticides, but some will damage crops planted on treated soils in following years.[109] In Newfoundland cabbage and rape have been damaged by linuron applied to carrot crops in previous years.[110] Picloram treatment has been reported to preclude planting of picloram-sensitive crops such as alfalfa for five years,[111] but persistence varies greatly with such soil properties as texture, organic content, pH, and moisture movement.

The most critical concern about the use of herbicides resulted from experience with 2,4,5-T as a defoliant in the Vietnam war. It was used in equal parts with 2,4-D in Agent Orange. The exact amount used is not known, but between 1962 and 1969, 4,119,960 acres were defoliated, and in 1967-68 the complete United States production, about 14 million tons per year, was commandeered for military purposes. Apart from the damage caused to natural vegetation and crops and associated soil erosion or laterisation, some 38,300

Table 5.4. Mammalian Toxicity of Some Common Herbicides (Oral LD $_{50}$)

2, 4-D acid	375–560 ppm	Simazine	5,000 ppm
2, 4, 5-T ester	300–550 ppm	Diuron	3,400 ppm
Dicamba	1000 ppm	Linuron	1,500 ppm
Dalapon	7,000–9,000 ppm	Paraquat	157 ppm
Atrazine	2,000 ppm	Diquat	400–500 ppm

Source: L. E. Warren, "Residues of Herbicides and Impact on Uses by Livestock," in *Herbicides and Vegetation Management Symposium*, pp. 227–42 (Corvallis, Ore.: School of Foresty, Oregon State University, 1967).

acres of commercial rubber plantations were damaged by spray drift.[112] Paralysis and death have also been reported in wildlife and domestic animals. [113]

Much more serious was the relationship of defoliant use to an unusually high incidence of human birth deformities. In Saigon Children's Hospital 4,002 abnormal births were recorded between 1959 and 1968; cleft palates and a spinal deformity known as spina bifida were especially frequent. Both increased markedly in incidence after the commencement of heavy spraying in 1966. Subsequent research by the Bionetics Research Laboratory under contract to the United States National Cancer Institute confirmed the suspicion that 2,4,5-T is teratogenic.[114] The abnormalities found during research included no heads, no eyes, faulty eyes, cystic kidneys, cleft palates, and enlarged livers.[115]

The Bionetics study was conducted on a sample of 2,4,5-T containing 27 ppm tetrachlorodioxin, which raised the suspicion that birth deformities resulted from the dioxin rather than from the 2,4,5-T. Dioxin is an extremely potent teratogen, reportedly much more so than thalidomide. More recent research has been carried out to examine this possibility. Dow Chemicals tested 2,4,5-T containing only 0.5 ppm dioxin in pregnant rats. A dosage of 24 ppm produced a 24 percent increase in birth defects compared with control samples.[116] Separate studies of the teratogenicity of dioxin showed that it does cause gastrointestinal haemorrhages but no increase in cystic kidneys in rats at dosages of 0.125 to 8 ppb.[117] In the Bionetics study dioxin dosage resulting from contamination of the 2,4,5-T sample could have been 0.124 ppb, which suggests strongly that 2,4,5-T is teratogenic independent of dioxin contamination, although synergism with dioxin is a possibility. The problem is to some extent academic, as pure 2,4,5-T is apparently impossible to produce.

As a result of the information presented to it the United States Department of Health, Education, and Welfare issued the following statement:

> *The use of currently registered pesticides to which humans*
> *are exposed and which are found to be teratogenic by suitable*
> *test procedures in one or more mammalian species should*
> *be immediately restricted to prevent risk of human exposure.*
> *Such pesticides, in current use, include Captan, Carbaryl;*
> *the butyl, isopropyl and isoctyl esters of 2,4,-D Folpet;*
> *mercurials; PCNB (parachloronitrobenzene); and 2,4,5-T. The*
> *teratogenicity of 2,4-D, the other salts and esters of both*
> *2,4-D and 2,4,5-T, and that of 1 PC (isopropyl-N-phenyl-*
> *carbamate) should be investigated further.*

It is a matter of real concern that despite strong evidence that it is a potent teratogen, 2,4,5-T is still licenced for use in Canada. Even more disturbing is the fact that information about the amount in use is impossible to obtain, as is any assessment of the amount of dioxin present. The information which is available is far from reassuring; the herbicide Brushkill, used quite extensively in the prairie provinces, consists of equal parts 2,4-D and 2,4,5-T, like Agent Orange used in Vietnam. In view of the research available, the continued use of 2,4,5-T is an unjustifiable threat to public health, and an immediate ban should be instituted. Evidence is not sufficient at the present time to support a ban on 2,4-D or MCPA, but their use should be restricted and carefully supervised pending the results of research.

Conclusion

The widespread use of pesticides has resulted in the spectacular control of some of mankind's worst diseases and has been responsible for dramatic increases in food production. Obviously this has been beneficial for the individuals involved, but it is questionable whether it is truly beneficial to mankind as a whole. If pesticide use had resulted simply in the improvement of public health and nutrition, it would have been incontrovertibly beneficial. Instead, it has resulted in greatly increased population growth, and despite enhanced food production, malnutrition and starvation are now more widespread than ever. Pesticide use has greatly reduced death rates, but it has not provided an adequate living standard for many of those who now survive, and without adequate population control it cannot do so. The real potential benefits of pesticide use are therefore as yet unrealised.

Ill effects to humans resulting from pesticide use are small by comparison. Some people have died by direct poisoning or by a variety of diseases probably induced by pesticides, and a number of deformed children have been born. Although these cases are tragic, the total number of people affected is small compared with the number who owe their lives to pesticide use. Concern is not so much for those ill effects which have occurred but for those which may occur. It is possible that the ill effects of pesticide use are also as yet unrealised.

We cannot say that all pesticides present a hazard to human health, but we can say that any release of chemical compounds into the environment may be dangerous unless all aspects of their metabolism and all their effects on organisms have been thoroughly researched. No synthetic pesticide currently in widespread use meets these criteria. Although published work on DDT could fill a small library, we cannot state that even this best known of all pesticides presents no threat to health. By comparison, the knowledge about other pesticides is minute. Since the Second World War we have released immense quantities of chemicals into the environment that are known to be toxic to mammals in some concentrations. We have assumed that application is sufficiently diffuse to ensure that dangerous concentrations will occur only rarely, but we cannot prove this assumption. Much pesticide use has been carried out by untrained personnel who have little or no knowledge of pesticide properties, and virtually all application has involved methods by which only a small percentage reaches the target species.

Adequate testing of a pesticide to ensure that it will never cause any ill effect is impossible; this would require generations of testing and the unacceptable use of humans as guinea pigs. We must accept the fact that any pesticide, like any medical drug, can only be partly tested. When introduced for use it will be believed harmless, but it cannot be proved so. Pesticide use will always be a gamble, but one where short-term benefits appear to outweigh long-term risks.

The inherent risk is acceptable only under certain circumstances. First, all use should be at the minimum level needed for satisfactory control. In the past, the use of many pesticides has been excessive for several reasons. The low cost of DDT in particular, encouraged such use. A fruitless attempt to eradicate certain pests, and the low efficiency of application techniques also contributed. Achievement of minimum pesticide use will require steady improvement in application methods to reduce drift loss, the abandonment of attempts to eradicate pests, and careful monitoring.

A second criticism of past pesticide use is the involvement of untrained personnel. It is obviously absurd to suggest that all users of pesticides be required to possess a degree in pharmacology, but some basic training should be demanded. Perhaps a system of licencing trained personnel could be introduced.

The third condition is that any use should be accompanied by continued research to monitor long-term effects. Once serious doubts about safety arise, the pesticide in question should be suspended pending complete results. The only proviso is that in some cases such suspension may cause more harm than it prevents. No general statement can cover all possibilities, for policies appropriate to developing tropical countries may not be applicable to Canada. In this country there is no reasonable justification for continued use of any pesticide that is believed to present a threat to public health.

References

1. R. A. Chapman, "Canadian Food and Drug Viewpoint on Pesticide Tolerances," *Canadian Medical Association Journal* 100, (1969): 192–196.

2. L. F. Davignon, J. St. Pierre, G. Charest and F. J. Tourangeau, "A Study of the Chronic Effects of Insecticides in Man," *Canadian Medical Association Journal* 92 (1965): 597–602.

3. J. C. Headley, "Pesticide Use by Agriculture," *Canadian Medical Association Journal* 100 (1969): 141–144.

4. R. Goulding, "Pesticide Residues as a Health Hazard," *Canadian Medical Association Journal* 100 (1969): 197–204.

5. J. L. Bergsteinson, "Potential Sources of Airborne Pesticides." Paper presented to the *12th*

Annual Meeting of the Canadian Committee on Agricultural Meteorology, Ottawa, Jan., 26-27, 1971.

6. S. G. Bloom and D. B. Menzel, "Decay time of DDT," *Science* 172 (3980) 1971: 213.

7. S. C. E. P., *Man's Impact on the Global Environment*, Report of the Study of Critical Environmental Problems (Cambridge: M.I.T. Press, 1970).

8. J. O. G. Tatton and J. H. A. Ruzilka, "Organochlorine Pesticides in Antarctica," *Nature* 215 (1967): 346-348.

9. C. Jonkel, "Polar Bear Research in Canada," in *Proceedings of the Conference on Productivity in Northern Circumpolar Lands, Edmonton, October, 1969*, edited by W. A. Fuller and P. G. Kevan, I. U. C. N. Publications New Series, No. 16, 1970, pp. 150-155.

10. H. V. Morley, "Analysis of Pesticides in the Air." Paper presented to the *12th Annual Meeting of the Canada Committee on Agricultural Meteorology*, Ottawa, Jan. 26-27, 1971.

11. G. A. Wheatley and J. A. Hardman, "Indications of the Presence of Organochlorine Insecticides in Rainwater in Central England," *Nature* 207 (1965): 486-487.

12. R. W. Risebrough, P. Reiche, D. B. Peakall, S. G. Herman and M. N. Kirven, "Polychlorinated Biphenyls in the Global Ecosystem," *Nature* 2220 (1968): 1098-1102.

13. L. M. Reynolds, "Polychlorinated Biphenyls (PCB's) and their Interference with Pesticide Residue Analysis," *Bulletin of Environmental Contamination and Toxicology* 4 (1969): 128-143.

14. R. B. Dahlgren and R. L. Linder, "Effects of Polychlorinated Biphenyls on Pheasant Reproduction, Behaviour and Survival," *Journal of Wildlife Management* 35 (2) (1971): 315-319.

15. C. R. Harris, W. W. Sand and J. R. W. Miles, "Exploratory Studies on Occurrence of Organochlorine Residues in Soils in S. W. Ontario," *Journal of Agriculture and Food Chemistry* 14 (1966): 398-403.

16. J. R. Duffy and N. Wong, "Residues of Organochlorine Insecticides and Their Metabolites in Soils of the Atlantic Provinces of Canada," *Journal of Agriculture and Food Chemistry* 15 (1967): 457-464.

17. J. G. Saha, C. H. Craig and W. K. Janzen, "Organochlorine Residues in Agricultural Soil and Legume Crops in N. E. Saskatchewan," *Journal of Agriculture and Food Chemistry* 16 (4) (1968): 617-619.

18. N. M. Chopra, "Persistence and Degradation of Heptachlor in Some Soils," *Journal of Economic Entomology* 59 (1966): 326-330.

19. J. B. Dimond, G. A. Belyea, R. E. Kadunce, A. S. Getchell and J. A. Blease, "DDT Residues in Robins and Earthworms Associated with Contaminated Forest Soils," *The Canadian Entomologist* 102 (1970): 1122-1130.

20. A. T. S. Wilkinson, D. G. Finlayson and H. V. Morley, "Toxic Residues in Soil 9 Years after Treatment with Aldrin and Heptachlor," *Science* 143 (1964): 681-682.

21. D. C. Abbott, R. B. Harrison, J. O. G. Tatton and J. Thompson, "Organochlorine Insecticides in the Atmospheric Environment," *Nature* 211 (1966): 259-261.

22. E. C. Tabor, "Contamination of Urban Air through the Use of Insecticides," *Transactions of the New York Academy of Science, Ser. 2* 28(5) (1966): 569.

23. C. A. Edwards, *Persistent Pesticides in the Environment* (Cleveland: C. R. C. Press. 1970).

24. J. R. Brown, "Organochlorine Pesticide Residues in Human Depot Fat," *Canadian Medical Association Journal* 97 (1967): 367-373.

25. L. A. Miller, J. R. W. Miles and W. W. Sans, "DDT and DDD Residues on Tomatoes Processed into Juice," *Canadian Journal of Plant Science* 37 (1957): 288-291.

26. G. G. Dustan and D. Chisholm, "DDT Residues on Peaches in Ontario," *Journal of Economic Entomology* 52 (1959): 109-110.

27. J. G. Saha and W. W. A. Stewart, "Heptachlor, Heptachlor Epoxide and Gamma Chlor-

dane Residues in Soil and Rutabaga after Soil and Surface Treatment with Heptachlor," *Canadian Journal of Plant Science* 47 (1967): 79.

28. R. H. Burrage and J. G. Saha, "Insecticide Residues in Spring Wheat Plants Grown in the Field from Seed Treated with Aldrin or Heptachlor," *Canadian Journal of Plant Science* 47 (1967): 114.

29. J. R. Duffy and D. O'Connell, "DDT Residues and Metabolites in Canadian Atlantic Coast Fish," *Journal of the Fisheries Research Board of Canada* 25 (1968): 189-195.

30. R. W. Risebrough, "Chlorinated Hydrocarbons in Marine Ecosystems," in *Chemical Fallout,*" edited by M. W. Miller and G. G. Berg (Springfield: C. C. Thomas, 1969).

31. D. R. Buhler and W. E. Shanks, "Influence of Body Weight on Chronic Oral DDT Toxicity in Coho Salmon," *Journal of the Fisheries Research Board of Canada* 27 (1970): 347-358.

32. P. F. Elson, "Effects on Young Salmon of Spraying D.D.T. over New Brunswick Forests," *Journal of the Fisheries Research Board of Canada* 24 (1967): 731-767.

33. C. D. Fowle, "The Effects of Phospamidon on Birds in New Brunswick," *Journal of Applied Ecology* 3 (Supp) (1966): 169.

34. K. J. Macek, "Reproduction in Brook Trout (*Salvelinus continalis*) Fed Sublethal Concentrations of DDT," *Journal of the Fisheries Research Board of Canada* 25 (1968): 1787-1796.

35. J. M. Anderson and H. B. Prins, "Effect of Sublethal DDT on a Simple Reflex in Brook Trout," *Journal of the Fisheries Research Board of Canada* 27 (1970): 331-334.

36. D. A. Jackson, J. M. Anderson and D. R. Gardner, "Further Investigations of the Effect of DDT on Learning in Fish," *Canadian Journal of Zoology* 48 (1970): 577-580.

37. R. Carson, *Silent Spring* (New York: Fawcett Publications Inc., 1962).

38. S. Cramp and P. J. Conder, "Fifth Report of the Joint Committee of the British Trust for Ornithology," *Royal Society for the Protection of Birds Report* 20 (1965).

39. J. O. Keith, "Insecticide Contamination in Wetland Habitats and their Effect on Fish-eating Birds," *Journal of Applied Ecology* 3 (Supp) (1966): 71-85.

40. J. H. Enderson and D. D. Berger, "Chlorinated Hydrocarbon Residues in Peregrine Falcons and their Prey Species from Northern Canada," *Condor* 70 (1968): 149-153.

41. J. O. Keith, "Reproduction in a Population of Herring Gulls (*Larus argentatus*) Contaminated by DDT," *Journal of Applied Ecology* 3 (Supp) (1966): 57-70.

42. L. F. Stickel, N. J. Chura, P. A. Stewart, C. M. Menzie, R. M. Prouty and W. L. Reichel, "Bald Eagle Pesticide Relations," *Transactions of the 31st North American Wildlife Conference* (1966): 190-204.

43. B. S. Wright, "Some Effects of Heptachlor and DDT on New Brunswick Woodcocks," *Journal of Wildlife Management* (1965): 172-185.

44. J. J. Hickey and D. W. Anderson, "Chlorinated Hydrocarbons and Egg Shell Changes in Raptorial and Fish-eating Birds," *Science* 162 (1968): 271-273.

45. D. W. Anderson, J. J. Hickey, R. W. Risebrough, D. F. Hughes and R. E. Christensen, "Significance of Chlorinated Hydrocarbon Residues to Breeding Pelicans and Cormorants," *The Canadian Field-Naturalist* 83 (1969): 91-112.

46. D. Decker, "Disappearance of the Peregrine Falcon as a Breeding Bird in a River Valley in Alberta," *Blue Jay* 25 (1967): 175-177.

47. F. W. Fyfe, J. Campbell, B. Hayson and K. Hodson, "Regional Population Declines and Organochlorine Insecticides in Canadian Prairie Falcons," *The Canadian Field-Naturalist* 83 (1969): 191-200.

48. T. Mosquin, "Toward Legislation to Protect Young Peregrine Falcons," *The Canadian Field-Naturalist* 83 (1969): 297-299.

49. W. H. Stickel, W. E. Dodge, W. G. Sheldon, J. B. DeVitt and L. F. Stickel, "Body Condition and Response to Pesticides in Woodcocks," *Journal of Wildlife Management* 29 (1) (1965): 147–155.

50. A. S. W. DeFreitas, J. S. Hart and H. V. Morley, "Chronic Cold Exposure and DDT Toxicity," in *Chemical Fallout*, edited by M. W. Miller and G. G. Berg, pp. 361–367 (Springfield: Charles C. Thomas, 1969).

51. D. B. Peakall, "Pesticides and the Reproduction of Birds," *Scientific American* 222 (1967): 72–78.

52. N. W. Moore and J. O. G. Tatton, "Organochlorine Insecticide Residues in the Eggs of Sea Birds," *Nature* 207 (1965): 42–43.

53. D. A. Ratcliffe, "Decrease in Egg-shell Weight in Certain Birds of Prey," *Nature* 215 (1967): 208–210.

54. R. D. Porter and S. N. Weimeyer, "Dieldrin and DDT: Effects on Sparrow Hawk Eggshells and Reproduction," *Science* 165 (1969): 199–200.

55. W. H. Stickel, L. F. Stickel and J. W. Spann, "Tissue Residues of Dieldrin in Relation to Mortality in Birds and Mammals," in *Chemical Fallout*, edited by M. W. Miller and G. G. Berg, pp. 174–204 (Springfield: Charles C. Thomas, 1969).

56. J. J. Hickey and D. W. Anderson, 1968, *op. cit.*

57. B. Switzer, V. Lewin and F. H. Wolfe, "Shell Thickness, DDE Levels in Eggs and Reproductive Success in Common Terns (*Sterna hirundo*), in Alberta," *Canadian Journal of Zoology* 49 (1971): 69–73.

58. C. R. Kury, "Pesticide Residues in a Marine Population of Double-crested Cormorants," *Journal of Wildlife Management* 33 (1969): 91–95.

59. J. Bitman, H. C. Cecil and G. F. Fries, "DDT-induced Inhibition of Avian Shell Gland Carbonic Anhydrase: A Mechanism for Thin Eggshells," *Science* 168 (1970): 594–596.

60. H. W. Cook and B. E. Baker, "Seal Milk. I. Harp Seal Milk: Composition and Pesticide Residue Content," *Canadian Journal of Zoology* 47 (1969): 1129–1132.

61. K. C. Walker, D. A. George and J. C. Maitlen, "Residues of DDT in Fatty Tissues in Big Game Animals in the States of Idaho and Washington in 1962," *United States Department of Agriculture Research Series* 33–105 (1965).

62. R. D. Morris, "Effects of Endrin Feeding on Survival and Reproduction in the Deer Mouse (*Peromyscus Maniculatus*)," *Canadian Journal of Zoology* 46 (5), (1968): 951–958.

63. F. F. Gilbert, "Effects of Natural Diet DDT Residues on Ranch Mink," *Journal of Wildlife Management* 33 (1969): 933–943.

64. A. Curley and L. K. Garrettson, "Acute Chlordane Poisoning, Chemical and Chemical Studies," *Archives of Environmental Health* 18 (1969): 211–215.

65. L. K. Garrettson and A. Curley, "Dieldrin: Studies in a Poisoned Child," *Archives of Environmental Health* 19 (1969): 814–822.

66. H. F. Kraybill, "Significance of Pesticide Residues in Foods in Relation to Environmental Stress," *Canadian Medical Association Journal* 100 (1969): 204–215.

67. R. Goulding, 1969, *op. cit.*

68. W. A. Brown, J. M. Witt, F. M. Whiting and J. W. Stull, "Secretion of DDT in Fresh Milk by Cows," *Bulletin of Environmental Contamination and Toxicology* 1 (1966): 21.

69. J. L. Henderson, "Insecticide Residues in Milk and Dairy Products," *Residue Reviews* 8 (1965): 74–115.

70. R. C. Laben, "DDT Contamination of Food and Residues in Milk," *Journal of Animal Science* 27 (1968): 1643–1650.

71. World Health Organization, "Pesticide Residues in Food," World Health Organization and Food and Agriculture Organization, Report 370, 1967.

72. E. P. Laug, F. M. Kunze and C. J. Prickett, "Occurrence of DDT in human fat and milk," *American Medical Association Archives of Industrial Hygiene and Occupational Medicine* 13 (1951): 245-246.

73. G. E. Quinby, J. F. Armstrong and W. F. Durham, "DDT in Human Milk," *Nature* 207 (1965): 726-728.

74. W. J. Hayes, *et al.*, 1958, *op. cit.*

75. J. A. O'Leary, J. E. Davies, W. F. Edmundson and G. A. Reich, "Transplacental Passage of Pesticides," *American Journal of Obstetrics and Gynecology* 107 (1) (1970): 65-68.

76. A. Curley, M. F. Copeland and R. D. Kimbrough, "Chlorinated Hydrocarbon Insecticides in Organs of Stillborn and Blood of Newborn Babies," *Archives of Environmental Health* 19 (1969): 628-632.

77. J. F. O'Leary, J. E. Davies, W. F. Edmundson and M. Feldman, "Correlation of Prematurity and DDE Levels in Fetal Whole Blood," *American Journal of Obstetrics and Gynecology* 106 (6) (1970): 939.

78. I. Hoogendam, J. P. J. Versteeg and M. deVlieger, "Nine Years Toxicity Control in Insecticide Plants," *Archives of Environmental Health* 10 (1965): 441-448.

79. D. P. Morgan and C. C. Roan, "Chlorinated Hydrocarbon Pesticide Residue in Human Tissue," *Archives of Environmental Health* 20 (1970): 452-457.

80. J. L. Radomski, B. Deichman, E. E. Clizer and A. Ray, "Pesticide Concentrations in Liver, Brain and Adipose Tissue of Terminal Patients," *Food and Cosmetic Toxicology* 6 (1968): 209-220.

81. E. Mastromatteo, "Hematological Disorders Following Exposure to Insecticides," *Canadian Medical Association Journal* 90 (1964): 1166-1168.

82. I. West, "Lindane and Hematologic Relations," *Archives of Environmental Health* 15 (1967): 97-101.

83. H. L. Falk, S. J. Thompson and P. Koten, "Carcinogenic Potential of Pesticides," *Archives of Environmental Health* 10 (1965): 848-858.

84. K. J. Davis and O. G. Fitzhugh, "Tumourigenic Potential of Aldrin and Dieldrin for Mice," *Toxicology and Applied Pharmacology* 4 (1962): 187-189.

85. U. S. Department of Health, Education and Welfare, *Report of the Secretary's Commission on Pesticides and their Relationship to Environmental Health*, Parts I and II, (Washington: U. S. Government Printing Office, 1969).

86. D. Kupfer, "Effects of Some Pesticides and Related Compounds on Steroid Function and Metabolism," *Residue Review* 19 (1968): 11-30.

87. A. W. A. Brown, "Insecticide Resistance and the Future Control of Insects," *Canadian Medical Association Journal* 100 (1969): 216-221.

88. Defence Research Board, 1965, *op. cit.*

89. C. D. Grant and A. W. A. Brown, "Development of DDT Resistance in Certain Mayflies in New Brunswick," *The Canadian Entomologist* 99 (1967): 1040-1050.

90. Department of Education and Science, "Further review of certain persistent pesticides used in Great Britain," *Report by the Advisory Committee on Pesticides and Other Toxic Chemicals* (London: H. M. S. O., 1969).

91. T. R. Fukuto and J. J. Sims, "Metabolism of insecticides and fungicides," in *Pesticides in the Environment*, ed. R. White-Stevens (New York: Marcel Dekker Inc., 1971), pp. 145-236.

92. J. R. W. Miles, G. F. Manson, W. W. Sans and H. D. Niemczyk, "Translocation of Diazinon from Planting Water by Cabbage and Tobacco Seedlings," *Canadian Journal of Plant Science* 47 (1967): 187-192.

93. J. H. Davis, J. E. Davies and A. J. Fisk, "Occurrence, Diagnosis and Treatment of Organophosphate Pesticide Poisoning in Man," *Annals of the New York Academy of Science* 160 (1969): 383-392.

94. W. Hayes, *Clinical Handbook on Economic Poisons*, U. S. Department of Health, Education and Welfare (Washington: U. S. Government Printing Office, 1963).

95. R. L. Metcalf, "Chemistry and Biology of Pesticides," in *Pesticides in the Environment*, edited by R. White, (New York: Marcel Dakker, 1971), pp. 2-144.

96. J. Greenberg and Q. N. Latham, "Malathion-Induced Teratism in the Developing Chick," *Canadian Journal of Zoology* 47 (1969): 539-542.

97. K. S. Khera and D. J. Clegg, "Perinatal Toxicity of Pesticides," *Canadian Medical Association Journal* 100 (1969): 167-172.

98. J. Miyamoto, "A Feature of Detoxication of Carbamate Insecticide in Mammals," in *Biochemical Toxicology of Insecticides*, edited by R. D. O'Brian and I. Yamamoto (New York: Academic Press, 1970), pp. 115-130.

99. C. S. Carpenter, C. S. Weil, P. E. Palm, M. W. Woodside, J. H. Nair and H. F. Smyth, "Mammalian Toxicity of I-napthyl-N-methyl Carbamate (Sevin Insecticide," *Agriculture and Food Chemistry* 9 (0000): 30-39.

100. K. J. Macek and W. A. McAllister, "Insecticide Susceptibility of Some Common Fish Family Representatives," *Transactions of the American Fishery Society* 99 (1970): 20-27.

101. D. J. Hennessy, "The Potential of Carbamate Synergists as Pest Control Agents," in *Biochemical Toxicology of Insecticides*, edited by R. D. O'Brien and I. Yamamoto, (New York: Academic Press, 1970), pp. 105-114.

102. D. V. Buchanan, R. E. Millemann and N. E. Stewart, "Effects of the Insecticide Sevin on Various Stages of the Dungeness Crab *Cancer magister*," *Journal of the Fisheries Research Board of Canada* 27 (1970): 93-104.

103. J. A. Butler, R. E. Millemann and N. E. Stewart, "Effects of the Insecticide Sevin on Survival and Growth of the Cockle Clam, *Clinocardium nuttalli*," *Journal of the Fisheries Research Board of Canada* 25 1968: 1621-1635.

104. N. E. Stewart, R. E. Millemann and W. P. Breese, "Acute Toxicity of the Insecticide Sevin and its Hydroylic Product I-naphthol to Some Marine Organisms," *Transactions of the American Fisheries Society* 96 (1967): 25-30.

105. J. F. Robens, "Teratologic Studies of Carbaryl, Diazinon, Norea, Disulfiram and Thiram in Small Laboratory Animals," *Toxicology and Applied Pharmacology* 15 (1969): 152-163.

106. A. H. Baumhover, A. J. Graham, B. A. Bitter, D. E. Hopkins, W. D. New, F. H. Dudley and R. C. Bushland, "Screw-worm Control through Release of Sterilized Flies," *Journal of Economic Entomology* 48 (1955): 462-466.

107. J. L. Bergsteinson, 1971, *op. cit.*

108. J. B. Jackson, "Toxicologic Studies on a New Herbicide in Sheep and Cattle," *American Journal of Veterinary Research* 27 (1965): 821-824.

109. T. J. Sheet and C. I. Harris, "Herbicide Residues in Soils and Their Phytotoxicity to Crops Grown in Rotations," *Residue Review* 11 (1965): 119-140.

110. R. F. Morris and B. G. Pennay, "Persistence of Linuron Residues in Soils at Killigrews, Newfoundland," *Canadian Journal of Plant Science* 51 (1971): 242-245.

111. W. H. Van den Born, "Picloram Residues and Crop Production," *Canadian Journal of Plant Science* 49 (1969): 628-629.

112. T. Whiteside, *The Withering Rain* (New York: E. P. Dutton and Co., 1971).

113. F. H. Tschirley, "Defoliation in Vietnam," *Science* 163(3869) (1969): 779-786.

114. United States Department of Health, Education and Welfare, *Teratogenicity of Pesticides*, Report of the Secretary's Commission on Pesticides and their Relationship to Environmental Health (Washington: U.S. Government Printing Office, 1969).

115. B. Nelson, "Herbicides: Order on 2,4,5-T Issued at Unusually High Level," *Science* 166 (1969): 977-979.

116. J. L. Emerson, D. J. Thompson, C. G. Gerbig and V. B. Robinson, "Teratogenic Study

of 2,4,5-trichlorophenoxyacetic Acid in the Rat," *Society of Toxicology, 9th Annual Meeting, Atlanta, Georgia,* 1970.

117. G. L. Sparschu, F. L. Dunn and V. K. Rowe, "Teratogenic Study of 2,3,7,8-Tetra-chlorodibenzo-p-dioxin in the Rat," *Society of Toxicology 9th Annual Meeting, Atlanta, Georgia,* 1970.

Chapter 6

Oil Pollution
and Arctic Development

Oil Pollution in Canada

During 1970 four separate incidents of oil spillage and pollution focused attention on the hazards of developing Canadian oil resources. At the beginning of February the 11,379-ton, Panamanian-registered tanker *Arrow* ran aground and broke its back on Cerberus Rock in Chedabucto Bay, Nova Scotia. The tanker was carrying a cargo of heavy grade oil, Bunker C, from Venezuela to Nova Scotia Pulp, Ltd., at Point Tupper. Badly damaged tanks in the bow section released 6,000 tons of crude oil into the bay, which spread rapidly along the coast of Cape Breton Island driven by winter storms, eventually polluting 170 miles of coastline and even affecting Sable Island, 100 miles offshore. Damage to bird life was extensive; 2,300 dead birds were recorded near Chedabucto Bay, and 4,800 on Sable Island.[1] Fishing and fish-processing operations along the coast were disrupted, but no extensive fish or shellfish kills were reported except clams, which suffered an estimated 25 percent loss due to suffocation. The cleaning and control operations took many months and were complicated by frequent storms and technical problems. Oil had to be pumped out of the stern section, which slid off Cerberus Rock and sank in 100 feet of water, and removed from many miles of coastline. Both tasks were made more difficult by the extreme viscosity of the crude oil, particularly when mixed with sea water, and sea temperatures as low as 28 degrees F. The eventual cost to the federal government was more than $3 million.

In June 1970 a break occurred in the main pipeline that carries oil from the Great Canadian Oil Sands plant at Fort McMurray, Alberta, to Edmonton. The pipe broke near a creek, by which the oil eventually reached the Athabasca River, which flows into Lake Athabasca. The exact quantity of oil lost is unknown, but it has been estimated at 490,000 gallons by a plant official. Of this, approximately half is believed to have soaked into the ground before reaching the creek. The problem differed from the Chedabucto Bay spill because the oil was partially refined and less viscous than Bunker C, and the amount involved was considerably smaller. Despite attempts to control its spread, the oil flowed downstream and passed into Lake Athabasca. Damage to birds was not apparently widespread, partly because the water was not high enough to flow into adjacent marshlands, which are important bird breeding grounds. No fish kills were reported, although the oil was shown by the Canadian Wildlife Service to be quite toxic. Commercial fishing was closed for the season on Lake Athabasca, which was particularly unfortunate for the fledgling fish copperative at Fort Chipewayan, which, it was hoped, would provide an alternative livelihood for trappers rendered idle by low water levels in the Peace-Athabasca delta.

The break in the Great Canadian Oil Sands pipeline was followed within a fortnight by fish kills near Smoke Lake, Alberta, following the accidental release of about 270,000 gallons of natural gas condensate from a Hudson Bay oil and gas plant. A few days later the Kinuso (Alberta) Fish and Game Association reported to the provincial government on oil well operation in the Swan Hills region, where 1,000 wells are active. The report provided evidence of more than 500 oil spills, of which 40 were classified as serious. Sixteen wells were concerned, eleven of which were operated by Home Oil Co., Ltd. Unlike the Chedabucto Bay and Athabasca spills, which were accidental, in the Swan Hills a certain amount of spillage appeared to be "normal," resulting primarily from careless operation. In addition to oil spillage, the report also provided evidence of damage to fishing caused by erosion and siltation resulting from careless road construction. Operations at a number of sites were suspended by the Alberta Oil and Gas Conservation Board until operating procedures were improved.

In September an unmanned barge, the *Irving Whale,* sank while it was under tow in bad weather in the Gulf of St. Lawrence. As with the *Arrow*, the cargo consisted of Bunker C oil, some of which escaped to form an oil slick that damaged beaches in the Isles de la Madeleine. The task force that was already cleaning up in Nova Scotia rapidly controlled the new spill, using some of the techniques developed in Nova Scotia, although the problem was slightly different, because the barge sank in 240 feet of water. The oil that remained in the barge could not be pumped out and was capped instead.

None of these incidents was particularly unusual; similar incidents had occurred in Canada and in other countries in the past. But because they occurred within a short time and involved a range of activities in the oil industry, they had a cumulative effect on public opinion. Public concern had already been aroused by marine oil pollution which followed the grounding of the *Torrey Canyon* on the Scilly Isles in 1967 and the spillage from offshore drilling rigs in the Santa Barbara Channel, California, and the Gulf of Mexico in 1969. Like virtually all maritime countries, Canada suffered persistent minor coastal oil pollution from accidents and from intentional clearing of oil from engines and bilges in coastal waters. One week before the *Arrow* grounded, the captain of a Liberian tanker, the *Sincerity,* was charged with polluting Burrard Inlet, Vancouver, with bilge oil and was fined $5,000. Up to 1967, forty-five such prosecutions had been made under the Canada Shipping Act and only two had failed.

The *Arrow* grounding was the first major spill on the Canadian coast. And although Canada had suffered less than many countries until the *Arrow* accident, it had ample reason to worry about the future. More than fifty oil companies were interested in offshore oil exploration around Nova Scotia, Newfoundland, and Labrador and in the Gulf of St. Lawrence, and some test drilling was done on the Grand Banks of Newfoundland in 1966 by Amoco Canada Petroleum and Imperial Oil.

In 1967 Mobil Oil Canada drilled to over 15,000 feet off Sable Island. In September 1969 Shell Canada began drilling a series of bores off Sable Island with a semisubmersible rig, which was subsequently joined by several rigs working for Shell Canada and other companies. Although Canadian regulations about concrete casings for marine wells were more stringent than those in the United States at the time of the Santa Barbara spill, there was worry that serious pollution might occur. The hazards of offshore drilling had already been demonstrated by several rig collapses in the North Sea off the British coast, and the Canadian Atlantic coast is subject to storms at least as severe as those in the North Sea. No restrictive action on offshore exploration was taken in the east, but the federal government banned exploratory drilling in the Strait of Georgia to prevent damage to a recreational area.

Arctic Oil Discoveries

Concern about offshore drilling, particularly in areas of scenic or recreational value, was significant, but the real anxiety focused on the development of Arctic oil reserves. Until the late 1960s only moderate oil reserves had been proved in the Arctic, and only two oil fields were in production—at Norman Wells, Northwest Territories, and at Cook Inlet on the Kenai Peninsula, Alaska. The Norman Wells field was discovered in 1920 but has been in production only since 1933; the Cook Inlet field has been producing since 1957.

Reserves at both fields were quite small, and although geologists had realised for many years that geological structures along the North Slope of Alaska were promising, nothing indicated substantial reserves. Certainly no one was prepared for the mid-1968 discovery of the major oil field at Prudhoe Bay, Alaska, in a test well drilled by the Atlantic Richfield Company and Humble Oil. The total extent of the reserves is unknown; an admittedly conservative estimate placed them at 4.49 billion barrels of high-quality oil and 0.72 trillion cubic metres of natural gas,[2] but it is now believed that the oil reserves may be as large as 20 billion barrels. The strike resulted in a spectacular wave of land acquisition and oil exploration in Alaska, culminating in the sale of oil rights to 400,000 acres of the North Slope for $900 million in September 1969.

The Prudhoe Bay discovery stimulated renewed interest in the possibility of oil reserves in the Canadian Arctic. Early studies had shown that geological structures in the Canadian Arctic Islands held considerable promise for the discovery of significant oil and gas reserves. In the late 1950s, following further favourable reports, oil rights leases were taken on 120,000 square miles. Several exploratory wells were drilled in the early 1960s on Melville, Cornwallis, and Bathurst islands, but less problematic areas such as the North Sea diverted capital. In 1967 a number of leading Canadian oil and mining firms joined a consortium, Panarctic Oils, in which the federal government acquired a 45 percent share. Panarctic started drilling in 1969 on Melville Island and proved the existence of substantial natural gas deposits.

In the meantime, the Prudhoe Bay discovery stimulated exploration, and between June 1968 and June 1969 lease holdings in the Canadian Arctic rose from 800,000 square miles to 1.7 million square miles. A number of older companies started drilling on both the islands and the mainland in 1969 and 1970, including Gulf Oil Exploration, King Resources, Shell Canada, and Imperial Oil. In January 1970 Imperial Oil discovered oil at Atkinson Point, near Tuktoyaktuk on the shore of the Beaufort Sea. (A second discovery took place in the same area in May 1971.) Later in 1970 immense reserves of natural gas were proved in a spectacular well fire on King Christian Island.

These discoveries are sufficient to ensure that exploration will continue in the immediate future, particularly with the eventual expansion of exploration by offshore drilling in the Beaufort Sea. It seems inevitable that a field comparable to those on the North Slope of Alaska will be proved in the near future. Current estimates of the Canadian Arctic reserves range from a low of 50 billion barrels of oil and 300 trillion cubic feet of gas (by the Canadian Petroleum Association) to a high of 100 billion barrels of oil and 650 trillion cubic feet of gas (by J. C. Sproule and Associates of Calgary).

Environmental effects of oil exploration

Three aspects of Arctic oil exploration and development cause concern: exploration, drilling, and transportation of oil to markets. The investigation of geological structures involves seismographic surveying and vehicles traveling along cleared seismic lines. The main problem of exploration is that damage may be caused by travel because of the peculiar character of soils and vegetation. Most of the exploration area lies within the tundra, which is characterised by very cold temperatures, high winds, and a thin snow cover throughout the year. Vegetation is restricted to low-growth habit plants such as mosses, saxifrages, and lichens, which can withstand the adverse conditions, with occasional stunted birches and willows in favoured sites. Only in the Mackenzie valley, where the river ameliorates the climate, do tall trees extend almost to the Arctic Ocean. Almost everywhere the soil consists of an accumulation of slow-decaying plant material which has built up into a thick dark organic sponge, overlying a variable thickness of mineral soil above bedrock.

The moisture in the soil and bedrock is frozen throughout the year to a variable depth that reaches over 1,300 feet in places, constituting what is known as *permafrost.*[3] Above the permafrost a thin surface layer, the *active layer,* melts in summer, saturating the soil. Beneath this layer much of the volume of the soil is ice—in places the weight of ice in ground sections is ten times that of dry material. As long as the surface vegetation remains undisturbed, summer melting is restricted to a thin surface layer, but if it is damaged or removed the insulating layer is destroyed, allowing heat to penetrate more deeply into the soil, causing extensive melting. Because of the volume of moisture, melting may produce serious subsidence and erosion, or *thermokarst erosion.*

Obviously thermokarst erosion takes place only in summer, but because plant colonisation of devegetated surfaces in the Arctic is extremely slow, many summers of erosion may take place before vegetation is restored. Therefore even rather minor disturbance of vegetation can affect the landscape markedly. J. R. Mackay, of the University of British Columbia, has described a clear depression which resulted from a dog being tethered in one place for ten days.[24] Thermokarst erosion will not occur everywhere; it is restricted to areas where the soil has a high moisture-holding capacity, which depends in part on the clay content. Sandy soils will generally suffer little damage.

On some early seismic lines damage to vegetation by vehicles caused marked thermokarst erosion. In northern Alaska, for example, siesmic lines from exploratory work during the Second World War are still clearly visible.[5] In addition to damage to the land surface, it was thought that seismic tracks might disturb animal movement, particularly the migration of caribou. Considerable research on these problems has been carrried on in recent years, and not all the results are yet available, but initial observations suggest that animals are not significantly deterred by seismic trails—in fact, some trails become preferred routes. The only seismic trails that appear to endanger caribou and moose are those that develop into mud-filled trenches, in which the animals may get stuck.

In Alaska damage to vegetation and the resulting thermokarst erosion have been considerably reduced by restricting the use of tracked vehicles to winter months, when the frozen surface is not as subject to damage. My own observation of some seismic lines run in the Mackenzie delta during the 1969–70 winter suggests that winter use of tracked vehicles may produce little damage, even on clay-rich soils. Timber clearing has been necessary for vehicle access, but disturbance of ground vegetation has been minimal. This is not to minimise the serious damage that has already taken place in the Canadian Arctic and Alaska as result of careless operations, but if strict regulations are laid down and enforced, particularly with regard to the summer use of tracked vehicles, extensive damage can probably be avoided. Every effort should also be made to develop forms of transport which cause the least damage. Hovercraft seem to offer possibilities, but it will probably be some time before large-scale use is economically feasible.

The chief worry has been vegetation damage and thermokarst erosion, but concern has also arisen about the potential direct disturbance of wildlife, particularly in connection with the seismic exploration of Banks Island by Gulf Oil Exploration and Geminex Canada, which started in the fall of 1970. The fauna of Banks Island supports one of the few remaining self-supporting Eskimo communities at Sachs Harbour. Fur-trapping, especially of Arctic fox, brings an annual income of around $250,000 to seventeen families in the community.[6] It was feared that exploration activity would disrupt fox burrows, as it has done in Alaska,[7] and that seismic work might drive caribou and seal from the island.

The proposed exploration raised much opposition, particularly from Banks Islanders, who had not been consulted before the federal government granted permits to twenty-two companies for exploration on the island, but exploration was allowed to proceed after the companies agreed to stringent regulations and posted bonds of $100,000. The federal government gave assurance that no ill effects would result, but virtually no studies exist upon which such assurances can be based. It does not seem that the possible benefits of the exploration of Banks Island justify the hazard to this model native community. Here, at least, exploration should have been postponed for a few years until potential damage could be realistically estimated.

Environmental effects of drilling and oil well operation

Environmental damage associated with well drilling could occur in many forms. The chief concern is over oil spillage caused by careless operations, as in the Swan Hills of Alberta. No inherent hazard in Arctic operations makes spillage more likely than in other oil fields, but it could cause more damage because of the delicate ecological balance. Vegetation destroyed by spillage would be restored very slowly. Many northern wildlife populations are barely adequate to ensure survival, and the balance could be tipped by such disruption. There is no evidence of spillage connected with any of the high Arctic operations, although Cook Inlet in southern Alaska suffers from persistent marine oil pollution.[8]

One problem with Arctic operations is that the tundra is so exposed that the results of careless operations are visible for many miles. All sorts of garbage and general carelessness are involved, but the most persistent cause of complaint is the accumulation of fuel drums, which most companies insist cannot be economically transported back to the south. The federal government should ensure their return, perhaps by a levy on oil leases or production. If they are not removed they will be a visual pollutant for many years, as in parts of Antarctica.

In addition to pollution caused by drilling, some contact has been made between wildlife and drill crews. Polar bears in particular are attracted into campsites and then must be shot. There are also tales of musk-oxen being chased by snowmobiles. Expanding exploration in the next few years will bring increased animal-human interaction, and unless it is carefully controlled, it will cause serious depletion of the populations of species such as the polar bear, the barren-land grizzly, and the musk-ox, all of which have already suffered serious decline. Sometimes animals are the offenders, as on Banks Island, where Arctic foxes have persistently gnawed through the insulation on seismic cables.

Transportation of oil from the Arctic

By far the biggest problem in Arctic oil development is the transportation of oil to markets. This problem has been primarily responsible for the delay in the development of Arctic reserves,[9] and it is the reason why fields like Norman Wells have never produced oil at their full capacity—the only economical market is the surrounding area. It has been stated that many of the producing fields further south, such as the Pembina field in Alberta, discovered in July 1953, would never have been brought into production had they been located in the Arctic. A field of Prudhoe Bay dimensions was necessary to justify the cost of developing effective transportation in the Arctic.

Surface tankers. Possibilities for oil transportation are theoretically endless, but the only three that are remotely feasible are pipelines, surface tankers, and submarine tankers. Surface tankers were particularly attractive at first, because they offered considerable scale economies in transportation and direct access to eastern American and European markets. If oil could be shipped direct from Prudhoe Bay to Europe, the journey would be about 8,000 miles shorter than that from the Persian Gulf oilfields. Reduced transport costs could offset high exploration and production costs and could thus ensure a profitable market. To realise this potential, however, it would be necessary to bring tankers through the maze of channels in the Canadian Arctic archipelago which constitute the Northwest Passage.

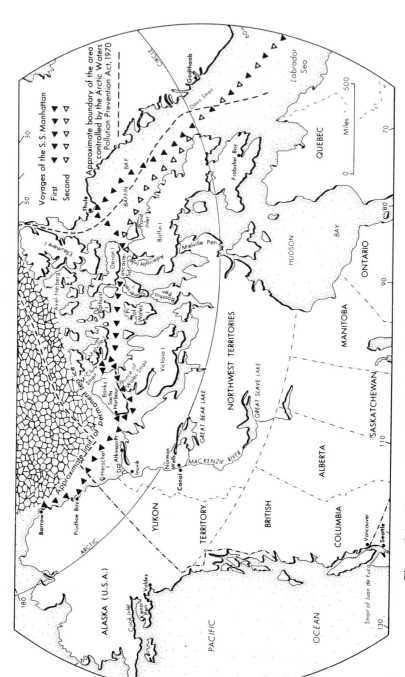

Figure 6.1.   Voyages of the S.S. *Manhattan* in the Canadian Arctic, 1969 and 1970.

The first successful penetration of the passage in one season was by the RCMP vessel *St. Roch* in 1940, although Amundsen in the *Gjoa* had worked his way through over a three-year period, emerging in 1906. Several icebreakers and ice-strengthened vessels have since passed through, but at the time of the Prudhoe Bay discovery no commercial vessel had successfully penetrated the heavy pack-ice that is jammed into the channels by Arctic storms and the outflow of surface waters. Following the Prudhoe Bay strike, the Humble Oil Company conceived the idea of sending an ice-strengthened tanker through the passage.

No suitable vessel existed, but an early supertanker, the *Manhatten,* had the potential for conversion. Because she was experimental when built, she was extremely strong and much more powerful than most tankers of similar displacement. Her loaded displacement was 155,000 tons, of which 115,000 tons was cargo weight,[10] very close to the cargo weight of the *Torrey Canyon.* With a length of 1,005 feet, a width of 150 feet, a draught of 53 to 55 feet, and 43,000 shaft horsepower, her displacement was more than seventeen times greater than that of the largest vessel that had been through the Northwest Passage, the Canadian Coast Guard icebreaker *John A. Macdonald.* In addition to her unusual strength and power, the *Manhattan* was particularly suitable because of her twin propellers and rudders. Substantial modifications included cutting the ship into four parts and fitting a new ice-breaking bow, a high tensile steel ice belt around the hull, double hull reinforcement around the engine room, and ice-strengthened propellers. The total cost of modifications was about $40 million.[11]

The modified *Manhattan* sailed north at the end of August 1969, entering the Northwest Passage with the *John A. Macdonald* and the United States icebreaker *Northwind.* At later stages in the voyage the U. S. icebreaker *Staten Island* and the new Canadian icebreaker *Louis S. St. Laurent* were also escort vessels. The *Manhattan* eventually reached Prudhoe Bay through the passage on September 19, after some difficulty and an enforced retreat from heavy ice in McClure Strait, through which no ship has ever passed.[12] The return journey was without apparent difficulty despite hull damage sustained on the outward journey.

Opinion was divided on exactly what had been proved by the *Manhattan's* voyage. The voyage itself was successful, although it might not have been achieved without the escorting icebreakers. It proved that commerical vessels could navigate the passage in moderate ice conditions toward the end of summer in some years. Contrary to some statements, the voyage certainly did not prove that tankers could consistently operate through the passage in heavy pack-ice throughout the year, particularly in the absence of icebreakers. It also failed to prove the economic feasibility of the route in view of the high cost of the much larger strengthened tankers which would actually be used, estimated at $100 million each.

In order to try the ship in heavy pack-ice approximating winter conditions, it was decided to return to the Arctic in the spring of 1970. Apart from a minor refit, no structural alterations were made before the *Manhattan* entered heavy pack-ice with the *Louis S. St. Laurent* in April. The ships performed penetration tests for several months in the pack-ice, and both sustained some minor damage before they returned south in June.[13]

No decision was immediately taken on the feasibility of tanker transport through the Northwest Passage. During the winter between the two voyages the spectre of potential oil pollution in the Arctic had been raised by the *Arrow* affair in Chedabucto Bay. Despite reassuring statements from the Department of Indian Affairs and Northern Development, the *Arrow* showed that much still needed to be learned about oil spill control, particularly in cold waters. Concern was raised about the effects of a supertanker sinking in the passage, where clean-up operations would be much more difficult and expensive than in Nova Scotia. No one knows what effects an oil spill under ice would have or whether an oil slick could make its way south with the Labrador Current to the Grand Banks of Newfoundland. Biodegradation of oil in the cold water would be very slow, if it occurred at all. The potential for serious damage to scarce Arctic wildlife seems high, with likely repercussions on many Eskimo communities. Concern was also raised about payment for clean-up operations. Obtaining compensation for oil-spill damage had proved difficult in the past; the experience of the French and English governments with the *Torrey Canyon* disaster showed that melodramatic measures could be necessary to obtain compensation, even where sovereignty over polluted waters was not in question. In this case the question about the ownership of waters within the Arctic archipelago had been highlighted by the *Manhattan*'s voyages.

Space does not permit a detailed consideration of all the complex issues involved in the question of Arctic sovereignty; these have been discussed comprehensively in a paper by G. W. Smith.[14] Canada's claims to sovereignty over the Arctic archipelago are based essentially on the so-called *sector principle,* which involves the poleward extension of mainland territories. This principle has also been used by Russia in the Arctic and by New Zealand, Argentina, and Chile in the Antarctic. The United States has generally opposed the sector principle in both the Antarctic and the Arctic but in practise has recognised Canadian sovereignty over the islands. The point at issue was whether such sovereignty also extends over intervening water and pack-ice. The Canadian government maintains that it does, although this has never been officially spelled out.[15] This extension of sovereignty would make all the Arctic area bounded by the 141st and 60th meridian Canadian territory, so that any tanker using the Northwest Passage would have to pass through Canadian territorial waters. If sovereignty extends only over land areas and the twelve-mile breadth of adjacent offshore waters, a tanker could stay in international waters throughout the journey except in the Prince of Wales Strait.[16] It was suggested that one reason the *Manhattan* attempted McClure Strait was that such a passage would allow the complete journey to be made in international waters.

Faced with the possibility of serious oil pollution without compensation, the Canadian government introduced the Arctic Waters Pollution Prevention Act in April 1970. Under this bill a twelve-mile territorial limit and a hundred-mile Arctic control zone were established, bringing the complete Arctic archipelago under Canadian control. Stringent regulations were laid down for ship structure, crew competence, cargoes, and fuel, and provision was made for demanding insurance bonds from any person exploring, developing, or exploiting natural resources in the Arctic as well as from ship owners. Pollution officers were given extensive powers, including the right to seize vessels, which could be sold by the government subsequent to conviction. Fines of up to $5,000 for individuals and $100,000 for ships were instituted. Finally the United Nations was informed that Canada no longer recognises the jurisdiction of the international Court of Justice over pollution disputes off the Canadian coast.

Predictably the new legislation drew mixed reactions from other countries, including diplomatic protests from the United States. The United States government still does not recognise the legality of Canadian claims, but in practise Canada does have de facto control. Very few icebreakers can operate safely in the Northwest Passage. These include the Soviet conventionally powered *Moskva*-class icebreakers and the nuclear-powered *Lenin,* the Canadian *John A. Macdonald* and *Louis S. St. Laurent,* and the United States Navy icebreaker *Glacier.* The *Glacier,* an up-rated Wind-class icebreaker more than twenty years old in concept and not really strong enough for the Northwest Passage,[17] is normally occupied much of the year in support of the United States Antarctic research program. The Canadian ships were therefore the only ones available for escort in the Northwest Passage, and the owners of the *Manhattan* posted an insurance bond of $6.5 million before the second voyage.

The new legislation evoked generally favourable reactions in Canada, although some felt that tankers were unlikely to get into difficulties in the Northwest Passage. This opinion is unconvincing in view of the performance of oil tankers elsewhere in the world and the loss of 600,000 tons of tanker shipping in the last half of 1969. Admittedly some tanker loss is caused by poorly maintained and ill-crewed vessels like the *Arrow,* but many lost vessels are in first-rate condition despite their registration under flags of convenience. The *Torrey Canyon,* registered in Liberia, was rated 100 A by Lloyds of London, the highest rating, for insurance purposes. A ship as carefully maintained and crewed as the *Manhattan* might run little risk, but it is difficult to visualise a tanker fleet of such high standard.

The dangers of running aground in the incompletely charted waters of the passage were indicated by a narrow miss on the *Manhattan*'s first voyage. Subsequently a number of reefs that would be dangerous for deep-draught tankers were charted. The risk of grounding is serious because a supertanker of the *Manhattan*'s size takes over two miles to stop. In addition to common navigational hazards, the ice conditions of the passage pose a severe threat. Tankers might be able to survive average conditions, but eventually a combination of ice conditions, winds, and currents would probably trap and crush a vessel like many vessels before. If the suggested shipping schedules were followed, four or five tankers might be caught simultaneously, causing a vast pollution problem and immense losses to the companies concerned.

Apart altogether from the local hazards of the Northwest Passage, the whole concept of supertanker transport came into question in early 1970. At the end of 1969 three supertankers were seriously damaged by explosions within a period of seventeen days. One, the brand-new, 207,000-ton Shell tanker *Marpessa,* sank off the coast of West Africa. The explosions have never been satisfactorily explained but are believed to have been caused by built-up hydrocarbon gases following oil discharge. A series of shipwrecks of large tankers and ore carriers in the Sea of Devils of Japan during early 1970 also generated concern about the structural safety of the new large bulk carriers.

In late 1970 the Humble Oil Company suspended work on ice-breaking supertankers. No reason was given except that analysis of data derived from the two *Manhattan* voyages indicated that tanker transport in the Arctic is not yet economical. There is no doubt that insurance costs were contributory factors: the explosions which wrecked the supertankers resulted in 25 percent increase in insurance rates for supertankers by Lloyds. In addition, all ships navigating north of 60 degrees north latitude are required to pay an additional premium, and insurance is usually obtainable only for July 23 to October 10.[18] The estimated cost of such premiums for the projected 300,000-ton tankers was over $2 million. The high cost of insurance bonds against pollution are an added deterrent, and it is doubtful if insurance adequate to cover the pollution risk of such large vessels could even be obtained. The $6.5 million bond posted for the second *Manhattan* voyage was the maximum amount which could be obtained from TOVALOP, the international insurance organisation set up to cover oil tanker pollution charges after the *Torrey Canyon* disaster.

In addition to high insurance costs and other risks, the shallow coastal waters of Prudhoe Bay will not allow supertankers closer to the shore than thirty miles. The necessary offshore terminals would be expensive and technically difficult to build because of the heavy winter pack-ice. A study of possible onshore terminal construction at Herschel Island and Mackenzie Bay has indicated costs of around $16 million per installation, and the cost of an offshore terminal would be much higher. One possible alternative is pipeline transportation under the Beaufort Sea for 200 miles from Prudhoe Bay to Herschel Island, but this would also be very expensive.

These factors make tanker transport in the Arctic economically unattractive at the moment, but the situation could change rapidly. Improved, extended hydrographic surveys and new technical innovations in ice navigation, like the Alexbow ice-breaking bow, may make bulk transport of both oil and metallic ores attractive within a decade. In the meantime other alternatives exist.

Submarine tankers. The idea of using submarine tankers for transport in Arctic areas is not new; it was tested by Sir Hubert Wilkins in 1931. Short voyages under ice had been made by Russian submarines off Vladivostock in 1905 and 1908, but the feasibility of transport under the Arctic ice cap was not demonstrated until the 1957 voyage of the United States nuclear submarine *Nautilus* under the North Pole. In 1960 another United States nuclear submarine, the *Seadragon,* passed through the Northwest Passage via McClure Strait under the ice, demonstrating the feasibility of such operations in confined waters.

The most recent research on submarine tanker feasibility has been carried out by the General Dynamics Boat Division in the United States.[19] Design studies have centred on large submarine tankers, in particular a tanker of 175,000 dead-weight tons, 900 feet long, with a 140–foot beam and an 88-foot depth. This tanker is designed to operate at a 350-foot depth; nuclear-generated power equivalent to 75,000 shaft horsepower would allow a sustained sea speed of 18 knots.

The main advantage suggested is that a submarine tanker should be able to operate year-round beneath the ice and the effect of storms. This claim is subject to the completion of hydrographic surveys in the passage. As the *Manhattan* voyages showed, reefs and shoal waters do occur which might require a deep-draught submarine to surface, which would be awkward in heavy pack ice. Also, the submarine would theoretically be able to travel at full speed, giving it a considerable advantage over surface tankers, which must travel at 1 or 2 knots while breaking ice, if they can move at all. Submerged travel would allow the vessel to travel in water of more or less stable temperature (hull distortion and fracture as a result of sharp temperature changes has been suggested as a possible cause of the loss of ships in the Japanese Sea of Devils).

In the General Dynamics design, the submarine tanker would be able to load and unload on the surface or while submerged. The deep draught of the proposed vessel would limit its use in the shallow waters off Prudhoe Bay, but a subsurface terminal could have advantages in pack-ice areas. The biggest question is whether detecting systems for underwater obstacles are adequate. This point is crucial, because the submarine tanker would take two and a half to three miles to stop from full speed. In the General Dynamics proposal the safety record of submarines is compared favourably with surface tankers. This comparison is accurate, but it is unjust, because no civilian-owned submarines are in commercial operation. It seems likely that safety would be at least as problematic as with surface tankers; unexplained sinkings of submarines have occurred, including a U. S. nuclear submarine.

The chief barrier to submarine tankers at the moment is cost. No construction costs have been suggested, but for a submarine tanker of 173,000 tons the cost should be well over $100 million, if the Humble Oil estimates for surface tankers are correct. The cost of submarine terminals and sonar buoys and operating costs would also be formidable. No precedent in commercial shipping allows the prediction of insurance premiums, but they would probably be considerably higher than for surface tankers, at least initially. Preliminary study suggests that submarine tanker transport would be considerably more expensive than surface tanker transport or pipelines unless the shipped volume of oil is less than 60 million tons per year. This study dates from before the *Manhattan* voyages and is based on many unknown factors. Many of the costs and difficulties of submarine tankers remain unknown, but the system deserves further study. Until some practical tests have been carried out it is difficult to foresee when such a system might come into use.

Pipelines. At present pipelines seem to be the most economically feasible and the least damaging method of moving oil out of the Arctic. Many environmental hazards are associated with pipelines, but we have more information on which to base protective measures than in the case of marine transport. The problems associated with pipeline transport are diverse and depend to an extent on how the pipeline is constructed.

A basic problem that will affect all pipelines is the disturbance of surface vegetation by vehicles transporting equipment and materials to the construction sites. This can be minimised by restricting transport and construction to winter, but even so, repetitive travel by heavy vehicles along the same route will eventually damage the surface vegetation. Such damage will almost inevitably lead to thermokarst erosion (subject to soil character) unless the area is rapidly recolonised by vegetation. This is not normal in the Arctic, but tests on induced grasses in Alaska suggest that it could be speeded up.

Actually the problem of vegetation damage is not so vital along the route, for it will be necessary in any case to build a permanent road for pipeline maintenance, and this would probably be laid during construction. Roads built across permafrost must be laid on a thick pad, or *berm,* of gravel.[20] An immense amount of gravel is necessary, which may create supply problems, particularly in Arctic Canada, where many soils are relatively fine grained. Alluvial gravels are the most likely source, but they would have to be obtained from many different stream beds to avoid unacceptable damage to the streams and a possibly disastrous increase in their erosional capacity. Even where gravel supplies are abundant it may be almost impossible to build satisfactory permanent roads due to mud flowage, as at Norman Wells.[21] A further problem is that the gravel becomes extremely abrasive at low temperatures, decreasing the tooth life of excavators from 4,000 feet per set to 50 feet per set.

The second major problem of pipeline operation is the temperature of oil passing through the pipeline.[22] The temperature of crude oil at the wellhead at Prudhoe Bay is about 150 degrees F. The oil will cool on its journey through the pipeline, although viscous flow may keep it fairly hot. The temperature must be kept if necessary by heating, or it will become too viscous to flow. If the heated pipeline comes into direct contact with the frozen ground it will cause melting. Pipelines can be laid on the surface, laid underneath the surface, or suspended above the ground. If the pipeline is buried beneath the surfact it will cause severe melting unless it is carefully insulated. The exact amount is not known, but a melted zone of 50 feet in diameter has been calculated for the 48-inch diameter pipelines which will be used. Melting would cause subsidence and erosion, and variations in ground materials and ice content would cause the subsidence to vary, which would lead to pipeline fracture and oil spillage. Adequate insulation of the pipeline would require immense quantities of gravel, with a thickness of four to six feet around the pipeline. Rough calculation suggests that more than a million tons of gravel would be required for a thousand-mile pipeline.

Laying the pipeline on the ground surface would also require insulation; inadequate insulation would again lead to melting and differential collapse of the ground, producing stresses in the pipeline and almost inevitably fracture. Gravel insulation would be essential only underneath the pipeline, although it would be useful to build it around the pipeline to protect against rapid temperature fluctuation. In either case the amount of gravel required would be less than for an underground pipeline, although it would still be substantial. One possible way to reduce the quantity needed is to use an intermittent berm, in which berm sections several hundred feet in length would be separated by thirty- to forty-foot spans where the pipeline would be unsupported.

The third possibility is to lay the pipeline above the ground on top of a trestle or a series of pilings. The most satisfactory material for such pilings is timber because it is a poor conductor of heat. An air gap between the pipeline and the ground would provide adequate insulation. One of the problems of above-ground construction is that the pipeline must be sufficiently high to allow large mammals to pass underneath it—a gap of at least seven feet. There is no technical difficulty involved, but the supply of timber would be expensive because local sources are not available throughout much of the north. Operating costs would also be high, as heat loss from exposed pipeline is rapid, so that pumping stations would be required.

Opinions differ on the most suitable system, but generally it is believed that the above-ground pipeline would cause the lease environmental damage, although some problems exist. Some wildlife experts wonder if animals will balk at passing beneath a pipeline even if it is built sufficiently far above the ground to permit passage. We do not yet know if this worry is valid, but if it is justified, the effects might be serious. Particularly disturbing is the possibility that the caribou migration might be disturbed. Results of recent research in Alaska indicate that the majority of caribou will balk at a pipeline, even if it is covered by a complete gravel ramp.[23]

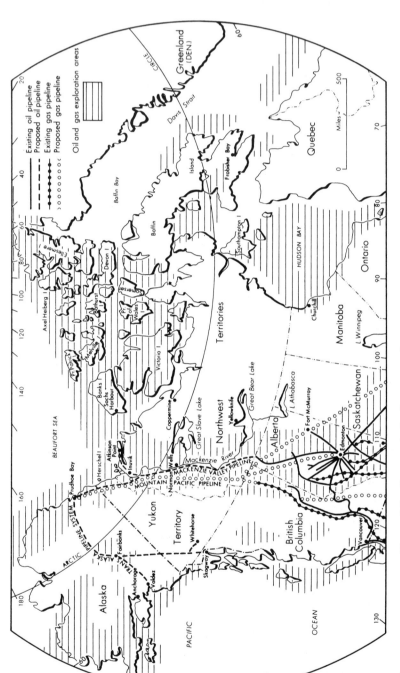

Figure 6.2.   Proposed pipeline routes from Alaska and the Canadian Arctic.

Pipeline breakage is, of course, a main problem. Exactly how much damage would occur is hard to assess. Rapid cooling of the oil would prevent it from spreading far on land, but cleaning up the mess would be difficult, and damage to vegetation might result. The degree of damage would depend on the amount of oil spilled, which would depend on the rapidity of detection, how quickly the oil could be shut off, and how far the break occurred from the nearest shutoff point. As a 48-inch diameter pipe would contain about 44,000 gallons per mile, these details are vital. If the break occurred ten miles from a shutoff point and detection and shutoff were instantaneous, nearly half a million gallons would be lost. A break would be even more troublesome if it occurred at a river crossing, releasing oil into the river. As crossings are the weakest points on pipelines, this is the most likely place for a fracture to occur. The probability of a break occurring is not easy to assess, but certainly the record of pipelines in Alberta, for example, would suggest that it is inevitable and would probably be frequent. Very little knowledge yet exists about the corrosion of pipelines in very cold climates, which could result in serious leakage and high replacement costs. In addition to detection of a break, getting a repair crew to the site in winter could be difficult due to blizzards and icy roads or poor flying conditions. Under some weather conditions it could easily be a week before a repair crew could reach the break. It is estimated that a break would have to be repaired within two weeks or oil would solidify in the pipe, preventing the resumption of pumping. None of these problems is insurmountable, but they must be overcome before construction begins.

Several different pipeline routes have been suggested to bring oil from the North Slope of Alaska, some of which could be adapted to bring oil from the Inuvik area if substantial reserves are found in the Canadian Arctic. Bringing oil from the Arctic islands to Inuvik would obviously create some problems. The best-known proposal is the so-called TAPS, or Trans Alaska Pipeline System, which would involve an 800-mile length of 48-inch diameter pipe running from Prudhoe Bay over the Brooks Range of northern Alaska to Valdez on Prince William Sound on the south coast. At Valdez transshipment to tankers would take place. Extensive storage facilities would be necessary at Valdez, which is close to the zone of the 1964 Alaska earthquake. A similar earthquake could damage facilities and cause spillage.

TAPS was originally planned for completion in 1972, but it has been held up by conservationists, who are not satisfied with the planning for environmental protection. Certainly the companies concerned were premature in assuming approval by the United States Department of the Interior; large amounts of piping are currently stockpiled and rusting at Valdez and Prudhoe Bay.

It is not possible to say how soon construction will start on TAPS, because a major legal battle is continuing. The general consensus of opinion seems to be that eventual construction is inevitable, although at the time of writing the Department of the Interior had not granted approval. The major advantage of the enforced delays is that studies leading to minimisation of ecological damage can be completed. It seems likely that delays and replanning to meet new requirements will put off any start on construction for at least two years. The cost will asmost certainly rise above the current estimate of $1.5 billion.

The fate of TAPS is of more than academic interest in Canada. If it is built it may cause serious damage along the coast of British Columbia. Oil shipped at Valdez will be transported southward along the coast and through the Strait of Juan de Fuca to the vicinity of Seattle. The dismal safety record of tankers indicates that some form of marine accident resulting in a major oil spill is inevitable, and this has raised considerable concern in Canada. Partially in response to this concern the Canadian government made strong overtures to American oil interests in early 1971 in an attempt to promote an alternative pipeline development along the Mackenzie valley. These overtures caused anxiety in Canada, for it appeared that the government was prepared to ignore all the objections which had been made to TAPS. Apparently government officials believed that a pipeline could be built along the Mackenzie without harmful effects, despite the almost complete lack of research results to support such a view.

The planning of additional or alternate pipelines has not been carried out in nearly the same detail as for the TAPS proposal. If the TAPS proposal is held up indefinitely, pressure to start building an alternative will increase. Even if TAPS is built, an additional pipeline will almost certainly be necessary, and apart from the TAPS route across Alaska, the only feasible route is along the Mackenzie valley. A pipeline there would be well situated to serve both the Alaskan North Slope and the Canadian Arctic and could also serve existing reserves at Norman Wells.

A consortium, Mackenzie Valley Pipe Line Research, Ltd., has already made preliminary studies costing about $2.5 million at Inuvik. Much more research is necessary before the technical and ecological problems can be solved, and a considerably larger volume of proven reserves in the Canadian Arctic will be necessary before a pipeline would become economically feasible. At present the most probable pipeline would run from Prudhoe Bay south of the Arctic Wildlife Refuge and through the Richardson Mountains to the Mackenzie valley near Fort Macpherson, where it would be joined by a spur from the Atkinson Point area. It would then follow the river southward and would eventually cut across country to join the existing Trans Mountain and Interprovincial pipeline at Edmonton. The total length from Prudhoe Bay to Edmonton would be about 1,600 miles. The Trans Mountain pipeline would provide transport for an additional 1,560 miles to Chicago. The cost estimates for the Prudhoe Bay-to-Edmonton section are as yet tentative and would depend on the diameter of pipe used but would be at least $1 million per mile—a total cost of at least $1.5 billion.

It will also eventually be necessary to transport natural gas south-

ward to market. Some thought has been given to a combined oil and gas pipeline, but safety considerations will almost certainly demand that the systems
be separate. Three proposals have been made for gas pipelines. The Mountain
Pacific Project would consist of a 48-inch diamer ultrahigh-pressure pipeline
1,085 miles in length, running from Prudhoe Bay to a bifurcation point near
Fort Liard, British Columbia. One line, of 40-inch diameter and 938-mile
length, would continue to the United States border at Kingsgate, British Columbia, and another would run southeast to Chicago. The Northwest Project Study
Group is studying a system which would follow a route similar to Mountain
Pacific to near Fort Simpson before passing southeast to Chicago. The Alberta
Gas Trunk Line proposal would follow a similar route in the northern section,
but would join the existing AGT system in Alberta, which is already linked
to many parts of Canada and the United States.

Detailed cost estimates have not yet been completed for the Mountain Pacific Pipeline, but a construction cost of approximately $725,000 per
mile has been suggested. The economic feasibility of any of the pipelines at
the present time has not been established, as it is uncertain how much of the
Prudhoe Bay gas will actually be available for marketing. An assured through-
put of 2 billion cubic feet per day for at least twenty years has been stated as
the minimum necessary to justify construction.

It has been suggested that of the alternative systems for transporting
Arctic oil to market, pipelines probably present the least environmental hazard,
but the potential for damage is still high. More information about environmental effects is essential before construction commences, and such construction should be strictly controlled. The Canadian federal government has already
stated its intent to ensure control both to protect the northern environment
and to ensure the participation of northern residents in construction programs.
No definite standards have yet been established, however, and the only definite
principle so far is that all pipelines in the Canadian Arctic will be within a
narrow corridor, and that initially, at least, there will be only one gas and one
oil pipeline. The "corridor" concept is designed to minimize the extent of
environmental disturbance, but is also makes sense for construction and maintenance.

Arctic Development

The discovery of substantial oil and gas reserves in the Canadian
Arctic and the potential which exists for further discoveries has emphasised the
necessity of establishing a coherent national policy for northern development.
The development which has taken place in the Arctic has been predominantly
unplanned and exploitative. The only value which has been clearly recognised
is the commercial potential of resources, to the neglect of such values as recreational potential, wilderness preservation, and the maintenance of stable,

economically healthy settlements. This means that the potential of the Canadian Arctic has been distinctly undervalued. Unless an attempt at rational planning is undertaken, the benefit to be derived by all Canadians from Arctic development will be much lower than the potential.

The Canadian north provides an unparalleled opportunity to establish a planned environment on the broadest scale; it could serve as a model for intelligent resource use in the rest of the country. Part of this planned environment must involve the extraction of some of the vast reserve of resources. But the north is the home of many unique plants and animals, and it contains many unique natural landscapes. A properly planned environment must provide adequate reserves of a variety of habitats to ensure the survival of all these species, and national parks must be established to preserve unchanged examples of all unique landscapes. Proposals have already been made for a national park at the eastern arm of Great Slave Lake. Other suggestions include a tundra park, a park to display the ice-cored mounds known as "pongos," and a park to display the landscape of the Mackenzie delta. The immense recreational potential of many areas not included in national parks must also be realised, particularly in view of rapidly improving transportation networks. The planned environment must also include northern residents in the benefits of development. In particular, phased exploitation of resources must be planned to ensure the disappearance of the "boom-and-bust" pattern of settlement development. Possibilities for the development of secondary industrial growth in selected areas must also be explored.

Northern development will probably run the gamut from complete exploitation to complete preservation, as in the remainder of the country. We have an opportunity to ensure that the mistakes which have been made in the rest of the country are not repeated in the north, and this has certain practical implications. To produce the sort of planned environment suggested, it is necessary to complete an inventory of resources, flora and fauna, landscapes, and potential forms of development and their environmental effects. No such inventory exists at the present time. In order to use the opportunity, therefore, a moratorium on development is essential. A complete moratorium is impractical, but as a compromise, wilderness areas and national parks should be tentatively established at once as areas free of development or exploration. If the areas set aside are subsequently found to be unnecessary or unnecessarily large, they can be opened to exploration or reduced in size. If they are not established soon, attempts to set up such areas in the future will be hampered by seismic lines and other evidence of exploration. The fact that an area may once have been a wildlife sanctuary does not preclude subsequent mineral exploration and extraction. On the other hand, if an area has been used for mineral exploration or extraction, it will be a long time before it can serve as a wilderness area or wildlife sanctuary, particularly in the north, where the changes made by man are slow to disappear.

In summary, it appears that northern policy should involve a brief

moratorium on all resource development. Ideally this would provide time
to complete an inventory, to develop a master plan, and to discover nondamaging methods of resource extraction and transportation. The exact length of
the moratorium is difficult to project, for it depends to a large extent on the
funds and manpower available, primarily from federal sources. To do the job
properly would probably require ten years, but even a respite of two years
would be invaluable. To the entrepreneurs waiting to start resource extraction
and to the northern inhabitants waiting for the jobs and prosperity that the
extraction will bring, this may seem a long time, but when it is measured
against man's past occupancy of the north, and hopefully against his future
occupancy, it is but a moment in time. Man will want to inhabit the north long
after the oil and the lead and the zinc are gone. To ask for a moment's respite
to ensure this future is surely neither presumptuous nor unrealistic.

Conclusion to Part Two

The few examples of pollution and the environmental impact of
development in Canada we have discussed are far from exhaustive. However,
they do indicate the type of problems we will face in the immediate future and
some of the difficult decisions we will have to make. The trend in the last few
years has been rapid passage from one environmental crisis to the next without
progress toward solutions; we have become involved in a succession of emergency operations to control the symptoms of pollution without making significant progress against the disease itself.

This situation has diverse causes, but it is perhaps primarily a result
of our failure to define environmental goals. We do not appear to be sure how
highly we value an unpolluted environment, and we must decide this before we
can make significant progress in pollution abatement. Most of our pollution
problems are the by-pruducts of a materialistic society, and maybe the quest for
pollution abatement will lead to a reduction in our material well-being. We must
decide whether such a reduction will be balanced by the physical and aesthetic
advantages of living in a clean environment.

So far we as a society do not appear to have made this decision—in
fact, many of us probably do not fully recognise or comprehend the dilemma.
As a result, we have not given a clear mandate for pollution abatement to our
governments. As a society we demand that governments institute and enforce
pollution controls, but we tend to become upset if this action results in higher
prices, unemployment, or increased taxes. Perhaps we do not yet realise that
if we are to have pollution controls we must be prepared to pay for them. In
response to electoral demand the government may attempt to enforce industrial
controls. The industries involved may then attempt to defray the costs involved either by decreasing their profit margins or by increasing their prices.
But market conditions may not allow either action: the profit margin may

already be so low that shareholders will not permit further reduction, and prices may be too high to allow further increase without overpricing the products. Under these circumstances industries may be unable to meet new control requirements and may be forced to close, creating unemployment. To avoid this the government may choose to subsidise the cost of pollution controls. Whichever situation arises, society as a whole pays for pollution abatement through higher prices, fewer jobs, or higher taxes. Admittedly this analysis is simplistic, and without doubt some industries could absorb the costs of pollution control without increasing prices or cutting staff, but it is an accurate general summary of the situation. If overall pollution control is to be instituted, we must tighten our belts. As a society we have not yet demonstrated that we are prepared to do this, although we may be if the issue is clearly explained.

Another factor postponing pollution control which has been suggested is a lack of suitable legislation. This is only partially true, for much legislation does exist and has for some time. Pesticide use may be controlled by the Experimental Farms Act, the Pest Control Products Act, and the Canada Grain Act. Pollutant criteria for foodstuffs can be established under the Food and Drug Act. Water pollution can be controlled under the Fisheries Act, the Canada Shipping Act, the Arctic Waters Pollution Control Act, the Migratory Birds Convention Act, and the Canada Water Act. Air pollution can be controlled under the Clean Air Act. If all else fails, the Criminal Law can be invoked to protect public health. A suitable legislative framework for federal action does exist, therefore, although significant portions, such as the Clean Air Act, the Canada Water Act, and the Arctic Waters Pollution Control Act, are of recent development and their effectiveness will not be demonstrated for some time.

Effective control of environmental quality has been hampered by fragmentation of authority, a situation that should be improved by the concentration of relevant authority in the new Department of the Environment. However, the new department will not solve the problem of the reluctance of the federal government to take action which infringes on, or appears to infringe on, provincial jurisdiction. The situation is complicated by the existence in most provinces of extensive legislation that parallels federal pollution control legislation. Authority often overlaps, and the exact delineation of authority has not been clearly established legally or constitutionally. This is unfortunate, because federal government may be reluctant to act for fear of going beyond its constitutional powers, even though some problems require solution on a national scale. It is also unfortunate because provincial governments tend to be more subject to the influence of local industrial pressure groups. If authority were more clearly vested in the federal government, uniform controls could be established across Canada to largely negate the effect of such groups. Furthermore, the way would be cleared for a unified, comprehensive approach to the maintenance of environmental quality.

In summary, therefore, if we wish to maintain or improve the quality of our environment, we must say so and be prepared to accept the costs involved. We must also break the administrative and legal logjam by vesting greater authority in the federal government—the only body capable of coordinating a national programme of pollution control.

References

1. Department of Transport, *Operation Oil: a report on the clean-up operations at Chedabucto Bay, Nova Scotia*, April, 1971.

2. J. C. Reed, "Oil Developments in Alaska," *The Polar Record* 15 (94) 1970: 7–17.

3. R. J. E. Brown and G. H. Johnston, "Permafrost and Related Engineering Problems," *Endeavour* 23 (1964): 89.

4. J. R. Mackey. Public address to Department of Geography, The University of Alberta, January, 1970.

5. D. R. Klein, "The Impact of Oil Development in Alaska," in *Proceedings of the Conference on Productivity and Conservation in Northern Circumpolar Lands, Edmonton, October 1969*, edited by W. A. Fuller and P. G. Kevan, IUCN Publication New Series, No. 16, pp. 209–242, 1970.

6. T. Pearce, "The Success Story of an Island," *North* 17 (3) (1970): 14–16.

7. R. B. Weeden and D. R. Klein, "Wildlife and Oil: a Survey of Critical Issues in Alaska," *The Polar Record* 15 (94) (1970): 60–61.

8. P. J. Kinney, D. K. Button and D. M. Schell, "Kinetics of Dissipation and Biodegradation of Crude Oil in Alaska's Cook Inlet," *The Northern Engineer* 2 (1970): 6–7.

9. J. R. K. Main, "Transportation as a Factor in Northern Development," *Resources for Tomorrow* 1 (1961): 579–596.

10. A. H. G. Storrs and T. C. Pullen, "*S. S. Manhattan* in Arctic Waters," *Canadian Geographical Journal* 80 (5) (1970): 166–181.

11. Anon., "Arctic Reconnaissance Voyage of S. S. Manhattan, *1970,"* *The Polar Record*

12. W. Slipchenko, "An *S. S. Manhattan* Diary," *North*, 17 (3) (1970): 1–10.

13. C. W. M. Swithinbank, "Second Arctic Voyage of the *S. S. Manhattan, 1970*," *The Polar Record* 15 (96) (1970): 355–356.

14. G. W. Smith, "Sovereignty in the North: The Canadian Aspect of an International Problem, in *The Arctic Frontier*, edited by R. St. J. MacDonald, pp. 194–255 (Toronto: University of Toronto Press, 1966).

15. L. B. Pearson, "Canada Looks 'down North,' *Foreign Affairs* 24 (4) (1946): 638–639.

16. N. W. Morris, "Boundary Problems Related to the Sovereignty of the Canadian Arctic," *The Musk-Ox* 6 (1) (1969): 32–58.

17. J. P. Morley, "Polar Ships and Navigation in the Antarctic," *British Antarctic Survey Bulletin* 2 (1963): 1–26.

18. Warnock Hersey International Ltd., *Arctic Transportation Study* for the Northern Economic Development Branch of the Department of Indian Affairs and Northern Development, 1970.

19. J. L. Helm, "Submarine Tankers." Paper presented at the *Canadian Fifth National Northern Development Conference*, Edmonton, 5th Nov., 1970.

20. D. R. Nichols and L. A. Yehle, "Highway Construction and Maintenance Problems in Permafrost Regions," *Proceedings of the 12th Annual Symposium on Geology and Applied Highway Engineering.* Bulletin 24m pp. 19–29, 1961.

21. R. J. E. Brown, *Permafrost in Canada* (Toronto: University of Toronto Press, 1970).

22. A. H. Lachenbruch, "Some Estimates of the Thermal Effects of a Heated Pipeline in Permafrost," *United States Department of the Interior, Geological Survey Circular* 632 (1970).

23. K. Child, "Reaction of Caribou to Various Types of Simulated Pipeline." Paper presented to the *International Conference on the Behaviour of Ungulates and its Relation to Management,* University of Calgary, November 2-5, 1971.

Part 3

Transfer and Export of Canadian Water

The W.A.C. Bennett Dam and Lake Willisden, British Columbia. (Credit: B. C. Hydro).

Chapter 7

Water Transfer
and the Canadian Water Resource

Some of the problems associated with the transfer or export of water were introduced briefly in a preceding chapter. A more extensive discussion is merited because of the potential repercussions on the Canadian environment and the public interest and alarm which have been aroused by proposed schemes. Alarm probably originated because of the Columbia River Treaty of 1961, which had nothing to do with water transfer but which raised related problems. It involved the construction of a number of dams for hydroelectric power generation in the Arrow Lakes area of southern British Columbia. The power was designated primarily for the power grids of the northwestern United States. Two of the many issues involved in the controversy are of particular importance: some people felt that the social values of the scenic and fertile valleys involved had not been adequately considered in the treaty; others felt that although the principle involved was reasonable, the Canadian negotiators had assented to a treaty containing minimal benefits to Canada. The two factors of environmental damage and Canadian nationalism were thus involved in the controversy and have remained in most water resource discussions since.

The basic environmental problems caused by water transfer bear some similarity to those caused by organochlorine pesticides, for example. In each case a benefit accrues and a cost is involved, and the controversy concerns the reality of the benefits produced and the magnitude of the costs to be borne. The analogy should not be carried too far, for there are obvious differences. The benefits of pesticides are demonstrable and the costs are the clearly defined, although long-term dangers to the health and life of humans and wildlife may be difficult to predict. The costs and benefits associated with water transfer are more nebulous and depend largely on subjective judgement. In assessing these costs and benefits one must balance the relative importance of the uses to which the water would be put at two different locations and the environmental and monetary costs of transferring the water. This might involve trying to balance the value of wildfowl nesting grounds in one location against the recreational virtues of grassed golf courses in another. Obviously the decision will depend on one's priorities.

Controversy has not arisen solely from the differing priorities, however; it has become associated with a considerable degree of mutual mistrust. This has probably originated because of the manner in which decisions on major water management projects have been based on the opinions of "experts" and the general secrecy involved. The use of expert opinion is fundamental to many aspects of government and is in many cases justified; on technical matters the opinions of experts in related fields are obviously more valuable than those of laymen. However, in aesthetic matters such as assessment of the social value of a beautiful valley experts are not more valuable than laymen. In such judgements all are qualified, and all opinions should be consulted. The difficulties of doing this have been outlined in Chapter One. Public hearings are probably the most widespread method, although these tend to provide a sounding board only for extreme viewpoints; the bulk of the public neither know nor care about them. This is perhaps not surprising in view of the cynicism with which some governments arrange hearings. One flagrant recent example was connected with the construction of the Big Horn Dam in Alberta. Initially no public hearings were scheduled, but eventually public and opposition pressure forced the provincial government to hold hearings. By this time, however, the decision to build the dam had already been made, and work at the site was under way. It is not surprising that many people have come to mistrust the motives of everyone who was involved with the decision.

The degree to which decisions that affect environmental quality are based on the opinions of experts alone is a disturbing aspect of the environmental crisis, made even more so when the experts are selected from a restricted range of disciplines. One common criticism is that water management authorities rely almost entirely on the advice of engineers, neglecting economists, biologists, sociologists, urban and recreational planners, and others who should contribute to decisions on water management. As a result, cost-benefit studies tend to concentrate almost entirely on engineering feasibility, neglecting the important social elements involved. A good example is the Saskatchewan-Nelson Basin Board, which is carrying out "a study of the water resources of the Saskatchewan-Nelson basin, including the potential additional supply by diversion or storage."[1] The board includes fifteen engineers and hydrologists but no representatives of other disciplines. Such a narrowly based study group is inadequate to prepare a balanced, broadly based report on which rational development of the water resources of the basin could take place.

Controversy over water transfer will probably continue for a long time, but if progress is to be made, some degree of compromise will eventually be necessary. Inevitably some water will be transferred within Canada; in some places it is being transferred at present. The conservationist's role is not to stop water transfer but to ensure that its necessity is objectively examined, that all opinions have been heard, and that all social and monetary costs considered.

The Canadian Water Resource

In its simplest statement, the case for water transfer in North America is that some parts of the continent have apparent surpluses of water, whereas in other parts development is limited by deficient supplies. Water transfer would help to eliminate the deficiencies, would stimulate growth and development, and would provide a source of revenue to the supply areas. To assess the validity of the case for water transfer we will examine first the existence of apparent surpluses and deficiencies.

Fresh water exists on the earth's surface in a number of forms: as ice and snow, lakes and ponds, streams and rivers, and as groundwater stored in soils and rocks. The water in ice caps and lakes and as groundwater is in storage and constitutes the "capital" of the water resource. It varies somewhat in amount from season to season and year to year in response to climatic fluctuations, but if natural processes are undisturbed, its total quantity will remain more or less in balance in a human life span. The capital of stored water may be tapped or "mined" for man's uses, but it then becomes a wasting resource which will eventually disappear, at least locally, although it will be replenished when withdrawal ceases. Water in streams and rivers is in transit to the sea, from which it is evaporated and eventually returned to the land by rainfall and snowfall. This water may be regarded as the "interest" of the water resource, although it is not governed in quantity by the amount of water in storage. It may be withdrawn and used for man's purposes without short-term effects on the capital of water stored. Such withdrawal may affect both the quantity and quality of water reaching downstream users, however, sometimes to a degree which precludes use.

Canadian river basins

As we attempt to assess the existence of a surplus of fresh water in parts of Canada that might be available for transfer or export, the amount of

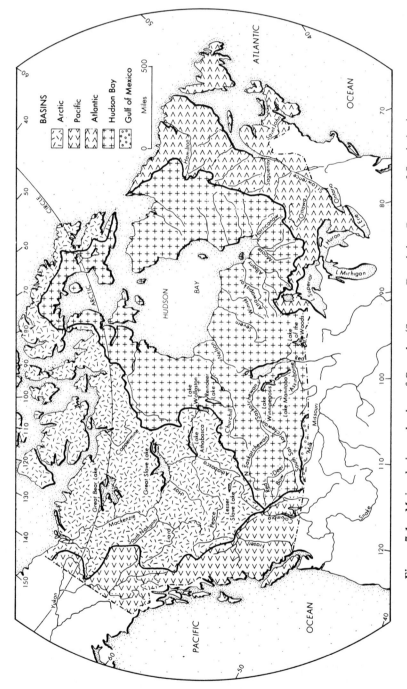

Figure 7.1. Major drainage basins of Canada. (Source: Dominion Bureau of Statistics.)

water in streams and rivers should be discussed, not the stored water. Included within Canada's borders are some of the longest rivers in the world—the Mackenzie (2,635 miles), the St. Lawrence (1,900 miles), the Nelson (1,600 miles), the Yukon (1,587 miles), and the Columbia (1,150 miles), some of which are shared with the United States. The rivers are located in four main drainage basins: the Arctic, Pacific, Hudson Bay, and Atlantic basins, which cover a total area of 4,209,375 square miles. The Milk River in southern Alberta drains into the Missouri-Mississippi system.

The Arctic basin, which contains 16 percent of Canadian water flow, covers an area of 1,399,687 square miles. It is dominated by the Mackenzie River, but it also contains abundant fresh water stored as permafrost beneath the ground and as lakes, the most important of which are the Great Slave and Great Bear lakes.

The Pacific basin includes all rivers rising on the western slopes of the Western Cordillera, most of which are relatively short but fast flowing, presenting a considerable potential for hydroelectric power development. The basin covers 424,218 square miles; the most important rivers are the Columbia, the Fraser, and the Yukon.

The largest basin is the Hudson Bay, which covers 1,578,125 square miles. The most important rivers, the Nelson and the Saskatchewan system, together drain Manitoba, most of Saskatchewan, and the southern part of Alberta. The Nelson also receives water from the Red River, which drains northward from the United States.

In terms of present population distribution, the most important basin is the Atlantic, which covers an area of 798,828 square miles and which is dominated by the Great Lakes–St. Lawrence system. This sytem is an unparalleled network of navigable waterways that has been of vital importance in the development of eastern Canada and the United States.

Measurement of streamflow

An estimated nine percent of the total world streamflow is in Canadian rivers, but to assess the accuracy of such estimates it is necessary to know how streamflow data is measured. Ideally streamflow should be measured by frequent or continuous monitoring, or gauging, of stream heights and velocities at intervals along the stream course. Using height and velocity data the streamflow, or *discharge,* can be calculated, usually in cubic feet of water passing the station per second. Obviously the accurate gauging of a stream in this way is expensive and must be continued over a long time period. Although there are approximately 3,400 stream gauges in Canada, many have been in position for a relatively short time. We still have no accurate discharge data for a considerable number of rivers. Most of the rivers that have been gauged for a significant time are concentrated in the southern part of the country. This is unfortunate, for any water "surplus," if it exists, will be mainly in northern rivers.

Estimation of streamflow

In areas where direct observations of streamflow are not available, estimates can be developed on the basis of meteorological data, particularly precipitation and temperature data. For any given conditions of temperature, air humidity, and wind, a specified amount of moisture will be evaporated from the ground surface. This is referred to as the *potential evapotranspiration,* for moisture is taken up both by direct evaporation from the surface and by transpiration from plants. Precipitation may not be adequate to fulfill potential evapotranspiration, particularly as some portion is lost by infiltration into the ground surface and contributes to changes in stored groundwater. When the actual evapotranspiration falls below the potential due to deficient rainfall or infiltration, the difference is referred to as the *deficit.* Any water in excess of the requirements of potential evapotranspiration is referred to as the *surplus,* and gives some measure of the availability of water for streamflow.

Direct measurements of evapotranspiration are available from very few sites, but estimates can be derived by various methods incorporating temperature data. The most common of these is the Thornthwaite method, which is useful but which takes no account of the influence of wind on evapotranspiration. Another difficulty with the water balance equation is the great variation in storage capacity in response to variations in soil and rock type, in vegetation, and in topography. This makes accurate estimation of infiltration difficult, for it varies not only from place to place but also at one place with time. Precipitation data are available from all meteorological stations, but completely satisfactory methods of measuring snowfall have not been developed. A serious limitation in the calculation of surplus is the sparse network of meteorological stations in the Canadian Arctic and sub-Arctic, many of which have been operational only for a few years.

The available water resource

The combination of available streamflow data with estimates derived from water balance equations permit a wide variety of estimates, varying from about 39,000 cubic metres per second, or 1 billion acre-feet per year, to about 137,000 cubic metres per second, or 3.5 billion acre-feet per year, (an acre-foot is the amount of water which would flood one acre to a depth of twelve inches; it is equivalent to 273,112 Imperial gallons). At present the best estimate of the total discharge of Canadian rivers is 100,700 cubic metres per second (2.6 billion acre-feet per year), which is just over half the total discharge for the rivers of the coterminous United States.[2] Of this total approximately 33 percent is within the Atlantic basin, 29 percent within the Hudson's Bay basin, 21 percent within the Hudson's Bay basin, 21 percent within the Pacific basin, and 16 percent within the Arctic basin.

Canadian water use

River water use may be broadly classified into *withdrawal* and *non-withdrawal* uses, depending on whether water is removed from the river. Withdrawal use may in turn be classified into *consumptive* and *nonconsumptive* use, depending on whether the water is eventually returned to the river. The amount of water actually consumed is variable, depending on the purpose for which it is used. Domestic uses involve about 10 percent consumption, irrigation about 60 percent, and industry about 2 percent.[3] An average consumption of about 25 percent has been suggested for Canada, under three headings: residential and commercial, industrial, and rural nonindustrial.

The total Canadian withdrawal use of water has been projected from 891 cubic metres per second in 1956 to 2,109 cubic metres per second in 1990, which represents about 2 percent of the available supply.[4] In addition, an estimated 10 percent of the total streamflow is at present in nonwithdrawal use for the dilution and transportation of waste materials.[5] If current philosophies on waste removal prevail, this may rise to 25 percent by the end of this century, but if society decides that this is no longer an acceptable use of river water, it may drop close to zero. Even allowing for considerable variation in estimates, it is unlikely that Canadian needs will rise to above 30 percent of the total available supply by the year 2000. If the Canadian population continues to grow at the present rate and the ratio of water used to population remains constant, supplies would be theoretically adequate until the year 2189. This very simplistic estimate assumes, for example, that the percentage of water used for irrigation would remain constant. In fact, other physical factors such as soil salinity limit the potential expansion of irrigation. The estimate does point out the fact that assessment of potential Canadian use of water resources should not be projected merely to the end of this century.

Another point often overlooked is the considerable difference between the toal amount of water in the country and the amount that is actually available to satisfy demands. In Canada most of the water supply is remote from large-scale demands, and the two can be brought together only with considerable expense and disruption. Further, the streamflow data quoted above are average figures. Planning for human needs should not be based on average streamflow but on minimum reliable flow rates.

Before leaving water use it is important to question the assumption that water not used for residential and commerical, industrial, or rural nonindustrial purposes is surplus, or not in use. In fact, all the water flowing in rivers is in use, supporting extensive aquatic flora and fauna, which in turn support other organisms in an intricate ecosystematic web. Any reduction in the quantity or quality of water flowing in rivers will cause important and perhaps irreversible changes in these flora and fauna. A growing number of people feel that such change is not desirable on aesthetic grounds, but there are also social and economic repercussions. Among the people most directly affected would be the many Canadians who have a strong recreational or commercial interest in water-based wildlife. Fishing and trapping are important to the livelihood of most of the native population of Canada. Any reductions in streamflow could endanger or destroy that livelihood, as demonstrated in the Peace-Athabasca delta of Alberta, which has been affected by the elimination of spring floods in the Peace by the W. A. C. Bennett Dam in British Columbia. (This is discussed in some detail in a later chapter.)

Many Canadian rivers are also used for transportation. For example, the Mackenzie River is a vital link in the eventual development of the western Canadian Arctic. Streamflow reduction in the Mackenzie caused by the filling of Williston reservoir behind the W. A. C. Bennett Dam was partially responsible for the enforced deepening of the Sans Sault Rapids at a cost of $500,000. Admittedly, improved flow regime in the river once the reservoir is full could eventually benefit navigation.

The examples indicate that some uses of river water are frequently not considered in discussions of water surpluses. All the water flowing in our rivers is being used for some purpose; we may be able to find more valuable uses for some of the water, but we should not ignore present use. If water is to be transferred from Canadian rivers it will involve abandoning one set of water uses in favour of another. The benefits might justify the losses, but these losses must be recognised and assessed and not merely ignored, as has often happened.

Water Transfer within Canada

The concept of water transfer is certainly not new in Canada; it has been part of agricultural practise since at least the end of the eighteenth century, when techniques for the subsurface drainage of poorly drained fields were developed. In principle, water transfer covers any movement of water away from its natural drainage network. When a farmer digs a ditch to drain melt water off his fields he is transferring water just as the engineer who transfers large amounts of water from the Arctic southward; the difference is only in scale. In minor transfer schemes the benefits derived are localised and the environmental disturbance produced is small. If someone miscalculates the balance of costs and benefits, the results are not too serious. Major schemes are of more concern; the potential benefits are greater and the possible environmental changes reach farther. If we miscalculate on this scale, the results may wreak havoc with part of our environment.

Before proceeding to ignore minor water transfer projects, we should point out that the sum effect of many small projects, which individually are of little consequence, may be a major environmental change. A good example is the extensive drainage of wetlands carried out in the western prairies, particularly since the Second World War.[6] To a large extent this has been on a single-farm basis in an attempt to extend crop acreages or to facilitate the operation of machinery. The wetlands form one of the most important breeding areas for wildfowl in the Western Hemisphere. The effect of each individual drainage project on wildfowl has been small, but the cumulative effect has been a great reduction in suitable breeding habitats and staging posts for migratory wildfowl. To balance this, the agricultural benefits have frequently proven illusory.[7] This example is a strong argument for integrated regional planning of water resource use.

Most major water transfer projects proposed for Canada also involve the export of water to the United States and are discussed in a later chapter. Although Canada is frequently cast in the role of a water supply region and the United States as a water demand region, there are areas of "surplus" and deficit in both countries. The deficiencies are more extensive and severe in the United States, but some areas of Canada could benefit from increased supplies of water, particularly the southern parts of the prairie provinces. Considerable development of water transfer on a relatively small scale has already been carried out to improve the water supply in this area, but before we discuss these developments we should examine two feasibility studies, both concerned with increasing the water supply to the prairies on a much larger scale.

Prairie Rivers Improvement Management and Evaluation

The so-called PRIME project originated in the mid-1960s as a "total basin development approach" to the planning of water resource use in Alberta. Officially it is regarded as a feasibility study for supplementing the water supply in southern river basins by water transfer. The project is envisaged as a phased development to take place as demands on the water supply in southern basins increase. As full utilisation of the existing supply is reached, additions would be made first by intrabasin transfers, then by transfers from neighbouring basins, and eventually by large-scale transfers from the Peace and Athabasca rivers. A variety of water transfer projects would be incorporated, involving canals, tunnels, and major reservoirs. The main features are shown in Figure 7.2. The project will incorporate an inventory of surface water and groundwater supplies, a study of related land uses, assessment of resource potential, population projections, and economic forecasts.

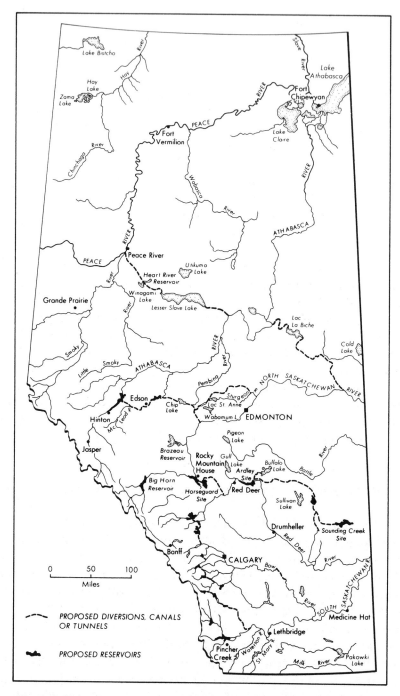

Figure 7.2. Water management proposals for Alberta made under the Prairie Rivers Improvement and Management Evaluation. (Source: Alberta's Blueprint for Water Development.)

The benefits projected for the scheme include an enhanced water supply for urban centres of central and southern Alberta to provide for urban industrial and domestic development and pollution abatement, particularly in the North Saskatchewan and Bow rivers. Additional benefits suggested are the provision of water supplies for the further development of irrigation agriculture in southern Alberta, the creation of potential hydroelectric power generation sites, the provision of flood control, and the possible recreational potential of reservoirs.

One major difficulty in discussing the PRIME project is finding out exactly what studies are being made. For example, in view of the emphasis placed on resource assessment in the objectives, an examination of wildlife habitat and potential should be involved, particularly as some phases of the project would significantly alter several wildlife habitats. However, up to the time of writing no ecologist has been employed in the study. In March 1971 Renewable Resources Consulting Services, Ltd., of Edmonton, was hired to examine the ecological implications of the project; the suggested time period for the study was eight months!

Another problem is the absence of detailed cost forecasts for the total project, without which it is impossible to make reasonable comparisons of even the economic costs and benefits. It has been suggested that such long-term projections are not necessary, that each stage of the phased project can be judged in isolation. In theory this is correct, but in practise the economic justification for some earlier stages is that they are necessary to permit the completion of later stages, which would restore a favourable cost-benefit ratio. In the absence of long-term projections the only economic justification for some of the later stages may prove to be the amount of capital already invested in the earlier stages. This criticism is not serious for a feasibility study; the main objection is that implementation of parts of the plan has already commenced without adequate data on either projected costs or the environmental alteration which would occur. The Big Horn Dam in the Kootenay Plains already exists, a joint project of the government of Alberta and Calgary Power that is economically justifiable only by its contribution to the PRIME project. Common sense alone decrees that a feasibility study should be completed and public hearings held before implementation begins. (In October 1971 the government of Alberta halted all research and expenditure on the PRIME project and on water export.)

The Saskatchewan-Nelson Basin Board

The Saskatchewan-Nelson Basin Board has been mentioned as an example of the restricted use of expert advice in the planning of water resource development. Like the PRIME project, it is intended only as study in which "consideration will be given to the feasibility and cost of many combinations of storage and/or diversion works needed to provide a firm water supply of varying amounts and with varying seasonal distributions, at various selected points along the river system."[18] The management proposals are grouped into four stages, each of which represents a potential increase in water supply to the prairies. The first provides for intrabasin storage and transfer, the second for the addition of water from the Athabasca and Churchill rivers, the third for alternative intrabasin transfers, and the fourth for importation of water from the Peace River and Lake Athabasca basins. These stages do not necessarily represent the eventual order of implementation.

The project is an engineering feasibility study, scheduled for completion in 1973. It is a narrowly based study involving, for example, no economic or ecological investigations. Even when complete it will not form an adequate basis for implementation despite its estimated cost of $5 million, which is being borne by the federal government and the governments of Saskatchewan, Manitoba, and Alberta.

Potential Benefits of Water Transfer in Canada

A number of potential benefits which might be derived in Canada from water transfer have been mentioned in passing. These depend on the detailed design of the projects involved and to some extent of their timing. The following discussion of possible benefits does not therefore suggest an order of importance or probability.

Irrigation

The area most likely to benefit from an increased water supply for irrigation agriculture is the southern part of the three prairie provinces. The irrigation potential there has already been developed to a considerable degree by numerous local and four major projects. The oldest of these is the St. Mary and Milk River Project, which began operation in 1901, supplying irrigation water originally to 3,600 acres and now to 296,000 acres in the area south of the Oldman River, Alberta. The Bow River Irrigation Project was started in 1909 and currently supplies water to 120,000 acres in the area north of the Oldman River. Another major project is the Eastern Irrigation District, east of the Trans-Canada Highway in Alberta, where some 200,000 acres are irrigated. The latest project, the damming of the South Saskatchewan River to form Lake Diefenbaker, was completed in 1968, with the capacity to irrigate 400,000 acres in the area between Outlook and Saskatoon in southern Saskatchewan. Undoubtedly there is physical potential for further development of irrigation agriculture in the prairie provinces, but it may be years before it is economically feasible.

Development of the St. Mary project was hindered for many years by

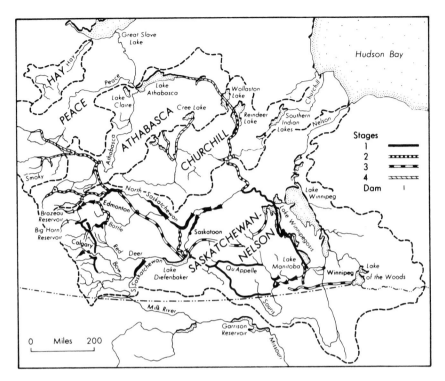

Figure 7.3. Water management proposals for the Prairie Provinces made by the Saskatchewan-Nelson Basin Board. (Source: Saskatchewan-Nelson Basin Board Annual Report, 1970.)

a lack of markets for produce from irrigated areas, and the potential for irrigation still depends not so much on the lack of water as on the lack of markets. The variety of crops which can be produced at a competitive price using irrigation is limited; the main ones are specialty crops such as vegetables and sugar beets, which provide high yields per acre. Vegetable production could be increased, but the available market could be satisfied by small acreages. For example, it has been estimated that the complete Albertan demand for carrots could be supplied from two quarter sections of land. There is a potential for increases in beet acreages, but a number of Canadian provinces already have sugar industries, so the possible home market is not very large. Perhaps the best potential for expansion in irrigation farming is through dairying and beef-fattening—using irrigated acreage for forage production. Production could be expanded in both areas, but produce would compete with existing supplies. For example, dairy produce from the prairie provinces has little chance of being marketed in the major population centres of Ontario, where a thriving dairy industry already exists, unless the prairie produce was heavily subsidized or subject to special agreement.

The acreage presently irrigated by some existing projects is significantly less than the projects are capable of serving. The St. Mary project irrigates only 60 percent of its potential, and the Bow River project irrigates slightly over 50 percent. The Lake Diefenbaker project currently serves approximately 40,000 acres, although it is designed to supply water for up to 430,000 acres. Under these circumstances it would seem that any potential for increase in irrigated acreage could be easily served by existing facilities for quite a long time. It is therefore not realistic to use irrigation benefits as a motive for major water transfer.

Urban supply and pollution abatement

The water supply has not restricted urban development in Canada on the grounds of quantity, although quality has sometimes been less than adequate, primarily because watercourses are used for the dilution and transport of domestic and industrial wastes. Heavily polluted water can be purified to a level suitable for most purposes, but the greater the pollution load, the more expensive such purification becomes. The main benefit of increasing the water supply to urban areas would be the abatement of pollution in rivers and lakes, which in turn should reduce purification costs. Water transfer could provide some pollution abatement, as in the North Saskatchewan, where the PRIME diversions could supplement low winter discharges. At present the main areas of excessive river pollution are in the densely settled parts of eastern Canada—in the Great Lakes-St. Lawrence basin—outside the sphere of influence of many proposed transfer schemes. Some proposals would augment the supply to the Great Lakes, which are suffering from accelerated eutrophication as a result of high waste inputs. This scheme might retard eutrophication, but the amount necessary to significantly alleviate pollution in the Great Lakes is much larger than the capacity of any proposed diversion.

Augmentation of water supplies may be necessary in some urban centres in the near future because of the expense of providing adequate waste treatment across the country. This sould not be regarded as a prime objective, however, but only as an interim measure until adequate treatment facilities are installed. Augmentation of the supply for pollution abatement without this proviso would simply encourage authorities at all levels to delay the implementation of adequate waste treatment. The only reason that cities such as Montreal are now belatedly installing facilities is the deterioration of natural water bodies to crisis levels.

Additional benefits

Several other benefits could result from water transfer or export, depending on the details of the plan involved. Some plans provide for development of hydroelectric power generation facilities. This is only a peripheral benefit, however—not a justification for transfer—for it is considerably cheaper to transport electric power than water. Therefore, if power generation is the primary objective it is normally cheaper to develop power stations at the source of the waterhead than at the market for the electricity. If the demand for power is very large it may even be economical to locate the demand at the power source, as in the case of the Alcan operation at Kitimat, British Columbia, but for most power demands location is determined by factors other than power supply.

Some proposed transfers would provide flood control benefits, particularly in the southern communities of Saskatchewan and Manitoba. Apart altogether from the question of water transfer, it is time that we reevaluated our ideas about flood control. It is economically impossible to protect against the largest flood which will ever occur, even if we could predict it accurately. Flood control measures normally involve a calculated risk, in which protection is provided against, for example, a 100-year or a 500-year flood. Statistically the 500-year flood should occur only once in 500 years, but it could take place the year after the control works are compelted. The provision of flood control encourages people to settle and develop areas which are inherently hazardous with a false sense of security. Flood control measures are obviously necessary on a short-term basis, but we should consider relocating settlements away from major hazard areas.

Any water management projects which involve extensive development of reservoirs have some potential for recreational development. A number of factors may limit this potential, particularly the rise and fall of the reservoir surface, or the *drawdown*. A reservoir with a minimal drawdown can be easily developed for recreation, depending on the shoreline characteristics, but where the drawdown reaches 50 to 100 feet it is much more difficult. This means, for example, that summer cabins built along the shore at the high water level would look out over mud flats at low water level. The amount of drawdown is also important in determining the possibility of using reservoirs as breeding grounds for wildfowl; most water birds nest close to the water's edge and are thus vulnerable to changes in water level. This is especially true for fledglings, which are unable to swim or to protect themselves against predators. (These problems are discussed more fully in a later chapter.) Another difficulty with the recreational use of reservoirs is that timber must be cleared from the area before flooding. This was not done in some existing reservoirs, including Lake Williston, in British Columbia, and Brazeau Dam, in Alberta; in both cases the recreational potential has been impaired.

The discussion indicates that there are possible benefits to be derived from water transfer in Canada, although some of them, such as pollution abatement, may not be beneficial in the long run. Potential benefits such as hydroelectric power generation and recreation are peripheral and certainly should not be used as a prime justification for diversions. The major potential benefits of water transfer do not lie within Canada, however, but in the revenue which might be derived by exporting water to the United States. In order to assess the market for Canada's water that might exist in the United States, we must discuss the water supply situation there in considerable detail.

References

1. Saskatchewan-Nelson Basin Board, Annual Report for the year ending March 31st, 1970.

2. Canadian National Committee for the International Hydrological Decade, *op. cit.*

3. D. Cass-Beggs, "Water as a Basic Resource," in *Regional and Resource Planning in Canada*, ed. R. R. Krueger, F. O. Sargent, A. deVos and N. Pearson, pp. 176–197 (Toronto: Holt, Rinehart and Wilson of Canada, Ltd., 1970).

4. D. Cass-Beggs, *op. cit.*

5. A. H. Laycock, "Canadian water for Texas?" *Water Resources Bulletin* 6 (1970): 542–549.

6. D. A. Munro, "Ducks and the Great Plains Wetlands," *Canadian Audubon* 25 (1963): 105–111.

7. R. W. Lodge, "Agricultural Use of Wetlands," in *Saskatoon Wetlands Seminar*, Canadian Wildlife Service Report Series, No. 6, pp. 11–15 (Ottawa: Queen's Printer, 1969).

8. Saskatchewan-Nelson Basin Board, *op. cit.*

Chapter 8

Water Supply
in the United States

We pointed out in the previous chapter tha the major benefit Canada might receive from water transfer is revenue inflow from the United States. Whether water export to the United States on a significant scale is possible depends at least as much on the existence of an American demand as it does on Canadian willingness to supply. Water supplies in the United States as a whole are adequate to meet demands. It has been suggested that current consumptive use is only 6 percent of the available supply and that by the year 2000 this will rise only to 10 percent and total withdrawals to less than half the available supply.[1] In many parts of the United States, therefore, the quantity of the supply is not a serious problem, although its quality may not be suitable for all, or indeed for any, purposes.

Several regions which have adequate precipitation and streamflow have already experienced a scarcity of good quality water, particularly the densely settled parts of the eastern seaboard, where rivers are expected to dilute and transport excessive loads of pollution from domestic and industrial sources. This has been supplemented by additional local pollution loads, such as acid water draining out of coal mining areas in Appalachia. The absurdity of this devastation of a reasonably abundant water supply is emphasised by the spontaneous combustion of the excessively polluted Cuyahoga River flowing through Cleveland, Ohio, in 1969 and by the severe restrictions on water use imposed in New York in the summer of 1965, while the Hudson discharged abundant but highly polluted water. In these heavily settled areas, water shortages could be corrected by adequate pollution control and by recycling water supplies without importing further water supplies.

The quantity of the supply is deficient in some parts of the country, notably the arid southwestern states. The United States Senate Select Committee on National Water Resources predicted that five of the nation's twenty-two water resource regions, the South Pacific, the Colorado River, the Great Basin, the Upper Rio Grande–Pecos River, and the Upper Missouri River, would all be using their complete supplies by 1980 if present growth trends continue.[2] An additional three, the Upper Arkansas Red River, the Western Great Lakes, and the Western Gulf, would be in the same situation by the year 2000. Discussion will focus on these areas of potential deficiency, all of which except the Western Great Lakes lie within the arid part of the country.

Water shortages have always been a barrier to human development in the southwestern states. J. C. Ives, in command of the first expedition to navigate the Colorado in 1858, damned the area as "altogether valueless" in an indictment resembling Palliser's view of the southern prairie provinces in Canada.[3] The development which has taken place was made possible by the creation of extensive water control and diversion measures. Both major river systems, the Colorado and the Rio Grande have been channeled, damned, stored, and diverted by elaborate engineering works, so that they are among the most extensively modified major rivers in the world. Among the southwestern states only California has a relatively abundant water supply, although this abundance is concentrated in the northern part of the state. In the south, around Los Angeles the available supply has been totally outstripped by explosive population growth, which has resulted in a rapid increase in water demands for municipal, industrial, recreational, and agricultural purposes, accentuated by a high per capita demand, as in many affluent societies. This per capita demand rose from 80 gallons in 1940 to over 160 gallons in 1960.[4] Satisfaction of this demand has required water importation from the Colorado and from the northern part of the state.

Despite their aridity other parts of the southwest have also begun to experience a rapid growth of population and associated water demands, such as Denver, Colorado, and the Phoenix-Tucson area of Arizona, which is one of the fastest growing urban areas in the United States. New Mexico has also experienced a rapid increase in population, especially in the basins of the San Juan River and the Rio Grande. However, in all the arid states the dominant consumptive use is still agricultural.

Water Demand for Irrigation

Most agriculture in the southwestern states depends on irrigation. Some 30 million acres are irrigated, the total annual water demand being about

110 million acre-feet, compared with a national total of 120 million acre-feet.[5] Most water is diverted for irrigation in unlined open ditches and canals, and waste by seepage and evaporation is immense; only a relatively small proportion of the water diverted reaches the fields. The loss is variable, depending on soil characteristics, weather conditions, and other local factors, all of which make estimation difficult. However, the annual loss for the whole nation has been estimated at 32 million acre-feet, or more than 25 percent of the water diverted.[6] Local losses are much higher, particularly in the southwest, where evaporation is rapid.

Much of the water which manages to survive the journey to the fields is wasted there because of inadequate knowledge of crop moisture requirements and poor water distribution systems. Considerable advances have been made by research on crop moisture requirements, but few farmers have an accurate idea of how these vary. Even if they did, few farms have an accurate means of measuring the amount of water supplied to the fields. The water supplied is unmetered on at least 75 percent of the irrigated farms of the United States.[7] The result is an erratic distribution of water that bears little relationship to crop needs and which is usually overabundant.

The combined wastage of diverted water in transport and by careless use is staggering. In Arizona it has been estimated that 10 to 50 percent of the water withdrawn is actually used for crops; in Utah, the home of modern irrigation in North America, the figure is just over 30 percent.[8] It appears that of the 120 million acre-feet withdrawn every year for irrigation in the United States, 58 percent is wasted. This situation is not satisfactory, especially considering that irrigation has been practised in the United States since at least 200 B.C., when the Hohokam Indians irrigated land in the Salt River plain of Arizona on the present location of Phoenix. The wastage is particularly significant because irrigation is by far the largest consumptive use of water in the United States.

Salinization

It is difficult to assess the future demands for irrigation water in the United States because the water is used to grow a wide range of crops, the market potential of which is limited more by political and economic factors than by physical ones. It is also clear that early estimates of the amount of potentially irrigable land were unduly optimistic. In most arid and simiarid lands salt deposits are found in the soil at some depth. This depth is variable, but in most arid parts of North America it is sufficiently great to allow plants to root without meeting toxic concentrations of salt. When excess irrigation water is applied to the soil it should percolate away through the soil and eventually make its way to drainage networks. Sometimes such percolation is prevented by impermeable subsurface soils or by a high water table. Then excess water is drawn back toward the surface by evaporation and capillary action, bringing with it soluble salts from the subsurface, which are redeposited in the root zone. Despite recent research in many countries there are still relatively few commercial crops that are not inhibited by such salinization, which occurs in almost all irrigated parts of the world and which has been blamed for the decay of several irrigation-based civilizations, such as that of Mesopotamia. In the United States salinization problems have already appeared in several irrigation districts, including the Imperial and Central valleys of California. It can be reversed only by leaching with abundant quantities of water over a lengthy period (about five years) after the provision of adequate subsurface drainage. The combined costs of subsurface drainage and irrigation may be sufficient to make farming uneconomical, particularly if measures to prevent soil erosion are also necessary. Salinization can occur in any soil of low permeability in an arid climate, and because many soils of arid lands are of low permeability, they are irrigable only with great expense, trouble, and risk of failure.

Future water requirements for irrigation

Because of limitations set by salinization, the irrigated acreage in the southwestern United States will probably not increase rapidly, at least until there is freer access to the agricultural produce markets of underdeveloped countries. An increase to a national total of nearly 56 million acres has been predicted for the year 2000.[9] The bulk of this increase would be in the east, where lower evapotranspiration rates permit greater efficiency of water use. However, an eventual increase of 70 percent in the irrigated acreage in California has been predicted.[10] The eventual national water requirement for irrigation has been estimated at 138 million acre-feet, or an approximate increase of 20 million acre-feet over present withdrawals.[11] This increase in demand is based on the available water supply rather than on physical limitation. It could be satisfied easily by increasing the efficiency of irrigation water transport, thereby eliminating the need for increased withdrawals from rivers or the construction of elaborate, expensive, and potentially damaging engineering works.

Increasing efficiency of water use

The immense wastage of water in irrigation agriculture has become the focus of much research. In particular, attempts have been made to reduce seepage through the beds of canals by installing impermeable linings. Chemical sealants have been tested in the Eden Reclamation Project in Wyoming, where a petroleum-based emulsion was found to reduce seepage loss by about 65 percent.[12] Another possibility is thin plastic sheeting, but this is rather vulnerable and tends to need frequent replacement. Concrete is a satisfactory lining, although its expense prevents large-scale use. In general seepage is a problem of economics rather than technology.

At least as important are attempts to reduce evaporation from canal and lake surfaces, most of which have involved films of hexadecanol one molecule in thickness spread over the entire surface. (Hexadecanol is a nontoxic chemical used extensively in the cosmetics industry.) Laboratory tests by the United States Bureau of Reclamation have produced evaporation reductions of up to 75 percent, although only 10 to 22 percent reduction has been attained in lake tests. The chief obstacle is the disruption of the monomolecular film by wind,[13] and difficulty has also been experienced with the application of the film over extensive water surfaces. Monomolecular films also interfere with reoxygenation and could therefore affect flora and fauna in reservoirs and canals. Despite difficulties, economical methods of reducing both seepage and evaporation losses can be expected soon.

General Water Demand in Deficit Areas

The only water resource area in early danger of water shortage apart from the southwestern states is the Western Great Lakes region, which includes some large cities, such as Chicago, Milwaukee, and Detroit, and a number of industries that have very high water requirements. With the neighbouring Eastern Great Lakes area, it shares the water supplies and problems of the Great Lakes with the area of highest population concentration in Canada. Most settlements around the Great Lakes use them as a depository for sewage and industrial wastes, which has resulted in high pollution levels, that have restricted the use of lake water, particularly in Lake Erie. Pollution levels have increased following population and industrial growth, and between 1952 and 1965 additional difficulties were created by a marked fall in water levels. Recent rises in water levels have removed this difficulty, however, and the chief problem now is pollution. This could be temporarily abated by additional water supplies diverted from Canada, although a very large diversion would be required to produce appreciable improvement. If pollution control is a major objective, it would be better achieved by adequate control over the effluents entering the lakes. Water diversions could be beneficial if water levels again drop severely, but long-term research on the frequency and duration of such declines is necessary before diversion for this purpose is seriously considered. Flooding of lakeshore settlements, as in 1952, might be more damaging in the long run than low water levels.

Local water shortages have appeared in several parts of the eastern United States, but these have been the result of mismanagement of water resources rather than of an overall supply shortage. Perhaps the most flagrant example of mismanagement of water resources has occurred in southern Florida, where extensive drainage for housing development and a jet airport, together with excavation for a ship canal across the peninsula, have seriously endangered Everglades National Park. The airport development was stopped in 1970 by the activities of conservation groups, and President Nixon stopped the ship canal early in 1971, but the future of the Everglades is still in jeopardy because of the water demands of urban development along the Florida coast.

Water demand in the southwestern states

Water supply for irrigation is the dominant demand throughout the southwest and will likely remain so. In California, agriculture demands about 30 million acre-feet per year, or 90 percent of the total state demand. This share is expected to drop to 80 percent of the "ultimate" state requirement. (The "ultimate" demand is a hypothetical level at which it is believed stabilisation will take place.) The "ultimate" urban, suburban, and industrial demand is predicted at only 16 percent of the total demand, or 8 million acre-feet per year.[14]

In Arizona also agriculture is responsible for most of the total annual demand of 6.6 million acre-feet. To cater to this demand Arizona is already mining groundwater reserves at a rate which exceeds the recharge rate by approximately 2.25 acre-feet per year. New Mexico and Texas also mine groundwater extensively. New Mexico supplies approximately half of its annual 2.9 million acre-foot demand from groundwater reserves. Groundwater reserves believed to have originally totaled over 200 million acre-feet exist in the High Plains area of Texas, although withdrawals have now made serious inroads on this supply.

California is the only high-demand state that has abundant surface water supplies, although these are estimated to vary between 18 and 135 million acre-feet per year.[15] Unfortunately 70 percent of this supply is concentrated in the northern half of the state, whereas 70 percent of the demand is in the south. The metropolitan area of Los Angeles and its satellites, which is the focus of the most rapid population growth in the United States, generates most of this demand. Its growth has helped to produce in California a water demand that dwarfs that of any other water-deficient state. The supply problems of the Los Angeles area predate the present popularity of the state by many years, however; Los Angeles was forced to supplement the local supply by water imports as early as 1913. In that year the 233-mile Owens River Aqueduct was completed at a cost of nearly $25 million, to tap the water supply of the High Sierra. This encouraged such rapid population growth that within ten years new sources of water had to be sought. The supply was supplemented in 1940 by the extension of the Owens River Aqueduct 105 miles further north to Mono Lake, at a cost of nearly $23 million and in 1941 by the $220 million Colorado River Aqueduct, by which water was diverted 240 miles over the mountains from Parker Dam on the Colorado River. This aqueduct currently carries 1.2 million acre-feet of water per year to the Los Angeles area, of which almost 25 percent is used to recharge depleted groundwater reservoirs.

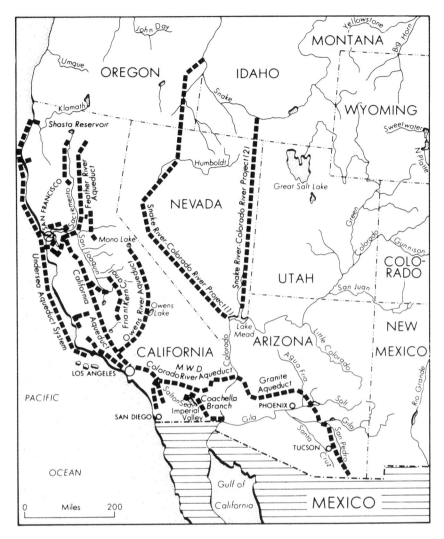

Figure 8.1. Major existing and proposed water management projects in the southwestern United States.

The additional supplies from the Sierra and from the Colorado were sufficient to support an explosive population growth triggered by the expansion of southern California aircraft plants and shipyards during the Second World War. They were sufficient until the late 1960s, when the expanding demand made it necessary to "twin" the Owens River Aqueduct. Even this addition has barely kept pace with the demand, and new sources of supply must be found if the population growth in southern California continues.

Even if the population growth does not continue, alternate sources of supply will be necessary in the near future. California at present withdraws a total of 5.2 million acre-feet per year from the Colorado. As a result of the Supreme Court decision of 1963, however, the Californian rights to water from the Colorado will be reduced to 4.4 million acre-feet; 2.8 million will go to Arizona, 0.3 million will go to Nevada, and 1.5 million will be transmitted by agreement to Mexico.[16] The normal flow of the Colorado is about 10 million acre-feet per year, of which almost 10 percent is lost by evaporation from reservoirs and from the river. This means that even in a year of normal flow, the complete discharge of the river would be necessary to fulfill the agreed allocation. At present Arizona does not withdraw its complete allocation, but it will do so when the Central Arizona Diversion Project is complete, forcing California to find the 0.8 million acre-foot difference between its present use and its allocation from other sources.

Potential sources of water supply for southern California

Water diversion and transfer within California. By the late 1950s it was obvious that planning on a greatly enlarged scale was necessary if the growth in the water demand of southern California was to be met with anything but stopgap measures. The immediate result was approval for a major extension of the Central Valley project in 1960. The original project, completed between 1935 and 1960, diverted part of the flow of the Sacramento to the southern part of the valley for irrigation and helped to fill the power and municipal water supply requirements of the area around San Francisco Bay. The extension, the California State Water Plan, will eventually transfer 4.23 million acre-feet annually from the northern part of the state to the southern San Joaquin Valley and southern California. The cost was originally estimated at $1.9 billion, but it will probably eventually cost at least $2.9 billion and possibly over $4 billion. Some parts of the original plan will probably never be completed because of potential environmental and economic damage. One worry is that the reduced flow of the Sacramento River will no longer be sufficient to keep the salt water of San Francisco Bay out of the Sacramento–San Joaquin delta and that agriculture will therefore suffer.

Water sources outside California. In addition to the major transfer schemes developed within California, a number of plans have been suggested for obtaining additional water supplies from outside the state. These include the Pacific Southwest Water Plan, which combines the State Water Plan and the Central Arizona Diversion Project into a major project involving the construction of dams in the Grand Canyon. This has been successfully stopped, at least for the time being, by the action of conservation groups led by the Sierra Club. The Snake River–Colorado River Water Project, involving supplementation of the Colorado by diversions from the Snake and Columbia rivers across Utah to Lake Mead, has been strongly opposed by the states of Washington, Idaho, and Oregon. These projects make provision only for the diversion of American water, at least in the initial stages; several plans that suggest major diversions of Canadian water to supplement the flow of the Colorado are discussed in more detail in a later chapter. One further plan which has been proposed is the Undersea Aqueduct System for the transfer of water from the Klamath and Eel rivers of northwestern California to the Los Angeles area. Provision is made for extension to Oregon and Washington, and presumably the aqueduct could also be extended to Canada or to Alaska. This plan is only a suggestion, but it is reasonable to question such an idea in a region known to be subject to frequent, severe earthquakes. The potential for earthquake damage to any water management network in southern California concerns state water management authorities. Such damage could seriously disrupt the water supply and endanger human life. The potential hazard was indicated by the crack which developed in the Van Norman Dam in the San Fernando Valley after the February 1971 earthquake; which necessitated a temporary evacuation of parts of the valley.

Alternative Means of Water Supply Supplementation

Cloud seeding

In addition to the variety of orthodox or unorthodox plans which have been presented for the diversion of surface water, additional supplies could be produced by weather modification. Cloud seeding to produce rainfall has been under study in several countries since the Second World War. Many clouds do not produce rain because of the absence of nuclei which would allow the combination of small droplets into drops large enough to reach the earth, as precipitation. Artificial nuclei can be introduced, or "seeded," into the cloud in the form of dry ice or silver iodide crystals. Most tests have involved seeding from aircraft, but this would be too expensive for large-scale operation. Cloud seeding on a commercial scale is feasible only where ascending air currents can carry crystals upward, usually on the windward side of major mountain chains. Local increases of precipitation have been effected; in northern Peru increases of 10 to 15 percent have assisted local irrigation.[19] Russian meteorologists have also claimed increases of 10 to 15 percent,[20] and more than three years of seeding winter cumuli clouds in Israel increased precipitation locally by 15 to 18 percent.[21] In Arizona, on the other hand, seven consecutive summers of seeding produced no increase.[22] Even if cloud seeding is successful, one problem is that the windward slopes of major mountain chains are not normally areas of severe water deficiency, and it would therefore be necessary to transport the water to deficient areas. In view of these problems it seems unlikely that cloud seeding will provide a realistic supplementary water supply for at least several decades, particularly because complex legal problems might be involved.

Desalination

A more realistic source for additional water supplies is desalinized sea water. Significant progress has been made in desalination processes during the last twenty years, resulting in a steady decrease in the cost of water produced. Several satisfactory processes exist for large-scale desalination, including thermal distillation, electrodialysis, and freeze separation, but none is yet capable of producing water at a price comparable to that of available water supplies.[23] Locally desalination plants can produce water competitively, as at Coalinga, in southern California, although the cost is almost $500 per acre-foot. The most hopeful possibility seems to be a reduction in the costs of thermal distillation by reducing fuel costs, particularly by using nuclear power. At the moment no desalination plants produce water at less than $230 per acre-foot. A nuclear-powered installation to be built for the Los Angeles Metropolitan Water District by the Bechtel Corporation looked promising, but it was shelved when estimated costs rose to $170 per acre-foot. There is no doubt that the costs of desalination will drop in the future, providing an economical alternative supply at the point of production. Whether the water thus produced will ever be cheap enough to permit transfer for agricultural purposes is doubtful.[24] Certainly the inland arid states cannot hope to benefit greatly, for the cost of transferring water from coastal production plants to interior regions such as central Arizona could be three to four times the cost of production, which would exceed the tolerable price for agriculture.

The Cost of Water Supplies

It is clear that a demand for more water exists in the southwestern United States. It is a demand rather than a need in the strict physical sense. This distinction is significant, because a need must be supplied regardless of cost, whereas satisfaction of a demand is optional. If the cost of supplying water for some of the more exotic demands rises too high, these demands will evaporate.

Many factors are involved in attempting to determine when a water price is too high for any purpose. In agriculture there is a fairly direct relationship between the market value of produce and the price which can be paid for water. This value will be extremely variable, even when produce is the same, depending on the location relative to population centres and on government policies. In the Rio Grande basin in New Mexico, the following tolerable prices for water have been suggested:[25]

Agriculture: $44–51 per acre-foot
Recreation: $212–307 per acre-foot
Industry: $3040–per acre-foot

These values are doubtless higher than general prices because of the deficient supply in New Mexico. Only a few industries could pay the price suggested, and industries with a very high water requirements, such as steel, could not survive economically in such an area. In California water prices have been quoted from a few dollars to over $100 per acre-foot for some municipal purposes. More generally applicable water values (per acre-foot) have been suggested by Ripley:[26]

On submarines:	$2,000	Chicago and New	
Kuwait:	$1,000	York:	$70
Coalinga:	$ 470	Metropolitan	
Canadian dry		Toronto:	$55
prairie town:	$ 250	California citrus	
Large-scale de-		crops:	$50
salination:	$ 163	Vancouver:	$35

A national average cost of water in the United States of $10 to $20 per acre-foot has also been suggested by Ripley.

The wide range of values and the general inadequacy of study on the subject make it difficult to state a definite tolerable cost for any place, but we can indicate some general principles. In water-deficient areas where potential alternative uses are in free competition, the use which can tolerate the highest price for water will capture the major part of the supply. This means that in virtually all regions where water is short, domestic and industrial use will tend to grow at the expense of agricultural use. This tendency is indicated both by the predicted future patterns of water use in Arizona and by the suggestion that up to 1 million acre-feet per year could be diverted from the desert agricultural region of the Imperial Valley to meet the demand of the Los Angeles Metropolitan Water District. If free competition between uses continued to its ultimate conclusion, it would lead to the elimination of agriculture from areas in which the existence of towns is not directly dependent on it. There are good reasons why this should not be allowed to happen, but the alternative is either subsidy of water supply for agriculture or government control of the expansion of other uses.

Competition between alternative water uses in the southwestern states has not yet grown to the point where the existence of agriculture is threatened, but the developing water shortage will be felt primarily by agriculture. Urban uses compete favourably with agriculture for local water supplies, so when the supply is deficient additional water supplies will be sought primarily for irrigation agriculture, although the real cause of the demand may be municipal expansion. This situation must be recognised in connection with the potential cost of water from new sources. If the supplementary water supply were to be used for municipal purposes it could probably remain competitive even with costs above $100 per acre-foot. As it will be used for irrigation, the maximum tolerable cost would probably be $50 to $60 per acre-foot for truck cropping and citrus and much less for other forms of agriculture. Higher costs could be tolerated only if irrigation agriculture were subsidised, as in the Salt River Project in Arizona. This should be considered in assessing the potential market for water transferred from Canada.

Very few proposed plans for the transfer of water from Canada to the southwestern states include an estimate of the eventual cost of the water. Costs ranging from $35 to $75 per acre-foot at delivery have been estimated for what is probably the cheapest plan, but they are not attached to precise delivery points. Water transferred by the California State Water Plan will cost at least $65.20 per acre-foot, and the tentative original estimate for water from the Snake-Colorado Project was $31.80 per acre-foot. If these estimates are accurate, those for water transferred from Canada are too low, perhaps by as much as $100 per acre-foot. (Details of transfer estimates are examined in the following chapter.) If the eventual delivery cost of Canadian water is going to be $100 to $150 per acre-foot, it is difficult to foresee any significant market. Obviously this subject should be studied much more carefully and extensively before consideration is given to proposals for water transfer.

Government Policy and Growth in Water Demand

Various water transfer plans and other sources of supply have been considered, but one alternative has been consistently ignored by the government authorities concerned. It has already been pointed out that there is no overall shortage of water in the United States, but merely a shortage in some areas of rapid population growth. No government appears to have considered that it might be more logical, cheaper, and ultimately more beneficial to encourage population growth in areas of abundant rather than deficient water. A growing body of opinion in the United States, as in other countries, holds that unrestricted population growth in any area is an extremely ill-advised policy. The disadvantages of unrestricted growth are obvious in southern California, where the population has increased tenfold in forty years. The most notorious problem is smog, which is produced by the interaction of car exhaust fumes and sunlight accentuated by temperature inversions and which is already a threat to public health in the Los Angeles area, and which has even damaged ponderosa pines in the foothills of the Sierra Nevada. Increasing population has also caused heavy pressure on recreational and national park areas, traffic congestion, and expansion of settlement into areas subject to dangerous chapparal fires or frequent flooding. Not so widely recognised is the destruction of agricultural land in California by spreading urbanisation. It is estimated that 375 acres of prime agricultural land are removed from agriculture each day, or 140,000 acres per year. Of the 16 million acres of land in California suitable for agriculture, only about 6 million acres are of prime quality. If the current rate of urban expansion continues, the lack of suitable land will diminish the agricultural demand for irrigation water.

In view of the problems associated with intense concentration of population growth, it seems probable that an attempt will eventually be made to locate industry, and therefore the major part of population growth, elsewhere. The current unemployment associated with the recession in the aircraft industry may hasten such an attempt in southern California. One instrument a government could use to encourage industrial relocation in California is the availability and cost of water supplies. It is neither likely nor desirable that Canadian attitudes to water export would influence industrial location policy in California or elsewhere in the United States, but it is likely that U. S. industrial location policy will determine the demand for or the feasibility of Canadian water export. It is therefore important that future trends in water use in the United States be carefully assessed, not for the next thirty years but for at least the next couple of centuries, if Canadian people are to avoid being burdened with a costly and destructive white elephant.

References

1. United States Water Resource Council, *The Nation's Water Resources*, Water Resources Council, Washington, D. C., 1968.

2. F. E. Moss, *The Water Crisis* (New York: F. A. Praeger, 1967).

3. W. H. Goetzmann, *Army Exploration in the American West, 1803–1863* (New Haven: Yale University Press, 1959).

4. F. B. Blanchard, "The Competition for Water Quantity: Domestic and Municipal Use," in *Water Policy Conference, Report No. 3,* edited by R. M. Hagan and V. Lawton, pp. 98–105 (Davis: University of California Water Resources Center, University of California, 1961).

5. Select Committee on National Water Resources, Report No. 29, to the 87th Congress, 1st Session, Washington, D. C., 1959.

6. K. A. Mackickan, "Estimated Use of Water in the United States," *United States Geological Survey Circular,* No. 398, 1960.

7. H. B. Hawkes, "Irrigation in the United States," in *Conservation of Natural Resources,* edited by Guy Harold-Smith, pp. 103–132 (New York: John Wiley & Sons, Inc., 1965).

8. H. B. Hawkes, *op. cit.*

9. Select Committee on National Water Resources, *op. cit.*

10. M. Fireman, "The Competition for Water Quality: agriculture," in *Water Policy Conference Report No. 3,* edited by R. M. Hagan and V. Lawton, pp. 49–56 (Davis: University of California Water Resources Center, University of California, 1961).

11. Select Committee on National Water Resources, 1959, *op. cit.*

12. W. H. Price, "Engineering Research in the Development of Water Resources," in *Land and Water, Planning for Economic Growth, Western Resources Conference,* edited by H. L. Amoss and R. K. McNickle, pp. 137–145 (Boulder: University of Colorado Press, 1961).

13. International Commission on Irrigation and Drainage, *World-wide Survey of Experiments on the Prevention of Evaporation Losses from Reservoirs,* New Delhi, 1967.

14. J. Humlum, *Water Development and Water Planning in the Southwestern United States,* (Kulturgeografisk Institut, Aarhus Universitet, Denmark, 1969).

15. G. M. Reith, "The State Water Project: Problems and Prospects," in *Opening Session Papers,* The Association of American Geographers, 66th Annual Meeting, San Francisco, 1970, pp. 41–81.

16. J. Humlum, *op. cit.*

17. G. M. Reith, *op. cit.*

18. L. B. McCammon and F. C. Lee, "Undersea Aqueduct System," *Journal of the American Water Works Association* 58 (1965): 885.

19. W. E. Howell, "Twelve Years of Cloud Seeding in the Andes of Northern Peru," *Journal of Applied Meteorology* 4 (1965): 693–700.

20. L. J. Battan, "A survey of Recent Cloud Physics Research in the Soviet Union," *American Meteorological Society Bulletin* 44 (1963): 755–771.

21. J. Gabriel, "The Israeli artificial rainfall stimulation experiment." An interim statistical evaluation of results, Hebrew University, Depart. of Statistics, Jerusalem, Israel, 23 pp., 1965.

22. L. J. Battan, "Silver Iodide Seeding and Rainfall from Convective Clouds," *Journal of Applied Meteorology* 5 (1966): 669–683.

23. R. Eliassen, "Saline Water Conversion, A Report of Committee 3210 P," *Journal of the American Water Works Association* 58 1966.

24. M. Clawson, H. H. Landsberg and L. T. Alexander, "Desalted seawater for agriculture: Is It Economic?" *Science* 164 (1969): 1141–1148.

25. N. Wollman, *The Value of Water in Alternate Uses* (Albuquerque: The University of New Mexico Press, 1960).

26. J. G. Ripley, "The Columbia River Scandal," *Engineering and Contract Record* April 49 (1964), April.

Chapter 9

Proposals for Water Export from Canada

Many people do not realise that water is already being exported from Canada to the United States, albeit in small quantities. One example is the sale of water by Coutts, Alberta, to Sweetgrass, Montana. Another is the permitted withdrawal by Chicago of up to 3,200 cubic feet per second from Lake Michigan to transport partially treated wastes via the Illinois River to the Mississippi.[1] Water withdrawn from the Great Lakes system is replaced in part by water diverted southward from the Ogoki and Longlac tributaries of the Albany River, Ontario, into Lake Superior. The purpose of these diversions was not water export but power generation by Ontario Hydro, but the result is a form of water export. The amounts diverted from Canada to the United States are trivial, but the principle of water export has been accepted. The question is therefore not whether water export should take place but whether it should be increased and, if so, from what sources and how soon. Unless a significant American demand develops, no large scale export will take place, regardless of Canadian views. This demand depends ultimately on the price of water. It is necessary to emphasise this point, for some emotional writing has created the impression that Americans are waiting to snatch our water as soon as our backs are turned. This is not the case. The review of the United States water supply situation indicates that the market for Canadian water may well be a reluctant one which could be established only by hard selling, and many of the proposals for water export are of Canadian, not American, origin.

The feasibility of water export depends on the price at which it could be delivered, which in turn depends on the transfer plan. Some of the plans proposed probably could never be economically feasible, but they are examined because their acceptance or rejection should be based on principle as well as on economic expedience. Many proposals involving widely differing costs and benefits have been made. This should be realised, for water export has been widely identified with grandiose plans to divert vast amounts of water from northern Canada, with far-reaching environmental effects. Such plans exist, but they are not the only, or even the most important, plans.

The North American Water and Power Alliance

The NAWAPA plan, proposed by the Ralph M. Parsons Company of Los Angeles in 1964[2] and subsequently slightly modified, has generated more controversy than any other water export proposal. It has been variously described as a "monstrous concept—a diabolical thesis"[3] and as "forward looking and challenging";[4] one of the plan's vociferous proponents, Senator

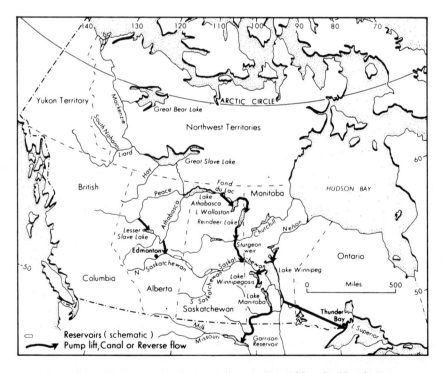

Figure 9.1. Water management projects proposed by the North American Water and Power Alliance. (Source: Committee on Public Works, United States Senate, 1966.)

Frank Moss of Utah, talks of its "grandeur and potential."[5] The core of the proposal is a diversion of "unused" water from rivers in Alaska, the Yukon Territory, and British Columbia southward through Canada to serve the water needs of arid and semiarid parts of Canada, the southwestern United States, and northern Mexico. What makes the project unique is not the basic concept but the scale of the proposed diversions and their potential effect on the Canadian environment.

The plan involves damming the Tanana, Susitna, and Copper rivers in Alaska and their diversion via reservoirs and tunnels into a joint reservoir formed with the dammed headwaters of the Yukon River. Water would be fed southward from the reservoir and pump-lifted to an altitude of 2,400 feet just south of Atlin, British Columbia, to join the waters of the Dease and Liard in a series of large reservoirs. From these, water would be pump-lifted into a series of reservoirs connecting with the existing Lake Williston, dammed by the Bennett Dam. The dam would have to be raised, but the headwaters of the Peace River would be added to the system. Water would be pump-lifted 670 feet out of Lake Williston into the Rocky Mountain Trench, a lengthy north-south valley which separates the Rocky Mountains from the Purcell, Selkirk, and other ranges in British Columbia.

Several major rivers issue from the Rocky Mountain Trench; the most important are the Fraser, the Thompson, the Columbia, and the Kootenay. Their headwaters would be dammed to create a reservoir 500 miles in length and between 5 and 15 miles in width, with a storage capacity of 74 million acre-feet. This immense reservoir would feed into Flathead Lake in Montana, from which water would be pump-lifted another 2,360 feet via six pumping stations to join another reservoir in the Sawtooth Mountains of central Idaho. Water would then travel to the Great Basin Waterway, via a 50-mile length of 80-foot diameter pipe, and then would cross the Snake River basin and northwest Utah, to culminate in a large reservoir in northeastern Nevada. South of the Nevada reservoir one branch would lead water to southern California and Mexico, with diversions to the Colorado, and another would cross Arizona to New Mexico and the valleys of the Rio Grande and the Pecos River.

Transfer of water southward along the western side of the continent is the dominant feature of the plan, but several other developments were also proposed. The Alberta-Great Lakes Waterway was proposed as a 30-foot draught unlined ship canal about 730 feet wide at the base, to extend from Peace River via Lesser Slave Lake and Edmonton to Moose Jaw, Saskatchewan. This would involve modification of the Peace, Smoky, Athabasca, and North Saskatchewan rivers. From Moose Jaw, one branch would follow the Qu'Appelle River into Manitoba, linking Lake Winnipeg into the system and eventually issuing into Lake Superior at Nipigon Bay. A southern waterway, the Dakota Canal, would leave Moose Jaw and cross the Dakotas to Minneapolis, diverting the headwaters of the Souris on the way. Its scope would be more modest—a mere barge canal of 12-foot draught.

The James Bay Seaway would also be built, linking Hudson Bay to Georgian Bay on Lake Huron, traversing a 900-foot watershed. A branch would serve the iron mines of Schefferville, in the Labrador-Ungava peninsula. Later modifications also provide for linkage to the New York Barge Canal and provision of water to the Hudson Valley and the New York megalopolis.

The Parsons Company has listed an extensive range of benefits to be derived from the NAWAPA plan, many of which are illusory and some of which are imaginary. The main benefit is the provision of water for irrigation and municipal purposes in Canada, the United States, and Mexico. Estimates of the actual amount to be made available vary, but it is suggested that Canada would receive 22 million acre-feet per year, the United States 78 million acre-feet, and Mexico 20 million acre-feet.[6] The total distribution of 120 million acre-feet per year could be expanded to 250 million acre-feet per year by additions to the basic plan. This would provide for an increase in irrigation agriculture of 10 million acres in Canada, 41 million acres in the United States, and 8 million acres in Mexico. The realism of a proposal to increase irrigation agriculture in Canada by 10 million acres is very doubtful. The Parsons proposal suggests that the NAWAPA plan would provide a water supply adequate for North American needs until the year 2050. What would happen after that year is not specified.

Power generation would be an important asset of the plan, although most of the power generated in Canada would be used to pump water southward. In total, some 30 million kilowatt hours (kwh) would be generated for sale in Canada, and a further 30 million kwh would be purchased by the system for pumping. Thirty-eight million kwh would be available for sale in the United States, and 2 million kwh in Mexico. The proposal suggests that Canada would receive up to $2 billion per year from the sale of power and the collection of shipping tolls.

Shipping tolls are probably the most illusory of the plan's benefits. Some shipping traffic could be generated on the Dakota Canal, although the existence of a substantial demand for freight flow between Moose Jaw and Minneapolis is not yet apparent. On the Canadian prairies cheap, efficient bulk transport is certainly scarce, and grain movement, particularly to Vancouver, has been impeded by inadequate rail service. It is doubtful, however, that freight movement would be helped by an expensive ship canal, which would inevitably charge high tolls and which could be frozen for half the year.[7] It is impossible to predict the patterns of freight flow thirty years in advance; there might be no demand by the time the canal was completed. Many countries have ship and barge canals which outlived their usefulness, sometimes before they were completed. One example is the Ludwig Canal, built in a grandiose plan to generate trade flow along a navigable waterway from the mouth of the Rhine to the mouth of the Danube. The mere existence of a ship canal is no guarantee that anyone will want to send ships along it. The experience of the St. Lawrence

Seaway indicates the ease with which potential traffic generation can be over-estimated. What has been said about the prairie ship canal applies even more emphatically to the James Bay and Schefferville canals, where uncertain freight flow, high tolls, and a long frozen period would almost certainly preclude significant shipping traffic.

A further benefit to be provided by the plan is the supply of 48 million acre-feet of water per year to stabilise water levels in the Great Lakes and to increase power generation on the Niagara River and the St. Lawrence. This benefit was suggested at a period when the water levels in the Great Lakes were falling rapidly and is less significant now that levels have reverted to their former position.

In addition to the $2 billion per year to be derived from power sales and shipping tolls, the planners forecast a yield of $2 to $3 billion per year in Canada and $3 to $4 billion in the United States during the construction period. Totaled over the projected twenty-year construction period, this could amount to $140 billion, somewhat above the suggested project cost of $80 to $100 billion.

The suggested distribution of the $80 to $100 billion estimated costs of the NAWAPA project is $16.6 billion for land acquisition, $8.9 billion for engineering, $64.5 billion for construction, and $10 billion for contingencies. The engineering and construction costs have been quite carefully examined and may be reasonably predictable, though probably underestimated by at least 100 percent, as with the California State Water Plan. The apparently arbitrary allocation of $16.6 billion to land acquisition and relocation is more difficult to assess and appears ridiculously low.

An American writer has said that "there will be minor problems associated with the displacement of some 60,000 people, largely in Canada."[8] This is surely the most nonsensical statement that has appeared on the subject. The NAWAPA plan would involve the flooding of Whitehorse, Prince George, Golden and a number of smaller communities. Financial costs of land acquisition and settlement relocation are unpredictable in detail, but they would probably be higher than the $16.6 billion suggested, particularly as the plan would involve relocation of both the Yellowhead and Trans-Canada Highways and both trans-Canadian rail systems. The social costs are to some extent predictable because they have already been encountered among Indian families displaced from Finlay Forks by the filling of Lake Williston. People displaced by misguided water development so far are few in number and lacking in political force, but it would be a rash politician who would willingly create a population of 60,000 discontented squatters in western Canada. The "minor problems" could assume a social significance of major proportions.

Apart from settlements that would be inundated and routes relocated, the NAWAPA project would involve flooding considerable agricultural land in British Columbia, acreage made significant by the scarcity of land suitable for agriculture. Arable land in the province has been estimated at less than 4 percent, much of which is in the major river valleys such as those of the Fraser and Kootenay. Substantial portions of both these valleys would be flooded.

By no means all the valleys which would be flooded are of high agricultural potential, but most are still important as winter range areas for wildlife. They are also of high recreational potential and include some of the most beautiful parts of the Western Cordillera. Part of the potential has already been developed, particularly in the Kootenay area of British Columbia. It would be possible to determine the financial costs involved in the loss of existing recreational installations, but no one has developed a method whereby the loss of the magnificent land which stimulated the recreational activity can be accurately assessed. The loss to the Canadian people may be immeasurable, and it is hard to see how it could be realistically balanced by the nebulous benefits which might accrue from the NAWAPA project. This may be damned as an emotional assessment, and it is; the appeal of magnificent scenery is emotional, not financial.

It has been claimed that flooding the Rocky Mountain Trench would create a lake with great recreational potential to balance or outweigh the amenity loss. The validity of this claim is indicated by Lake Williston, which was also touted as a potential recreation facility. There recreation has been rendered impossible, or at least extremely hazardous, by landslipping and erosion along the shore and by floating driftwood, a problem that could have been largely eliminated by logging the area before flooding. No estimates for the cost of logging the Rocky Mountain Trench before flooding have been included in the Parsons proposal, and the experience of the Big Horn reservoir in Alberta shows that they would not be covered by the sale of the timber extracted.

Landslipping and shore erosion are normal in a newly created reservoir, but in Lake Williston they are sufficiently severe to endanger boats. A reservoir in the Rocky Mountain Trench could generate landslides of major proportions. The Western Cordillera already suffer from considerable instability, as shown by the Hope Slide in British Columbia, the Frank Slide in Alberta, and numerous smaller slides. The potential danger, not only to boaters but also to dam installations, was demonstrated by the Vaiont Dam disaster in the Italian Alps in 1963, where a major landslip produced a wave which overtopped the dam and drowned 3,500 people in the Piave Valley.[9] The dam survived, but the reservoir was unusable because of accumulated debris. There is also a possibility of deep-seated seismic effects produced by the immense weight of water, as experienced in connection with the Kariba Dam on the Zambezi in Africa.[10] In northern areas the creation of reservoirs of unfrozen water over permafrost could also result in subsidence, landsliding, and thermal erosion.[11]

A problem that could be catastrophic for recreation on the reservoir is the occurrence of sudden severe storms. The size of waves is partially governed by the length of the water body over which wind blows. This length, or *fetch*, in the Rocky Mountain Trench would be 500 miles, orientated more or less parallel to the direction of the strongest winds, which would be funneled between high mountains in a steep-sided valley. The waves could subject dam installations and recreational facilities to serious damage and could promote extensive bank erosion, which would be accentuated by fluctuations in the reservoir water level.

The NAWAPA plan is based on the concept of "unused" water in the major rivers involved although most are not "unused," even in a traditional definition of the term. The Fraser and the Columbia, for example, are both heavily used. Damming and diversion of headwaters, particularly during the reservoir filling stage, would result in unusually low flows which would have serious ecological repercussions (because these are common to all forms of diversion they are discussed collectively in the next chapter). The effects of low flows in the Fraser and the Columbia would also be felt by urban areas. Vancouver would be affected by low flows on the Fraser, which is important for shipping and for the dilution and transport of municipal waste, while low flows on the Columbia could disrupt power supplies in the northwestern United States.

Space does not permit the discussion of all aspects of the NAWAPA plan or all its potential repercussions. Some possible effects are discussed with those of other plans in the next chapter; others were thoroughly examined in a series of reviews in the Bulletin of Atomic Scientists in 1967. In such a far-reaching plan the potential problems inevitably cover a wide spectrum of disciplines and include such questions as the economic feasibility,[12] the degree to which Canadian sovereignty would have to be vested in a supranational authority,[13] the possible climatic effects,[14] and the engineering problems that would be faced.[15] Among the latter would be construction of the 1,700-foot-high Chitina dam on the Copper River, Alaska, which would be 710 feet higher than the highest existing dam, the Nourek Dam in the Soviet Union. There is little doubt that 1,700-foot dams can be built eventually, but a 70 percent increase is a big rise in magnitude for one step. The engineering profession is a bit wary of such rapid progress, particularly since the Fréjus Dam disaster in France in 1959. Another problem for the Chitina dam and the 880-foot Watana dam on the Sisitna River is their proximity to the active earthquake zone of southern Alaska. Movement along the southward extension of the same feature was responsible for the destruction of the Baldwin dam in California.

The basic problem with the NAWAPA plan is that too many unknowns are involved. There is not doubt that the costs, both financial and social, would be immense, although perhaps incalculable in detail. Even neglecting the cost of necessary research and using the very limited data available, there is no possibility that a demand would exist for water at the price that would be involved. Becuase of this, few water resource workers believe in the feasibility of the plan, although it is still being promoted in some quarters. Senator Moss apparently feels that a large portion of the Canadian population are in favour of the proposal, although he provides no evidence to support this belief.[15] If he is correct, the majority of the Canadian population have been seriously misled, for the plan is manifestly absurd and destructive. It should not be ignored but actively opposed for precisely these reasons, rather than on the question of Canadian national ownership of water supplies. Opposition to the NAWAPA plan should not lead automatically to the rejection of more realistic and less damaging proposals for water export.

The Kuiper Diversion Scheme

Some of the most detailed, extensive studies of water transfer and export have been made by E. Kuiper, of the University of Manitoba, resulting in the production of a transfer proposal in 1966.[16] This plan perpetuates the myth of "unused" water flowing into the Arctic Ocean, but it is based on careful examination of the flow characteristics of four major rivers—the Nelson, the Churchill, the Mackenzie, and the Yukon. From this study Kuiper concludes that some 230 million acre-feet per year would be available for diversion in the northwestern part of Canada. The proposal consists of several stages, the first involving only water transfer within Canada. A storage dam on the Peace River would impound water, which would be pump-lifted to the Athabasca River via Lesser Slave Lake. Further pump-lifting from the Athabasca River would bring water into the Saskatchewan system, where it would be joined by water diverted and pumped from the Churchill River via the Sturgeon Weir River. A series of steplike reservoirs is proposed for the Saskatchewan system between Lake Winnipeg, Diefenbaker Lake, and Edmonton, from which water could be pumped to any site in the prairie provinces by a network of pumping stations, pipelines, and open canals. In total about 80 million acre-feet could be made available at an estimated cost of $1 billion per year; the estimated delivery cost for water would be $10 per acre-foot.

The water export section of Kuiper's proposal would involve sequential development of diversions from Lake Winnipeg up to Lake Athabasca. The first export stage would require the pumping of water from Lake Winnipeg via Cedar Lake and Lake Winnipegosis to Lake Manitoba, then up the Assiniboine River and the Souris River to reach the Great Plains area, at an estimated cost of $20 per acre-foot. In the second stage water from the Winnipeg River, Rainy River, and Lake Winnipeg would be pumped over the height of land near Port Arthur to Lake Superior, to be used there for lake level stabilisation or for diversion via Chicago and the Des Plaines River to the Mississippi. The estimated cost for delivery of water to Lake Superior would be $5 per acre-foot.

In the third stage water would be moved from Lake Winnipeg to the Souris River, as in the first stage. From Minot on the Souris it would be pumped over the watershed to Garrison Reservoir and thence would descend via Garrison Dam, Oahe Dam, and Fort Randall Dam to Kansas City. Distribution from

Kansas City to the vicinity of Dallas would-be via a series of pumping stations, pipelines, and canals, to give a water supply in central Texas at an estimated $35 per acre-foot. After the use of the "surplus" of the Nelson River via Lake Winnipeg, the supply could be further supplemented from the Churchill River via the Sturgeon Weir River and Cedar Lake, at an estimated additional cost of $1 per acre-foot. The final step would be the incorporation of Lake Athabasca via Fond du Lac River and Wollaston Lake into the Reindeer River and thence to Lake Winnipeg. The estimated additional cost would be $5 per acre-foot.

Kuiper's plan uses existing natural waterways extensively, thereby reducing the cost of engineering works, but is not complete, inasmuch as water is delivered only to the Great Plains or to central Texas, some distance from the demand areas. When the costs of eventual delivery to these areas are aded, the economic attraction of the transferred water becomes questionable. In the plan the idea of "opportunity costs" was introduced, to include

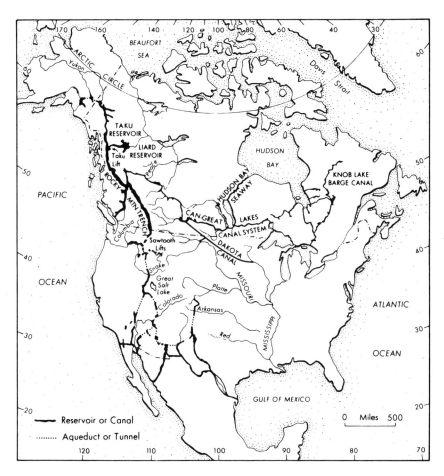

Figure 9.2. Water management and diversion proposals in the Kuiper scheme. (Source: Kuiper, 1966.)

compensation for the value of amenity lost to Canadians. If these are added to the transfer costs, the price of water would become prohibitive. The Kuiper plan, like others, would produce considerable fluctuation in the lakes used for storage purposes. The effects of such fluctuation on lake flora and fauna are discussed in the next chapter, but extensive bank erosion could also follow falling levels, a result of maintained soil pore water pressure forcing unsupported banks outward. Bank erosion would lead to a reduction of the storage capacity through siltation.

The Central North America Water Project

This project was developed by E. R. Tinney as a reaction to some of the far-fetched aspects of the NAWAPA plan, in the belief that the plan did not conform to the important engineering principles of using as few artificial structures and causing as little disruption of the natural environment as possible.[17] It is similar to parts of the proposed Kuiper diversion but extends the distribution network in the United States to water-deficient areas. The project involves the transfer of water from the MacKenzie, Churchill, and Nelson rivers along a route using many natural lakes as reservoirs, including Great Bear Lake, Great Slave Lake, Lake Athabasca, Wollaston Lake, Reindeer Lake, Lake Winnipegosis, Lake Winnipeg, and Lake Manitoba. These are relatively closely spaced, so that canal construction would be minimised. The estimated total length of canal construction to the Lake Winnipeg–Lake Manitoba collection centre is 900 miles. Construction would be assisted by generally flat topography, eliminating the need for extensive pump-lifting.

Some water would be transported by canal from the collection site via Lake Nipigon to Lake Superior. A second canal, the Central American Canal, would move water from Lake Manitoba across North Dakota to join the Missouri near Bismarck. The Missouri would be used as a channel almost to the Nebraska border, then water would be diverted into the Southwest American Canal, to traverse Nebraska, the North and South Platte rivers, eastern Colorado, the Oklahoma Panhandle, and northwest Texas. From Texas it would turn southwest across the Pecos River in New Mexico to join the Rio Grande. From the Rio Grande it would be transferred by canal to the Gila River, flowing westward across Arizona to join the Colorado near Yuma. The project would provide water to northern Mexico via the Rio Grande and the Colorado and to the water-deficient parts of New Mexico, Arizona, and California via existing pipelines from the Colorado.

CeNAWP was presented as a conceptual alternative to the NAWAPA project rather than as a detailed plan and some reservations about large-scale water export were expressed. No costs have been attached to the project and no potential yield of water has been suggested. Considerable canal construction would be necessary, possibly as much as 2,500 miles, despite the use of natural waterways. Even so, the costs should be less than those of the NAWAPA plan because of the less extravagant engineering works involved. The potential environmental effects have not been studied. One effect would be a reduction of flow in the Mackenzie, Churchill, and Nelson rivers, which could destroy the muskrat in the Mackenzie delta. Muskrat form the basis of the livelihood of a significant population of trappers in the lower Mackenzie valley. Diversion would also affect water transport along the Mackenzie. The main diversion would be upstream of the Sans Sault Rapids and would therefore require further blasting operations to deepen the channel for freight barge traffic. It is difficult to estimate the cost of such deepening without more detailed knowledge of the amount of water to be diverted, but the deepening operations already carried out indicate that an eventual cost of up to $10 million might be involved. Fluctuations of levels in lakes used as reservoirs could be expected

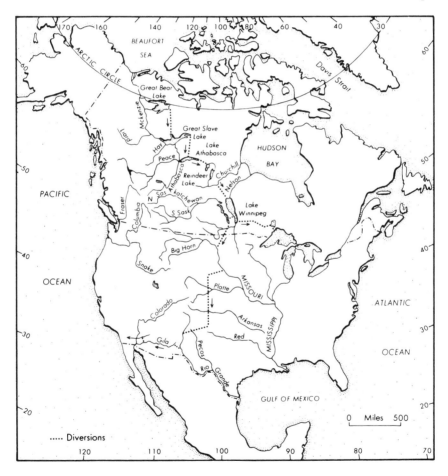

Figure 9.3. Water management and diversion proposals in the Central North American Water Project. (Source: E. R. Tinney, "N.A.W.A.P.A.: Engineering Aspects," *Bulletin of the Atomic Scientists* 23 [1967]: 21–27.)

to have considerable repercussions on lake flora and fauna and possibly on surrounding settlements. The project has not been presented in sufficient detail to determine the exact amount of fluctuation that would be involved or the amount of water which could be added to existing lakes without extensive flooding.

The Western States Water Augmentation Concept

This plan, proposed by L. G. Smith,[18] is another elaborate alternative to the NAWAPA project, which would involve diversion of the Laird and part of the Mackenzie from near Fort Simpson by a series of dams and pumping stations. The water collected would be transferred into the Peace system via the Kickika and Finlay rivers, and thence pump-lifted into the Fraser River in the Rocky Mountain Trench. Three alternative proposals are suggested for subsequent transfer. The first is to allow flow down the Fraser before diversion under the Cascades to the Columbia system, presumably from the vicinity of Hope, on the Fraser. The second proposal would involve damming the Fraser further upstream and reversing its flow into the headwaters of the Columbia. The third requires the diversion of both the Columbia and the Fraser through the Trench into the Kootenay. Water exported via the Columbia would be diverted through the Snake and Salmon rivers, pump-lifted to the Lemhi River and thence via a tunnel to a major reservoir in the Centennial Valley in southern Montana. If the water were to come down the Kootenay, it would be transferred to the Salmon River by canal, and then would follow the same route to the Centennial Valley, where the reservoir created could store approximately 50 million acre-feet.

From the Centennial Valley a complex series of canals, tunnels, and aqueducts would transfer water to a variety of demand points in the southwestern states. The main artificial canals necessary would be a transfer system into Nevada and California and a diversion across Utah to the Colorado. Another canal would traverse the North and South Platte, the Arkansas, and Canadian rivers to the Pecos along a route similar to that proposed in CeNAWP

The estimated yield of water would be approximately 38 million acre-feet per year, and construction costs have been estimated at $75 billion. Of this total, $12 billion would be spent on the collection system to the Centennial Valley, $51 billion on water-distribution systems, and $12 billion on hydroelectric generating facilities. These figures refer only to the cost of construction works and do not include any assessment of the value of amenity lost in either Canada or the United States.

A later addition is the Prairie Water Exchange Concept, which would greatly affect the environment of western Canada. It would include diversion of the Smoky River into the Athabasca via Lesser Slave Lake, followed by sequential diversion of the Athabasca into the North Saskatchewan via the McLeod and Pembina rivers. This water would replace flow lost from the North Saskatchewan by a diversion to the Red Deer near Rocky Mountain House, Alberta. A further diversion lower down the North Saskatchewan would carry water to the South Saskatchewan and subsequently southward, while the final diversion would be via a canal to the Souris River or via the Qu'Appelle River.

This project closely resembles part of the NAWAPA plan, although it avoids the single most controversial feature, the reservoir in the Rocky Mountain Trench. It does involve considerable loss of water from the Mackenzie which could not be removed without serious ecological effects in the Mackenzie delta, as described in connection with the CeNAWP. Damming of the Liard and the resulting backing of water up the South Nahanni valley would destroy one of the finest wild rivers in Canada, which was recently incorporated into a national park. Some of the rivers involved in the United States have similar

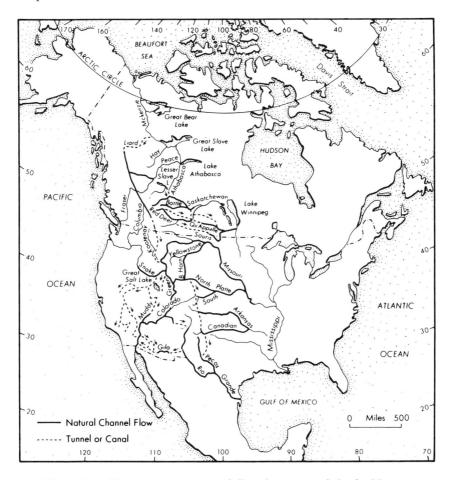

Figure 9.4. Water management and diversion proposals in the Western States Water Augmentation Concept. (Source: L. G. Smith, *Western States Water Augmentation Concept* [Federation of Rocky Mountain States, 1968].)

credentials, and the Centennial Valley is an important nesting ground for the endangered trumpeter swan. The potential for damage to the salmon fishing rivers of British Columbia, Washington, and Oregon must also be considered, although salmon runs have already been greatly reduced by other water management projects, by pollution, and by pulp-mill operations. The plan would appear to cause significantly less environmental damage than the NAWAPA plan, but the final cost of water in the southwestern states would probably not be appreciably lower, and the existence of a market is therefore doubtful.

The Magnum Diversion Scheme

Like many proposals for water export, the Magnum scheme was put forward more as a suggestion for further consideration than as a detailed plan.[19] The proposal would involve diversion of the Liard River into the Peace River and storage in Lake Williston. Water would be diverted from the Peace below Bennett Dam into a canal leading to Lesser Slave Lake. Subsidiary storage would be established on the Smoky River for diversion by another canal to Lesser Slave Lake. The storage capacity of Lesser Slave Lake would be increased to allow the level to rise twenty to forty feet, so that it could receive water from the Athabasca River as well as from the Peace and the Smoky. From the Lesser Slave Lake reservoir water would be transported by canal across the North and South Saskatchewan rivers and the Qu'Appelle River to

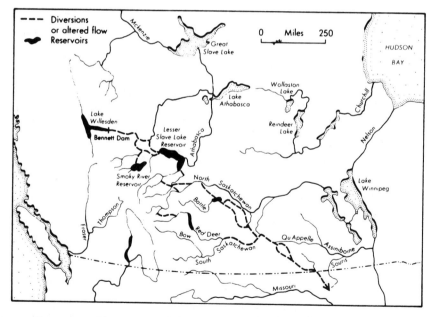

Figure 9.5. Water management and diversion proposals in the Magnum scheme. (Source: K. Magnusson, unpublished brochure, 1967).

the Souris, while another canal would tap the Souris in North Dakota, moving water south to the Missouri and thence by canals to demand areas.

No estimate of development costs are included, although it is suggested that $1 billion per year would be involved during the construction stages. The proposal is insufficiently detailed for accurate assessment, but it does not appear to offer significant improvements on the Kuiper scheme. It would involve inundation of considerable areas adjacent to Lesser Slave Lake and the proposed reservoir on Smoky River, which would apparently involve relocation of the town of Grande Prairie, although this point is uncertain.

The GRAND Canal

The Great Replenishment and Northern Lakes Development Canal was proposed primarily to solve the problem of fluctuating water levels in the Great Lakes, but it would also provide for extended withdrawals from the lakes up to the year 2000.[20] The proposal is specifically linked with Lakes Michigan and Huron and would regulate the remainder of the Great Lakes indirectly. At the time the plan was proposed, the chief problem in the Great Lakes was the decline in water levels, but provision was also made for reducing high water levels by increased withdrawals. The proposed source of supply would be some of the rivers flowing northward into James Bay—the Albany, the Moose, and the Harricanaw. Damming and storage on these rivers would be followed by pump-lifting over the 950-foot watershed into the Ottawa River. Diversion from the Ottawa would be along the Mattawa River to an expanded Lake Nipissing and thence to Georgian Bay on Lake Huron.

The proposal has been termed a "level-conditioning plan" and would depend for success on the acceptance of 50 percent increase or decrease clauses in the water supply contracts signed by cities withdrawing water, such as Chicago. For example, if Chicago were contracted to receive 10,000 cubic feet per second (cfs), the actual supply might vary from 5,000 cfs to 15,000 cfs, depending on lake levels. This clause would be essential to the project, but it is doubtful if a major urban area could base its development on such a variable flow. No attempt has been made to assess the costs, financial or otherwise, of the plan. Apart from the ecological effects of reduced flow in the Albany, Moose, and Harricanaw rivers, which could affect the beaver populations of the James Bay area, the plan might necessitate the relocation of parts of North Bay due to the increased level of Lake Nipissing.

Part of the area around James Bay which would be affected by the GRAND Canal is currently under scrutiny in connection with the proposed James Bay power development. This would involve damming several rivers on the eastern side of the bay, including the East Main, Rupert, Broadback, Nottaway, and Harricanaw, to form a vast reservoir, which would eliminate all wildlife from the southeast side of the bay and destroy the beaver conservation

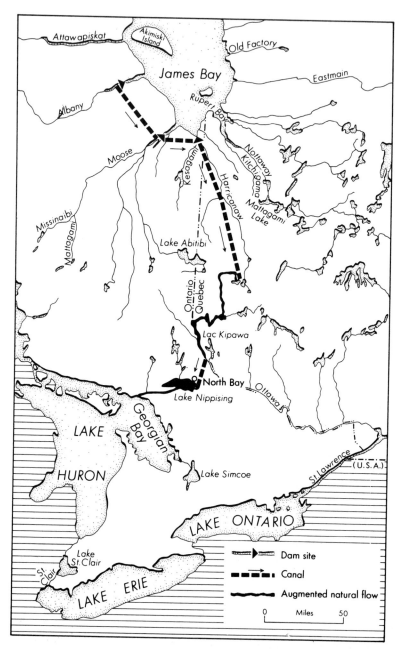

Figure 9.6. Water management and diversion proposals in the G.R.A.N.D. Canal scheme. (Source: T. W. Kierans, "The G.R.A.N.D. Canal Concepts," *Engineering Journal* 48 [1965]: 39–42.)

project at Rupert's House Reserve, discussed in chapter 11. The project might also cause climatic changes in Quebec and Ontario. An ecological study has been carried out, although it had not been released at the time of writing. As in many water management projects, the decision to proceed appears to have been taken (by the Quebec government) before assessment of potential ecological effects is complete. In outline the project appears to have a much greater potential for ecological destruction than the GRAND scheme, but it may now be too far advanced to halt.

Other Proposals

All the plans for water diversion and export discussed above require extensive engineering construction. There is little doubt that the technical ability exists to carry out construction of the structures suggested (with the possible exception of the Rocky Mountain Trench reservoir and the northern dams of the NAWAPA plan), but whether the water demand in the United States will ever grow sufficiently to support the costs involved is doubtful. Certainly a present or future demand has not been proven, despite the assurance from Senator Moss of Utah that "you will find a profitable market for it (water) south of the border in the United States and Mexico."[21] In the absence of proven demand, there is little likelihood that any major projects will be started in the near future. However, possibilities do exist for water export on a much smaller scale with proportionally fewer disadvantages.

No particular diversion plan has yet been proposed, but several of possibilities exist. Diversion of more northward-flowing rivers into the Great Lakes could provide for greater withdrawals in the U. S. Western Great Lakes water resource region without involvement in schemes on the GRAND scale. Such possibilities exist in the east, but because of the increasing water demands of the Toronto-Montreal urban development, western diversions are more likely. In the prairies water supplies could be made available on a moderate scale by further extension of the plans of the Saskatchewan-Nelson Board and the PRIME project in Alberta. Obviously the amounts of water available from such projects would not compare with the potential yield of major continental transfer schemes, but they could provide benefits in the United States.

It has also been suggested that without actually starting any export at the present time, Canada could commit itself to supplying agreed amounts of water in the future to the United States. If some U. S. demand areas were assured of future Canadian supplies, it is argued that they would be able to mine groundwater reserves without concern for eventual exhaustion. Obviously such a commitment would be as binding as physical export at the present time. The only apparent advantage over other plans would be the possibility that long-range planning in Canadian supply areas could alleviate or avert some of the ecological or social repercussions. The possibility exists, but little in the past record encourages belief in such farsightedness. It is impossible to judge the concept of small-scale transfers adequately in the absence of detailed plans of specific diversions, but the general concept would appear to merit more consideration than any of the large-scale plans discussed.

References

1. A. H. Laycock, "A Review and Comment on Canadian Water Export Proposals and of Studies Relating to Them." Paper presented to the 20th Meeting of the Western States Water Council, Many Glacier Lodge, Montana, 1970.

2. Ralph M. Parsons, Inc., *N. A. W. A. P. A., North American Water and Power Alliance,* company brochure, 606–2934–19, 1966.

3. A. G. L. McNaughton, "A Monstrous Concept, a Diabolical Thesis," in *Water Resources of Canada,* edited by C. E. Dolman, Royal Society of Canada (Toronto: University of Toronto Press, 1967), pp. 16–25.

4. H. B. Hawkes, "Irrigation in the United States," in *Conservation of Natural Resources,* ed. edited by Guy Harold-Smith, pp. 103–132 (New York: John Wiley & Sons, 1965).

5. F. E. Moss, *The Water Crisis* (New York: F. A. Praeger, 1967).

6. Ralph M. Parsons, Inc., 1966, *op. cit.*

7. T. Lloyd, "A Water Resource Policy for Canada," *Canadian Geographical Journal* 73 (1966): 2–17.

8. H. B. Hawkes, 1965, *op. cit.*

9. G. A. Kiersch, "Vaiont Reservoir disaster," *Civil Engineering* 34 (1964): 32–39.

10. W. R. D. Sewell, "Pipedream or Practical Possibility," *Bulletin of the Atomic Scientists* 23 (1967): 9–13.

11. N. W. Radforth, "N. A. W. A. P. A. and Permafrost," in *Water Resources in Canada,* edited by C. E. Dolman, Royal Society of Canada, pp. 27–28 (Toronto: University of Toronto Press, 1967).

12. J. A. Crutchfield, "Economic Considerations," *Bulletin of the Atomic Scientists* 23 (1967): 17–21.

13. V. Ostrom, "Political Feasibility," *Bulletin of the Atomic Scientists* 23 (1967): 13–17.

14. H. H. Lamb, "Climatic Variations and our Environment Today and in the Coming Years," *Weather* 25 (1970): 447–455.

15. E. R. Tinney, "N. A. W. A. P. A. — Engineering Aspects," *Bulletin of the Atomic Scientists* 23 (1967): 21–27.

16. E. Kuiper, "Canadian Water Export," *The Engineering Journal* 49 (1966): 13–18.

17. E. R. Tinney, 1967, *op. cit.*

18. L. G. Smith, *Western States Water Augmentation Concept,* Federation of Rocky Mountain States, Inc., 1968.

19. Alberta Department of Agriculture, Water Resources Division, *Water Diversion Proposals of North America,* prepared for the Canadian Council of Resource Ministers, Edmonton, Alberta, 1968.

20. T. W. Kierans, "The G. R. A. N. D. Canal Concept," *The Engineering Journal* 48 (1965): 39–42.

21. F. E. Moss, "Toward a North American Water Policy," in *Water Resources of Canada,* ed. edited by C. E. Dolman, pp. 3–16, Royal Society of Canada (Toronto: University of Toronto Press, 1967).

Chapter 10

Potential Effects
of Water Export in Canada

In discussing proposals to export water to the United States it is difficult to avoid the suspicion that the whole subject has become a sort of game. It would be facetious to suggest that all proposals for exporting water from Canada to the United States have originated purely as mental exercises, but many do share with mapping games an Olympian disregard for detail. This makes it difficult to discuss the proposals in detail and to examine carefully their potential effects. For example, it is difficult to find mention in any proposal of the amount of surface fluctuation in reservoirs and storage lakes. This information is absolutely critical in assessing both the amount of ecological damage which might occur and the potential recreational function the reservoirs might serve. The proposals have been advanced as broad concepts, yet their feasibility can be judged only by careful and detailed analysis. Certainly none of the proposals has considered the full range of costs involved or examined rigorously the benefits which might accure. The Kuiper plan probably came closest to the degree of careful analysis necessary (despite some controversial conclusions about future population densities in the prairie provinces), yet it dispenses with ecological effects in one sentence. Much more study in greater detail of all of the potential effects of the proposals is essential before any action is taken.

Financial and Political Effects

The potential demand for water in the United States has already been discussed in some detail. Satisfaction of this demand and the resulting inflow of revenue to Canada would be the chief benefit of water export to Canada. None of the major proposals makes any attempt to predict this revenue, yet it is a vital issue, for the revenue is the only valid reason for Canada's involvement in water export. Perhaps the only estimate of potential revenue which has been presented is the $1 billion per year suggested by Laycock as a possible yield from small-scale diversions, probably through the prairie provinces.[1] This figure is calculated at a rate of $40 per acre-foot on an export of 1 percent of Canadian streamflow, or approximately 25 million acre-feet per year. It is not clear whether this $40 is the sale price or the profit. If it is the sale price, the real revenue would be much less than the $1 billion suggested, because opportunity costs and such expenses as upkeep of diversion channels would have to be subtracted. If it is envisaged as profit, the cost of water transfer and opportunity costs would have to be added to the $40 to produce an unspecified total cost, which must be much higher. The final cost would depend on exactly where the water was to be sold, the opportunity costs involved, and so forth. It is not possible to make a realistic generalised statement of revenue to be derived from water export without specifying clearly the origin, destination, and route of transfer. The purpose for which exported water would be used must also be specified, as this greatly affects the price that could be paid.

As an example of the type of complications involved in assessing the existence of a market and the revenue to be derived, water could perhaps be brought to Texas by the Kuiper plan at a cost of $35 per acre-foot. This figure is the actual transfer cost and does not include any profit margin. Alternative water supplies there cost less then $35 per acre-foot, so the water would not be marketable. If water could be brought to the San Juan Valley of New Mexico for the same price, it could be sold for irrigation at $64 per acre-foot, yielding a profit of $29 per acre-foot, but this is unfortunately not possible. Using the costing of the California State Water Plan as a guide, it would probably cost well over $100 per acre-foot. At this price the water could not be sold in New Mexico, at least for irrigation purposes.

There are many areas in the United States where exported water could not be sold, let alone sold at a profit. It could be sold in areas such as Coalinga, California, but the amounts needed are not large. If the major demand areas were adjacent to the Canadian border, water could undoubtedly be sold. The only demand area so situated is the Western Great Lakes water resource region, and some Canadian water could probably be sold there in the near future, possibly at $40 per acre-foot. There is no realistic possibility of selling Canadian water in the major demand areas of the southwest, even at cost price. The project would not only be unprofitable, it would almost certainly lose money.

Obviously there are limitations to the general assessment of potential revenues in this way, the main one being lack of information on costs. None of the major projects has been costed in detail, and this is essential because the benefits to be derived in Canada must be shown clearly and in detail, so that they can be compared with costs. The revenue derived must be sufficient to balance all potential environmental, economic, and social ill effects. At present it appears that the potential revenue has been considerably overestimated, but without further study this is not certain. The experience of the Columbia River Treaty of 1961 should have warned us to study the alleged benefits of international water management very carefully before signing any agreements. The general opinion now is that the treaty was misguided in plan, if not in concept. An unnecessary dam, the High Arrow, was built at a cost of at least $190 million, flooding 20,000 acres of the scarce arable land of British Columbia. British Columbia received a cash settlement of $56.3 million for perpetual flood control downstream, plus half the power benefits for thirty years. These "benefits" must compensate not only for the loss of arable land, the relocation of 2,200 people, and the loss of the valuable recreational resource of the Arrow Lakes, but also for the cost of maintenance of the dam in perpetuity.

Unless the revenue to be received outweighs the costs, water export should not be undertaken. However, some peripheral benefits might appear in addition to the revenue received. Obviously some employment would be generated by the construction work involved. The actual value of this to Canada is doubtful, because the work would require primarily skilled labour and would not be drawn from the normal pool of unemployed. Much of the construction work would probably be carried out by American companies or their Canadian subsidiaries, if some current views on the availability of Canadian investment funds are accurate. It is also probable that the actual inflow of capital to Canada would be relatively small and short-lived.

Some political benefits might arise, but any discussion of these is purely theoretical. The United States might agree to reduce import restrictions on Canadian oil and gas as a trade-off against future water deliveries, but such reduction, and possibly the elimination of restrictions, will probably take place without any trade-off. It is debatable whether the removal of restrictions would be in the long-term Canadian interest. Certainly it would not be in Canadian interests to enter agreements to exploit oil and gas reserves to extinction before future energy requirements can be accurately predicted, or to sell a resource which will gain immensely in value within the next decade at a low price now. Other political effects are even less predictable. Obviously extensive continental development of water resources would tie the United States and Canada more closely together than at present even without the supranational authority the NAWAPA plan would necessitate. This would probably not be regarded as a desirable side effect by most Canadians.

Many suggest that if the United States really wants Canadian water it will come and take it, but this extreme view would be difficult to support, although as United States Senator Neuberger stated in 1949, failure to become involved in joint water management could be considered "an unfriendly act between nations."[2] The implications of this threat were not spelled out, but American business and industrial interests, with an investment of $23.3 billion in the Canadian economy, are well placed to exert pressure. Nevertheless it is hard to believe that American interest in Canadian water is yet sufficiently strong to provoke such pressure.

Some Canadians are concerned that in becoming party to a water export agreement Canada would sell the right to use her water as she wished and therefore some of her sovereignty. Conversely, it has been suggested that in signing a water export agreement Canada does not need to deliver water rights but only the marketable commodity of water. In this view Canada could insist on an agreement ot cease supply or to reduce it by a specified amount at the end of a predetermined period, such as twenty-five or fifty years.[3] Canada could certainly insist on such a contract, but whether she could enforce it is another matter. It is difficult to see how export could be stopped after considerable expenditure on water transfer networks and development of population concentrations and industries dependent on the augmented water supply. Any water export agreement must effectively involve the sale of Canadian water rights in perpetuity, or for as long as the water is wanted in the United States. At least one of the proposals, the Western States Water Augmentation Concept, specifically demands agreements for transfer in perpetuity because of the capital costs involved.

Ecological effects

The ecological effects of stream diversion and water export can be discussed only in broad generalities unless reference is made to specific projects. The possible direct results can be summarised as (1) flooding of wildlife habitats and timber reserves (2) reduction of streamflow (3) drying up of marshes and lakes and (4) increased fluctuation of lake levels. These effects would not all necessarily occur.

Flooding of wildlife habitats

All proposed methods of exporting water involve some form of water impoundment, resulting in inundation of appreciable land areas. The exact ecological significance would depend on their location and extent. Inundation could be relatively harmless if it occurred in an area of low faunal density or one without any endangered species, but it would be more serious if it occurred in a major breeding area or food range of abundant wildlife or of wildlife in danger of extinction. This would apply in the Western Cordilleran valleys, most of which are important winter range areas. Any reduction of range areas by flooding might finish several threatened species such as the grizzly bear and mountain caribou. Loss of areas like the Nahanni Valley or the Rocky Mountain Trench would be disastrous. Worry has also been expressed about The Big Horn Dam and reservoir in the Kootenay Plains of Alberta will reduce the winter range of the Rocky Mountain bighorn sheep when filling is complete. This species is not yet near extinction, but the breeding stock could be reduced. Some projects would do extensive damage simply because large areas flooded would interrupt migration routes.

A large amount of potentially valuable timber would be flooded. Admittedly this could be removed before flooding, as has been done in a number of reservoirs. In assessing the cost, however, allowances must be made not just for standing timber but also for the productive capacity of the land area in perpetuity. Compensation for the loss of future productivity has not been adequate in many projects involving flooding, such as the Skagit valley in British Columbia, discussed previously.

Reduction in streamflow

Water diversion results in decreased total discharge in the rivers involved, although the flow regime of the river may be improved by storage and phased release. Such improvement could involve the elimination of both extremely low flows and flood peaks, although the latter may not be an unmixed blessing. The effects of the diversion proposals on streamflow vary considerably. All the proposals would produce significant flow reduction during the initial stages of reservoir filling. Once this stage had passed, the more modest proposals, involving, for example, the diversion of a total of 1 million acre-feet from a number of streams, would produce little flow reduction. Major diversions, such as the 120 million acre-feet involved in the NAWAPA project, would seriously reduce flows.

Reduced streamflow causes a number of changes in rivers. Turbulence, and therefore the reoxygenation rate of the river, might decrease, resulting in generally low dissolved oxygen contents that could inhibit aquatic fauna, particularly in winter, when low oxygen levels could cause extensive fish kills. Changes in flow patterns could also affect aquatic vegetation and therefore the general productivity of the stream by increasing the scouring and erosional capacity of the stream. Any river carries a load of debris during its journey to the sea: dissolved chemicals, fine particles in suspension, and a slowly moving *bed load* of course material. The erosional capacity of the river is in equilibrium with this debris load and would increase if the load were decreased. One of the effects of dam construction is to remove this bed load and sometimes other debris, thereby increasing the erosional capacity and causing scouring and bank erosion downstream. The increase would be balanced in part by a decrease due to reduced streamflow. Nevertheless, for some distance downstream from any major dam there would be an increase in bank erosion and scouring until a full bed load is restored to the stream.

An increase in scouring would damage the habitat of bottom-feeding fish such as whitefish and could destroy the spawning beds of anadromous fish (fish that spend part of their life cycle at sea but migrate up freshwater streams to spawn and die) such as salmon. It would also contribute to the destruction of rooted aquatic vegetation, which would indirectly reduce the food supply for fish as well as the photosynthetic oxygen supply. The effects of dam construction on anadromous fish populations have been demonstrated in many countries, although these are frequently the result of the fishes' inability to negotiate dam structures during spawning runs rather than a result of flow reduction. In the Susquehanna River, in the United States, dams have cut off migrations of white shad and reduced the spawning area of striped bass.[4] On the Columbia and Snake rivers in Washington and Oregon a series of dams connected with the Columbia River hydroelectric projects has greatly reduced salmon populations.[5] A similar problem has resulted from the Kama-Vychegda-Pechora project in the Komi Republic of the Soviet Union, which involves the southward diversion of part of three major rivers flowing into the Arctic Ocean.[6] The dam also greatly alters the stream characteristics, changing circulation, temperature, and currents, so that anadromous fish may be unable to navigate the reservoir.[7] This may be one of the reasons why hatchery stocking does not eliminate population reduction. Siltation in the channel upstream from the dam may cover spawning beds and aquatic vegetation and thus decrease fish productivity. The only conclusion that can be drawn from these observations at the moment is that although we do not have sufficient information to predict the effects of water diversion and export on Canadian fisheries in detail, the prospects do not look promising.

The effects of reduced streamflow also appear in sea areas around the mouths of diverted rivers. Significantly reduced flow in the Mackenzie would reduce the input of fresh water to the Beaufort Sea, resulting eventually in increased salinity. The effects of such increases on fauna in the Beaufort Sea have not yet been studied, but they have been observed in other parts of the world.[8] In the eastern Mediterranean increased salinity caused by the reduced flow in the Nile associated with the Aswan High Dam has caused the virtual elimination of the local sardine fishing industry. On the Gulf coast of the United States commercial shellfishing has also been reduced by increasing estuarine salinity caused by reduced flows.[9] Generally increased salinity causes the replacement of commercial by noncommerical species and increases the incidence of shellfish infection.[10] It is not known to what extent these results might be applicable in the Arctic.

It has also been suggested that a major decline in the flow of relatively warm fresh water into the Arctic Ocean would produce changes in climate. These potential changes have been studied in some detail in connection with the Kama-Vychegda-Pechora project. In this study it was predicted that the area climatically affected by the diversions would be four times greater than the actual reservoir area, the major change being a general reduction in the continentality of climates. A similar result could be predicted for the reservoir areas in Canada, but the effect of reduced discharge in downstream areas would be to remove a warming influence and therefore to increase continentality. The reduction of "warm" river water flowing into the Arctic Ocean could cause a local decrease in ocean temperatures and increased sea ice thicknesses, but as Lamb has pointed out, the major effect would be increased salinity in the Arctic Ocean and therefore a decrease in sea ice thicknesses.[11] In connection with the Kama-Vychegda-Pechora project,the predicted increase in salinity was from 2.0 ppm to 2.3 ppm. The important feature is the transfer of water from an area where temperature changes greatly with season. Data from tropical and subtropical reservoirs such as Lake Volta in Ghana and the Kariba reservoir are not really applicable. The potential repercussions of these changes need careful study before they are assessed as beneficial.

Another potential climate change which requires study is the effect of moving large amounts of water in open canals and reservoirs into a water-deficient area. Evaporation loss would be substantial—estimated at approximately 14 million acre-feet for the NAWAPA project.[12] The addition of such a large amount of water to the atmosphere in the arid southwest would certainly alter climate patterns, probably increasing precipitation. This might be beneficial from a human standpoint, but it would alter the habitat of arid land flora and fauna and could lead to widespread soil erosion.

Drying up of marshes and lakes

None of the proposed plans suggests the removal of water from any lakes without replacement by river diversion, but diversion would result in the drying of lakes. Many lakes in deltaic areas of northern Canada are supported by a seasonal reversal of flow. During most of the year water drains out of the lakes to an adjacent river through narrow outlet channels. When the river is in flood in spring, the level of water in the main river rises above that of the lake, and flow in the outlet channels is reversed, causing the lake to fill with a water supply which lasts through the remainder of the year, when drainage is outward. Obviously this reversal depends on a seasonal fluctuation of the water level in the river. If the high flow of the river in flood is eliminated, flow reversal cannot take place and the water supply of the lake is cut off. Under these circumstances flow regime stabilisation is ecologically harmful if it eliminates peak flows.

Probably the best-known examples of lakes suffering the effects of diminished flow from feeding rivers in Canada are the shallow lakes which lie in the composite delta of the Peace and Athabasca rivers, at the western end of

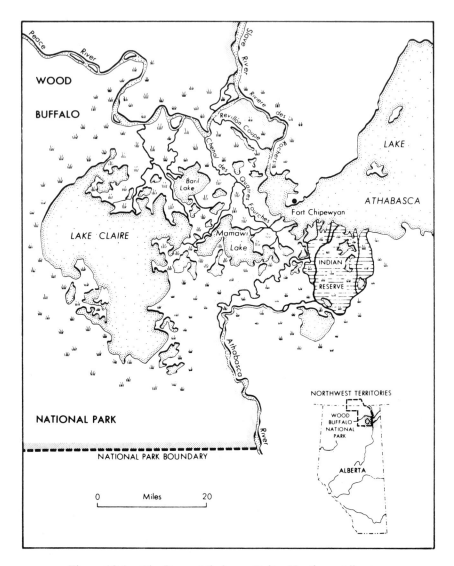

Figure 10.1. The Peace-Athabasca Delta, Northern Alberta.

Lake Athabasca. These lakes used to be nourished by the Peace River, the seasonal flow of which used to vary between 350,000 cfs in spring and 15,000 cfs in winter. During the spring floods on the Peace, flow in the outlet channels was reversed, and the lakes refilled. Completion of the Bennett Dam and the filling of Lake Williston caused marked reduction in the flow of the Peace. This will be partially restored when filling is complete, but the spring floods will disappear, because the full volume cannot pass the dam structure. Elimination of spring floods has been described as a major advantage of the dam in a federal report,[13] but it will lead inevitably to the destruction of the lakes.

Spring flooding has now been absent from the delta since 1968.

Certainly dry spells have occurred before, but never for such a prolonged period. As a result of the loss of the annual influx of flood waters from the Peace River, a number of serious ecological changes have taken place. Many of the shallow lakes in the delta have dried out or have been seriously reduced in area. Dirschl has assessed the reduction at 28 percent of the total lake area, or if the largest lake, Lake St. Clair, is excluded, 55 percent.[14] In addition to reductions in major lakes, twenty-five small lakes have dried out completely. These reductions have diminished the populations of pike and pickerel in the lakes, for even when water remains, many of the lakes are now so shallow they freeze to the bottom in winter. Even in Lake Athabasca itself low water levels have endangered fish spawning areas. The serious decrease in fish populations is overshadowed by a decline in beaver and muskrat, which were formerly abundant in the shallow lakes and marshes.

Apart from their importance to fish and wildlife, the lakes of the Peace-Athabasca delta form one of the most important habitats for waterfowl in western North America, both as a breeding ground and as a staging post for migratory wildfowl. Birds from all four major North American flyways congregate in the delta. Among those found are twenty-two species of duck, five species of geese, swans, pelicans, grebes, and many others. Soper describes the area as

the most important known stopping place of Ross' goose in

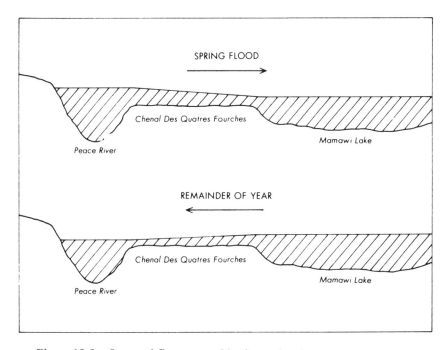

Figure 10.2. Seasonal flow reversal in the outlet channels of the Peace-Athabasca Delta.

*Canada. It is believed that almost all the existing flocks visit
there in spring and autumn migrations to and from the
breeding grounds at Perry River, N.W.T. The latest evidence
suggests that the total number of the species is only about
2,000. Its position may therefore be described as precarious.[15]*

The reduction or elimination of most of the lakes would damage one of the
most important bird sanctuaries in western Canada, which is part of Wood Buffalo National Park, and would undoubtedly lead to a decline in bird populations
and possibly to the extinction of such rare species as Ross' goose.

It has been claimed that alterations in the Peace-Athabasca delta
caused by the construction of the Bennett Dam are not entirely destructive. It
has been suggested, for example, that some lakes which were formerly too
deep to provide a suitable habitat for muskrat or beaver may now do so. This
is theoretically sound, but in fact virtually none of the lakes affected are in this
category. Another possibility is that plant succession on the exposed mud flats
would provide increased forage for the bison of the national park. This would
be true only for a short period, as the *Carex* meadows upon which the bison
feed are only a stage in succession. Any temporary increase brought about by
succession onto the mud flats would be balanced by the replacement of *Carex*
meadows by willow thickets in areas surrounding the lakes. The only species
which might eventually benefit is the moose, which thrives in willow thickets,
but as Fuller and LaRoi have pointed out, this would probably result in a
reduction in total biomass production, as terrestrial ecosystems are less productive than those of wetlands.[16] If biomass production is accepted as a
criterion of benefit or loss, the results of succession induced by drying the lakes
would be negative. The successions described are already progressing quite
rapidly, so that even if the lakes are restored habitats will be disrupted due
to decay of vegetation, which will induce accelerated eutrophication. (In
October 1971 the report of a federal study of the Peace-Athabasca delta recommended the construction of a retention dam on one of the outflow channels
to alleviate conditions.)

The effects of flow reduction in the Peace River caused by the
Bennett Dam would be magnified many times if diversion of the Peace, proposed in several plans, took place. Diversion of the Athabasca as well, proposed
in the Magnum plan and the Albertan PRIME project, would entail the complete destruction of the delta and a reduction in the level of Lake Athabasca.
Although the lakes of the Peace-Athabasca delta are undoubtedly unusual,
many small lakes in the Mackenzie delta depend on a similar flow reversal.[17]
Any reduction in the flow of the Mackenzie would certainly have consequences
in the delta, particularly to the abundant muskrat population, which depends
on lakes of adequate depth.

Creation of lakes of fluctuating level

The lakes of the Peace-Athabasca delta and Lake Athabasca itself are subject to appreciable annual fluctuation of water level even under natural conditions. In Lake Athabasca the fluctuation is generally four to eight feet. Wildlife dependent on the lakes is usually adapted to these minor fluctuations. Many ducks, such as the lesser scaup, pintail, and various species of teal, and other birds, such as the Canada goose, trumpeter swan, white pelican, and various species of grebe, all nest close to the water's edge. A steady drop of four to eight feet during the summer allows them to rear chicks safely before high water returns. Other species are less tolerant of water level fluctuations; a variation of only two feet has been shown to have adverse effects on mallard and redhead populations.[18]

None of the diversion proposals presented provide a sufficiently detailed analysis to permit estimation of the fluctuation of lake and reservoir levels. In some of the projects little fluctuation would probably occur; in others it could reach 150 feet, particularly in those that function partly as flood control works. Such fluctuation in a natural lake would affect waterfowl and in an artificial reservoir would greatly restrict any possible use for waterfowl breeding. The low level would be much lower than those naturally present, exposing mud flats between the shore and water. Young chicks, particularly of species like the pintial, would suffer severely increased predation from hawks and magpies if they were forced to travel extended distances to water. High water levels higher than those at present would drown out suitable nesting habitats around the shore and on islands, where birds like the Canada goose and white pelican nest. Destruction would be permanent, for the fluctuation would prevent plant colonization. The extensive bank erosion generated by the fluctuating levels would also contribute to the destruction of nesting habitats and to lake siltation. (Some of these problems have already appeared in Lake Diefenbaker.[19] Siltation would reduce the capacity and life span of the lake or reservoir, would hamper fish spawning, and would destroy the food supply of bottom-feeding ducks, as already demonstrated in Lake Louisa and Lake Oprongo, Ontario.[20]

It is impossible at this time to estimate accurately the reduction in bird populations which would result from water diversions. Some decline would certainly take place, and possibly some species would become extinct. The trumpeter swan has been on the border of extinction for the last thirty years, and Ross' goose is also threatened. Reduction of duck and goose populations, accentuated by wetland drainage elsewhere in the prairies, could cause economic losses.

The financial losses could almost certainly be balanced by population increases by stocking some species on artificial reservoirs, as already practised with irrigation projects in southern Alberta. This would, of course, be limited to those reservoirs without appreciable water level fluctuation. The loss involved if a species should become extinct, on the other hand, would be irreparable and very difficult to justify.

Economic and Social Effects

Most decisions we make about our environment are not binding on our descendants, but if we do not value a species highly enough to prevent its extinction, our decision, however faulty, is for all time. All species are of value, although this value may not be easy to quantify. In later chapters some practical objections to species extinction are discussed, but the issue here is the social rather than the practical value. This is the core of environmental conservation, which recognises qualitative and aesthetic values as well as financial ones. Unless we recognise the existence of human values which cannot be expressed in financial or material terms, we have no right to regard ourselves as more advanced than other forms of life.

The effects of water diversion can influence at least some people directly. Many of the native population of Canada still depend on wildlife for their livelihood. Any diversion of water will affect the wildlife population and will reduce or eliminate native trapping. The effects on the fishing industry in Lake Athabasca have already been mentioned. These effects would be reproduced in many other lakes, such as Lesser and Great Slave lakes and Great Bear Lake, where fishing is also important. Although the contribution of native industry to the Canadian gross national product may not be large, this is no reason why it should be destroyed. The independent livelihoods destroyed could be partially replaced by welfare payments, but few, if any, native people would willingly replace a self-supported existence by one based on welfare. Undesirable social effects of water management have already appeared in Finlay Forks, British Columbia, due to the filling of Lake Williston; in Fort Chipewyan, Alberta, caused by reduction of flows in the Peace; and on the Kootenay Plains of Alberta, due to the flooding of the Big Horn reservoir. Similar problems have also affected other Canadians, results of the Arrow Dam in British Columbia and the Mactaquac Reservoir in New Brunswick, where long-established vegetable farmers were forced to move. The people who would benefit most from water transfer are not those who would suffer the greatest loss.

The destruction of wildlife, particularly wildfowl, associated with water diversion could damage the recreation industry of Canada. The financial loss is difficult to assess, but it could be large, as indicated by the closure of the hunting season for upland wildfowl in Alberta in 1969 (discussed in chapter 4). If assessment of the value of potential loss in hunting values is problematic, it is even more so for other recreational pursuits such as boating, bird watching, and the general use of weekend cabins. No definite figures are available, but it is generally recognized that these pursuits are now of greater financial importance than hunting and have greater social significance. Canals and reservoirs associated with water transfer might have a recreational potential, but this would be severely limited for reservoirs that had large fluctuations of water level. The illusory nature of proposed recreational benefits has been demonstrated by Lake Williston and Duncan Lake Reservoir in British Columbia; the balance of effects on the recreational industry would probably be negative.

Conclusion to Part Three

The need for water export to the United States or the existence of a demand for it has not been demonstrated. That benefits might be generated in Canada is undeniable, although many potential benefits are ill defined and have perhaps been overestimated. Ill effects might well outweigh the benefits, particularly in view of the changing values of our society. Assessments of potential demand, benefits, and costs are all subjective because of the lack of adequate research data. If the subjects of water export and water transfer within Canada are to be seriously discussed, such research must be carried out. If water is to be diverted and exported, the costs involved must be fully realised and accepted. Furthermore, there must be clearer provision for adequate compensation to the people who suffer most directly than has sometimes been the case. To enter any agreement or treaty for water export is premature in the present state of knowledge, and unless this knowledge is significantly extended, it will remain premature for many years.

References

1. A. H. Laycock, "Canadian water for Texas?" *Water Resources Bulletin* 6 (1970): 542–549.

2. D. C. Waterfield, *Continental Waterboy: The Columbia River Controversy* (Toronto: Clarke, Irwin, 1970).

3. A. H. Laycock, "A Review and Comment on Canadian Water Export Proposals and of Studies Relating to Them." Paper presented to the 20th Meeting of the Western States Water Council, Many Glacier Lodge, Montana, 1970.

4. R. J. Mansueti, "Effects of Civilization on Striped Bass and Other Estuarine Biota in Chesapeake Bay and Tributaries," *Proceedings of the Gulf Caribbean Fisheries Institute,* Nov. (1961): 110–136.

5. M. E. Marts and W. R. D. Sewell, "The Conflict between Fish and Power in the Pacific Northwest," *Annals of the American Association of Geographers* 50 (1960): 42–50.

6. P. P. Micklin, "Soviet Plans to Reverse the Flow of Rivers: the Kama-Vychegda-Pechora Project," *The Canadian Geographer* 13 (1969): 199–215.

7. R. R. Whitney, "The Susquehanna Fishery Study, 1957–1960: a Report on the Desirability of Passing Fish at Conowinge Dam," Maryland Department of Research and Education, Contribution no. 169 (1961): 1–81.

8. H. C. Davis, "Survival and Growth of Clam and Oyster Larvae at Different Salinities," *Biological Bulletin* 114 (1958): 296–307.

9. B. J. Copeland, "Effects of Decreased River Flow on Estuarine Ecology," *Journal of Water Pollution Control Federation* 38 (1966); 1831–1839.

10. P. S. Galtsoff, "Ecological Changes Affecting the Productivity of Oyster Grounds," *Transactions of the 21st North American Wildlife Conference* (1956): 408–419.

11. H. H. Lamb, "Climatic Variation and our Environment Today and in Coming Years," *Weather* 25 (1970): 447–455.

12. Committee on Public Works of the United States Senate, Special Subcommittee on western water development, *Western Water Development*, Washington, United States Government Printing Office, 1966.

13. A. Coulson and R. J. Adamcyk, "The Effects of the W. A. C. Bennett Dam on Downstream Levels and Flows," *Inland Waters Branch Technical Bulletin*, 18 (1969).

14. H. J. Dirschl, "Ecological Evaluation of the Peace-Athabasca Delta." Paper presented to the *Peace-Athabasca Delta Symposium*, University of Alberta, Edmonton, January 1971.

15. J. D. Soper, "Waterfowl and Related Investigations in the Peace-Athabasca Delta Region of Alberta, 1949," Canadian Wildlife Service, *Wildlife Management Bulletin*, Series 2, 2 (1951).

16. W. A. Fuller and G. H. LaRoi, "Historical Review of Biological Resources of the Peace-Athabasca Delta." Paper presented to the *Peace-Athabasca Delta Symposium*, University of Alberta, Edmonton, January 1971.

17. D. A. Gill, "Damming the Mackenzie: a Theoretical Assessment of the Longterm Influence of River Impoundment on the Ecology of the Mackenzie River Delta." Paper presented to the *Peace-Athabasca Delta Symposium*, University of Alberta, Edmonton, January 1971.

18. K. Wolf, "Some of the Effects of Fluctuating and Falling Water Levels on Waterfowl Production," *Journal of Wildlife Management* 19 (1955): 13–23.

19. R. O. Van Everdingen, "Diefenbaker Lake: Effects of Bank Erosion on Shorage Capacity," *Inland Waters Branch, Technical Bulletin* 10 (1968).

20. N. V. Martin, "Effects of Drawdowns on Lake Trout Reproduction and the Use of Artificial Spawning Beds," *Transactions of the 20th North American Wildlife Conference* (1955): 263–271.

Part 4

The Status and Conservation of Wildlife in Canada

Polar bears. (Credit: Canadian Wildlife Service).

Chapter 11

The Use of Wildlife
in Canada

At several places in earlier chapters I referred to the importance or value of wildlife in connection with various aspects of environmental conservation. The survival of at least some species of wildlife often conflicts with the apparent progress of society and so becomes a central issue in conservation. The status of wildlife therefore deserves more careful study.

Attitudes toward Wildlife

Whether wildlife in general or any particular species will survive in our society depends entirely on the value we place on it. If the majority of the population place a high enough value on wildlife, provision will be made for its survival. The value we place on wildlife is closely bound up with our attitudes towards and awareness of it, or wildlife *perception*. Few studies of wildlife perception have been attempted, so there is little quantitative data on which to base a discussion, but presumably awareness of wildlife can be graded from those who are completely unaware to those who are highly aware. Obviously only those who are aware of wildlife can have any attitude toward it, and it is probable that the greater the degree of awareness, the stronger the attitude becomes. Some people have little awareness of wildlife, and their attitude is therefore nonexistent or one of indifference; these people place a very low value on wildlife.

The attitudes of people who are highly aware of wildlife may vary from acute antagonism to enthusiastic advocacy, and between these extremes are many complex, subtle variations. Study is difficult because attitudes are changeable and are not clearly defined or articulated by many people. Further, some people are emotionally involved with wildlife to such a degree that they may be reluctant to respond accurately to questioning. Space does not permit a detailed discussion of all the variations of attitude which may exist, but a brief discussion of the extreme viewpoints is useful.

Acute antagonism toward wildlife may be based in part on fear resulting perhaps from an unhappy or painful encounter. More often it appears to be a relic of the "pioneer" attitude, which is also based to some degree on fear, or at least uncertainty, and is characterized by an urge to demonstrate dominance over nature and wildlife. Its origins are complex and atavistic, being closely involved with the effectiveness of man as a hunter, food producer, and protector. This involvement with functions associated with virility is undoubtedly one reason why attitudes toward wildlife are so difficult to study. Perhaps antagonism toward wildlife is so deeply engrained in the human character that it can be regarded as an instinct. Certainly at present in Canada it seems that to be favourably inclined toward wildlife requires more explanation and justification than to be antagonistic.

Favourable attitudes toward wildlife are as complex in origin as antagonism and are less easily defined. Their net expression is the desire to coexist with wildlife as an integral part of the natural environment. The origin of favourable attitudes may be admiration for the beauty and grace of wildlife or the perfection of its environmental adaptation, refined by millions of years of evolution and selection. Perhaps it is partly a recognition of the value of such perfect adaptation in a world in which our own imperfect adaptation becomes increasingly obvious. Admiration of the characteristics of wildness and freedom, which most of us lack, may also be involved. Certainly the recognition that each species is a unique part of the natural environment and experience is fundamental. If a species becomes extinct, the possible range of human experience is reduced, in somewhat the same way as it would be if a great work of art were destroyed. On a more pragmatic level, many species of wildlife have been of direct use to man, particularly in medical research. Often these were classic example of a "useless" plant species which became invaluable. It is impossible for us to predict which species may become useful or even vital for mankind in the future, but we can at least protect our interests by even vital for mankind in the future, but we can at least protect our interests by doing everything we can to ensure the survival of all species.

Basic attitudes toward wildlife are important, but to suggest that they control the values placed on wildlife would be a great oversimplification.

This would not take into account, for example, the hunter who may be antagonistic to wildlife, but who values it highly so that he will have something to hunt. If wildlife is to survive in significant quantity and diversity we must attempt to understand such complexities of attitude, but we should also realise that all attitudes cannot be successfully dissected and analysed. Perhaps we must recognise ultimately, as Aldo Leopold did, "that there are some people who can live without wild things, and some who cannot.[1]

Objective study is as yet too scant to give an accurate idea of the attitudes of the Canadian people toward wildlife. Available results suggest that in general Canadians are highly aware of wildlife and are favourably inclined; certainly this viewpoint has been expressed by several authorities.[2] Favourable attitudes are not enough to ensure survival, however, for many people are largely ignorant of the needs of wildlife. We can eliminate wildlife just as thoroughly by ignorance as by shooting or poisoning.

Wildlife as a Resource

Canadian wildlife is unusually abundant and varied and constitutes a natural resource of substantial material and aesthetic value. Wildlife can be exploited in a number of ways which are to some extent related to the state of development of a society. In a primitive society wildlife is used directly as a source of food, clothing, and sometimes fuel and shelter. As the society progresses it becomes more complex; settlement, agriculture, and commerce with neighbouring societies develop. The direct use of wildlife declines in importance as other sources of food and clothing become available, but it is replaced by the use of wildlife as a commodity in trade and in recreational hunting. Eventually an interest in wildlife for its own sake may develop, creating a primarily aesthetic use for the resource.

As Cowan [3] has pointed out, all these uses coexist in Canada. In the north wildlife is used primarily as a source of food and to a lesser degree as a source of clothing and fuel. These uses are declining rapidly as the area is opened up and more convenient sources become available, and they are giving way progressively to the use of wildlife for recreational hunting, as in an earlier age father south. Throughout Canada in the twentieth century and locally much earlier, interest in the aesthetic appeal of wildlife has developed rapidly, resulting in protection of some species and the setting aside of substantial areas as sanctuaries for wildlife.

Wildlife is a renewable resource which can be harvested on a recurrent basis, provided that the annual harvest and the natural mortality do not exceed the annual increment. If this happens, the resource will dwindle to exhaustion. Wildlife thus resembles other renewable resources, such as timber. Unlike timber, however, the annual increment and the natural mortality are subject to sudden changes which are only partly predictable. As a result, it is difficult to adjust annual harvests to maintain a stable population, due partly to the inflexibility of the administrative systems which control harvests. This inflexibility is increased by the great variation in population dynamics between different types and species of wildlife; the annual harvest established for one species may be totally inappropriate for another.

A further complication in establishing harvest limits is the complex interrelationships between species. Harvesting a prey animal, such as the wapiti, may result in a decline in the population of a dependent predator, such as the wolf. On the other hand, harvest of the wolf may increase the population of wapiti as a result of decreased predation, which will result in greater demands for forage by the wapiti herd, perhaps in excess of the capacity of available range. This may result in extensive starvation and die-off, and also in reduction of the health of survivors. It will also result in the overuse of available vegetation, which may produce semipermanent damage. It may take years for the range to recover, and in the meantime soil erosion and siltation in fishing streams can occur. In this way simple acts which apparently cause little damage may upset one link in an ecosystem and generate extensive repercussions, the outcome of which may be difficult to predict. All forms of wildlife are components of ecosystems and are therefore subject to these complex controls. This does not mean that the wildlife resource should not be used and harvested, but such use may result in population instability unless we acquire knowledge of the ecosystematic relationships of the species involved.

Analysis of the status of a resource in a social context demands the examination of the costs it incurs as well as the benefits it confers. Although wildlife is a resource of considerable value, its nature demands that its use be carefully regulated if full benefit is to be derived. This can be regarded as a cost to society, for effective regulation involves expenditure on fish and game authorities, issuing licences, policing bag limits, and prosecuting offenders. It is fair to say that such expenditure is often more than balanced by revenue derived from the sale of licences. Other costs may be caused by the interaction between wildlife and humans, including the consumption of swathed grain by wildfowl, damage to aircraft by collision with wildfowl, destruction of seedlings by deer browsing in forestry areas, and damage to farm fences by large mammals. It is impossible to obtain comprehensive figures for such damage, but the costs can be substantial.

Another important cost is the loss of development potential because of wildlife habitat requirements. These include food supply, shelter, the absence of disturbance, and space, and they are extremely variable. Some species are catholic and tolerant in their requirements and will adapt easily; others suffer severely from any disturbance of their specialised habitats. The physical requirements of most species are fairly well known, but data on the psychological needs of space and absence of disturbance are deficient, particularly data about the territorial demands of wildlife. Patterns of territoriality vary immensely; some species apparently demand no exclusive rights over territory, whereas individuals of other species may battle violently to protect it. Some species will defend territory only against intruders of the same species; others will defend against all comers. Some will defend their territory only during a brief period of the year; others will defend at all times. Successful planning for all species would require a knowledge of and provision for such behaviour patterns. To cater adequately to the habitat requirements of wildlife requires the setting aside of tracts of land from development. This implies a loss of revenue from other potential uses of the land, which must be weighed against the value of the resource protected.

The costs of maintaining a wildlife population can be assessed in monetary terms, as can some of the benefits. Some benefits cannot be expressed so readily, however, including the aesthetic benefits of wildlife and its function as part of the national heritage. Attempts have been made to assess these quantitatively, but this is perhaps neither wise nor realistic, because it puts a price on something which is fundamentally priceless and irreplaceable. The existence of such a tag invites competition with other potential, and possibly more demonstrably valuable, uses of the land. The whole point of attempts to conserve environmental quality, whether directed to wildlife, clean air, or unpolluted water, is that quality cannot be assessed in monetary terms. At the same time it is realistic to recognise that values which cannot be quantified, particularly in monetary terms, tend to be ignored. Conservationists must ensure that they are not ignored.

Use of the Wildlife Resource

Wildlife as a primary food source

Little quantitative information exists on the importance of wildlife as a source of food, clothing, and shelter in Canada, either now or in the past. A comprehensive picture cannot be drawn, but sporadic references show that in the past these uses of wildlife were of great importance. Apparently the use of wildlife was the only major use of natural resources prior to European settlement. Almost the entire indigenous population appears to have depended on hunting and gathering, although some commercial use of wildlife did precede European settlement, both internally and on a sporadic basis between Indians and European fishermen along the east coast. Cartier described fur trading in the St. Lawrence area following his voyage of 1534, but it appears to have been minor. It included fur made into clothes, and in some cases the Indians "bartered all they had on to such an extent that all went back naked without anything on them."[4]

Only scattered references to the species used for food are found, and undoubtedly there was much variation. In the east small game, fish, beaver, moose, and deer were eaten—moose meat is specifically referred to in a 1626 source quoted by Innis.[5] Champlain also encountered moose meat used as a trade item among the Montagnais, Etechemin, and Algonquin Indians in the Saguenay region in 1603.

In the western plains by far the most important animal was the plains bison, although beaver and antelope were also used. The bison appears to have been a target species for hunters since the retreat of the Pleistocene ice sheets, and its use possibly preceded the last glacial advance. Certainly by the early Christian era extensive hunting of bison was carried on despite a lack of both firearms and horses, and many artifacts of this period are connected with bison slaughtering. The bison was a dominant food source until the late nineteenth century, by which time the herds had been almost completely wiped out. Although the use of the bison had continued for thousands of years, the most rapid depletion apparently followed the arrival of the fur trade and the introduction of firearms. At times the slaughter was extremely wasteful, and frequently only small portions of each animal, particularly the tongues, were removed.[6]

In northern Canada the barren-ground caribou served as a source not only of food but also of bones for implements, sinews for sewing, and skins for kayaks, tents, and clothing. The chief users were inland Eskimo groups living in the valleys of the Dubawnt, Kazan, Thelon, and Back rivers and several Indian tribes, including Yellowknives, Dogribs, Loucheux, and Chipewyans. Eskimo groups living along the coast depended primarily on hunting seal, walrus, and whale, but expeditions were often made inland in late summer to hunt caribou. Again the use made of wildlife was sometimes very wasteful. In the narrative of his journey from Churchill to the Coppermine River in 1771, Samuel Hearne mentioned that "the deer were plentiful and the Indians killed great numbers, frequently only for the fat, marrow, and tongues."[7] The killing of caribou and bison in large numbers was facilitated by the size of the herds in which they traveled and the fact that both were easy to kill.

There was obviously great variation in the species and type of wildlife used for food and in the way this use declined. After European settlement more diversified societies developed, and agriculture grew in importance. In the east wildlife ceased to be a significant primary source of food after the beginning of the nineteenth century, although it persisted in the west until the end of the century. The decline spread westward and northward, until the present situation was reached. Now wildlife is a primary food source only in parts of the north, and these areas are shrinking rapidly with the spreading influence of the major urban population centres in the north. This use will probably not survive on a large scale for more than a few decades, although undoubtedly it will persist in small enclaves.

As the use of wildlife as a primary food source declined, other uses became progressively more important. The most significant was the fur trade, which coexisted with the earlier use in many areas. From a resource point of view, the chief difference was that the developing fur trade led to much more rapid depletion of fur-bearing animals than hunting for food alone would have done.

The fur trade

Historical development. The history of the development of the fur trade in Canada is long and complex and is essentially the history of Canada, at least up to the beginning of the nineteenth century. It has generated an immense literature, so only the major features are outlined here.

The initial stages of the trade were apparently informal interchanges between Indian tribes and European fishermen in the east at the end of the fifteenth century, but the trade was of minor importance until the mid-sixteenth century. Not until the wearing of beaver hats became fashionable in Europe in the latter half of the century did the trade grow rapidly. As it grew, beaver colonies around the Gulf of St. Lawrence were trapped to extinction, and traders were forced to penetrate into the interior along the Saguenay, St. Maurice, and Ottawa rivers. This penetration was contended by some Indian tribes, but by 1623 the trade had moved sufficiently far west for bison skins to appear in the trading reports.[8] By mid-century French fur traders reached Lake Superior and Lake Michigan, but thereafter progress was slowed by competition with English traders operating through Hudson Bay.

In 1670 the Hudson's Bay Company was formed by royal charter and granted a trading monopoly in the northern and western parts of Canada named Rupert's Land.[9] The best quality beaver pelts traditionally came from the vicinity of James Bay, where the Hudson's Bay Company had a trading advantage: its ships could sail directly to the trading posts, whereas the French traders had to negotiate the difficult river routes from the Ottawa Valley. Despite this competition the French traders were still able to send 92,000 pelts to France during 1677.

During the last quarter of the seventeenth century trading was disrupted by skirmishing between English and French traders. Not until the treaty of Utrecht, 1713, was the monopoly of the Hudson's Bay Company established beyond contention. For half a century thereafter trading was concentrated in fortified trading posts around Hudson Bay. In 1754 a declining supply of beaver forced the company to send Anthony Henday westward to trade with the Indians of the plains, followed in 1771 by Hearne's northward journey to persuade the Copper and Dogrib Indians to bring their furs to the trading posts.

Despite these journeys, trade in the interior was restricted by the renewal of competition from French Canada. In 1783–84 French Canadian traders formed the Northwest Company to operate from Montreal, thus starting the most intense rivalry yet seen in the fur trade. In response the Hudson's Bay Company finally abandoned its policy of waiting for furs by the coast and opened fortified trading posts in the western interior, including Manchester

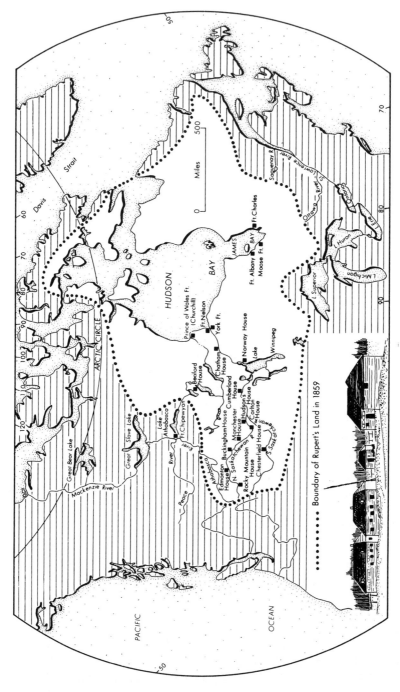

Figure 11.1. Selected fur trading posts and the location of Rupert's Land in 1859. (Source: Adapted from *Atlas of Alberta*.)

House, Cumberland House, and Edmonton House on the Saskatchewan, and Chesterfield House on the Red Deer. The Northwest Company also built trading posts, the best known of which was Rocky Mountain House, opened in 1799. The Northwest Company took an early initiative, and by 1797 it "controlled virtually the whole fur capacity of Canada,"[10] but this was lost during the six years it took to find a way through the Western Cordillera to the coast. By 1816 the two companies had driven out all competitors and had reduced each other to the verge of bankruptcy, and in 1821 they merged under the umbrella of the Hudson's Bay Company.

The Canadian monopoly established by the merger of 1821 enjoyed immense prosperity in the fur trade during the following forty years. Returns fluctuated considerably from year to year, but between 1821 and 1833 they averaged £83,316 per year, and between 1833 and 1840, £84,800. Thereafter they declined, averaging only £65,573 per year.[11] This era of the fur trade ended in 1859, when the exclusive trading rights of the Hudson's Bay Company in Rupert's Land terminated and the western plains were opened to agricultural settlement.

The fur trade prospered during the first half of the nineteenth century, but during this period it ceased to dominate the Canadian economy, although it has continued in importance as a secondary export. The value of wild fur production still fluctuates considerably from year to year, but it averages about $15 million per year. This fluctuation is partly due to variations in the market price for pelts and partly to the number of pelts taken; in recent years the number of pelts has varied from just under 3 million in 1920-21 to just under 7 million in 1950-51.[12]

The production revenues above represent the actual payments made to trappers for pelts. Although the production is not of great significance in the Canadian economy as a whole, its real significance, as Cowan has pointed out, is that it comes primarily from parts of the country where agriculture is impossible and which until recently have produced virtually nothing else. It is still an important source of income for much of the Indian, Eskimo, and Métis population.

The role of the beaver. The fur trade was built primarily on beaver pelts, and the fortunes of the beaver to a large extent governed the fortunes of the trade. The development of the trade is a classic example of the destructive exploitation of a species and a resource. Although excessive hunting had raised queries as early as 1635, not until the early nineteenth century, when possibilities of further westward migration no longer existed, did authorities in the trade become seriously concerned. In the years of intense competition before 1821 the decline was particularly serious, partly because of the use of steel traps and baiting with Castoreum. The first attempts to conserve beaver were made after the 1821 merger, and hunting was discouraged, particularly of cub beaver and beaver out of season. By 1841 the problem was sufficiently serious

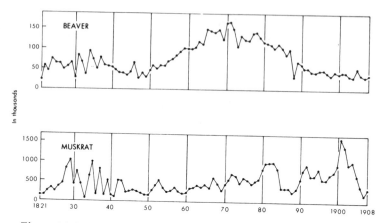

Figure 11.2. Fluctuations in beaver and muskrat returns of the Hudson's Bay Company. (Source: E. Seton-Thompson, *The Arctic Prairies* [New York: C. Scribner's Sons, 1911].)

to merit the sacking of company officers who did not conserve beaver and the payment of bonuses to Indians who did not hunt beaver. The policy also encouraged beaver conservation by paying higher prices for less valuable furs such as muskrat. Partly as a result, the number of beaver taken after 1841 declined dramatically until 1850. (The decline was also due to the replacement of beaver by silk as a hatting material and to fluctuations of beaver populations.)

After 1850 the number of beaver taken continued to fluctuate, but a general overall decline appears to have occurred in response to unrestricted hunting and to the clearance of beaver habitat by agricultural settlement. By 1916 the decline had reached such an alarming level that the establishment of beaver sanctuaries in the Northwest Territories, northern Ontario, and Quebec was recommended.[13] In 1919 a closed season for beaver was introduced for the first time, but even so, beaver dominated the fur market until 1922, when muskrat finally surpassed it in value, totaling $4,707,043.[14] Muskrat then declined until in 1933 it was surpassed in value by silver fox. The rise of silver fox can be attributed largely to fashion, and it remained dominant until the end of the Second World War, after which it dropped to a very low level. Since the Second World War muskrat and beaver have been restored to some of their former importance, aided by fur management and conservation projects undertaken in the late 1920s and 1930s which began to bear fruit at the end of the 1940s.

Fur conservation. The principles of fur animal conservation are the control of harvest to the annual surplus, the improvement of habitat and carrying capacity, the establishment of species in favourable habitats from which they are absent, and the improvement of fur quality. The first measure apart from closed seasons was the registered trap line system introduced in British Columbia in 1926. Under this system, still operated, a trapper is given exclusive

Table 11.1. Pelts of Fur-Bearing Animals Taken in
the Year Ending June 30, 1967

Animal	Number of Pelts	Value	Animal	Number of Pelts	Value
Beaver	371,533	$4,731,570	Coyote	17,458	$115,629
Muskrat	1,732,404	$1,695,245	Racoon	33,911	$106,857
Hair seal	153,390	$1,373,096	Polar bear	724	$92,660
Mink	88,614	$1,017,947	Fisher	6856	$78,283
Fur seal	12,830	$672,782	Black bear	1810	$43,055
Arctic fox	34,126	$536,052	Wildcat	3658	$36,033
Marten	55,042	$498,537	Wolf	1453	$26,124
Squirrel	635,058	$390,056	Rabbit	50,672	$21,457
Lynx	13,038	$362,103	Grizzly	215	$17,821
Otter	16,411	$299,096	Wolverine	602	$14,950
Cross and			Badger	1163	$8852
red fox	29,984	$170,657	Silver fox	287	$4252
Ermine	133,592	$130,873	Blue fox	189	$1889
			Skunk	298	$132

Total number of pelts: 3,395,309
Total value: $12,446,008

Source: Dominion Bureau of Statistics.

rights to the fur in a defined area and the responsibility for the conservation
and management of fur-bearing wildlife in the area. Registration of a specific
trap line is renewable on an annual basis, provided that satisfactory conservation
practises have been followed. Obviously the efficiency of the system varies
with the individual trapper, but in general it appears to work well. It has been
extended to fur harvesting in all but the Atlantic provinces, which retain only
small areas of Crown land, and the Northwest Territories. Among the Atlantic
provinces only in Newfoundland has the trap line system appeared, yielding
about one-third of the beaver harvest in 1968. Although most registered trap
lines are on Crown land, in Saskatchewan they also extend to private lands,
on which owners and occupants receive first consideration. In 1946 northern
Crown lands in Saskatchewan were set up as the Northern Fur Conservation
Block, which functioned as an effective management unit under the joint
administration of Indian, Métis, and white trappers.

The earliest attempt at conservation of fur-bearers by management
in reserves was the Rupert's House Reserve set up in 1932 by the Hudson's
Bay Company in the portion of Quebec bordering James Bay. In this reserve,
7,500 square miles in area, the beaver population in 1930 was estimated at
a couple of hundred, and by 1944 it had increased to over 10,000.[15] The
success of this project led to the creation of further reserves in Quebec, and
twelve reserves now exist, covering a total area of 327,400 square miles and including some areas originally trapped out in the seventeenth century.

Manitoba was the first province to attempt fur-bearer conservation
by habitat manipulation, in the Pas project, set up in 1932 on a reserve of

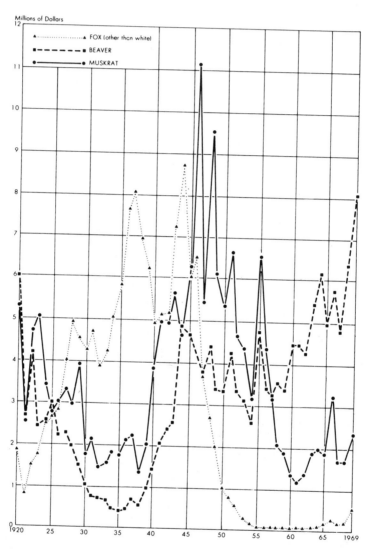

Figure 11.3.   Relative values of annual pelt production for leading fur producers. (Source: Dominion Bureau of Statistics.)

80 square miles. Management of water levels increased the muskrat population
from an estimated 300 in 1932 to over 60,000 in 1937. The large-scale Summer-
berry project was started in 1936 on some 230 square miles. A closed season
of four years followed the planting of a seed stock of 5,000 muskrat in 1936. In
1940 the population was estimated at 200,000, and 126,000 pelts were taken,
valued at $180,000; in 1941 191,562 pelts valued at $361,179 were taken. The
major achievement of the project was perhaps the raising of 1,800 families
above the welfare level.[16]

These examples are representative of fur-bearer conservation activity
in all provinces and territories. With these developments the fur trade had
changed from a purely destructive form of resource exploitation to a stable
industry based on sustained-yield management principles. It is obvious that fur-
bearers will never again enjoy the abundance which preceded European settlement, but the fur trade's change of policy should ensure that most fur-bearing
species will not become extinct through overhunting. At the same time, it is
disturbing to see that the fur returns still list species such as the grizzly bear and
polar bear, which face other challenges to survival and whose situation is
serious. Also, because seal are only under the partial control of Canadian
authorities, they cannot be managed in the same way as beaver and muskrat. In
general, however, it can be said that the fur trade no longer constitutes a threat
to any species, but there are no grounds for complacency, because many
methods of trapping are extremely cruel, particularly the leg trap.

Recreational hunting of wildlife

Separation of the use of wildlife for recreational hunting from that as
a primary food source may seem unnecessary, as much of the wildlife killed by
recreational hunters is eventually used for food. However, the differences in
motives that underlie the killing, could be of considerable significance in
determining management practises and possibly the eventual survival of some
species. There is also a social difference between the two forms of hunting;
"food" hunting is done primarily by low-income groups, particularly by
Indians, Métis, and Eskimos, whereas recreational hunting is dominated by
white Canadians and foreign tourists, many of whom are affluent by comparison. A further difference is the relative economic importance of the two
forms of hunting. Recreational hunting is directly or indirectly responsible for a
considerable amount of employment, and it generates a substantial flow of
currency, both within Canada and from foreign sources. "Food" hunting, on
the other hand, generates virtually no currency flow and little employment,
although much time may be spent in its pursuit.

It is impossible to determine exactly when recreational hunting began
in Canada, although organised group hunting existed in Toronto at least as
early as 1860.[17] Presumably it developed gradually as a change in the prime

motive of hunters, and obviously its origin is an individual matter, but it probably did not become important until the twentieth century, and the really significant increase probably postdates the Second World War. Cowan, for example, quotes an increase in the number of big game licences issued in British Columbia from 37,648 in 1943 to 85,313 in 1951.[18] It is difficult to obtain an accurate picture for the complete country for several reasons: statistics are collected on a provincial basis, and frequently data are not easily comparable; return periods vary, the amount of revenue derived cannot always be obtained; and there are differences between provinces in the type of licences issued. Ontario, for example, offers fifteen different hunting licences, and Alberta issues twenty-five. Nevertheless, the data do indicate the way in which hunting patterns have changed. The most conspicuous feature is the sharp, though irregular, increase in the number of licences issued after the Second World War, which reached a peak in Nova Scotia in 1953–54 and in Alberta and Ontario six or seven years later. Recent declines have now ceased, and hunting appears to have reached a stable level.

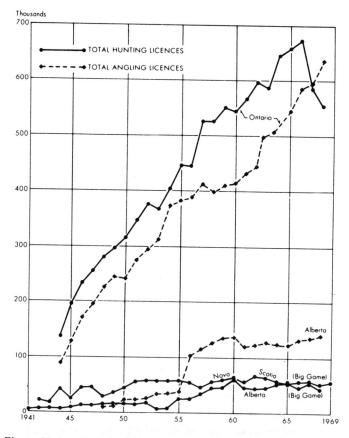

Figure 11.4. Annual values of hunting and angling license sales, (Source: Annual reports, Department of Lands and Forests, Alberta, Nova Scotia and Ontario.)

Perhaps because of the difficulty in obtaining comparable data, few attempts have been made to assess the flow of currency generated by recreational hunting. The data available for Albertan licence sales show that this has fluctuated considerably even in recent years, but the overall importance is indicated by a revenue of $6,285,930 derived from the sale of angling and hunting licences in Ontario in 1966.[19] The sale of licences, of course, measures only the direct, immediate returns of hunting and takes no account of indirect revenue in the form of salaries for guides and outfitters, expenditures on equipment, motel accommodations, travel, and other ancillary expenses. Studies in the Atlantic provinces,[20] Alberta,[21] and British Columbia and for the whole country, together with studies in the United States, have attempted to assess the importance more comprehensively. These studies indicate that the ratio between expenditures on licences and total expenditures vary with the type of hunting, ranging from 1:7 to 1:50. In Benson's study of the whole country in 1961, the ratio for all forms of hunting was 1:27, and the expenditure for the complete country was $87,345,925; the comparable ratio for angling was 1:143; the total expenditure was $187,651,082.[22]

No study comparable to Benson's has been carried out since 1961, but there is no reason to suppose that the importance of hunting and angling has declined. In fact, the data for Alberta, Nova Scotia, and Ontario suggest that 1961 was a year of moderate licence sales, despite subsequent declines, which have been partly offset by increased licence fees. Revenue from angling in Alberta, for example, was $434,999 in 1968 compared with $168,400 in 1960, although the increase in the number of licences sold was only 13.5 percent. It is obvious that even if it is judged solely by its capacity to generate currency flow, recreational hunting is important in Canada.

Although the currency flow generated is substantial, it represents only a partial accounting of the value of this resource use in Canadian life. No one has attempted to measure the social significance of the recreational benefit obtained. At the time of Benson's study 12.6 percent of the population over fourteen years of age were either hunters or anglers or both. Considerable regional variation was reported: the Atlantic region, 11.1 percent; Quebec, 17.9 percent; Ontario, 37.9 percent; the prairies, 20.5 percent; and British Columbia, 12.6 percent. No attempt was made to analyse or discuss the significance of these returns, but any activity which plays a part in the recreational activity of up to 37.9 percent of the population is of great social significance. The variation between areas is undoubtedly affected by many factors, such as income, age structure, weather patterns, and cultural background. At the same time, the importance of hunting and angling in Ontario may be partly a reflection of the high concentration of the population in urban areas.

Recreational hunting and angling seem to serve as a release from the pressures of urban life, and they are thus important in making urban life tolerable. One could argue, of course, that such release could be obtained merely by visiting rural areas. This is true, but it is probable that without the incentive of a clearly defined objective, fewer people would visit the country. It is also possible that hunting, and to a lesser degree fishing, act as a safety valve for aggressive tendencies, without which our society might deteriorate rapidly. If one of the alternatives to reduced hunting is an increase in violent crime, it seems perferable that hunting be encouraged.

If wildlife is used as an outlet for aggressive tendencies the implications for land-use planning should be clearly understood. Benson's study showed that 60 percent of hunters and anglers stayed within a 100-mile radius of their homes, and 90 percent stayed within 300 miles. This indicates that if recreational hunting and angling have an important social function, adequate provision must be made for these activities within the immediate surroundings of large cities. This need is pressing, for Benson's study showed that the average hunter or angler is not particularly affluent—87.9 percent have a family income of less than $7,500—so that frequent long-distance travel is not possible.

The prime purpose behind hunting and angling is recreation, but the food produced does play an important role in the diet of many Canadians. No one has attempted to estimate the food production of recreational hunting separately from that of hunting for primary food production. However, in 1952 Solman[23] estimated the total utilisation of game meat at 48.4 million pounds, consisting of 38 million pounds of big game, 6 million pounds of waterfowl, and 3 million pounds of upland birds. Data are not available to assess current utilisation, but general increases in hunting since 1952 would suggest a conservative estimate of 80 million pounds per year. In 1954 the approximate value of venison was computed at $1.50 per pound.[24] A current estimate of $2.00 per pound is probably conservative, but even this would indicate that the total annual value of wildlife as a food source is around $160 million. The importance of this source is therefore considerable, particularly in view of the relatively low average incomes of many hunters.

The figure given does not include the value of fish produced either by anglers or by commercial fishermen. No records are available for the weight of fish caught annually by anglers. If this is assessed arbitrarily at ten pounds per angler, and the fish is valued at $0.80 per pound, the annual value of the food produced by anglers is about $10.5 million. This does not include anglers in the Yukon and Northwest territories, where fish is an important dietary item. Commercial fishing has not been discussed in this chapter, but it is worthy of mention. In 1966 the total weight of fish caught was 2,631,533 pounds—2,509,923 by sea fisheries and 121,610 by inland fisheries. The value of the fish caught totaled $172,542,000, with $156,966,000 for sea fisheries and $15,756,000 for inland fisheries.[25]

Although this discussion has relied heavily on estimation, it is possible to derive some idea of the approximate financial value of fish and wildlife in Canada. The breakdown of these values is given in table 11.2. The tabulation is inaccurate and incomplete, and it certainly underestimates some values. Nevertheless, it indicates that wildlife, with an annual value of

Table 11.2. Estimates of the Annual Value of
Various Wildlife Uses in Canada

Recreational hunting	$87,345,935
Recreational fishing	$187,651,082
Hunting food—production	$160,000,000
Recreational fishing—food production	$10,500,000
Commercial fishing—food production	$172,542,000
Wild fur production	$15,000,000
Total	$633,039,017

about $650 million, is a resource of economic importance in Canada comparable to that of wheat. It should be emphasised that this financial value represents only a fraction, possibly a small fraction, of the real value of wildlife in Canadian life.

Nonconsumptive uses of wildlife

This classification to includes a gradation of passive interests in wildlife which cannot be easily assessed in monetary terms; most do not include the killing of animals or fish. The simplest nonconsumptive use is as an object of interest to sightseers, an interest that is often fleeting and ill-informed but nevertheless important. It is impossible to determine how prevalent such interest is, but it seems that very few people have absolutely no interest in wildlife; certainly attendance figures at zoos would support this view. Wildlife is an important drawing factor in national and provincial parks. Clarke[10] quotes the results of an inquiry which found that the experience visitors to Banff National Park most desired was to see a bear. An additional role of significance for wildlife—in urban parks—has been indicated by the success of nature walks in a number of cities.

The next gradation of nonconsumptive use is typified by bird watchers, who have a continuous and usually a well-informed interest. This is probably the most poorly documented and underestimated use of wildlife, because most bird watchers are relatively undemonstrative about their interest and are not readily identifiable as a group. It is impossible to determine the size of this class, even with the directory of organisations recently published by the *Canadian Field-Naturalist,*[26] as many people do not belong to formal organisations. There is no doubt that they are numerous, as indicated by the case of the telephone service set up in Toronto to provide information on bird migration: the service had to be discontinued because the volume of enquiries was so large that the telephone system became jammed. The value of such nonconsumptive uses cannot be easily quantified, but these uses are apparently of social significance. Nature observers also probably contribute substantially to the economy through the purchase of equipment, especially photographic equipment. In 1966 naturalists were estimated to number 800,000, of whom only 2 percent belonged to organised clubs. The Calgary Bird Club suggested operating expenditures of $202 and capital expenditures of $155 per capita. Extrapolated to the total number of naturalists, this would suggest a possible total annual expenditure of $162 million for the whole country.[27] This figure needs much refining and examination, but it does suggest that the value of this type of nonconsumptive use is large.

The most intensive nonconsumptive use of wildlife is scientific research, which includes the use of wildlife in schools and universities for teaching and research and research to improve management practises. Accurate data are not available, but these cases have increased considerably in the past decade. Much research is related to other uses, such as that directed toward higher productivity for hunting. Another research value is that wildlife acts as a sensitive monitor of environmental quality; both the physical and mental reactions of wildlife to environmental stress may indicate possible human reactions.

The most extreme nonconsumptive uses of wildlife are those which require no contact; the mere existence of wildlife may be sufficient to fulfill these functions. The function of some species as a national heritage and sometimes as national symbols typifies such use. The symbolism is sometimes ironic; Manitoba uses the plains bison as its symbol, despite the bison's virtual extinction, and California uses the Californian grizzly bear, which has been extinct since 1922. These uses are perhaps important, but they are less so than the satisfaction many people derive from the simple knowledge that wildlife exists. No physical use or contact may be intended, yet wildlife still has a value that may become apparent chiefly as a loss of satisfaction if a species is wiped out.

Any of the reasons discussed may justify provisions for the maintenance of wildlife, but the basic reason to preserve many species is still emotional. The real reason for preserving the grizzly bear is not because of the value of its hide in the fur trade or because tourists want to stare at it or even because it is a symbol and part of the national heritage. Rather, it the unforgettable psychic impact of encountering a grizzly at close quarters. We should preserve the grizzly because it is a magnificent animal and because the world will be poorer if we allow it to be killed off.

References

1. Aldo Leopold, *A Sand County Almanac and Sketches Here and There* (New York: Oxford University Press, 1949).

2. C. H. D. Clarke, "Wildlife in perspective." Background papers for the *Resources for Tommorrow Conference*, pp. 837–844 (Ottawa: Queen's Printer, 1961).

3. I. McT. Cowan, "Wildlife Conservation in Canada," *Journal of Wildlife Management* 19(2) (1955): 161–176.

4. H. P. Biggar, *A Collection of Documents Relating to Jacques Cartier and the Sieur de Roberval* (Ottawa: Public Archieves of Canada, 1930).

5. H. A. Innis, *The Fur Trade in Canada* (Toronto: The University of Toronto Press, 1962).

6. L. G. Burpee, "The Journal of Anthony Henday, 1754–1755," edited by L. G. Burpee, *Proceedings and Transactions of the Royal Society of Canada,* 3rd Series, 1 Section KK, pp. 307–354.

7. Samuel Hearne, *A Journey from Prince of Wales' Fort in Hudson's Bay to the Northern Ocean . . . in the Years 1769, 1770, 1771, 1772* (London: Strahan and Cadell, 1795).

8. H. P. Biggar, *The Early Trading Companies of New France* (New York: Argonaut Press, 1965).

9. E. E. Rich, *The Fur Trade and the Northwest to 1857* (Toronto: McClelland and Stewart Ltd., 1967).

10. E. E. Rich, 1967, *op. cit.*

11. H. A. Innis, 1962, *op. cit.*

12. Dominion Bureau of Statistics, *Canada Year Book,* 1920–1921 (Ottawa: Queen's Printer, 1921).

13. F. H. H. Williamson, "Game Preservation in Dominion Parks," in *Conservation of Fish, Birds and Game,* Commission of Conservation, Canada, pp. 125–140 (Toronto: The Methodist Book and Publishing House, 1916).

14. Dominion Bureau of Statistics, *Canada Year Book,* 1923 (Ottawa: Queen's Printer, 1923).

15. Dominion Bureau of Statistics, *Canada Yearbook,* 1944 (Ottawa: Queen's Printer, 1944).

16. I. McT. Cowan, 1955, *op. cit.*

17. C. H. D. Clarke, "The Bob-white Quail in Ontario," Ontario Department of Lands and Forests, Technical Bulletin, Fish and Wildlife Series, No. 2, *Bulletin of the Federation of Ontario Naturalists* 63 (1954): 11.

18. I. McT. Cowan, 1955, *op. cit.*

19. Ontario, Annual Report of the Department of Lands and Forests, 1967.

20. D. A. Benson, "Some Dollar Values of the Wildlife Resources of the Atlantic Provinces," *Wildlife Management Papers,* pp. 5–10, *21st Federal-Provincial Wildlife Conference,* Department of Northern Affairs and Natural Resources, Ottawa, 1957.

21. W. S. Pattison, *Economics of moose hunting in Alberta.* Unpublished M. A. thesis, Department of Agricultural Economics and Rural Sociology, The University of Alberta, 1970.

22. D. A. Benson, *Fishing and Hunting in Canada,* The Canadian Wildlife Service, National Parks Branch, Department of Northern Affairs and Natural Resources, 1961.

23. N. E. Solman, *Minutes of the 16th Annual Federal-Provincial Wildlife Conference,* 1952.

24. I. McT. Cowan, 1955, *op. cit.*

25. Dominion Bureau of Statistics, *Canada Year Book,* 1969 (Ottawa: Queen's Printer, 1969).

26. T. Mosquin and M. T. Myers, "Directory of Natural History, Conservation and Environmental Organizations in Canada," *The Canadian Field-Naturalist* 84 (1970): 75–87.

27. M. T. Myres, "A Sample Survey of the Expenditures of Naturalists," *Canadian Audubon* 30 (1968).

Chapter 12

The Decline of Wildlife in Canada

We have no accurate estimate of the amount of wildlife that existed in Canada before European settlement. Not until the end of the nineteenth century did accurate counts begin, and for some species none exist even today. Assessment of original populations must be based on the impressions of travelers like Cartier and Champlain in the east, Kelsey, Henday, and the La Vérendrye brothers in the west, and Hearne in the north. These give only a subjective and often nonspecific account of wildlife, but they indicate a great abundance of animals and birds. Many species have since dwindled, some to the point of extinction; bison herds no longer move like a brown carpet across the prairies, and branches have ceased to break under the weight of passenger pigeons. On the other hand, species such as the moose and white-tailed deer have adapted well to the changed conditions and have increased in number. If we are to make intelligent provision for the preservation of wildlife, the reasons for these changes must be understood.

The Effect of Hunting Pressure

The principle of sustained-yield hunting has already been stated: the harvest and natural mortality should not exceed the increment. The earliest

206

cause of wildlife decline, other than natural evolution or cyclic fluctuation, was unrestricted hunting that far exceeded the natural increment. Beaver extirpation from eastern Canada in response to the heavy demands of the fur trade has already been described. Although the decline of beaver was rapid in many areas, the beaver would probably not have become extinct even without control because much of its domain was inaccessible, and its tendency to group in small numbers made wholesale killing difficult. The destructive potential of overhunting is better demonstrated by two other species, the plains bison and the passenger pigeon. In both cases the decline in Canada closely reflected events in the United States, for both species traveled freely across the border.

No one knows how many bison used to wander the grasslands of North America, but it is generally believed that the population at the beginning of the nineteenth century was about 60 million. A number of accounts tell of heavy hunting pressure and wasteful killing even before this period, but the dramatic decline took place during the nineteenth century with the spread of fur trading posts and firearms. A wholesale slaughter took place—for food, for hides, and sometimes just for the sake of killing. The toll was so great that even before mid-century some Indian tribes had difficulty finding enough bison for food. At one time upwards of 300,000 plains Indians in the United States and Canada appear to have depended on the bison herds for food.[1]

By the late 1860s and early 1870s the large-scale exploitation of bison for leather had begun. Although this use was largely confined to the United States, it did extend into the southern Canadian prairies as well. By 1879 the decline was so widespread that starvation threatened many of the Indian tribes; during that year some 600 of the Blackfoot tribe died,[2] partly due to competition with bands of Sioux, driven northward across the border by the decline of bison in the United States. It was also related to the destruction of the bison winter range (much of the winter was actually spent in the aspen poplar parkland, where trees provided some shelter from the searing wind) by fire and to local overhunting.[3] The incidence of drowning while herds crossed rivers also became serious as the herds dwindled in size. For these reasons the bison herds had been reduced to a very low level by the time the Canadian Pacific Railway reached the prairies in 1881. The bison were used even after death, however; the immense piles of bones which littered the prairies were moved eastward by rail for use in the fertilizer industry.

By the end of the 1880s the bison had virtually ceased to exist south of the Peace River, but a small herd of wood bison survived around the western end of Lake Athabasca. This herd was estimated at 500 in 1893, when Parliament enacted protective legislation, although this was not enforced until 1911.[4] Another reserve, the Buffalo Park at Wainwright, Alberta, was established in 1907 to maintain a small herd of plains bison. In 1922 the reserve near Lake Athabasca was established as Wood Buffalo National Park, and between 1925 and 1928 plains bison from Wainwright were introduced. Most of the animals presently in the park are hybrids of wood and plains bison, although small herds in the isolated northwest of the park apparently still represent the true wood bison strain. Between 1923 and 1949 the herd increased from 1500[5] to between 10,000 and 12,500.[6] Despite turberculosis, brucellosis, anthrax, recreational hunting, and occasional poaching, the population is now more or less stable, allowing a periodic harvest to be taken. The herd also used as a source of stock for other areas in Canada and the United States, as is the smaller herd in Elk Island National Park, Alberta. The Buffalo Park at Wainwright ceased to exist at the start of the Second World War, when it was taken over for military training purposes.

The history of the plains bison is undoubtedly the most dramatic example of the reduction of a species by extreme hunting pressure. Thanks to good fortune, the isolation of the northern herd, and the eventual action of the Canadian government, it did not end in extinction, however, and survival of the bison now seems assured. Other species were less fortunate. Passenger pigeons were at one time so numerous in North America that their flocks darkened the sky and trees broke under their weight. Aldo Leopold records an 1871 estimate of 136 million pigeons in a small area of Wisconsin alone,[7] and in 1877 an Ohio State senate committee investigating the need for protecting passenger pigeons reported that there was "no need of protection, as the pigeons were in such countless numbers that they could not possibly be exterminated."[8] The pigeon was adapted to a very specific habitat—climax stands of oak, beech, and chestnut. Where good feeding was found the flocks would congregate in great density, which probably led to overestimation of their abundance. Certainly the vast flocks were not immune to hunting pressure, and in 1916 the last passenger pigeon died in a Cincinnati zoo. Although hunting pressure has generally been blamed for its demise, it has been pointed out that it showed little ability to adapt to habitat change.[9] The removal of the climax stands of deciduous forest for agricultural settlement would probably have sealed its fate even without overhunting. Either way, the passenger pigeon became extinct because we did not make room for it in our society.

In Wyalusing State Park, Wisconsin, a monument to the passenger pigeon was dedicated in 1947, for which Aldo Leopold wrote:

> We have erected a monument to commemorate the funeral of a species. It symbolizes our sorrow. We grieve because no living man will see again the onrushing phalanx of victorious birds sweeping a path for spring across the March skies, chasing the defeated winter from all the woods and prairies of Wisconsin.
>
> Men still live who, in their youth, were shaken by a living wind. But a decade hence only the oldest oaks will remember, and at long last only the hills will know.
>
> There will always be pigeons in books and in museums, but

*these are effigies and images, dead to all hardships and to all
delights. Book-pigeons cannot dive out of a cloud to make the
deer run for cover, or clap their wings in thunderous applause
of mast-laden woods. Book-pigeons cannot breakfast on new
mown wheat in Minnesota, and dine on blueberries in Canada.
They know no urge of seasons; they feel no kiss of sun, no
lash of wind and weather. They live forever by not living
at all.* [7]

The passenger pigeon is the most celebrated species we have extin-
quished by hunting, but it is only one of several, including the great auk and
the Labrador duck. Others will go the same way in the near future unless they
are protected and allowed the necessary habitat. We must realise that had the
bison herds not been diminished almost to extinction by hunting, they would
have suffered the same fate eventually due to the westward progress of agricultural settlement and the fencing of their ranges. Huge, free-roaming herds of
bison are incompatible with a settled, agricultural society.

Reduction of Habitat

Hunting has been an important cause of decline for some species in
Canada, but in most cases decline was the inevitable result of competition
between wildlife and agricultural settlement. Essentially wildlife and humans in
Canada coexist in three situations. Outside the area of agricultural settlement
wildlife habitat is disturbed only through hunting, resource exploration and
extraction, and forestry. Along the border with the settled agricultural area
there is active competition; expansion of the agricultural area by clearing and
fencing is reducing the habitat of some species of wildlife, and these species are
struggling to survive in the dwindling habitat. Often the competition is made
more severe by the introduction of domestic species which compete with wildlife for food. The result is a reduction in wildlife populations through habitat
reduction and also considerable damage to farm equipment and fences and
predation on crops and livestock, which creates demands for the removal of the
species believed to be responsible for predation, such as the black bear, the
grizzly bear, the wolf, and the coyote.

The third zone has been agriculturally settled for a considerable
period of time, and here wildlife (except species which thrive on agricultural
land) exists only in areas unsuitable for agriculture. The wildlife population may
bear little relation to the original population in species composition, as many
predators may be absent or severely restricted in number. The removal of these
natural checks may result in violent population fluctuations. Rapid increases
generate overuse of available food supplies and damage to the range, which in
turn may cause widespread starvation and die-off, particularly among young

animals. The surviving animals are usually in poor condition and are vulnerable to disease, so the stock is eventually reduced again to a low level, perhaps below the original population. Such a cycle due to the disappearance of predators is common, but many other factors may also be involved in the fluctuation of wildlife populations, some of which are not yet well understood. Certainly fluctuations can and do occur even without man's intervention.

Before European settlement virtually the whole of Canada was in the first zone identified above. Only minimal agriculture was carried out by the Iroquois, and elsewhere the wildlife population was probably approximately in balance with the carrying capacity of the environment. Population fluctuation would have occurred in response to natural disasters such as forest fires or heavy snowfalls and perhaps partially in response to factors such as crowding, but the average population was probably more or less constant. The indigenous people coexisted with wildlife and depended on it for survival. Most important, however, they were nonagricultural and often migratory and made few competitive demands on wildlife habitats; their only impact, through hunting, was minor because they were few and used hunting methods of limited effectiveness. Even so, the evidence of the fossil fauna in the Rancho la Brea tarpits near Los Angeles indicates that some species had been extinguished, possibly by hunting, even before the arrival of European settlers and firearms.

The arrival of European settlers accelerated the decline of wildlife, the range shrinking as agricultural settlement spread north and west. This expansion was slow and by the middle of the nineteenth century was still virtually confined to the Atlantic provinces and the Great Lakes–St. Lawrence basin. The area of agricultural land was still small enough so that most of it could probably be regarded as lying within the agricultural fringe of human-wildlife interaction. Rapid agricultural expansion did not take place until the Hudson's Bay Company relinquished its control over Rupert's Land in 1869.

During the late nineteenth and early twentieth centuries reduction of wildlife habitat was rapid, until the agricultural fringe reached approximately its present position in the 1920s and 1930s. This position may be reasonably regarded as a stable, for agricultural settlement now covers virtually all suitable land. Many species may be able to survive in the area that remains beyond the agricultural fringe, but this will depend on the proper regulation of hunting and careful study of the impact of mineral and water resource development.

Agricultural settlement significantly reduced many species of wildlife in Canada but also resulted in increases of some species, such as moose, deer, and grouse. To understand this, one must realise that climax coniferous forest is not an ideal habitat for many species, and a change to earlier successional stages may result in the increase of some species. Edwards[10] has demonstrated this effect in Wells Gray Provincial Park in British Columbia. Before 1926 a dense cedar-hemlock forest covered the lower parts, giving way to an alpine forest of spruce and fir with increasing altitude. It supported a mixed wildlife of mountain caribou, black bear, grizzly bear, wolverine, marten, beaver, mountain goats, and mule deer. Fires in 1926, 1930, and 1940 destroyed much of the original vegetation, which was succeeded by willow, birch, and aspen poplar, resulting in marked changes in wildlife species. The mountain caribou herd, which depended particularly on lichens in the ground cover and on lower branches, both destroyed by the fires, almost completely disappeared, as did wolverines and martens. On the other hand, mule deer increased, and moose appeared, encouraged by an abundance of suitable browse, bringing timber wolves in their wake, and ground squirrels also invaded the burned area in large numbers. The net effect of the fires was to reduce species dependent on climax vegetation and to promote these which thrive on lower successional vegetation.

Many forest fires have natural causes but their frequency has been increased by settlement and human penetration into forests. This has been noted in connection with the development of the Canadian Pacific Railway through the Rockies,[11] where fires promoted by settlement caused significant changes in the proportions of various species. The dwindling of woodland caribou populations in response to expanding settlements, for example, has been well documented.[12] This effect was largely restricted to the forest zone, although the importance of fire in connection with bison populations has been mentioned. On the northern margin of the prairies, aspen poplar parkland is an almost permanent feature believed to be a subclimax vegetation type induced by frequent prairie fires. Agricultural settlement there probably did not greatly increase the incidence of fire; lumbering and agricultural clearing were probably more significant causes of successional vegetation changes.

Successional disturbance obviously does not constitute a serious threat to wildlife as a whole because it encourages some species, but it does threaten species that depend on climax vegetation. These are more or less confined to the area beyond the agricultural fringe, in northern and western parts of the country. With the rapid expansion of human activity there for mineral exploration and recreation, the incidence of successional disturbance by fire will certainly increase. Even as early as 1889 this had been noted.[13] Any forest fire which occurs in northern areas in difficult to control because of inaccessibility and lack of labour. The million-acre fire in the Yukon in 1967 and the fire which threatened Inuvik for some weeks in 1969 both show the dangers of forest fires near the edge of the tundra. In tundra areas the surface becomes highly inflammable if it dries out, and fires once started may burn for months underground. This is one hazard that accompanies the construction of oil and gas pipelines. Any significant diversion of water away from these areas could also greatly increase the fire hazard by reducing marshes and shallow lakes.

The effect of fire in reducing the population of barren-ground caribou has been discussed by many writers. Leopold and Darling,[5] working in the interior of Alaska, felt that it was the dominant factor that caused decline of caribou herds, while G. W. Scotter, of the Canadian Wildlife Service, demonstrated the extensive damage caused by fire to both the ground and arboreal forage of caribou herds.[15] Damage to lichens was particularly significant becuase of their slow growth rates and their importance in the winter diet of caribou;[16] seventy to a hundred years are necessary to restore lichen to full abundance after a fire. Although Scotter felt that the destruction of range by fire was not the prime factor limiting barren-ground caribou populations, he believed that it was probably partly responsible for reducing herds to a level at which other factors such as hunting became important.

Predator Control

Several species of wildlife have been subjected to systematic destruction because they prey, or are believed to prey, on either domestic animals or on other species of wildlife. (The function of predator control has already been mentioned in connection with agricultural settlement.) Predators are

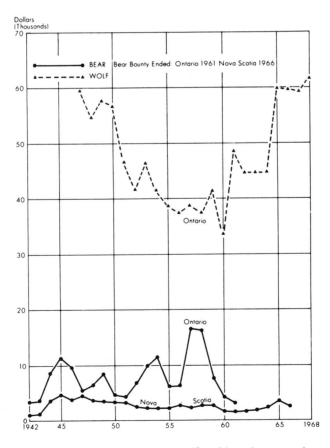

Figure 12.1. Payments made under wolf and bear bounty schemes in Nova Scotia and Ontario. (Source: Annual reports, Department of Lands and Forests, Nova Scotia and Ontario.)

rather like weeds, in that the term may be applied subjectively to any form of wildlife believed to be a nuisance. Reports of hearings in Ontario in 1892 on the identification of vermin which should be destroyed stated that witnesses listed "the names of every bird and animal found in the Province, from the Sparrow to the Beaver."[17] Recent studies along the northern agricultural fringe in Alberta showed a similar difference between the actual damage caused by animals and that which is attributed to them by farmers.[18] Despite wide interpretations of the term *predator,* the most consistent control efforts have been directed at relatively few species, particularly wolves, coyotes, cougars, bears, crows, magpies, and goshawks.

Two basic approaches to predator control have been followed in Canada. The earliest was the "bounty" system, whereby people who kill one of the target species are remunerated. The origins of this system are obscure but it was in use for wolves in the eastern United States in 1630. Pimlott states that in Ontario the system can be traced back to the eighteenth century,[19] whereas in Alberta and Saskatchewan it started in 1899 and in British Columbia in the early 1900s. The chief targets have been the wolf and the coyote (referred to in Ontario as the "brush wolf"). In general the system has proved expensive and somewhat ineffective. In 1951, when virtually all provinces operated bounty systems, the bounties paid in the whole country totaled $180,000.[20] Pimlott notes that between 1900 and 1961 Ontario paid over $1 million in bounties for wolves and coyotes. Between 1960 and 1965 the payments averaged $50,479 per year; 8,662 and 5,355 coyotes were killed.[21]

Because of its cost and ineffectiveness most provinces have abandoned the bounty system as a means of controlling wolf and coyote populations in favour of more highly organised government control systems. Saskatchewan abandoned wolf bounties in 1954, and British Columbia, Alberta, and Manitoba followed suit in 1955. Quebec abandoned them in 1960, although they have apparently been reintroduced locally. Ontario is the only province which retains bounties for wolves, payment being $25 for an adult (over three months old) and $15 for a cub. As Pimlott has pointed out, in Ontario wolves are killed indiscriminately under the bounty system simply because they exist, not because they do any damage. In many parts of the provincial moose ranges the presence of wolves is beneficial as a check to population growth and overbrowsing. (Early in 1972 Ontario terminated wolf bounties.)

A number of provinces also extended the bounty system to cover bears. Ontario operated a bear bounty programme from 1942 to 1961 which provided $10 for each animal over twelve months old and $5 for each cub. During the duration of the programme bounties totalling $149,660 were paid and 15,992 black bears were killed; the annual average was $7,483 and 799 black bears. In 1961 bears were placed under the protection of the Ontario Game and Fisheries Act and classified as big game requiring a hunting licence.[22] In Nova Scotia a similar program was operated from 1942 to 1966; the average annual kill was 228 and the payments $2,494. As in Ontario the programme was terminated by the accordance of big-game status.[23]

The second approach to predator control has been through government-supervised programs of organised poisoning. The chief targets of poisoning have been coyotes and wolves; the most common poisons, strychnine and "1080," which is particularly popular because it is water soluble and is deadly for canine species. Baits are usually dropped from aircraft except in the Northwest Territories, where ground baiting has been more effective.

There is no doubt that the poisoning programme can be effective in reducing populations of wolves and coyotes, but often only at the expense of broadcast and indiscriminate poisoning. Perhaps the most notorious example was in Alberta between 1951 and 1956, when "normal" demands for predator control were reinforced by a rabies scare. During this period 39,960 cyanide guns, 106,100 cyanide cartridges, and 628,000 strychnine pellets were distributed in the province in addition to "1080" bait stations which numbered 800 in 1956. While the programme lasted, an estimated 246,800 coyotes were killed, of which only a minute percentage were rabid. No study was made of the extensive nontarget kills which must have occurred or of the cost-effectiveness of the programme.

A number of authorities now question the whole concept of predator control, or at least the indiscriminate way in which it is practised. Pimlott believes that programmes have been instituted in the past not so much where they were needed but where they were demanded, and cites the case of ranching areas in central British Columbia, where overpopulation of moose has caused extensive deterioration of the range, resulting in incursion onto farmland. Despite the obvious advantages of maintaining a wolf population in the area to control moose herds, ranchers there have steadily demanded poisoning of the wolves. In the mountain national parks the removal of wolves has resulted in overpopulations of wapiti, necessitating periodic culls by park authorities to prevent range deterioration. The effects of overpopulation and starvation of ungulates in Jasper and Banff national parks in the late 1940s can still be observed through tooth marks on the trunks of aspen.

In Arctic and sub-Arctic Canada wolves have been subject to extensive poisoning because of their role as predators on barren-ground caribou. The population of barren-ground caribou has declined dramatically in this century, particularly between 1949 and 1955, when the estimated population dropped from 670,000 to below 300,000.[24] Overhunting by humans was by far the most important cause—responsible for about 56 percent of the decline; wolves were believed to be responsible for 19 percent. Although wolves were not the prime culprits, Pimlott felt that the wolf control programme was justified in this case, for the low levels of the caribou population rendered even this predation significant. He also felt that unless wolves were seen to be controlled, local residents would not cooperate in restricting hunting.

The subject is still controversial, but it is obvious that at least some authorities agree with Dasmann[25] that "the importance of predator control has been oversold," although they might not agree that "it is difficult to find records of any serious studies which show where predator control has accomplished anything of value." It certainly seems that there is sufficient doubt about its value to justify its restriction, at least until more research is completed. The system of massive overkill by indiscriminate poisoning should definitely be stopped, and the use of slow-acting poisons like "1080" in predator control is just as indefensible on humanitarian grounds as the use of leg traps in the fur industry.

References

1. D. L. Allen, *Our Wildlife Legacy* (New York: Funk and Wagnalls, 1962).

2. J. G. MacGregor, "The Impact of the White Man," in *Alberta - A Natural History*, edited by W. G. Hardy, pp. 303–319 (Edmonton: M. G. Hurtig Publishers, 1967).

3. F. G. Roe, *The North American Buffalo*, 2nd edition (Toronto: The University of Toronto Press, 1970).

4. W. A. Fuller, "The Biology and Management of the Bison of Wood Buffalo National Park," *Wildlife Management Bulletin Series 1*, No. 16, Canadian Wildlife Service, Department of Northern Affairs and Natural Resources, 1962.

5. M. Graham, "Canada's Wild Buffalo," Canada, Department of the Interior, Ottawa, 1923.

6. W. A. Fuller, "Aerial Census of Northern Bison in Wood Buffalo Park and Vicinity," *Journal of Wildlife Management* 14 (1950): 445–451.

7. Aldo Leopold, *A Sand County Almanac and Sketches Here and There* (New York: Oxford University Press, 1949).

8. F. K. Vreeland, "Prohibition of the Sale of Game," in *Conservation of Fish, Birds and Game*, Commission of Conservation Canada, Committee on fisheries, game and fur-bearing animals, pp. 93–99 (Toronto: The Methodist Book and Publishing House, 1916).

9. A. Starker Leopold, "Adaptability of Animals to Habitat Change," in *Future Environments of North America*, edited by F. Fraser Darling and John P. Milton (New York: The Natural History Press), pp. 66–75.

10. R. Y. Edwards, "Fire and the Decline of a Mountain Caribou Herd," *Journal of Wildlife Management* 18 (1954): 521–526.

11. J. G. Nelson and A. R. Byrne, "Fires, Floods and National Parks in the Bow Valley," *Geographical Review* 56 (1966): 226–238.

12. A. T. Cringan, "History, Food Habits and Range Requirements of the Woodland Caribou of Continental North America," *Transactions of the 22nd North American Wildlife Conference*, 1957, pp. 485–501.

13. R. Bell, "Forest Fires in Northern Canada," *Proceedings of the American Forestry Congress*, 1889.

14. A. S. Leopold and F. F. Darling, "Effects of Land Use on Moose and Caribou in Alaska," *Transactions of the 18th North American Wildlife Conference*, 1953, pp. 553–562.

15. G. W. Scotter, "Effects of Fire on Barren-ground Caribou and Their Forest Habitat in Northern Canada," *Transactions of the 32nd North American Wildlife Conference*, 1967, pp. 246–259.

16. G. W. Scotter, "The Winter Diet of Barren-ground Caribou in Northern Canada," *The Canadian Field-Naturalist* 81 (1967): 33–39.

17. C. H. D. Clarke, "Wildlife in perspective." Background papers for the *Resources for Tomorrow Conference*, pp. 837–844 (Ottawa: Queen's Printer, 1961).

18. M. C. Jansson, *Farmer response to depredation by wildlife on agriculture in the Athabasca area.* Unpublished M. Sc. thesis, Department of Geography, The University of Alberta, 1970.

19. D. H. Pimlott, "Wolf Control in Canada," *Canadian Audubon* 23 (1961): 145–152.

20. I. McT. Cowan, "Wildlife Conservation in Canada," *Journal of Wildlife Management* 19(2) (1955): 161–176.

21. Ontario, Department of Lands and Forest, Annual report of the Minister, 1966.

22. Ontario, Department of Lands and Forests, Annual report of the Minister, 1962.

23. Nova Scotia, Department of Lands and Forests, Annual report of the Minister (Halifax: Queen's Printer).

24. A. W. F. Banfield, "Preliminary Investigation of the Barren-ground Ground Caribou," *Wildlife Management Bulletin,* Series 1, No. 10 a and b, Canadian Wildlife Service, Department of Northern Affairs and Natural Resources, 1956.

25. R. F. Dasmann, *Environmental Conservation* (New York: John Wiley and Sons, 1968).

Chapter 13

Some Threatened Species

Several of species of Canadian wildlife have suffered decline, but only a few, such as the Labrador duck and the passenger pigeon, have become extinct. However, the populations of some species have sunk so low that their eventual survival is a matter of some doubt. Five species of Canadian mammals are listed in the Red Book of endangered wildlife produced by the International Union for the Conservation of Nature[1] —the polar bear, the Atlantic walrus, the ribbon seal, the black-footed ferret, and the wood bison. To this list the Canadian wildlife Federation adds the Arctic hare, the black-tailed prairie dog, the Vancouver Island wolf, the northern kit fox, the sea otter, the barren ground grizzly, the Newfoundland pine marten, the eastern cougar, the Rocky Mountain bighorn sheep, and the California bighorn sheep.[2] Five species of birds are listed in the Red Book: the Eskimo curlew, the Hudsonian godwit, the sandhill crane, the whooping crane, and the prairie chicken. The Federation adds the bald eagle, the osprey, the prairie falcon, the peregrine falcon, the Ipswich sparrow, and Richardson's pigeon hawk. Among the species listed as endangered are also nineteen reptiles, nine amphibians, and sixteen fish. Some species are seriously threatened on a slightly longer time scale or have recently recovered from the edge of extinction, including the grizzly bear, the barren-ground caribou, the wolf, the musk-ox, the cougar, the trumpeter swan, and Ross' goose.

The decline of these species is a response to various types of stress. The wood bison, for example, is threatened by interbreeding with the remnant plains bison, by poaching, and by disease. The black-footed ferret shares the burrows of the prairie dog and declined following extensive poisoning of its host species with "1080"; killing on roads, shooting, and trapping have also taken their toll. No recent sightings have been recorded in Canada and the species may now be extinct here. The whooping crane is really a Pleistocene remnant, of proven antiquity as a species. Its population declined from about 1,400 in 1860–70 to 23 in 1941,[3] but recovered to about 45 in 1967. Hunting, habitat destruction, and migratory mortality, appear to have been the chief causes of decline. The species is now found wild only in Wood Buffalo National Park and in the Aransas refuge on the west coast of the Gulf of Mexico (the birds winter at Aransas and migrate north in the spring). Because of recent increases there is some hope for survival, particularly as there is a breeding zoo population of ten birds at Patuxent, New Orleans, and San Antonio, Texas, but such a small population allows little safety margin.

Space does not permit a detailed discussion of all endangered species, but some are described as examples.

The Barren-Ground Caribou

There is no complete agreement on the exact number of species and subspecies of caribou found in Canada. All belong to the genus *Rangifer* and are closely related to the European reindeer that are successfully herded by the Lapps in northern Scandinavia. Banfield[4] classifies all Canadian caribou as members of one species, *tarandus,* with five subspecies, of which one, *dawsoni,* appears to be extinct. In this classification the barren-ground caribou is *Rangifer tarandus groenlandicus.*

The barren-ground caribou is well adapted to withstand the severe climate of the tundra and boreal forest where it lives. Its stocky build reduces heat loss and improves the heating efficiency of circulation; its heavy fur provides an effective windbreak and insulation and also provides buoyancy during river crossings. Its hooves are widely splayed for support on soft snow and muskeg and are adapted for shoveling through the snow to the preferred food supply of lichens, mainly *Cladonia* and *Cetraria.* Russian studies on reindeer suggest that the average caribou must eat between 4.5 and 6.5 pounds of forage per winter day to maintain body weight, and much of the winter is therefore spent excavating a food supply. Heavy snow cover can be disastrous, especially if heavy icing occurs.

The caribou winter in the partial protection of the boreal forest. A typical range consists of open black spruce, scattered tamarack, and a dense ground cover of lichens and moss. The extent of the winter range varies considerably but may reach southward almost to Lake Winnipeg and westward to the

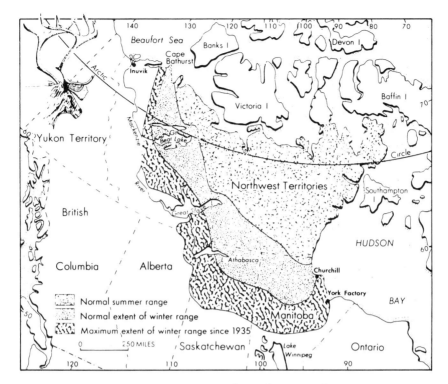

Figure 13.1. Ranges of the Barren-Ground Caribou. (Source: J. P. Kelsall, *The Migratory Barren-Ground Caribou of Canada*, Canadian Wildlife Service, Department of Indian Affairs and Northern Development [Ottawa: Queen's Printer, 1968].)

Mackenzie valley. Around the middle of April the caribou begin to migrate in large herds toward the tundra, although some movement may start earlier. The migration is a purposeful, direct movement which may include the crossing of many miles of void of landmarks. It tends to follow clearly defined routes but varies in detail from year to year. The distance, which ranges from 100 to 800 miles, is usually completed by June, when the calves are born.

Through the summer months movement is irregular and nomadic; the search for food, insects, and weather conditions keep the herds in continuous motion. By late July or early August the caribou start to drift southward to the tree line. The autumn migration is much less purposeful than the spring one, but it gathers momentum during October and November, in the rut season, and terminates in December.

No one knows the size of caribou populations before European settlement and the introduction of firearms. Seton-Thompson's well-known estimate of 30 million[5] is far too large. Estimates based on the carrying capacity of available ranges[6] indicate that a figure of between 1,750,000 and 3,840,000 is more realistic; Kelsall[7] suggests on the basis of available material that the correct figure would be about 3,395,000.

The impact of firearms on the easily hunted caribou has already been quoted, and many records tell of large-scale slaughter and its effects in reducing the number of animals and their range. Hunting was the major cause of decline; the annual kill by man has been estimated at 20,000 as late as 1940. Even at present hunting is often heavy and frequently pointless despite the dramatic drop in caribou populations. Harper[8] reports cases such as that of a trading family at Nueltin Lake who took 500 caribou per year for the use of the family and twenty-three dogs and the finding of many unused carcasses at Duck Lake that had been killed by the local Chipewayans. The effects of such continued slaughter throughout the Keewatin district undoubtedly make tremendous inroads into the population.

The first census, made by aerial survey in 1949, produced a population estimate of 668,000 animals. By 1954 the population had decreased to 278,000,[9] and in the 1957–58 winter the herd was estimated at only 200,000.[10] Hunting was recognised as the prime cause of decrease, but wolf predation and reduction in range capacity by fire were also important. The decline appeared to have reversed as a result of good calving years, reduced hunting pressure, and reduced predation; a range-wide survey in 1967 showed an increase to an estimated population of 385,500. When the data from the 1954–55 survey is reinterpreted according to the methods used in 1967–68, however, the population at that time would have been 390,500.[11] It is therefore believed that the decline of the barren-ground caribou herds is continuing, and commercial exploitation which was started in 1968 on the basis of an apparent increase in population would now appear to be ill-considered, although only 85 carcasses were sold in 1970 for approximately $6,000. A succession of bad calving years combined with heavy snows on the winter range or serious fires could bring the species to the brink of extinction.

Hunting has constituted the main threat to the continued existence of the barren-ground caribou, but hunting bans or closed seasons cannot work effectively over such a vast area without the active support of local residents. It now appears that development associated with resource exploration and extraction may well constitute a greater long-term threat by disrupting ranges and interfering with calving.

The Polar Bear

Until recently it was believed that polar bears all belonged to a single world population that migrated freely throughout the Arctic except during the denning period, but tagging of animals indicates that this is not the case, at least for polar bears in Canada. Five major groups of polar bears appear to exist: Svalbard-Nova Zemlya-East Greenland, Hudson's Bay, Canadian Arctic islands, northwest Canada and eastern Alaska, and western Alaska and eastern Soviet Union.[12] Some zoologists once believed that two species of polar bear

Figure 13.2.   Distribution and major denning areas of Polar Bears.
(Source: R. Perry, *The World of the Polar Bear* [Seattle, Wash.: University of Washington Press, 1966].)

existed, *Ursus maritimus* in the west and *Ursus marinus* in the east, but the distinction was not well documented. Information on the extent of home ranges and the travel patterns of individual bears is limited, but as more tagging information becomes available it should be possible to identify discrete groups in much smaller areas. As information becomes more abundant a lot of guesswork should be taken out of management and conservation programmes for the bears, which have been hindered by the bears apparently extensive migrations.

The polar bear is one of the largest carnivorous mammals; males average 900 pounds in weight and seven to eight feet in length. The main dietary item, particularly during the winter, is seal. As a result, most of the polar bear's year is spent on the drifting open pack-ice of the Arctic Ocean, where seals surface for air. Sometimes the bears penetrate far northward—they have been reported at latitude 88 degrees north—but normally they avoid the area of permanent sea ice. During spring breakup they abandon the sea ice and live on whatever food can be found on land—berries, roots, carrion, or any foodstuff available. The fully-grown male bear remains migratory throughout the year, but the female goes into hibernation in October, usually in snow-covered banks close to the coast. She remains in den until March or April, but the metabolic rate does not slow as it does in some hibernators; the bear will awaken and will possibly appear if disturbed.[13]

Although polar bears essentially form individual family groups, denning tends to be concentrated in certain areas, the most important of which are on Southampton Island in the Canadian Arctic and near York Factory, Manitoba, approximately nineteen miles south of Churchill, where a major denning site was discovered in May 1970. Cubs are born in December and usually remain with the mother for eighteen months.

Records of polar bear hunting date back for many centuries. It was apparently well established by Viking times, and polar bear hides appeared as a trade item during the eleventh century.[14] Trading statistics for the polar bear in Greenland go back to 1793. In early years the impact of hunting on the bear population was probably not severe because of the isolation of the bear's habitat and the danger of hunting such a formidable animal armed only with a spear. With the arrival of firearms the polar bear became extremely vulnerable, as it will stand to defend itself rather than fleeing. In the nineteenth century depletion was severe in association with the Norwegian, Dutch, and Russian whaling industries in the eastern Arctic. Polar bears were essentially ancillary, however, until the whaling industry declined in the mid-nineteenth century. In the sealing industry which followed, polar bears were highly prized, and severe hunting pressure developed in both the European and Canadian Arctic. Even before the turn of the century this resulted in appreciably fewer bear sightings.

At present the main danger to the polar bear is hunting for the fur trade and for trophies. In particular, hunting from aircraft, snowmobiles, and power boats with high-velocity rifles has negated the polar bear's defences of speed and isolation. Another particularly serious cause of decline is the market in live polar bear cubs for zoos; capture of the cubs almost inevitably involves killing the mother. Perry estimates that 1,000 polar bears are in captivity in zoos, most of which have been captured as cubs, and further, that as many as 50 percent of the captured cubs die in the course of capture or during transit to zoos.

The polar bear population appears to have declined alarmingly in recent years; it has been suggested that between 1924 and 1940 the population in the European Arctic was halved, and the United States Wildlife Service believes that the total population has decreased by about 10,000 in the decade 1960–70. As with the caribou, a clear picture of the decline is precluded by a lack of accurate population data due to the difficulty of identifying sightings in a migratory population. The population was placed as high as 17,000 to 19,000 in 1959,[15] and as low at 5,000 to 6,000 in 1961.[16] Against this small population a heavy annual harvest must be set. The latest available estimates[17] indicate that Canada has the largest harvest—about 600 per year—and Alaska has 292, Greenland 100, and Norway about 324, totaling 1,316 animals (which, of course, varies considerably from year to year). Before 1956, when strict controls were introduced, the Soviet Union had an annual harvest of about 120. In view of the indefinite size of the total population it is impossible to know how this harvest compares with the annual surplus, but the apparent decline suggests that it may be too large. It is difficult to plan adequate management for the polar bear until more accurate population data are available from research using marked animals.[18]

Faced with the decline in polar bear populations, the circumpolar countries and representatives of the International Union for the Conservation of Nature and Natural Resources (IUCN) and the Arctic Institute of North American convened an international conference on polar bears at Fairbanks, Alaska, in 1965. This meeting primarily identified a need for further information, but recommended that each country take steps to protect polar bears, particularly cubs and females with cubs.[19] As a result of this conference a major international program of bear tagging and tracking was started. By the time a second conference was held, at Morges, Switzerland, in 1970, approximately 450 marked bears were being traced in the Arctic. All the interested countries have followed the conservation proposals in some degree, although only the Soviet Union has banned all killing.

The Canadian delegation to the 1965 conference proposed the following regulations for Canada:

> 1. That the hunting of polar bears with the aid of any motorised vehicle (for example, snowmobile, motor toboggan, aircraft) be forbidden;
>
> 2. That the number of polar bears taken by one hunter be limited to six per year and that no hunter be allowed to fill the bag limit of another hunter.
>
> 3. That a closed season on polar bears be enforced from May 15 to October 1;
>
> 4. That hunting of mothers with cubs up to two years of age and cubs up to two years of age be forbidden.

In 1967 the government of the Northwest Territories limited the Canadian harvest of polar bears to 422 animals. At this time licences to hunt polar bears could be obtained only by Indians and Eskimos. However, in 1970 the Council of the Northwest Territories at Yellowknife voted to permit natives in two communities, Sachs Harbour and Resolute Bay, to sell their hunting rights to white hunters. The argument is that if the native hunters shoot their quota themselves they are limited in income to the value of the hide, which averaged only $127 for the 1966–67 winter. Under the new regulations they could sell their permits to white hunters for $2,000 and also gain from guiding fees, as the regulations demand that the hunt be carried out by dog sled.

The decision raised considerable protest in Canada and in other countries, which was in some degree an overreaction. The two communities actually have an annual quota of only eighteen bears, and the Eskimos allowed only four permits to be sold. In the first year of the hunt only three bears were killed by white hunters, and the gross revenue to the communities of Sachs Harbour and Resolute Bay was $12,250. It is obvious that the killing of these bears is not going to materially affect the survival of the species. On the other hand, the main justification for permitting the hunting of an endangered mammal is that it is a vital part of the native culture, and this does not justify the sale of hunting rights to a culturally disinterested hunter.

Because of the questionable cultural significance of polar bear hunting there would appear to be reason to ban the hunting of polar bears in Canada and other countries. Native communities can be compensated for lost incomes by grants or preferably by subsidised employment opportunities. It should be realised, however, that a hunting ban could not be effectively policed over the whole Arctic area, although the marketing of furs could be checked. A hunting ban would probably increase the illegal killing of the bears, at present estimated at twenty to forty animals per year.

Hunting is the most serious threat to the survival of the polar bear, but human interference by settlement and resource exploration will have an increasing effect. The arrival of polar bears at drilling sites such as the Pan-arctic camp at Rae Point on Melville Island was referred to in chapter 6. Obviously such incidents will lead to defensive killing of bears, as has happened already at Rae Point. It is difficult to argue with such unlicenced killing, and it is impossible to judge the reality of the danger claimed. A ban on hunting could increase such "defensive" killing.

In Manitoba the juxtaposition of settlements and denning areas has created a real problem of interaction between men and bears. Several incidents have occurred in the vicinity of Fort Churchill, including the death of a boy in 1966 and another in 1968. In both cases the bear involved had apparently been provoked. Careful, enlightened management has so far avoided many incidents, encouraging the hope that settlement and polar bears will not prove to be completely incompatible. The discovery of such an important denning area in a fairly accessible position also poses a threat of poaching while females and cubs are in hibernation. Some protection is essential, and the Manitoba government is planning measures despite the complication of oil exploration leases in the area. Unless such protection is effective, this important part of the polar bear population could swiftly disappear.

The Musk-Ox

The present population of musk-ox, *Ovibus moschatus,* is a relic of a more widespread one which roamed much of North America, the northern Soviet Union, and northern Europe at the end of the Pleistocene glacial epoch.

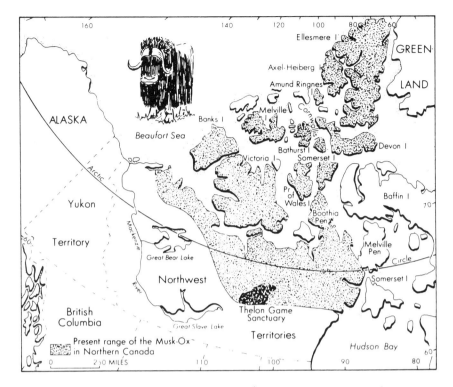

Figure 13.3   Range areas of Muskoxen. (Source: J.S. Tener, Muskoxen, Canadian Wildlife Service, Department of Indian Affairs and Northern Development, (Ottawa: Queen's Printer, 1965)).

The species apparently evolved in Asia and spread to North America via the Bering Strait. It has become extinct throughout most of Europe and Asia and is now found wild only in Arctic Canada, Greenland, Norway, Svalbard, and on Nunivak Island off the coast of Alaska. Herds in the last three locations are descended from transplanted animals.

The musk-ox is one of the few mammals that lives on the tundra throughout the year. It is confined entirely to the tundra, except in the Thelon Game Sanctuary, where the treeline extends northward along river valleys. It is well adapted to survive the harsh climate, with its stocky build, short appendages, and heavy fur. The fur consists of a fine, dense inner layer and an outer layer of long guard hairs; the inner layer is shed in spring and summer.[20] Another adaptation is the slow, deliberate movement by which the animal conserves energy and reduces heat loss. Life on the open tundra requires specialised defensive behaviour, for there is little cover from predators. The musk-ox herd joins in a defensive phalanx, which may be either a line or a circle. The circle, which capitalises on the animals' effective defence against a frontal attack while protecting the vulnerable hindquarters, is particularly common in the presence of wolves. Young animals may be protected in the centre of the circle. Behaviour during blizzards is similar; the adults form a tight wedge around calves, with the lead bull at the apex.

Musk-oxen browse and ruminate, moving almost continually throughout the year. They travel only a short distance, however; seasonal migration is rarely longer than fifty miles and is often much less. The musk-oxen's behaviour is not as regular as that of the barren-ground caribou, and ranges may vary greatly from year to year. Moss and lichen are important in the diet, but many other plants are also used, including willow, ground-birch, Labrador tea, blueberry, and various flowering plants. In winter snow may seriously impede the search for forage, particularly if it is deep and dense or includes many ice layers. It has been suggested that climatic factors may restrict the musk-ox range, for the animals do not thrive in milder areas such as parts of Greenland, where rain and sleet may build up impenetrable ice layers.

Musk-oxen are definitely herd animals, although occasional solitary bulls may be seen. Herds vary greatly in size, sex ratios, and calf-adult ratios. The mating season is in late July and August, preceded by fighting between bulls, which increases in intensity at the height of the rut. Some mortality probably occurs, but accurate data are not available. Gestation is believed to last eight or nine months, with calving in late April and May. Calves apparently are produced in alternate years, although sometimes one will be born every year, a frequent occurrence in captivity. They start to graze within a week of birth, but a strong parental relationship persists for at least a year. High calf mortality occasionally occurs if the weather is bad, but the survival rate to yearling age is generally 50 percent or better.

The musk-ox has been used in the Arctic for many years for food, clothing, and a variety of other purposes, although it was always secondary in importance to the barren-ground caribou. It was also used as a food source by explorers, which apparently resulted in considerable killing, although few quantitative records exist. Musk-ox hides have undoubtedly been in use from an early time, but they first appeared in the fur trade in 1862. Between that year and 1916 the Hudson's Bay Company traded 14,490 hides, the Arctic mainland forming the almost exclusive source area. The returns reached a maximum in the late 1880s, after which a dramatic drop took place, indicating the decline of mainland herds.

Accurate data are not available to show the decline of the musk-ox herds, but in 1930 the mainland herds were estimated at only 500 despite the complete legislative protection given to musk-oxen after 1917. Since 1917 killing has been sporadic, although it is estimated that up to 2,300 may have been killed while capturing calves for zoos or for transportation [21] (this figure applies to the complete population, not just the Canadian or mainland herds). Apparently the most common technique of capture was to shoot all the adult members of a herd. Despite such depredation, mainland herds appear to have increased and are now estimated at 1,500. The largest single group lives in the Thelon Game Sanctuary, set up in 1927 for their protection. All travel within the sanctuary is strictly limited.

On the Arctic islands the population is larger, and it probably never suffered the heavy loss of the mainland herds. The estimated population in 1965 was 8,300, with a distribution as shown in table 13.1.

Table 13.1. Distribution of Musk-Oxen in the Canadian Arctic Islands

Banks Island	100	Bathurst Island	1,160
Victoria Island	670	Melville Island	1,000
Prince of Wales Island	100	Amund Ringnes Island	10
Somerset Island	100	Axel Heiberg Island	1,000
Devon Island	200	Ellesmere Island	4,000
Cornwallis Island	50		

Source: J. S. Tener, *Muskoxen*, Canadian Wildlife Service, Department of Indian Affairs and Northern Development, Ottawa, Queen's Printer, 1965.

A number of islands have no musk-oxen, although evidence shows that their departure from some of these is recent, probably due to deterioration in the range, unusually heavy snowfall, and disease. On some islands, such as Amund Ringnes Island, the populations are so small that they could be very easily extirpated.

Slow recovery of the herds has resulted in their spread into areas from which they had disappeared. The recovery stimulated the Council of the Northwest Territories to propose recreational hunting of musk-oxen by white hunters at $4,000 per animal in 1967. In response to public pressure the proposal was dropped, but in 1969 the ban on killing was raised, and in 1970 Eskimo hunters from Resolute Bay and Grise Fiord were allowed to take twelve animals. A renewed proposal to allow recreational hunting was defeated, but this was again under consideration by the Council of the Northwest Territories at the time of writing. Restricted hunting by Eskimos will probably have little effect on the total population and may be beneficial where the carrying capacity of the range is exceeded. Recreational hunting has no ethical justification, however, and either form of hunting could endanger the species, particularly because killing musk-oxen, who do not run or hide, requires no skill. As Sverdrup observed, "It is plain butchery; it requires little skill and causes no excitement."[22] Despite this there will probably be a ready market for "recreational" hunting.

If the present close control is maintained the musk-ox will probably survive. Some poaching will always take place but a more serious threat than poaching is the disturbance of the animals by oil and mineral exploration. Reports have been made of workers chasing musk-oxen on tracked vehicles. This may not kill or be intended to kill the animals, but it will deplete their energy reserves and reduce the animals' chance of surviving a severe winter. Capture of calves for zoos also poses a continuing threat, although methods have changed.

On the positive side, musk-oxen have been bred and raised successfully in captivity. A number were bred in Vermont by F. Teal following author-ised capture in the Thelon Game Sanctuary in 1954 and 1955.[23] The success of the Vermont experiment led to the establishment of an experimental do-mestic herd at College, Alaska, in 1964, with support from the W. K. Kellogg Foundation. Breeding began in 1966, and by 1970 the original stock of thrity-four had increased to seventy-eight. In 1967 Teal set up another domestic herd at Fort Chimo, Quebec. In 1969 a farm at Bardu in northern Norway was also started, stocked with twenty-five animals captured in east Greenland. The ranched herds are used as a wool source, but eventually a market for meat is a possibility. In the first year of the Fort Chimo operation fifty-eight pounds of wool, or quiviut, were collected from fourteen yearlings and sold for $50 per pound. A mature bull will usually yield about six and a half pounds of quiviut, which is comparable in quality to the wool produced by cashmere goats.[24]

Some people may regret the domestication of yet another species as one more deletion from wild nature, but domestication does provide one of the strongest safeguards against extinction. The development of domestic ranch herds should be sufficient to ensure the survival of the musk-ox, but if it is to survive as a wild part of the northern heritage, maintenance of the present careful control is still essential.

The Grizzly Bear

The grizzly bear has a reputation unmatched by any species in North America and perhaps anywhere in the world. This respect originated long before the arrival of European settlers in North America; the grizzly had an honoured place in Indian folklore as "the animal that walks like a man." Its reputation grew from its great size, its ferocity as a fighter, its depredations on early farmsteads, and its courage when cornered or trapped. Although feared, it has usually also been respected, and this respect appears to have been recipro-cated. Although most grizzlies could kill a man easily with one blow of a paw, relatively few people have been killed by grizzlies. Commonly the victim is mauled, often not seriously. Despite such evidence of forebearance by grizzlies, the species still suffers from the image of a destroyer.

The grizzly is one of the largest of all carnivores, although this claim is confused by the bewildering variety of sizes, shapes, and colours in which the grizzly occurs. In 1918 Merriam classified eighty-four species in North Amer-ica.[25] By 1924 this had increased to eighty-six species and subspecies, and in 1955 seven forms were recognised in Alberta alone. Eventually sanity was restored by Rausch,[26] who classified all grizzlies under one species, *Ursus arctos Linnaeus.* Two subspecies were recognized, *U. arctos horribilis,* the silvertip or plains grizzly, and *U. arctos middendorffi,* the Alaskan brown bear or Kodiak bear. Both are now generally considered conspecific.

The silvertip is found in the northwestern part of the contiguous

United States, western Canada, and Alaska. It used to range widely over the western plains but is now almost completely confined to the Western Cordillera, except in the Yukon and Northwest territories. The species of grizzly which wanders over the tundra in the Canadian Arctic and part of Alaska is sometimes regarded as a separate form, the barren-ground grizzly, which is believed to be extending its range toward the east at present.[27] The Kodiak bear is restricted to southern Alaska, in the Alaskan peninsula and the islands of Afognak and Kodiak; part of the latter is set aside as the Kodiak National Wildlife Refuge.

The classification of grizzlies is still controversial and is rendered more difficult by interbreeding and some overlapping of ranges. The Kodiak bear is generally the largest of the grizzlies and is usually heavier than the silvertip, although exceptionally large grizzlies have been found in the Swan Hills of Alberta, believed by some to be the last remnants of the old plains grizzly population. One of these bears measured ten and a half feet in length; another that was caught in an 850-pound trap dragged the trap for a quarter of a mile before escaping.[28] The average size of the grizzly is appreciably smaller than these giants; the length is usually six to eight feet and the weight around 500 pounds, although bears up to 900 pounds are not uncommon. The heaviest grizzly recorded, taken on the West Coast in 1923, weighed 1,500 pounds; one of the heaviest in recent years was a 1,200-pound bear taken in Tweedsmuir Park, British Columbia, in 1969.

The grizzly varies immensely in colour and shape but is usually medium to dark brown. Silver or white-tipped guard hairs commonly give a silver sheen to the coat, hence the names "grizzly" and "silvertip." The face is often described as "dished" or concave but as Schoonmaker[29] has demonstrated, this feature varies so much that it cannot be used for identification. The best identification is the pronounced hump on the shoulders of the grizzly, which the black bear lacks. Further, a grizzly older than about one year cannot retract its very long claws (often six inches long in spring), unlike the black bear. As a result the grizzly track leaves clear claw imprints. This fact also ensures that the grizzly is a much less efficient tree climber than the black bear, and it is often stated that grizzlies older than one year do not climb trees. However, at least one case of an adult Kodiak bear climbing a tree has been recorded,[30] and it appears that the hindrance is reluctance more than inability.

Grizzlies are usually classified as carnivores, but in reality they are omnivorous; 80 or 90 percent of their diet is vegetable, and predatory activity on wildlife is largely restricted to young or sick animals and to small mammals such as ground squirrels. Of course, once cattle and sheep ranching penetrated into grizzly country the sedentary domestic animals provided a ready source of meat,[31] although relatively few grizzlies prey on domestic cattle. They will feed happily on carrion and there are indications that they prefer matured meat, so that grizzlies have often been blamed for predation caused by other animals. Grizzlies are expert anglers, and along the West Coast, fish, particularly salmon, and seal supplement the bears' protein intake. Ants, grubs, roots, and berries are other chosen foods, and Russell reports that they are not averse to a juicy car battery![32] Whether grizzlies will kill human beings for food is unsettled. I am aware of only one case in which suspicion was very strong—when a hunting guide from Fort St. John, British Columbia, was killed in 1970—and the suspect animal was an old bear in very poor condition.

Mating between grizzlies starts in late May and reaches a peak from mid-June to mid-July. This season is frequently marked by titanic battles between rivals. The usual gestation period is 184 days. The bears go into den in late October in the northern part of the range and in late November on the coast. Dens are usually located on north-facing or shaded areas, so that the snow does not melt and soak the den before the end of hibernation. During the winter the bears go into a deep sleep but not a true hibernation; they have been known to come out for a quick snack during the winter if aroused. The male grizzly usually emerges from the den six to eight weeks before the sow. Cubs are born in January or February and are extremely small, but by the time the sow leaves the den, in April or May, they are quite robust and weigh twenty to twenty-five pounds. Sows usually produce two cubs, but three are not uncommon. The cubs nurse all summer and are not completely weaned until late fall, before they go into den. They will den with the mother for a second winter, and they stay with her until the mating season in the second summer.

It is believed that the grizzly, like the musk-ox, originated in Asia and reached North America during Pleistocene times by a land bridge in the Bering Strait. It spread over most of western North America, particularly in the mountains but also in the plains, where the bison herds provided a ready food supply. There is no accurate evidence of the size of the pristine grizzly population, but estimates have been as high as 1.5 million for the contiguous United States and the population in Canada and Alaska was probably around 1 million. Hunting of the grizzly is probably as old as man in North America, but the earliest record of a grizzly being killed by white men in the plains was on the Kelsey expedition to western Canada in 1691. The early impact of hunting was probably not great, for primitive weapons were not particularly effective against the grizzly. In fact, in California the population appears to have increased considerably after the arrival of Spanish settlers, due to the extensive shooting of other wildlife, which provided carrion for the bears.[33] The real decline in grizzly populations came after the introduction of large-calibre, breech-loading rifles to the western United States in 1848.

This was also the period in which the western states were being opened up for ranching, and conflict with grizzlies resulted. This conflict did not arise until appreciably later in Canada because of the monopoly of the Hudson's Bay Company. Apart from hunting to protect the lives of humans and stock, bears were also hunted for meat and for hides. The impact of hunting was immense, probably because of the relatively low annual birth rate, and by 1950 the total population in the contiguous United States had shrunk from 1.5 million to 856.[34] Their range was a fraction of its former extent; the bears were found only in Idaho, Montana, Washington, Wyoming, and possibly Colorado. After the great decline of grizzly populations in the United States, their main stronghold is now in the mountains of Canada and Alaska. In neither of these areas has an accurate census of grizzly bears been taken. In Alaska the population is estimated at 17,000 to 18,000, an important portion of which is in protected areas such as the Kodiak National Wildlife Refuge and Mt. McKinley National Park. Outside these areas hunting is still active, and in 1966, 856 grizzlies were killed in Alaska.[35]

In Canada the remnant grizzly population is confined to British Columbia, Alberta, the Yukon Territory, and the western part of the Northwest Territories. In British Columbia the population is estimated at 10,000, with an average harvest of 400 to 500 bears. In Alberta the estimated population is around 500; some hunting is allowed, and the yearly kill is twenty-five to thirty. In the Yukon and the Northwest territories, as in Alberta, no accurate estimates exist, but in the Yukon the average annual kill is sixty-two bears. In the Northwest Territories MacPherson has estimated that the total population of barren-ground grizzly is not more than 1,000 and is probably only 500.[36] The estimated kill in the territories is about thirty animals per year. As a result of a 1963 decision of the Council of the northwest Ter-

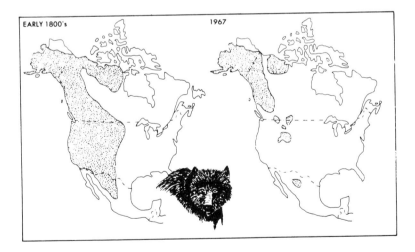

Figure 13.4. Changes in the range areas of Grizzly Bears. (Source: From *The World of the Grizzly Bear* by W. J. Schoonmaker. Copyright, ©, 1968 by W. J. Schoonmaker. Reproduced by permission of J. B. Lippincott Company.)

ritories, this is the only part of their range where grizzlies have no protection whatsoever, apart from the small remnant range of the Mexican grizzly in the Sierra del Nido, north of Chihuahua, where twenty-five bears are believed to exist.

The total surviving population of grizzlies in all range areas is believed to be between 28,000 and 37,000. If this assessment is accurate, the grizzly is in no immediate danger of extinction. It is based on the scantiest information, however, and may be very inaccurate. It is extremely difficult to complete an accurate census of grizzlies because of the extent of their range and frequently its heavily forested nature. Even if the estimate is accurate, a population decline from 2.5 million to around 30,000 in less than two centuries is dramatic.

The status of the grizzly is not immediately serious, except in Mexico, where hunting and poisoning with "1080" endanger it, but there is no cause for complacency. Because of its fearsome reputation there will always be pressure for its elimination, and this will almost certainly increase as developing recreational use of the grizzly ranges in the western mountains leads to greater contact. Like the timber wolf, the grizzly has a totally exaggerated reputation as a threat to man, a reputation greatly increased by the killing of two girls in Glacier National Park in the United States on the same night in 1967. The two incidents were separated by twenty miles and were entirely coincidential, but they were followed by a public outcry against grizzlies. In fact, there are few recent cases of people being killed by grizzlies, although there have been many encounters and a number of maulings. Most of the encounters have taken place in national parks, where the natural instinct of most animals to retreat from man is reduced. In all the national parks in North America, only sixty-six grizzly attacks have occurred this century, nine of these being in Canada, and only five deaths have resulted. The injury rate from grizzly attacks is only one or two per million visitors in national parks.[14] It seems, therefore, that the danger has been greatly overrated.

The future of the grizzly bear depends not so much on protective legislation as on the development of peoples' knowledge and attitudes. If we are prepared to learn about the grizzly, to respect it, and to make some provision for its needs, it will survive. At present we need greater knowledge of the behaviour, territorial needs, and the population of the grizzly. The most hopeful research development is the use of telemetry (radio tracking), developed for the grizzly by the Craighead brothers in Yellowstone National Park,[37] but a much greater expansion of research efforts is necessary.

Wildlife Management and Conservation

The major constraint on attempts to maintain or improve the status of wildlife in Canada is the attitude of the population at large. Unless the majority of the population recognise the aesthetic and monetary values of wildlife and understand the measures necessary for protection, wildlife in Canada will become progressively more impoverished.

There are signs that attitudes are gradually changing, but some species are too close to extinction for gradual changes to be effective. The immediate protection of wildlife in Canada depends on enlightened government action, but this is constrained by existing legislation, administrative structures, and equally important, by limited knowledge. If action is to be effective, it must be based on adequate knowledge of each species' environmental requirements, which can come only from extensive research supported with adequate funds and carried out over a sufficient time period.

The legal background

Wildlife in Canada belongs to the Crown while it is alive, but when dead it becomes the property of the landowner on whose land it falls. This right is rarely claimed, and landowners usually exert their rights only through trespass regulations. In addition, because the bulk of wildlife is on non-agricultural lands, the most important landowner is the Crown.

In Canada the authority of the Crown is divided between federal and provincial governments. The British North America Act does not clearly define the jurisdiction within which wildlife lies, except for coastal and inland commercial fisheries, which are specifically assigned as a responsibility of the federal government. Provincial governments have taken the responsibility for the administration of other natural resources, including wildlife but excluding migratory wildfowl, which ceased to be a provincial responsibliity in 1916. In that year a treaty signed with the United States, the Migratory Birds Convention Act, vested the prime authority over migratory birds in the federal governments. In the Yukon and Northwest territories the federal government is still the prime authority in most matters, but some powers have been vested in the territorial councils. In both territories the government has retained control over lands, minerals, and waters.

All provinces except Nova Scotia have enacted separate legislation to control wildlife, as have the territories. In Nova Scotia the relevant legislation is included in the comprehensive Lands and Forests Act. The extent of control and the type of powers provided by the legislation varies greatly. In Newfoundland broad nonspecific powers are provided, whereas in other provinces, such as Quebec, specific provisions for bag limits and hunting seasons are laid down. As stressed earlier in the discussion of wildlife, it is important that wildlife administration be flexible so that the harvest can be easily adjusted from year to year in relation to population dynamics. Where bag limits and open seasons are defined by provincial legislation this flexibility is lacking, and efficient wildlife management is obstructed.

Provincial wildlife legislation in general is concerned primarily with the control of the harvest, but it also deals with rights of access to private and public land for the pursuit of wildlife. Legislation also provides for the establishment of wildlife sanctuaries and deals with the issuing of hunting licences. Licences differ greatly in number and type between provinces, but in all provinces a distinction is made between resident and nonresident hunters. Some provincial and territorial legislation also makes provision for unlicenced hunting in emergencies, particularly important in the Northwest Territories.

A controversial and legally troublesome problem in wildlife administration is the question of Indian rights. These are derived from a variety of Indian treaties, the status of which is very complex in international law. The situation is further complicated by legal differences between Treaty Indians, non-Treaty Indians, and Métis. The treaties were concluded with the federal government and thus transcend provincial or territorial authority. As a result, most of the wildlife legislation in Canada does not cover Indian peoples. The legal situation is unclear, but courts are generally not prepared to convict natives for infractions of game regulations. This undermines wildlife management and conservation, and the areas most affected are those where wildlife is most endangered.

Administrative structure

The administration of wildlife is carried out in the provinces by provincial agencies, except national parks or Indian reservations. Organisation varies in the degree of decentralisation of authority and the separation of wildlife from other natural resources. As Munro has pointed out, comparison of the efficiency of different systems is almost impossible, because the competence of individual field officers is of paramount importance.

The number of employees actually involved in the administration of wildlife legislation also varies between provinces. In 1968–69 provincial authorities employed 117 scientific personnel in wildlife work and 107 in fisheries. [38] In some provinces employees are shared by several departments and spend only part of their time on wildlife administration. Expenditure also varies greatly between provinces. Ontario and Quebec have the largest shares of the total budget for all provincial authorities, which in 1968–69 was $3,876,000. In most provinces expenditures are balanced or exceeded by the revenue derived from licence sales.

The federal administrative body primarily concerned with wildlife is the Canadian Wildlife Service, a branch of the Department of Indian Affairs and Northern Development. It was formed in 1947 as a research and advisory body with particular responsibility for the study of wildlife problems in the Yukon and Northwest territories and in national parks. It administers the Migratory Birds Convention Act in conjunction with the RCMP and provincial authorities, and the ninety-five migratory bird sanctuaries in Canada, which have a total area of 44,942 square miles. Approximately 200 people are employed by the service, in addition to students employed during the summer.

Research on wildlife

Wildlife legislation and administration must be based on adequate research. In Canada this is done by the Canadian Wildlife Service, the Fisheries Research Board, provincial authorities, and universities, in addition to that carried out under the auspices of international organisations, mostly in connection with fisheries.

The exploratory stage in Canadian wildlife research is complete. Both the species that occur and their general distributions are reasonably well known, but detailed knowledge of distributions and population is sporadic, particularly on a provincial basis. The extent of ranges, the frequently rough terrain, and extreme weather conditions make census taking difficult. Aircraft have been used in census taking, particularly in Arctic and northern areas, but techniques have not yet been developed to their full potential.[39] Research on population dynamics is also of great importance for management purposes, particularly among animals and birds subject to recurrent, apparently cyclic, population fluctuations. Among these are many important game birds, such as the blue and ruffed grouse, and fur bearers, such as the beaver, lynx, and marten.

Research on the physiology and life histories of individual species is well advanced, particularly for waterfowl. Much research on wildfowl originated in the prairie, where the major flyways converge. Recent research of particular significance is the study of waterfowl lead poisoning by the ingestion of lead shot from the bottoms of lakes and marshes. By comparison, research on mammals is patchy. Excellent studies have appeared on the mule deer, the barren-ground caribou, the musk-ox, the moose, and the wapiti, but information is comparatively lacking on the bighorn sheep, the Rocky Mountain goat, the pronghorn antelope, and the cougar, although studies on some of these species are in progress.

Recently considerable research effort has been directed toward range surveys and habitat evaluation, much of which has been carried out in connection with individual species. The whole question of habitat quality is closely related to wildlife management; some impressive examples of wildlife management—the management of muskrat and beaver—have been involved habitat modification. Habitat and range studies are becoming progressively more involved with the question of land use values for wildlife production and the problem of losses incurred through wildlife, particularly by agriculture. The most costly damage is caused by waterfowl feeding on crops. This is important along the major flyways in Alberta, where losses due to waterfowl depredation were estimated at about $6 million for 1968. Considerable progress has been made in reconciling wildfowl needs and agricultural activity, but more research is needed.

The problem of wildlife depredation on agriculture is partly a question of human attitudes toward wildlife. The whole subject of interactions between wildlife and humans, both physical and perceptual, is one that has been largely neglected. We need information on the way in which attitudes are formed and influenced, formed and influenced, and the relationship they bear to physical reality. We need more information on animal behaviour, particularly in connection with hunting. Such studies go beyond the professional zoologist's normal field of study and will require interdisciplinary research, but they may ultimately determine the eventual fate of many species.

Conclusion to Part Four

The current general status of wildlife does not cause concern. The populations of most species are at a reasonable level, providing an adequate safety margin against extinction. Major declines in some types of habitat and in the populations of some species have taken place in the last two centuries in response to the spread of agricultural settlement, but the present situation appears to be stable. Undoubtedly further reductions of habitat will take place, but in scale these should not approach the changes that have occurred in the recent past. The remaining range of habitats and the existing legislative and administrative framework are probably sufficient to ensure that wildlife in general will not decline severely.

While the general situation is satisfactory, a number of species are in a precarious position. They include animals which by character or habitat requirements are incompatible with human settlement, such as the grizzly bear, polar bear, and bison, and those that are vulnerable to heavy hunting pressures and to habitat disruption, such as the musk-ox and the barren-ground caribou. Also included are marine mammals such as the fur seal and the Atlantic walrus, which can be adequately protected only by international agreement. This applies to migratory wildfowl as well, some of which, such as the trumpeter swan, the whooping crane, and the sandhill crane, are dangerously close to extinction. Another endangered bird is the peregrine falcon, which has declined as a result of organochlorine pesticide poisoning.

The legal and administrative situation in Canada is not adequate to ensure the protection and survival of most of these species. For example, it should not be within the power of a local authority, such as the Council of the Northwest Territories, to control the hunting of species like the musk-ox and polar bear, the survival of which is a matter of international concern. The same principle applies to the government of British Columbia, which until recently permitted the removal of peregrine falcons from nesting areas. In the protection of endangered species the authority of the federal government should override that of local or provincial governments. Reallocation of authority would help, although this would not guarantee survival. The federal government, for example, has permitted serious disruption in Wood Buffalo National Park by lumbering and by hydroelectric power development. No evidence has shown ill effects on either bison or whooping crane populations, but it is disturbing that the federal government is not prepared to provide adequate protection to wildlife sanctuaries. In some cases it is prevented from doing so by Indian treaties. Where this may result in the extinction of a species, it is essential that some new agreement be negotiated.

What is necessary in Canada is a recognition that the legislative and administrative framework which is adequate to protect the status of most wildlife in the country is not adequate for some species. Some sort of extraordinary framework applicable only to endangered species is necessary. It should also be realised that provision for policing and protection must be made, even though major logistic and budgetary problems would arise in connection with species like the grizzly bear and barren-ground caribou.

The discussion has so far concentrated on the maintenance of the present status of wildlife. However, many people feel that the time is ripe for a reappraisal of this status. This would involve a more general recognition of the extensive economic and social benefits which can be derived from wildlife in perpetuity if adequate management is permitted. There is also great potential for the development of some species for domestic or food purposes. Throughout much of northern Canada wildlife is a major natural resource, but at present it does not approach the potential which could be realised by management and habitat improvement. The potential for domestication of wildlife is indicated by the success of reindeer herding in Scandinavia and northern Russia. An experimental reindeer herd has been operated in the Mackenzie district of the Northwest Territories, but it has survived only with heavy subsidisation. The domestication of musk-oxen also has great potential, and some successful bison ranches are in operation. In the northern part of Canada wildlife achieve a productivity much higher than that of species currently domesticated [40] and would give a higher food return. This realisation is important in assessing land use in the agricultural fringe areas; in some of these areas the most intelligent land-use practise would be to buy out farmers and to restore the land to wildlife.

Above all, what is necessary in Canada is a realisation that wildlife is not something we have been saddled with, to grudgingly endure or eliminate. Neither is it a luxury to be discarded in times of economic stress. Canada is immensely fortunate in its endowment with a wealthy and abundant fauna. If the endowment is properly managed and provided for, the long-term returns may well prove at least as significant in the national economy as the short-term returns from oil and mineral resources.

References

1. J. Fisher, N. Simon and J. Vincent, *The Red Book, Wildlife in Danger* (London: Collins, 1967).

2. Canadian Wildlife Federation, *Endangered wildlife in Canada,* 1970.

3. R. P. Allen, "A Report on the Whooping Crane's Northern Breeding Ground." A Supplement to *Research Report No. 3 of the National Audubon Society,* New York, 1956.

4. A. W. F. Banfield, "A Revision of the Reindeer and Caribou, Genus *Rangifer,*" *National Museum of Canada Bulletin* (1962): 177.

5. E. Seton-Thompson, *The Arctic Prairies* (New York: C. Scribner, Sons, 1911).

6. A. W. F. Banfield, "Preliminary Investigation of the Barren-ground Caribou, *Wildlife Management Bulletin, Ser. 1,* No. 10 A and 10 B, Canadian Wildlife Service, Department of Northern Affairs and Natural Resources, 1954.

7. J. P. Kelsall, *op. cit.*

8. F. Harper, *The Barren-ground Caribou of Keewatin* (Lawrence, Kansas: University of Kansas, 1955).

9. J. P. Kelsall and A. G. Loughrey, "Barren-ground Caribou Resurvey, 1955," *Canadian Wildlife Service,* Report c, 277, mimeographed paper, 1955.

10. J. P. Kelsall, "Co-operative Studies of Barren-ground Caribou, 1957-58," *Wildlife Management Bulletin, Ser. 1,* No. 15, Canadian Wildlife Service, Department of Northern Affairs and Natural Resources, 1960.

11. G. R. Parker, "Trends in the Population of Barren-ground Caribou of Mainland Canada over the Last Two Decades: a Re-evaluation of the Evidence," *Canadian Wildlife Service, Occasional Papers,* No. 10, 1971.

12. International Union for Conservation of Nature and Natural Resources, "Second Working Meeting of Polar Bear Scientists," 1970, *The Polar Record,* 15 (1970): 348-349.

13. C. R. Harignton, "Denning Habits of the Polar Bear (*Ursus maritimus* Phipps)," *The Canadian Wildlife Service Report Series,* No. 5, Department of Indian Affairs and Northern Development, Ottawa, 1968.

14. R. Perry, *The World of the Polar Bear* (Washington: University of Washington Press, 1966).

15. R. F. Scott, K. W. Kenyon, J. L. Buckley and S. T. Olsen, "Status and Management of the Polar Bear and the Pacific Walrus," *Transactions of the 24th North American Wildlife Conference* (0000): 366-373.

16. S. M. Uspenskii, "Animal estimates in the Soviet Arctic," *Priorda* 8 (1961): 33-41.

17. Anon., "The status of the polar bear," *The Polar Record* 13(84) (1966): 327-336.

18. J. W. Lentfer, "Polar Bear Tagging in Alaska, 1968," *The Polar Record* 14(91) (1969): 459-462.

19. Anon., *The Polar Record,* 1966, *op. cit.*

20. J. S. Tener, *Muskoxen,* Canadian Wildlife Service, the Department of Indian Affairs and Northern Development (Ottawa: Queen's Printer, 1965).

21. F. Bruemmer, 1970, *op. cit.*

22. O. Sverdrup, *New Land: the Norwegian expedition of 1898-1902* (London: Longmans, Green and Company, 1904).

23. P. F. Wilkinson, "The Domestication of the Musk-ox," *The Polar Record* 15 (1971): 683-690.

24. F. Bruemmer, "Muskox Farming," *Canadian Audubon* 32(1) (1970): 5-8.

25. C. H. Merriam, "Review of the Grizzly and Big Brown Bears of North America (Genus *Ursus*)," *Biological Survey, North American Fauna,* Vol. 41, United States Department of Agriculture, 1918.

26. R. L. Rausch, "On the Status of Some Arctic Mammals," *Arctic* 6(2) (1953): 91–148.

27. A. W. F. Banfield, "Distribution of the Barren-ground Grizzly Bear in Northern Canada," *National Museum of Canada Bulletin* (1958): 47–59.

28. J. D. Soper, *The Mammals of Alberta* (Edmonton, Alberta: The Hamly Press, Ltd., 1964).

29. W. J. Schoonmaker, *The World of the Grizzly Bear* (Philadelphia and New York: J. R. Lippincott Company, 1968).

30. R. J. Kramer, "Adult Brown Bears Climb Trees," *Journal of Mammalogy* 35(4) (1958): 588.

31. A. Murie, "Cattle on Grizzly Bear Range," *Journal of Wildlife Management* 12(1) (1948): 57–72.

32. A. Russell, *Grizzly Country* (New York: Alfred A. Knopf, 1965).

33. T. I. Storer and P. T. Lloyd, *California Grizzly* (Berkeley, Cal. University of California Press, 1955).

34. W. J. Schoonmaker, *op. cit.*

35. J. W. Lentfer, "Report on 1966 Bear Studies, Annual Project Segment Report," Alaska Department of Fish and Game, V. 8, April, 1967.

36. A. H. MacPherson, "The Barren-ground Grizzly Bear and its Survival in Northern Canada," *Canadian Audubon Magazine* Jan.-Feb., 1965.

37. F. C. Craighead and J. J. Craighead, "Tracking Grizzly Bears," *Biological Science*, 15 (1965): 88–92.

38. D. H. Pimlott, C. J. Kerswill and J. R. Bider, "Scientific Activities in Fisheries and Wildlife Resources," *Background Study for the Science Council of Canada, Special Study* No.15, June, 1971.

39. D. A. Benson, "Use of Aerial Surveys by the Canadian Wildlife Service," *The Canadian Wildlife Service Occasional Papers*, No. 3, 1962.

40. A. De Vos, "Ecological conditions affecting the production of wild herbivorous mammals on grassland, in *Advances in Ecology*, pp. 137–179, edited by J. B. Cragg (New York: Academic Press, 1969).

Part 5

National Parks in Canada

Cameron Lake, Waterton Lakes National Park. The summit ridge on the far side of the lake is the international border. Some of the point of the International Peace Park has been defeated by the controversial demarcation of the international boundary by a twenty foot wide chemically defoliated zone.

Chapter 14

The Origins and Development of the National Park System

The National Park Concept

The origins of the national park concept are obscure and were probably as diverse as the present purposes of national parks, but one theme underlies the creation of all national parks: the protection or preservation of some facet of nature. The concept of nature preservation is very old. It had certainly evolved by the time the Normans arrived in England in the eleventh century, for nobles and kings protected lands for game preserves and royal forests. The most famous of these, created under William Rufus, still survives as the New Forest. The Norman aristocrats probably had no particular liking for nature or general desire to protect it; indeed, they were probably a little uneasy in natural areas like their successors. Their chief concern was to save their game from poaching commoners.

The general feelings of people toward nature are indicated by Daniel Defoe, who in the late seventeenth century passed through the area that is now the Peak District National Park in England and referred to it as a "barren, howling wilderness." This view of nature appears to have been common until at least the end of the eighteenth century. At that time, however, a reappraisal began to take place, led by such men as Jean-Jacques Rousseau and William

Wordsworth, who believed in an immanent diety in nature. This first appearance in a Western society of appreciation of nature for its own sake rather than for its capacity to produce game was almost certainly a partial reaction against the squalor of the industrial revolution and the ravages of deforestation to build the ships of the Napoleonic wars. The growing feeling for nature in Europe eventually brought results, and a small reserve in the Forest of Fontainebleau, near Paris, was set aside in 1858. This was the result of the action of a group of painters, and the reserve was really an open-air studio rather than anything resembling a modern national park. It was in North America rather than in Europe that the growing feeling for nature developed into the modern national park concept.

The change and destruction of nature in Europe, although accelerated at the start of the nineteenth century, was essentially the continuation of a slow erosion that had been going on for centuries. In North America, particularly in the United States, the change was sudden and dramatic as a flood of settlers swept westward, cutting forests, fencing grasslands, and slaughtering wildlife. It was not long before the destructive potential of man, even in this abundant continent, was realised. Men like George Catlin (in 1832) and George P. Marsh (in 1849) began to call for a readjustment of the relationship between man and nature and for the establishment of nature preserves. The practical result was that in 1864 the Yosemite Valley of California was established as a preserve to protect the scenery and giant sequoias for public use and recreation for all time. This preserve was not formally entitled a national park but was designed to fulfill some of the same functions. The first national park was created in 1872, when an act of Congress established Yellowstone National Park in Montana, Wyoming, and Idaho. The stimulus for this action was partly a forest fire which destroyed 1.5 million acres in Peshtigo, Wisconsin, during the previous year.

The primary purpose of Yellowstone was to protect the geysers and hot springs, although the rich flora and fauna, including grizzly bears, black bears, and plains bison, also benefited. Even at this early stage in the development of the national park concept a diversity of purpose had appeared, although its significance was probably not realised at the time. Catlin and Marsh had been interested primarily in the protection of nature in an undisturbed form as wilderness areas, and this remained an important purpose. At the same time, however, the feeling developed that the protection was for the use and recreation of man, and this was specifically stated in connection with Yosemite. In the United States a third concept also developed: national parks were and are looked upon as part of the American heritage, almost as shrines. This is important, for in this century it has generated a tourist traffic that has some of the elements of a pilgrimage.

The three purposes that developed were in conflict. If the primary purpose was to protect nature, then every effort should have been made to keep human interference to a minimum. The designation of these as recreation areas and as national monuments encouraged visitation, although no one in the nineteenth century foresaw the immense growth in leisure time and recreational demand that would occur in the twentieth century. In the nineteenth century it was believed that recreation was a nonexploitive use of natural land areas and was therefore compatible with the preservation of nature. It is apparent that this is not so—that recreation is instead a form of resource use and exploitation which is sometimes incompatible with wilderness preservation. This incompatibility has arisen in two ways. First, types of recreational activity that have arisen since the nineteenth century are recognisably at odds with wilderness preservation because they require machines or artificial installations. Second, types of recreational activity which were originally thought to be compatible with wilderness preservation, such as hiking, trail riding, and bird watching, have become incompatible simply because of the number of people now involved. As Darling and Eichorn have pointed out, "Even the purest of nature lovers has physical weight and boots on his feet."[1]

The conflict of purpose inherent but unrealised in the establishment of the Yosemite and Yellowstone parks is important, for these were the first parks of their kind and they strongly influenced the development of national parks in other countries. It might almost be said that the establishment of the American national parks defined the term *national park*. In Canada the current concept is identical to that which developed in the United States. Many operational problems which are beginning to occur in our national parks have their origins in the conflicting purposes of this concept. Most of these problems have already been experienced in the United States system, and we can thus learn from the American example and perhaps avoid some of the difficulties that have arisen there. The basic problem is that the concept of the national park developed in the United States is now out of date. Unless we rethink the concept, our national parks system may fail to achieve any of its objectives completely. The concept of the national park appropriate in the United States in 1872 is not necessarily so in all countries, or in any country, a century later.

In some countries the concept of national parks has undergone substantial change. Some countries have strongly emphasised wildlife preservation to the virtual exclusion of other purposes. The national parks of Africa, developed under the influence of the 1933 London Convention for the Protection of African Flora and Fauna, are in this category. On the other hand, in some densely populated countries, such as Japan and Britain, the term *national park* has been applied to areas which include a wide range of human activity, such as urban settlement, industry, and mining. This use of the term *national park* has been criticised, although such criticism negates the significant social value of these parks and neglects an instructive example of the way in which national parks can be operated in areas of dense population. In North America the same principles could be applied to park development in the major areas of settlement concentration, such as the Great Lakes–St. Lawrence basin, with substantial social and recreational benefit.

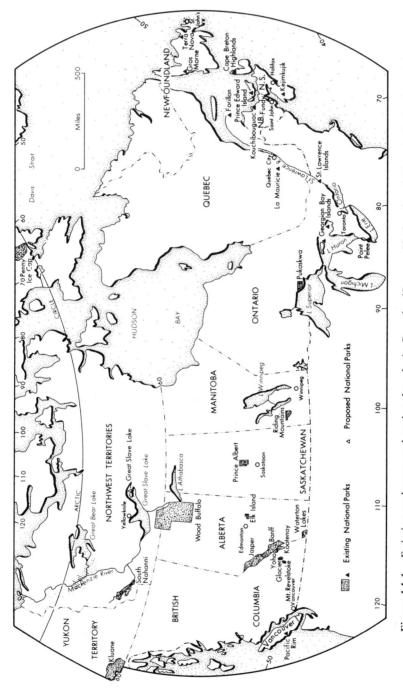

Figure 14.1.   Existing and proposed national parks in Canada. (Source: National and Historic Parks Branch.)

The Development of National Parks in Canada

The official protection of the Yellowstone Hot Springs started a chain of thought, and when hot springs were discovered in Sulphur Mountain, near Banff, Alberta, in 1883, a move was made to protect them. Actually, two enterpreneurial railworkers from Canadian Pacific Railway first saw the potential of the springs and established a log bathhouse at the site in 1884. In 1885, however, an area of ten square miles centred on Banff Station and including the springs was set aside as a reserve by the federal government. It is interesting to note that the prime motive was not protection of nature but the potential "of great sanitary advantage to the public." In 1887 the Banff Hot Spring Reserve was enlarged from ten to 260 square miles and was established as Rocky Mountains Park—"a public park and pleasure ground for the benefit, advantage, and enjoyment of the people of Canada"—by the Rocky Mountains Park Act.[2] It remained the Rocky Mountain Park until 1930, when it was renamed Banff National Park, having by that time grown to an area of 2,564 square miles.

The creation of the Banff Hot Springs Reserve in 1885 was followed by the establishment of two other reserves in 1886 in British Columbia. One was of ten square miles near Mount Stephen in the Rockies and the other a twenty-square-mile reserve in the Selkirks; these formed the nuclei of the present Yoho and Glacier National Parks. Waterton Lakes Reserve was established in 1895 in southwestern Alberta, and Jasper reserve was established in the Athabasca Valley of the Rockies in 1907. All these gained national park status under the Dominion Forests and Parks Act of 1911.

The 1911 act was the first official establishment of a national park system in Canada. Until that date the Rocky Mountains Park had been the only official park, and no specific administration had been established. The 1911 act separated park administration from the Dominion Forestry Branch and established as director a commissioner of dominion parks, paving the way for rapid expansion of the national park system between 1911 and 1930. During this period nine national parks were added to the five in existence, to provide fourteen parks with a total area of 28,668 square miles. The parks currently included in the system are shown in table 14.1.

It was not by chance that most parks created before 1930 are in Western Canada and that most parks created since are in Eastern Canada. It was pointed out in a previous chapter that the British North America Act did not clearly define the jurisdiction of federal and provincial governments over lands and natural resources but that this is now exercised by the provincial governments. Until 1930, however, the federal government retained the jurisdiction in Alberta, Saskatchewan, and Manitoba and in the railway belt and the Peace River area of British Columbia. The federal government was therefore able to establish national parks in these provinces. Because national parks could only be established with the agreement of the provincial government,

Table 14.1. The Canadian National Park System

Park	Province	Area (Square Miles)	Date Established
Banff	Alberta	2,564	1885
Glacier	British Columbia	521	1886
Yoho	British Columbia	507	1886
Waterton Lakes	Alberta	203	1895
Jasper	Alberta	4,200	1907
Elk Island	Alberta	75	1913
Mt. Revelstoke	British Columbia	100	1914
St. Lawrence Islands	Ontario	0.4	1914
Point Pelée	Ontario	6	1918
Kootenay	British Columbia	543	1920
Wood Buffalo	Alberta, Northwest Territories	17,300	1922
Prince Albert	Saskatchewan	1,496	1927
Riding Mountain	Manitoba	1,148	1927
Georgian Bay Islands	Ontario	5.4	1929
Cape Breton Highlands	Nova Scotia	367	1936
Prince Edward Island	Prince Edward Island	7	1937
Fundy	New Brunswick	79.5	1948
Terra Nova	Newfoundland	153	1957
Kejimkujik	Nova Scotia	145	1969
Kouchibouguac	New Brunswick	90	1970
Forillon	Quebec	90	1970
La Mauricie	Quebec	160	1970
Gros Morne	Newfoundland	775	1970
Pacific Rim	British Columbia	160	1970
Pukaskwa	Ontario	725	1971
Baffin Island	Northwest Territories	8,290	1972
Kluane	Yukon Territory	8,500	1972
South Nahanni	Northwest Territories	1,840	1972
East Arm of Great Slave Lake	Northwest Territories	2,860	?

Total 52,890.3

only three parks with a total area of twelve square miles were established in the eastern provinces; two are island reserves in Georgian Bay and the St. Lawrence, and the third is the unique area of Point Pelee, extending into Lake Erie.

In 1930 the federal government ceded control over land resources of the western provinces by the Transfer of Resources Agreeement. Since then, all new national parks have been created by a tortuous system whereby the provincial government must obtain the rights to any area involved and transfer these to the federal government. The system can work only if the federal and provincial governments are in agreement on the principles of national park operation. Several major obstacles to park development have arisen, particularly with the use of natural resources in park areas. Although provincial governments have authority over Crown lands, in most areas resource exploration and sometimes exploitation leases have been sold, and in order to obtain free title to the lands the provincial government must buy back these leases, often at considerable expense. For a number of reasons they are often reluctant to do this. The money derived from lease sales is usually rapidly expended in provincial budgets and is not readily available for lease repurchase. Even if it were, governments are not anxious to lose lease revenues, in addition to the tax revenues and employment associated with resource development. Resource development cannot be accommodated within national parks, for the federal government insists that they be free of such development, although this policy has not been consistently followed in the past, and some contradictions still exist.

Timber-cutting leases in Wood Buffalo National Park were sold to the Swanson Lumber Company of Edmonton, and they will not expire for another hundred years. The cost of lease repurchase is estimated at $3 to $5 million. Instead of repurchasing the leases, the National Parks Branch has suggested that the national park boundaries be redrawn to exclude leased areas, where trees have been removed by clear cutting without any attempt at reseeding. This raises doubt about the ability or will of the National Parks Branch to protect parks against development pressure, it compromises the principles on which the Canadian national park system rests, and weakens the negotiating position of the federal body in attempting to set up new national parks free of resource exploitation.

The loss of revenue that would be derived from resource exploitation has deterred provincial governments from attempting to set up new national parks, particularly in the poorer Atlantic provinces. Difficulty in achieving agreement on the status of resource development in parks delayed the opening of Forillon National Park in Quebec until 1970 and is currently delaying the opening of Gros Morne National Park in Newfoundland. This was originally scheduled for 1972 but will now probably take place in 1973.

The history of the development of Gros Morne in the Bonne Bay area of western Newfoundland is an unfortunate example of the difficulty of establishing new national parks. Discussions have been proceeding since 1965 but have been persistently hampered by a lack of cooperation from the provincial government. (The history of these discussions has been thoroughly examined by Pruitt.) [3] The former Newfoundland government was reluctant to include any area with even the most remote potential for resource exploitation with the park, which made it difficult to map out coherent area for park development. The provincial government offered a series of small areas, none of which was sufficiently large to be ecologically viable. The problem of buying back oil exploration leases granted in 1951 and 1952 to Bison Petroleum and Minerals, Ltd., was also raised, but the federal government offered financial assistance in this repurchase. Another bone of contention was the manner in which the park would be operated. The National Parks Branch wished to establish the area as essentially a wilderness, whereas the provincial government wanted it as a recreational playground. Throughout the negotiations the Newfoundland government displayed a total lack of appreciation of the objectives of national parks or of the social benefits which can be derived.

All provincial governments have not been as uncooperative as the former Newfoundland government, but in general they have been reluctant to hand over control of any provincial territory to the federal government unless it has been thoroughly explored and found deficient in potential resource development. This is particularly manifest in Alberta, which contains a greater area of national land than all other provinces combined. Not only is the provincial government reluctant to hand over control of more provincial land to the federal government but steady pressure has been maintained on the federal government to relax its control over existing national parks. In the past this has concerned primarily Jasper and Banff National Parks, where it is claimed that the National Parks Branch policy is impeding the Alberta tourist industry. Several suggestions have been put forward, including the removal of Jasper and Banff townsites from the national parks and the creation of provincially controlled transportation corridors. More recently pressure has also developed against Wood Buffalo National Park, which, it is claimed, impedes the development of important resources, particularly gypsum deposits at Peace Point.[4] The return to the provincial government of the portion of the park which lies within Alberta is being pressed.

The federal government retains its control over Crown lands only in the Yukon Territory and the Northwest Territories, and those areas therefore offer the best opportunity for the establishment of new national parks. The only legal obstacle is the need to retain Indian and Eskimo hunting rights that were established under the British North America Act. There is also strong opposition to the establishment of national parks by local inhabitants, mining companies, and oil companies, who fear that national parks will restrict not only resource development but exploration as well. Opposition has also come from hydroelectric power development corporations that are interested in the potential of some northern rivers. As a result, no national park was created in northern Canada between 1922, when Wood Buffalo National Park was established, and 1972, when three new northern parks were announced.

Full details of the parks had not been released at the time of writing. The largest park will be in the Yukon Territory and will have an area of 8,500 square miles. This borders the Alaska Highway and Kluane Lake and encompasses a large portion of the St. Elias Mountains, including 19,820-foot Mt. Logan, the highest peak in Canada. The park will protect part of one of the largest nonpolar ice fields in the world and will provide sanctuary to a wide variety of wildlife, including the golden eagle, the grizzly bear, and the Dall sheep. The Baffin Island National Park—8,290 square miles in the vicinity of Pangnirtung on the Cumberland Peninsula—encloses the 2,200-square-mile Penny Ice Cap and surrounding tundra areas and also protects fiords where whale, walrus, seal, and narwhal are found. The establishment of the third park on the South Nahanni River culminated a long struggle between conservationists and power developers. The 1,840-square-mile park reserves one of the most dramatic and challenging rivers in North America, including Virginia Falls— over 300 feet high, a gorge known as Hell's Gate, and a canyon nearly 4,000 feet deep. It is also an area with an intriguing and mysterious history of exploration—several explorers have died in the Nahanni and their bodies were found headless. The Nahanni is also inevitably associated with Albert Faille, of Fort Smith, who at an age when most men are comfortably retired made annual solitary and extremely arduous journeys up the river in search of gold. By any standard the Nahanni park is a major asset to the park system, even though the area reserved is smaller than recommended by an ecological survey.

A reserve of 100 square miles is also being considered in the Mackenzie delta, and a core area of 2,860 square miles has been reserved to form the nucleus of a national park to include Artillery Lake and part of the East Arm of Great Slave Lake.[5] This park would cover the transition from the boreal forest to the tundra and would encompass some magnificent scenery, including the scarp of the McDonald Fault and Christie Bay, which is the deepest fresh-water body in North America. It includes one of the most important nesting sites for the bald eagle in North America and supports a range of small mammals and several larger species, such as wolves, black bears, moose, and caribou.

Opposition to the Slave Lake park has come from mining concerns that are interested in possible wealthy mineralisation along the McDonald Fault, which is the structure associated with the lead and zinc deposits of Pine Point. Occurrences of copper, uranium, nickel, silver, and cobalt are all known in the area, and the announcement of plans to create a park triggered a claim-staking rush. The core reserve was eventually established in the area of least mineralogical interest. Indians of the adjacent area of Snowdrift also opposed the park because it would interfere with hunting areas. This problem has not been solved but has been temporarily circumvented by allowing hunting in the area to continue until the park is officially designated—postponed until a road is built from Pine Point, which is expected to take five years. A similar problem in the Nahanni was solved by safeguarding the hunting rights, so that the temporary solution may well become permanent.

Great progress has recently been made in extending the national parks system; with the three new northern parks and Pukaskwa in Ontario, all established in 1971, a total of nine parks have been established in the 1970s. (Announcement of a third national park in Nova Scotia is expected in late 1972.) Nevertheless, the park system is still far from complete, particularly in Ontario, Quebec, and the prairies. Obviously the establishment of new national parks will be slow in the future unless great changes take place. There is little realistic possibility of gaining the additional forty to sixty national parks in Canada by 1985, suggested as an objective by the minister of Indian affairs and northern development in 1968.[6]

Development of a Canadian National Park Policy

Canadian national parks have existed for almost ninety years, longer than in any country except the United States, and inevitably national park policy and its interpretation have undergone changes. Inasmuch as the present system and some of its problems are a legacy of earlier policies, we should examine the major changes in some detail.

As already stated, the Banff Hot Springs Reserve was established in the interests of sanitation rather than from a zeal for wilderness preservation or recreation. Apparently it was the only place where workers of the Canadian Pacific Railway could conveniently get a hot bath. The significance of the reserve was not, however, restricted to local utilitarian interests. The government of John A. MacDonald was firmly committed to a policy of developing western Canada as a means of cementing the newly established Confederation. The link in this policy was a transcontinental railway, which had been demanded by British Columbia as a condition for joining the Confederation. The government borrowed heavily to construct the Canadian Pacific Railway and narrowly survived a number of crises in parliament. The development and expense involved could not be justified to MacDonald's supporters (or his opponents) on the nebulous grounds of wilderness for nature preservation; abundant supplies of exploitable natural resources formed the collateral.

The most important keys to the national parks policy under which the early parks were established are the Rocky Mountains Park Act (1887) and the House of Commons debates associated with the passage of the act. (These are examined and discussed in an excellent study by Brown.[7]) The primary purpose of the act appears to have been provision of a legal framework for resource exploitation--the tourist potential of the hot springs—rather than nature protection. The park centred on the springs was to be a fashionable watering place and tourist centre, on par with the spas of Europe. Not only was wilderness preservation ignored but in the debates it became clear that some people felt that the reserved area constituted only the raw material for a park which would subsequently have to be developed. This concept of a developed park had little to do with the ideals of Catlin or Juhn Muir and seemed closer to the eighteenth century English and French concept of a landscaped estate park complete with elegant buildings and formal gardens. The townsite which developed around Banff Station was a planned community, and its rapid growth was encouraged.[8]

The development of a profitable, fashionable resort was the primary objective of the act, but other forms of exploitation were also envisioned, although they were opposed in the parliamentary debates on the bill. Provisions were made for lumbering, grazing, and mining. Coal mining had started before the formal creation of the park, at Anthracite, near Banff. In addition to the impact of the mine operation itself, lumbering for pit props also appears to have been of some importance. Mining continued at Anthracite until 1904, when it became uneconomical. In the same year a new mine was opened at Bankhead, near Banff. Far from being regarded as a blot on the landscape, these mines were regarded by some as added attractions. The superintendent of the park reported:

The new village of Bankhead, instead of being a detriment to

the beauty of the park will, on the contrary add another to
the many and varied attractions of the neighborhood. [9]

Opinions have changed, especially since the Bankhead mine closed in 1923, but it is interesting to note that the mine is still listed as an attraction in the current Banff National Park brochure.

A small copper mine existed at Silver City, between Banff and Lake Louise, until 1886.[10] Metallic ore mining also developed in Yoho National Park; the Monarch lead mine started operations on the slopes of Mount Stephen in 1893. In Jasper National Park small coal mines were operated from 1911 to 1920 at Pocahontas and Miette. Lumbering, quarrying, and dam construction for hydroelectric power also appeared in some parks. In a number of cases, leases for resource extraction were sold, although exploitation did not take place until much later, after significant changes in park policy had occurred. The best example is the lease for the Kicking Horse lead mine in Yoho National Park, granted in 1910. The mine did not come into production until 1941, and the lease was eventually bought out in 1958. Timber leases were also sold in Glacier, Yoho, and Banff national parks, some of which have been bought out or have expired only within the last few years.

The dominant theme of the national parks policy in the early years was therefore resource exploitation, and the Canadian national park concept evolved to resemble that of the United States by a somewhat different route. Certainly the parks were controversial even during this period, but the clash was not between preservation and exploitation, but between exploitation for tourism and that for minerals or timber.

The next significant development in national parks policy was the passage of the Dominion Forest and Reserves Parks Act in 1911. During the intervening years public ideas had changed considerably in North America. The mainspring of this change was the first conservation movement, which developed in the United States in the 1890s. It started as a reaction against the destruction of natural areas but developed into a social and political movement of far-reaching significance, albeit with nebulous ideals. It soon evaporated in controversy, particularly between John Muir and Gifford Pinchot, but before it did so new ideas and some practical conservation activity were generated. These ideas must certainly have influenced Canadian thought even before the Canadian representation at the 1909 North American Conservation Conference in Washington. The Dominion Forest Reserves and Parks Act of 1911 was primarily designed to reorder the administration of the Dominion forest reserves, which was placed under the authority of a commissioner of Dominion parks. The first commissioner under the act was J. B. Harkin, who was to become the most important figure in Canadian national parks history.

The purpose of the act was mainly administrative reorganisation, but it also represented a change in policy—a gradual evolution from exploitation toward protection. Resources would still be exploited and leases would be respected, but control would be stricter. Use for recreation and preservation to that end were now of paramount importance. With regard to recreation, however, an important point was established during the debates on the bill:

> *It is not proposed that these parts of reserves set aside for purposes of recreation shall be primarily places of business. There will be no business there except such as is absolutely necessary for the recreation of the people.*

The effects of this change in emphasis were not immediately apparent, for Harkin embarked upon a policy of attempting to attract tourists to the parks in large numbers. Encouragement may not have been necessary, for between 1897 and 1912 annual visits to Banff had increased from 3,000 to 73,725. Harkin's policy was a recognition that the national park system could survive at that time only if it could be shown to be self-supporting. Criticism of government expenditure during the debates in 1887 had been diverted only by the claim that such investment would be profitable. Harkin was certainly not the first person to realise that recreation had a commerical potential, but he was one of the first to realise its magnitude:

> *Mountain parks are worth 300 million dollars per year to the Canadian people.* [11]

It would be a complete injustice to suggest that Harkin had little appreciation of nature or the aesthetic aspects of national parks. In fact, he was vitally interested and concerned in the preservation and protection of the parks, and it was largely through his influence that wilderness conservation became an important function of national parks. His views are indicated in a paper written in 1918:

> *National parks are reservations of the wilderness—the most beautiful areas in our country. They constitute a national recognition of the necessity for recreation; they afford our people unique facilities to satisfy their instinct for recreation; they provide those charms of beauty and grandeur which enchant and stimulate the imagination and the soul; they throw open to everyone opportunities for satisfying that persistent, subconscious desire for getting in touch with the mysteries of the wilderness.* [12]

In this and other writing,[13] Harkin leaves little doubt that he regarded recreation in its original meaning of re-creation.

The rapid expansion of the national parks system under Harkin's administration ended in 1930. In that year the Transfer of Resources Agreements were completed and the National Parks Act—still the basic legislation

under which parks are administered—was passed. The policy established in the
act is the product of the interaction of Harkin's ideas and the 1911 act, shown
by Section 4 of the National Parks Act:

> *The parks are hereby dedicated to the people of Canada for*
> *their benefit, education and enjoyment, subject to the pro-*
> *visions of this Act and the regulations, and such Parks shall*
> *be maintained and made use of so as to leave them unim-*
> *paired for the enjoyment of future generations.* [14]

Although the emphasis in national parks policy had definitely
changed to one of preservation or nonimpairment, in fact the wording of the
act allows too much scope for interpretation—the emphasis can be varied to
justify almost any course of action. At the same time, extensive powers were
given to the governor-in-council to establish regulations, to grant permits
for grazing and lumbering, and to grant certain leases. Substantial powers of
enforcement were given to park wardens and officers, but these powers, like the
penalties available to magistrates trying offenses under the act, are not manda-
tory and are somewhat less than effective.

Despite the change of policy to one of nonimpairment, existing
leases were honoured by the 1930 act, as shown in the case of the Kicking Horse
mine. However, it is not easy to understand how the granting of new leases
after 1930, such as the timber leases in Wood Buffalo National Park, could be
justified. The 1930 act was so open to misinterpretation, either willful or
accidental, that it became necessary for the National Parks Branch to clarify it
by a statement announced in the House of Commons in 1964. The first provision of the statement is that:

> *National Parks are established to preserve for all time the*
> *most natural and outstanding features of Canada for the*
> *benefit, education, and enjoyment of all Canadians as a part*
> *of their natural heritage. They are dedicated forever for one—*
> *to serve as sanctuaries of nature for rest, relaxation and en-*
> *joyment. No exploitation of resources for any purposes is*
> *permitted. All development must contribute to public enjoy-*
> *ment and conservation of the parks in a natural condition.*

A second provision of the 1964 statement, which is of great importance, is that:

> *National Parks cannot meet every recreational need; the most*
> *appropriate uses are those involving enjoyment of nature*
> *and activities and experience related to the natural scene.*

This principle was elaborated and further clarified in a comprehensive declara-
tion of national parks policy issued in 1969, which states that:

*Each park has been set aside primarily to preserve for all
time, representative samples of the country's terrain, which,
by reason of outstanding physical or historical qualities, have
national significance.*

*Our obligation to protect the areas against impairment implies
not only protection against private exploitation, but also
guarding against impairment by overuse, improper use and
inappropriate development.* [15]

The statement continues:

*Provision of urban-type recreational facilities is not part of
the basic purpose of National Parks.*

The official national parks policy is therefore clearly one of preservation; all other objectives are subsidiary. In practical application, however, the statement recognises that national parks in Canada serve a diversity of purposes which sometimes conflict. It comments specifically on the fact that this problem is perpetuated by a park system which does not adequately cater to such diversity of purpose but restricts classification to two categories, national parks and national historic parks and sites.

References

1. F. F. Darling and N. O. Eichorn, *Man and Nature in the National Parks: Reflections on Policy* (Washington D. C.: The Conservation Foundation, 1967).

2. J. I. Nicol, "The National Parks Movement in Canada," in *The Canadian National Parks: To-day and To-morrow*, edited by J. G. Nelson and R. C. Scace, pp. 35–52, Studies in Land Use History and Landscape Change, National Park Series No. 3, University of Calgary, 1969.

3. W. O. Pruitt, "The Newfoundland National Park Potential," *The Canadian Field-Naturalist* 84(2) (1970): 99–115.

4. A. O. Fimrite, "Wood Buffalo National Park," brief presented to the Legislative Assembly of the Province of Alberta, March 1970.

5. P. G. Kevan and L. N. Evernden, "A National Park for the Northwest Territories — the East Arm of Great Slave Lake and Artillery Lake," *The Canadian Field-Naturalist* 83(2) (1969): 169–172.

6. J. Chretien, "Our Evolving National Parks System," in *The Canadian National Parks: To-day and To-morrow*, edited by J. G. Nelson and R. C. Scace, pp. 7–14, Studies in Land Use History and Landscape Change, National Park Series No. 3, University of Calgary, 1969. pp. 7–14.

7. R. C. Brown, "The Doctrine of Usefulness: Natural Resource and National Park Policy in Canada, 1887–1914," in *The Canadian National Parks: To-day and To-morrow*, edited by J. G. Nelson and R. C. Scace, pp. 94–110, Studies in Land Use History and Landscape Change, National Park Series, No. 3, University of Calgary, (1969).

8. R. C. Scace, *A Cultural Historical Study of Land Use and Management in a National Parks Community to 1945*, Studies in Land Use History and Landscape Changes, National Park Series No. 2, University of Calgary, 1968.

9. Annual report of Park Superintendent. Quoted by A. R. Byrne in, "Man and Landscape Change in the Banff National Park Area Before 1911," unpublished M.A. thesis, The University of Alberta, Calgary, 1964.

10. S. B. Jones, "Mining and Tourist Towns in the Canadian Rockies," *Economic Geography* 9(4) (1933): 368–378.

11. J. B. Harkin, "Conservation is the New Patriotism," typescript, Sept. 1st, 1922, Library of the Department of Indian Affairs and Northern Development, Ottawa.

12. J. B. Harkin, "Our need for national parks," *Canadian Alpine Journal* 9 (1918): 98–106.

13. Department of Northern Affairs and Natural Resources, *The Origin and Meaning of the National Parks of Canada: Extracts from papers of JR. Harkin* (Saskatoon: H. R. Larson Publishing Company, 1957).

14. Department of Northern Affairs and Natural Resources, National Parks and Historic Sites Services, *The National Parks Act,* Consolidated for Office Purposes (Ottawa: Queen's Printer, 1955).

15. Department of Indian Affairs and Northern Development, National and Historic Parks Branch, *National Parks Policy* (Ottawa: Queen's Printer, 1969).

Chapter 15

Problems and Conflicts in the National Parks

The previous chapter showed how the Canadian national park system originated and how it has evolved in response to changing ideas and pressures. Some of the purposes for which the parks were established, such as mining and lumbering, have clearly evolved out of national park policy, but sufficient diversity of purpose remains to ensure that a national park is a compromise. Some problems involved in the operation of national parks originated in this diversity of purpose; others have been caused by external changes. By far the most important problem at the present time is the dramatic rise in visitor attendance in recent years.

Visitation to National Parks

Between 1957 and 1970 visitation to Canadian national parks increased from 3,529,976 to 13,605,049, an increase of 288 percent. The biggest increase took place in the decade 1957-67, during which visitation rose 222 percent, or 22 percent per year. Between 1956 and 1966 the total population of Canada increased by only 24.5 percent, so the increase in visitation to national parks cannot be explained by population increase alone. In fact, the increase is not an exclusively Canadian phenomenon or one confined to national parks. Participation in all forms of recreation has increased in many countries since the Second World War, but nowhere more dramatically than in North America. The impact of this increase has been felt particularly in national parks, but it is affecting all types of recreational facilities.

Many factors have caused and influenced this sudden rise in demand, but the most important are increases in population, income, leisure, and travel. The increase in population has certainly been important, but as pointed out, it has been less rapid than the increase in visitation. An increase in leisure time has also been significant. Over the past hundred years the average work week in Canada has almost halved, and the amount of leisure time has grown by about 300 percent.[1] However, the increase in leisure time during the period in question has been only about 14 percent and can therefore explain only a relatively small part of the increase in visitation.

Affluence, or spending power, in Canada has undoubtedly increased despite persistent inflation and between 1957 and 1967 the personal expenditure on consumer goods and services grew from $15.6 billion to $37.7 billion, an increase of 141.7 percent. Obviously a general increase in affluence affects the amount of money available for expenditure and recreation, although we do not know to what extent.

A fourth major factor is the greater mobility of the Canadian population since the Second World War—a response to many factors, including cultural changes and changes in personal incomes. Two important factors have been general improvement in road networks and increasing ownership of cars. Road construction has traditionally been a provincial responsibility, but the federal government is becoming more involved in joint road construction and paving projects. Two of the most important roads, from a national parks point of view, are the Trans-Canada Highway and the Yellowhead Highway, neither of which is yet complete. (The sections through the Western Cordillera were opened in 1962 and 1969, respectively.) Increasing car ownership has also changed recreation patterns. Between 1958 and 1967 the total number of motor vehicles registered in Canada rose from 4,723,825 to 7,495,203, an increase of 56.7 percent. Ownership of private cars during the period increased from 3,572,963 to 5,876,691, 64.5 percent; the average number of persons per car decreased during the same period from 5 to 3.5.

Increases in leisure time, population, affluence, and mobility explain much, but not all, of the rise in national park visitation; many other factors are involved. One of the most important factors is the emergence of the recreation equipment industry, which has been particularly concerned with downhill skiing, in which participation has grown at a startling rate. Another factor is the extensive advertising coverage of national parks, which originated in early attempts to make the national parks self-sufficient and in the efforts of the Canadian Pacific Railways to promote its hotels at Banff and Lake Louise. Between 1930 and 1933, before the formation of the Government Travel

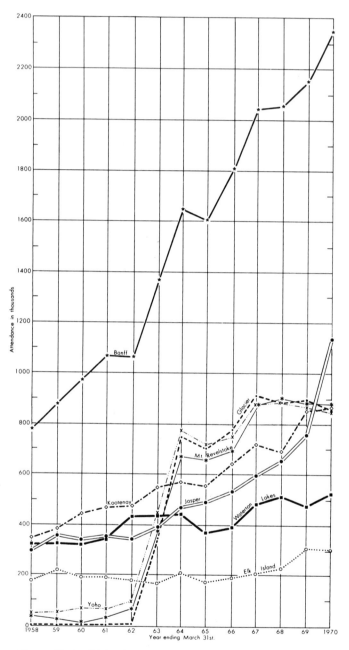

Figure 15.1. Visitation to Canadian national parks. (Source: Dominion Bureau of Statistics).

Figure 15.2.   Visitation to Canadian national parks, II.

Bureau, the National Parks Branch functioned in part as a federal tourist agency. At present advertising is carried out primarily by Canadian National Railways and Canadian Pacific Railways and by various provincial travel bureaus.

Two other factors have been significant. Public controversy has increased environmental awareness and has probably stimulated the desire to see natural areas, and Canadian national parks are being increasingly used by foreign tourists, particularly Americans. Part of the increased visitation to Canadian national parks has thus originated because of social factors and pressures outside Canada, including the increasing overcrowding of the American national parks. This influence has been felt mainly in the western national parks. It is not hard to visualise that overcrowding at Yellowstone, for example, could result in a diversion of visitors northward to Banff.

All these factors have contributed to the recent increase in national park visitation, but they have not all been important in every area. Comprehensive information on visits to different parks has been readily available only since 1958, but even the records of this comparatively short period indicate differences between parks. The major increase in park visitation has taken place primarily in the western mountain parks. Most important in terms of numbers has been Banff, where visitation increased from 790,910 in 1958 to 2,303,852 in 1970, an increase of 190 percent. The most dramatic increase, however, has been in Glacier National Park, where visitation increased from 222 to 885,947 during the same decade. The increase was partly a reflection of a general increase in movement to parks and was reproduced on a smaller scale by Fundy, Cape Breton Highlands, and Prince Edward Island national parks in the east. In the east, however, the increase was slower and more diffuse, spreading over the complete decade. In Banff, Yoho, Glacier, and Mount Revelstoke national parks the increase was concentrated particularly in 1962–63 and 1963–64, following the opening of the mountain section of the Trans-Canada Highway, which passes through these parks. This traffic indicates the demand for such a highway, but it is not such a clear demonstration of a demand for national parks, because it is difficult to separate park visitors from other traffic on the highway. The data do suggest that some of the increase was caused by curiosity to travel over the new road, for visitation in these parks declined slightly in 1964–65, after the novelty wore off.

Among the western mountain parks, Kootenay, Waterton Lakes, and Jasper were not greatly affected by the opening of the Trans-Canada Highway. This is readily understandable in the case of the last two, but it is interesting to note how few of the people passing along the Trans-Canada Highway diverted down the Banff-Windermere Highway to Radium Hot Springs. During the decade 1958–68 Kootenay and Jasper both showed approximately the same increase in visitation; Kootenay's increase was 97 percent and Jasper's 96 percent. Although these increases are much lower than in some other parks, they are still greater than can be explained by a population increase alone. After showing a steady but undramatic increase during the previous decade, Jasper's visitation suddenly rose from 652,186 in 1967 to 1,135,558 in 1969–70, an increase of 74 percent. This again reflects the importance of the opening of a major paved highway, the Yellowhead Highway.

Waterton Lakes showed a more modest increase during the 1958–68 decade—only 66 percent. This mountain park is equal to the other mountain parks in scenic and wildlife attractions and facilities, so the much lower increase must reflect the park's isolation from major highways. Waterton Lakes Park still seems to serve a primarily local recreational demand. Other national parks which cater to a primarily local demand, such as Riding Mountain and Prince Albert national parks, also showed comparatively minor increases over the decade. Several parks function essentially as provincial or even municipal resort parks, such as Elk Island, which acts almost as a municipal park for Edmonton. The Georgian Bay Islands and St. Lawrence Islands parks also serve a primarily local function. In both cases increases in visitation have been moderate because the parks are small and they must be reached by boat. Restricted size has also limited the increase of Point Pelée to 21 percent, slightly less than the population increase for the decade. Only two other parks were in existence for the complete decade. Of these, Terra Nova has supplied visitor returns from 1961–62. In the seven-year period, the increase has been over 1,300 percent, and the rate of increase is steepening. The other, Wood Buffalo, does not supply visitor returns, but visitors almost certainly number below 1,000 per year.

The Impact of Increasing Visitation on Roads and Accommodation

It is obvious that although the national parks system as a whole is experiencing rapid increase in usage, the brunt of this increase is falling on relatively few parks. To what extent can these parks continue to absorb visitors before visitors begin to suffer diminished "park experience," before the facilities they demand defeat the purpose of the park, or before physical and ecological damage occur? The answer to these questions depends on the purpose of the park and what people want to do in it.

If the purpose of the park is to preserve natural features, any encroachment of man-made features will diminish its success. The greater the encroachment, the greater the diminution, until eventually it cannot be said to preserve nature successfully at all. On the other hand, if parks are primarily playgrounds for people, facilities such as roads, motels, and restaurants must be provided. It can be argued that if the visitor is prepared to walk, to sleep under a tree, and to cook over a fire, such man-made features are unnecessary. This is true, of course, but most people apparently do not like to walk long distances and do not like to sleep under trees, particularly if the trees contain large animals. Therefore, if most people are to enjoy national parks, these facilities must be provided. The degree of natural disruption caused by visitors can be partially assessed by the type of facilities they demand.

Living and transport facilities are demanded even if the visitor has no intention of doing anything but driving through the park. Pressure has been felt already in a number of national parks, particularly in Jasper and Banff National Parks, where sizable towns exist as a focus for demands. There has been considerable pressure on the National Parks Branch from inhabitants of both towns to permit expansion of townsite facilities to cater to more tourists. It is difficult to imagine a trend that could destroy the parks more rapidly than satellite urbanisation.

The most coherent demands for increased facilities come in parks which contain urban centres, but it would be a mistake to assume, however, that the increase in visitation affects only townsites. There is also a steady demand in most national parks for increased campground facilities. Campgrounds are less disturbing aesthetically than urban developments, but their impact can be severe because they are spread throughout the national park. One of the problems of campgrounds, of course, is that they cater to a seasonal demand. Most national parks still show a pronounced visitation peak in summer, and in some parks campground facilities are full only during the summer holiday weekends. Throughout the remainder of the year the demand could be handled with fewer facilities and less disturbance. Seasonality of demand applies to urban facilities as well, but if these are privately owned they tend not to cater to peak demands.

The most serious threat posed by the demand for facilities is widespread travel by car. In all the national parks that have suffered increased visitation, road systems are a major form of disturbance. Cars also cause air pollution and noise and pose a direct threat to wildlife. Provision of a road is soon followed by demands for service station facilities and parking lots. We seem to be making the same error in our national parks that we have in our cities—devoting an excessive amount of space to cars. If it is appropriate to make downtown areas free of traffic, surely it is also desirable to reduce motor traffic in national parks.

Increasing numbers of visitors accompanied by their cars inevitably cause traffic congestion and traffic jams are already a recognised part of the park experience in several national parks at peak visitation periods. This happens particularly in Banff and Point Pelée, although in the latter park cars and camping are now being phased out. Faced with traffic congestion, the National Parks Branch can follow three courses of action: it can restrict entry to the national park; it can attempt to expedite the flow of traffic; or it can build more roads. The first course will be discussed below; here it is sufficient to say that the National Parks Branch has not yet seen fit to restrict entry to any national park.

The policy followed to alleviate traffic congestion in most parts of North America is to "improve" roads by paving, straightening, and widening, permitting people to travel more rapidly in comparative safety. Improvement has all sorts of gradations, but the logical end point is a high-speed highway along which cars travel at sixty to seventy miles per hour. Although this may be reasonable in other parts of the country, it does not seem appropriate in a national park, where the park experience would require somewhat slower travel. This would seem obvious, yet a high-speed highway—the Jasper-Banff Highway— is exactly what has been created. If high-speed freeways such as the Spadina in Toronto and the Embarcadero in San Francisco are objectionable in cities because they make urban life intolerable, surely they are even more out of place in national parks. The Trans-Canada and Yellowhead highways are also examples of high-speed roads in national parks, but both were developed for transcontinental communication and are essential for that purpose. It is an unfortunate accident of history that the two most suitable routes through the Western Cordillera happen to traverse national parks.

It is to be hoped that the National Parks Branch will avoid developing high-speed motorways in national parks in the future. However, the third course of action is equally disruptive in the long run. The extension of road systems in national parks creates a tentaclelike disturbance of natural areas, which the parks system is intended to preserve unimpaired. Despite this apparent incompatability between road development and the objectives of the national parks system, the policy of the National Parks Branch in the western mountain parks is to promote road development, demonstrated by the provisional master plans for Jasper, Banff, Kootanay, and Yoho national parks.[2] In Point Pelée National Park road traffic is being phased out, which would indicate an apparent confusion of aims in the National Parks Branch. If road traffic conflicts with the purposes of Point Pelée, it must also conflict with the same purposes in other national parks. An interesting point is that the United States National Park Service has now rejected a similar policy of road extension in U. S. national parks. It is reasonable to surmise that is we follow the previous American practise of extending roads, we will eventually experience the same problems.

The promotion of road extension in the national parks is supposedly based on demand, yet relevant data and methods of collection have not been made public. Without this information it is impossible to assess the validity of the demand. The method of ascertaining the demand is important. A survey of visitors to national parks might indicate a demand for more roads, but the parks do not belong only to park visitors—they belong to all the people of Canada. Some of these may never visit national parks, yet they may derive substantial benefit from the knowledge of their existence. It is therefore important that the preferences of the total population be assessed. Table 15.1 shows the results of a comparative study carried out in the Albertan communities of Edmonton, Westlock, and Jasper, in which respondents were asked if they would like to see more paved roads in the national parks. The results are based on a small sample, but they suggest that the demand used for planning pur-

Table 15.1. Response to the Question, Would You
Like to See More Paved Roads in National Parks?

	Edmonton	Westlock	Jasper
In favour	40.7%	39.6%	54.1%
Not in favour	47.9%	48.5%	40.8%
No opinion	10.8%	11.9%	5.1%
Sample number	194	101	98

Source: Questionnaire survey carried out by the author in 1969 and 1970.

poses by the National Parks Branch may not represent the views of the majority
of Canadians.

The Impact of Visitor Activity in National Parks

We have shown that visitors conflict with the objectives of national
parks simply by their large numbers, but the degree of conflict depends to some
extent on the types of facilities demanded by the visitor. Many visitors are
content simply to sightsee along roads in national parks, but an increasing
number take part in various other activities, some of which greatly increase the
disturbance.

Classification of activities by disturbance caused is fairly straightforward. Obviously snowmobiling causes more disturbance than nature observation, but we can develop a more subtle classification, depending on the ancillary
facilities required as well as on the activity itself. Downhill skiing causes more
disturbance than hiking, for example, because it requires the artificial installation of ski lifts and the cutting of trees on ski runs. It should be understood
that this is a ranking of relative disturbance. All activities cause some disturbance, and many hikers can be just as disturbing to a park as a small number
of downhill skiers. However, unit for unit, downhill skiers cause more
disruption.

Once we have established a gradation of activities by the disturbance
they cause, we can identify some activities that are so disrupting that they
have no place in a national park. Among these snowmobiling is perhaps the
worst offender. Many reports of disturbance of wildlife by snowmobiles (admittedly not from national parks) exist, and damage is also caused to vegetation.
High and unnecessary noise levels are irritating and can be heard for miles,
particularly in mountain regions. At the time of writing snowmobiling is permitted in the western mountain parks; the National Parks Branch has taken the
position that it should be allowed until it can be proved to cause damage. Even
if proof of ecological damage is not forthcoming, snowmobiles destroy the
serenity of a park and therefore conflict with park objectives. Use of powerboats falls into the same category.

Other activities mentioned are considerably less disturbing. The degree of artificial installation involved in downhill skiing causes visual disturbance, but there is no indication that it causes physical damage or disturbance to wildlife. Its visual impact can be minimised by carefully planning ski facilities so that they cannot be observed from a wide area; the Marmot Ski area in Jasper National Park is largely hidden, whereas the ski runs at Lake Louise in Banff National Park are visible for miles. The same principle applies to the provision of cable car facilities to transport visitors to viewpoints; careful planning of such facilities can reduce their impact, but they still impair the natural condition and detract from wilderness preservation.

Several activities could be removed from national parks, although they do not cause extensive damage. These include such activities as tennis and golf, which do not depend in any way on the setting of a national park for their successful pursuit. It is a wasteful use of the national park resources to permit activities which can be carried on successfully in other areas. Although they do not cause great disturbance, they detract unnecessarily from the unimpaired natural condition of the park and conflict with current official interpretations of the National Parks Act.

The first classification of uses—by disturbance—can be used to determine the basic compatibility of activities with concepts of national parks. A second—use intensity—permits determination of the maximum number of people that should be allowed to participate in any activity in a given area. For example, swimming, fishing, and downhill skiing are intensive uses which can accommodate large numbers of people in relatively small areas. Cross-country skiing, hiking, and nature observation are extensive uses which can tolerate fewer people. The permissible user density for any activity can be termed the *carrying capacity,* an extension of a concept derived from wildlife biology.[3] The carrying capacity for any particular use may be determined on the basis of three criteria:

1. Will the number of participants cause mutual danger or danger to those taking part in other activities?

2. Will the number of participants reduce pleasure from the activity?

3. Will the number of participants cause physical or ecological damage to the park environment?

These criteria would appear to be fundamental to any management of outdoor recreational areas, but surprisingly little work has been done on any of them. The first criterion does not apply to all activities. Some activities, such as mountaineering, are inherently dangerous regardless of the number of people involved; others, such as sightseeing, are inherently safe. The activities concerned are those which are reasonably safe when participants are few but which become dangerous when crowding occurs. A good example is water-skiing. Some activities are obviously incompatible with one another, such as water-skiing and swimming.

The second criterion is difficult to apply because the pleasure derived from participation in an activity is subjective and depends on many factors other than user density, such as weather, mood, and performance. The principle of a relationship between user density and quality of experience can be clearly established, however. A density of 100,000 people per square mile may be entirely appropriate for a football game and may increase the pleasure derived, but the same density on hiking trails would cause an acute reduction of pleasure. After sufficient study it should be possible to determine the optimum and maximum densities for all activities carried on in the park. Very little study has been completed on the quality of experience in outdoor recreation, although it is a critical subject in park management.

The first two criteria apply only to carrying capacity in relation to recreational use of national parks. The third criterion is of greater importance, for it relates to the whole question of visitation in relation to impairment of natural areas, regardless of the purpose of the visitation. If too many people are allowed into a park area, physical deterioration will occur. Deterioration may take many forms, such as a decline in the quality of lake waters used for recreation and destruction of vegetation on heavily used trails and campgrounds.[4] Frequently damage to vegetation will also trigger soil erosion or slumping, with rapid extension of damage.[5] Little is yet known about the physical effects of recreational use in Canada although studies of the impact of use on lake quality the ecological effect of trail use are in progress. Of particular interest is the resistance and recuperative power of various ecosystems, a serious concern along high-altitude trails in the mountain parks, where ecosystems are as sensitive to damage and as slow to recuperate as those in Arctic and subarctic areas.

Mountain trail use is the subject of a thorough study in Banff and Yoho national parks by J. W. Thorsell, [6] which, although it is strongly oriented toward user response, does provide examples of overuse. Use in some areas was so heavy that hard surfacing became necessary to avoid severe damage. Obviously this use and the remedy impairs natural preservation and does not conform to the present national parks policy. As Thorsell points out, however, the damage was not always due to overuse, but sometimes to the use of bulldozers to "create" trails. On the higher trails the frequent use of packhorses and trail riders was particularly damaging, and on the lower, more popular trails conflict developed between trail riders and hikers.

Visitors and Park Wildlife

The rapid increase in visitors and consequent overcrowding are the fundamental problems facing national parks in this country; most other difficulties are caused or are strongly influenced by this situation. Interaction between visitors and wildlife is a prime example. As visitation increases and road networks extend into formerly wild areas of the parks, home ranges are intruded upon, and inevitably contact and conflict arises. This may cause immediate danger to visitors, although the long-term effect is almost inevitably to the disadvantage of wildlife. Before discussing such contact in detail, one point should be made. Many people who have studied wildlife in national parks agree that many animals are aware that they are in a wildlife sanctuary and therefore no longer retain their innate fear of humans and are more frequently met.

Most encounters between animals and humans are unintentional, at least initially, and are by-products of the activities involved. Three situations may arise: chance meetings in back areas of parks, collision with wildlife along highways, and the attraction of wildlife to campgrounds and settlements. All these situations are potentially dangerous or destructive.

Chance meetings in areas remote from roads are relatively frequent and become more so as roads are extended. Most meetings involve hikers and are usually random, although they tend to occur along game trails, which are convenient for hikers. The degree of danger depends entirely on the species encountered and the circumstances. The meeting is usually sudden and often results in mutual flight. It is generally agreed that few animals will attack under such circumstances unless their line of retreat is barred or their offspring are present. It is difficult to generalise, but it appears that the instinct to flee is a sound reaction except in encounters with grizzly bears. The etiquette for such occasions has not been clearly established, but to run is certainly not correct. The grizzly is curious and has poor eyesight; to run is to excite curiosity yet to remove the means of satisfying it, thereby inviting an angry charge. There are nine recorded incidents with grizzly bears in Canadian national parks, all of which took place more or less in back areas. Only one was fatal (in 1929), and there was no definite proof that a bear was in fact responsible for the death. Presumably more encounters have remained unreported because no ill effects resulted. Bears were involved in most of the recorded episodes,[7] although some meetings with cougars are also on record. All recorded incidents took place in Jasper, Banff, Yoho, and Kootenay national parks.

No data are available on the incidence of collision with wildlife along highways or railroad tracks, but discussions with park officials and others suggest that these are increasing in frequency. Canadian National Railways workers interviewed in Jasper feel that the amount of wildlife killed along railway tracks is significant, particularly in winter, when the tracks form an easy route through deep snow. Highways serve the same function, and road kill is particularly high in fall and winter, when animals are driven down from high areas in search of food. Considerable damage also occurs to cars, and sometimes occupants are severely injured. One highway problem that is becoming serious with increased park visitation is the occurrence of traffic jams wherever animals are close to the road. This involves chiefly deer or black bears and in the mountains, bighorn sheep. The problem is serious because the location is unpredictable and because of the high-speed travel in some parks. It is only a matter of time before a car traveling at 60 mph will come around a blind corner and plough through an assorted collection of animals, tourists, cars, and cameras. Will we wait until then to question the wisdom of encouraging high-speed travel in national parks?

The most frequent encounters between animals and humans occur in campgrounds and campsites, where animals are attracted by scraps and foodstuffs. Here unintentional and intentional contact tend to merge. Animals, particularly bears, are attracted by the ready food supply of town garbage dumps and campground garbage cans. The original attraction is therefore unintentional, but the animals rapidly become a centre of attraction. Until recently, the town garbage dumps in Jasper and Banff were recognised as prime bear-viewing areas. Some hotels try to attract bears for the delectation of guests, despite the fact that this was one of the primary causes of the 1967 Glacier National Park disaster in the United States.[8] The National Parks Branch has recently closed the open dumps in Jasper and Banff and has forbidden access to visitors, but it will be some time before the effect on the bears' behaviour disappears. In the meantime, bears accustomed to feeding at garbage dumps will look for other sources of food, particularly in campgrounds. This has already been reported in some United States national parks, where a similar policy has been followed.

The problem of attracting animals to campgrounds is perhaps more serious, for there is a greater potential for contact, particularly with children. Inevitably someone will try to feed the animals despite instructions to the contrary. In a questionnaire study we found that many people are prepared to feed animals, although they know that this is not permitted. People expect an animal to be able to distinguish between the food it is allowed to have (that is, the food it is offered) and that which it is not. When the animal attempts to extend its attention to the forbidden supply, conflict results. The fundamental difficulty is that people do not respect the fact that the animal is wild and expect it to react as a human being or a domesticated animal. The origins of this "zoo" mentality are unknown, but it is almost certainly influenced by the array of humanised animals with which we are all familiar, such as Smoky the Bear, Gentle Ben, and Winnie the Pooh.

The discussion has concentrated on bears, for these are the most dangerous animals with which most park visitors are liable to come in contact. It is important to emphasise, however, that virtually all the animals in national parks are potentially dangerous if not treated with respect. A mule deer in velvet with razor-sharp hooves is a formidable and dangerous animal, made more so by the fact that most visitors would not regard it in this light.

The immediate effect of interaction between wildlife and people may be human injury, but the eventual outcome is to the detriment of wildlife. After any incident, particularly one involving serious injury, an outcry arises that parks are for people and dangerous animals should be eliminated. This reached major proportions after the Glacier deaths.[9] To their credit, national park authorities in both Canada and the United States refused to be stampeded into rash action. However, a series of incidents of this sort would probably generate irresistible public pressure, which could result in the elimination of some species from the parks.

The dangerous forms of wildlife are not the only ones to suffer from human impact on the national parks. The shy species of birds also suffer, particularly if roads approach nesting areas. Roads close to lakes are especially damaging, because many species, such as loons, nest along the lake margins. On the other hand, some birds have no objections to humans—the "whiskey-jack" certainly thrives in campgrounds. However, the net effect of an increase in all forms of interaction between wildlife and humans will be a decline of wildlife populations and probably of species.

Wildlife Management in National Parks

Interaction between people and animals in national parks inevitably results in some need for wildlife management. This may involve hunting and shooting a bear that has attacked a person, removal to a remote area of a bear that has caused damage, and many other forms of management. This is controversial, for it apparently conflicts with the maintenance of an unimpaired natural environment. Part of the conflict arises from the difficulty of establishing parks that can operate as ecological units in isolation; all but the very largest parks are affected by conditions in surrounding areas. It is also partly caused by an early belief that parks should be maintained as "museums of nature," with the clear understanding that they should not change. This is unrealistic, for no natural system is static and any attempt to make it so will result in imbalance necessitating reparative management. This creates a vicious circle in which some management begets more management.

One of the most troublesome wildlife problems in national parks is the explosion, or irruption, of some ungulate species that lack strong territorial demands. The wapiti has been particularly difficult, although the real problem dates from the period when predation was generally regarded unfavourably and wolf populations in the park were reduced to a very low level. (In fact, the wolf was virtually extirpated from many parks, partly intentionally and partly because parks did not include the animals' complete range, and they were persecuted in the portions lying outside the parks.)[10]

Reduction in natural predators removed the natural check on wapiti, and the resulting irruption caused severe overuse of the range. To keep wapiti populations in check it has been necessary to make periodic culls in the parks under the strict supervision of park authorities. This has generated controversy, for strict preservationists believe that such management is at odds with park objectives, while hunting groups feel that the need to cull herds is a good reason to allow recreational hunting in national parks. However, recreational hunting in national parks conflicts with all current ideas on the purpose of national parks, and there are sound practical reasons why it should not be permitted. First, recreational hunting is difficult to control and would probably result in loss of human life and frequent wounding and maiming of animals, as it has virtually everywhere that it occurs. National parks should be one area where both wildlife and humans have some protection—to permit public hunting in national parks would be to drive a wedge into parks policy that would eventually destroy the complete national park ideal. Second, hunters would tend to produce an unnatural population by killing older, large male animals for trophies, virtually ignoring other age and sex groups. The Leopold Committee report on wildlife management in the United States national parks opposed recreational hunting in parks after an extensive review.[11]

One alternative to shooting excess animals is to plan parks carefully so that part of the animals' winter range lies outside the boundaries.[12] Animals would then be subjected to recreational hunting in this portion of the range. This solution has been successfully applied in Waterton Lakes National Park. It has some advantages over culling within the park, but it does not overcome the difficulty of selective killing, producing unnatural populations. Another possibility is the trapping and transportation of excess animals, but as the Leopold Committee pointed out, this is expensive ($50 to $150 per animal) and depends on an understocked range to receive the animals. The ideal but difficult solution would be to restore natural predators to a level at which they could again act as an effective population control.

Overpopulation of ungulates in some national parks is also partly caused by continued reduction in the available range as a result of protection against fire and road construction. Protection against fire was an inevitable consequence of the early view of parks as museums and reflected a general belief that forest fires detract from nature preservation. In fact, forest fires are an entirely natural occurrence even in the absence of man. At the present time some 70 percent of the forest fires in the western mountains of North America have natural causes, most frequently lightning. The effect of repeated fires has been to maintain areas of open grassland and parkland—lower successional stages which, as pointed out in chapter 12, are more suitable for many species than climax forests. Because of protection from fire, lower successional stages are gradually being eliminated, and climax forest is encroaching. This has been important in the Bow and Athabasca valleys, in Banff and Jasper national parks, where mature spruce forests are invading aspen parkland.

Another problem associated with prolonged protection against forest fires is the accumulation of large quantities of fire fuels, such as dead and dry timber. The result is an increasing danger of serious forest fires which could damage parks for many purposes. A dry summer in many parks creates a tense situation, particularly because rising visitation greatly increases the risk of accidental or intentional ignition. Many people feel that some form of selective, controlled burning is advisable, for both wildlife and human safety. The problem now is that in some parks the build-up of fuels has reached a point where the introduction of selective burning could be hazardous, and there is some doubt whether technical expertise is adequate for controlled burning on the scale necessary.[13]

The second factor, road construction, has been of particular significance in the western mountain parks. Most roads follow valley bottoms, which are almost without exception important winter wildlife ranges. Road construction reduces the area of range available, and although the actual percentage of the land area affected may be small, it is of immense importance to the species which depend on these winter ranges. Most of the upper mountain ranges are not only inaccessible in the winter but are too severe climatically for many animals. The unique importance of the valley bottoms has not been generally recognised in park planning, particularly in Banff National Park, where few valleys now remain free of roads.

The need for wildlife management in national parks will continue in the future because of the inherited situation and increasing visitation. With the artificial absence of fire and predators, this will promote atypical, unbalanced flora and fauna. Thus, although the parks may serve as important recreational or wilderness areas, they may be of little use as natural control areas for scientific research.

Leases and Concessions in National Parks

Most of the problems of park management and operation discussed so far are directly related to the numbers of visitors. Some problems are essentially independent of visitation, although they are affected to some extent by it. One contentious issue in Canadian national parks in recent years has been the continued existence of privately held leases. The problem of resource exploitation leases has already been discussed, but in some parks private residential or commercial leases are equally problematic.

The policy of granting leases in the national parks originated in the Rocky Mountains Park Act of 1887 to provide a means whereby the government could encourage development in the parks without relinquishing control over it. Leases were originally for periods of forty-two years at nominal rents, with provision for repeated renewals of forty-two years. The federal government retained considerable rights over leaseholds, including rights of rental review, restrictions on land use, review of lease renewal, and control over lease transfer.[14] However, these rights have not been strictly exercised and rents have been allowed to remain absurdly low, ranging, for example, between $8 and $100 per year in Banff. Unrestricted and profitable transfer of leases has been effected without profit to the Crown but with profits of up to

$20,000 to the lessee. Leases have also been renewed without close examination of the advisability of such extension. The effect of this policy is that many of the original leases have become virtually perpetual.

The real problem of the leasehold situation did not become apparent until the mid-1950s, when visitation to some parks began to increase sharply. Increased pressure on facilities encouraged unrestricted development, resulting in extensive urban sprawl and construction of summer cottages. In response to this, official control was increased after 1958. The policy of granting leases with perpetual renewal was ended, and most new leases were for forty-two-year periods, with provision for only one renewal of twenty-one years or in some cases no renewals. Appreciably stronger control over buildings standards and land use has also been exercised.

Although the new policies will improve the degree of control over townsites in the parks in the future, the problem of existing perpetual leases still remains. Eighty-five percent of these leases are in either Banff or Jasper national parks. In 1970 the federal government moved to end these leases and to replace them by forty-two-year leases without renewal. This was prevented by a decision of the Supreme Court of Canada, which ruled that the perpetual leases could not be converted without lessees' consent. Strong objection has also been raised by attempts to institute a realistic rental fee for leased lands. The result is that an appreciable area of national parkland is still reserved for the exclusive use of a very small number of people, a situation that is not in the best interests of either the national parks system or the people of Canada. In addition to leased land, a small amount of freehold land also exists in some national parks. The largest portion is in Jasper and Banff national parks and is held by the Canadian Pacific Railway or Canadian National Railways. Point Pelée also contains an appreciable number of private freeholdings, which are gradually being bought out.

A problem closely related to the leasehold situation is the management of concessions in national parks. Park policy has been to encourage the development of services by private concerns. This arose because the park system developed at a time when the government was not prepared to vote extensive financial support. Although circumstances have now changed, the National Parks Branch still adheres to this policy.

It seems appropriate to ask three questions about the operation of services in parks: Is it necessary or desirable that they be privately operated; are they all necessary; and do they encourage exploitation of the parks? Some private concessions may be necessary, but others could be operated just as efficiently and perhaps with more moderate costs by the National Parks Branch. If profits accrue from concessions within parks, it would seem appropriate that they be used to the benefit of the national park system as a whole. Some services are essential, but others could be removed. It is not easy to understand how Madame Tussaud's waxwork gallery in Banff complements the attractions of the national park.

The third question is perhaps more crucial to the long-term welfare of the park system. Concessionnaires in some national parks are in a favoured position. Their operations are based in the pick of Canada's scenery, and a large clientele is virtually assured, drawn by the advertising of government agencies. In the case of ski area operations, roads into their facilities are constructed, maintained, and cleared by park authorities, giving them a competitive advantage over operators outside the parks. The ultimate result must be to encourage the development of facilities within parks, thereby increasing disruption. It seems that the best interests of the park system would be better served by stimulating developments beyond park boundaries.

References

1. L. Brooks, "The Forces Shaping Demand for Recreation Space in Canada." in Background papers for the *Resources for To-morrow Conference* (Ottawa: Queen's Printer, 1961), pp. 957–968.

2. Department of Indian Affairs and Northern Development, *Provisional master plans for Jasper, Banff, Kootenay and Yoho National Parks* (Ottawa: Queen's Printer, 1970).

3. J. A. Wagar, "The carrying capacity of wild lands for recreation," *Forest Science*, Monograph 7 (1964).

4. S. S. Frissell and D. P. Duncan, "Campsite Preference and Deterioration in the Quetico-Superior Canoe Country," *Journal of Forestry* 63(4) (1965): 256–260.

5. J. Densmore and N. P. Dahlstrand, "Erosion Control on Recreation Land," *Journal of Soil and Water Conservation* 20(6) (1965): 261–262.

6. J. W. Thorsell, *A Trail Use Survey, Banff and Yoho National Parks 1967*, Recreational Research Report, 33, National Parks Service — Planning, National and Historic Parks Branch, Department of Indian Affairs and Northern Development, 1968.

7. S. Herrero, "Human Injury Inflicted by Grizzly Bears," *Science* 170 (1970): 593–598.

8. A. Russel, "The People versus the Grizzlies," *Field and Stream* March, 1968.

9. G. B. Moment, "A New View of Conservation: Bears and People Don't Mix," *The National Observer* Feb. 24th, 1969.

10. W. A. Fuller, "National Parks and Nature Preservation," in *The Canadian National Parks: To-day and To-morrow*, edited by J. G. Nelson and R. C. Scace, pp. 185–198, Studies in Land Use History and Landscape Change, National Park Series No. 3, University of Calgary, 1969.

11. A. S. Leopold, S. A. Cain, C. H. Cottam, I. N. Gabrielson and T. L. Kimball, *Wildlife Management in National Parks*, Report of the Advisory Board on Wildlife Management to the Secretary of the Interior: (Washington D. C.: The United States Department of the Interior, 1963).

12. I. McT. Cowan, "The Role of Ecology in the National Parks," in *The Canadian National Parks: To-day and To-morrow*, edited by J. G. Nelson and R. C. Scace, pp. 931–939, Studies in Land Use History and Landscape Change, National Park Series No. 3, University of Calgary, 1969.

13. M. L. Heinselman, "Vegetation Management in Wilderness Areas and Primitive Parks," *Journal of Forestry* 63(6) (1965): 440–445.

14. R. G. Ironside, "Private Developments in National Parks," *Town Planning Review* 44(4) (1970): 305–316.

Chapter 16

Toward a Comprehensive
Canadian National
Park System

Despite the changing objectives of national parks policy and the variety of problems and conflicts which beset it, the national park system has survived without major impairment. It cannot do so in the future unless some management practises are changed. After almost a century of operation, the time is now ripe for a complete reconsideration of the objectives, functions, and success of our national park system.

There never has been general agreement on the purposes of the park system, but it is possible to identify four major functions among the welter of activities occurring in parks. The park system attempts to satisfy a demand for outdoor recreation in areas of magnificent scenery, to provide sanctuaries for the protection of wildlife, to preserve areas of wilderness, and to preserve parts of the Canadian national heritage. The order in which these are listed implies no priority, for all are legitimate functions serving genuine needs in Canadian society. It is important that all be accommodated; the question is the way in which this should be done.

Only in recent years has the national park system attempted to serve all four functions, and this has been done within a framework specifically designed for none of them. It was really not designed at all; rather, it grew in response to a variety of demands, pressures, and expediencies. It is therefore not surprising that the system is somewhat less than adequate. The remarkable feature about the system is not that it is inadequate but the degree of success with which it has operated so far. Despite this limited success, the park system is inadequate to meet the demands on it in two ways: the number and area of parks and the incompatibility of the activities encouraged in them.

Inadequate Area

Some of the problems of determining the area adequate for any activity have already been outlined. Practical application of the carrying capacity concept is in its infancy, so no precise measurement of the areal inadequacy of the park system as a whole is yet available, but some idea can be obtained from generalised data. The total area of national parks in Canada by the end of 1972 will be 52,890 square miles, which represents 1.37 percent of the total area of land and inland waters. Although the percentage of total land per se is of little significance, it is interesting to compare this with 1 percent for the United States, 5 percent for Africa, and 9 percent for England and Wales.

If the complete population of Canada chose to visit Canadian national parks at the same time, the population density in the parks would be 397 per square mile, a density exceeded only in urban areas. This is of little meaning, for it assumes that access is freely available to all parks, whereas in fact the northern parks are virtually unused by visitors because of their inaccessability. If the figure is adjusted to leave out these parks, the density becomes 1,597 per square mile. The question of access is important in determining the use which can be made and which is made of park areas, and in this respect the Canadian national park system is clearly inadequate. Only 6 percent of the total national park area is in the eastern provinces, where 73 percent of the population live, and most of the eastern parks are remote from major population centres.

These data are presented only to show the dimensions of the problem. Of course the complete population cannot visit the parks at once, but many foreign visitors contribute to attendance figures. At best, the total population gives some idea of the extent to which park visitation might grow and some indication of the sort of contingency planning that is needed. In recent years federal ministers have concentrated on the rate of growth needed in the number of national parks, but the number is of little importance compared with the area, for this will largely determine the success of the system.

Between 1957 and 1967 visitation to national parks increased 222 percent, but the area of national parks increased by only 0.5 percent. Since 1967 the increase has been 59 percent, including the large area of northern parks added in 1972, whereas visitation had increased by 19 percent according to the 1970-71 returns. The ratio of increase in visitation to increase in area is now favourable due to late additions, but it is not realistic to suggest that this favourable ratio will be maintained. Even if it is maintained, the brunt of visitation will continue to fall on a few parks. If the present level of park quality is to be maintained, some control over entry to these national parks is inevitable.

Restriction of entry to national parks

There is a general reaction against the possibility of controlling and perhaps restricting entry to national parks, but the example of the United States would suggest that restriction is inevitable if the national parks are to continue to serve any of their present functions. In U.S. parks it has been necessary to introduce a variety of entry controls to prevent overcrowding, including concession-operated campgrounds of limited capacity, as at Crater Lake National Park, Oregon, and ticket-controlled tours at Mesa Verde, Colorado.

Apart from a general reluctance to consider entry restrictions, two practical problems exist. The first is the question of carrying capacity. Until more study has been carried out on this subject we will have no precise idea of an appropriate level at which to start applying restrictions. The second problem is exactly which type of restriction to introduce. Rationing visits would be the most democratic form of control to introduce, but it is difficult to develop a system which would not become a costly, unworkable bureaucratic nightmare. In a rationed-visit system, for example, would a Torontonian have the same ration of visits to Banff National Park as a Calgarian, despite the fact that he may wish to visit it only once in five years? What would their relative ration status be at Riding Mountain National Park, for example? How would foreign tourists be incorporated into the system?

A more reasonable alternative is to control entry by modifying park entry fees, which are now far too low. It costs $2 for a permit to enter all Canadian parks as often as one wishes in one year, some of the eastern parks have free entry which, in a decade when one ticket to a football game costs two to four times as much, would appear to be a gross undervaluation of national parks. A fee of $5 to $6 would be more reasonable and would scarcely cause any hardship compared with other costs involved in park visits. The increased income could be set aside for land purchase to create further parks.

A mere increase of the park entry fee to $5 would probably have no effect at all on visitation, but if the fee were raised sufficiently to deter visitors, those deterred would presumably be from low income brackets. This form of discrimination is unacceptable, and any increase would therefore have to be differential. One possibility is to charge differential fees depending on the form of transport used to enter the park. The logic is that motor vehicles are a primary cause of disruption, and visitors should be discouraged from bringing them into park areas. The result would still be unfair, discriminating against people who are not mobile and against less wealthy motorists.

A differential fee based on the nationality of the visitors has been suggested. Some Canadians feel that because a relatively large percentage of visitors are foreigners, particularly in the mountain parks, it is appropriate to charge them more for visiting privileges. Apart from the undertone of xenophobia, some of the attributes of the Canadian national parks, particularly wildlife, are the property not only of Canadians but of all people, and all people should have equal visiting privileges. Perhaps of more importance, the institution of a differential price tag for our national parks would inevitably encourage somebody to regard them as a resource which should be sold to the highest bidder. National parks are too important for too many reasons to be regarded in this light!

The possibility of limiting visitors by restricting available facilities, particularly overnight accommodation, appears to be the fairest system. Such a system operates in some parks at peak visitor periods, although it is partially nullified by people who sleep in vehicles. A limit on overnight accommodation would not affect parks where day visitation is important, such as Banff, but it would help some. The major problem is that it would have to be run on a "first come, first served" basis, which would give local residents a distinct advantage. Also, it is not difficult to visualise the reaction of a person who drove from Victoria to Gros Morne, only to be told that the park was full.

None of the restrictions suggested are attractive and all involve some sort of unfairness. Yet if the choice is between an imperfect form of entry restriction and a deteriorating park system, we should opt for restriction. In doing so, however, we should maintain a flexible policy which would recognise that only a few parks yet face a visitation crisis. The major obstacle to the institution of any form of restriction is the difficulty of convincing authorities that the problem is serious and that the difficulties experienced in United States national parks will also arise here unless appropriate action is taken in time.

Uneven use of park areas

The problem of rapidly increasing visitation to national parks in both Canada and the United States is accentuated by the concentration of use around roads and tourist facilities. Even in the most crowded parks large areas are virtually unused; Yosemite National Park, portions of which have been likened to an urban slum, it has been estimated that 75 to 85 percent of the park area is almost devoid of visitors. This tendency for concentration was clearly shown by Thorsell's study, carried out in Banff and Yoho national parks.[1] He found, for example, that only 14 percent of the visitors who passed the east entry to Banff found their way onto trails in back areas. Even more significant, only 8 percent of trail users, or 1 percent of all visitors, penetrated more than eight miles from the highway. Similar results could probably be recorded in a number of other parks. It is clear that, inadequate as the total area of parks is, most visitors are in fact crammed into a much smaller area. It is not surprising that acute local overuse has resulted. If the reasons can be understood, some of the problems of the park system might be alleviated without the addition of large areas of land.

Several possible explanations for the intensely concentrated use of national parks can be suggested. The easiest is that most people are simply too lazy to walk any appreciable distance from their cars. Simple gregariousness may also be involved, and there are undoubtedly people whose visit to a national park is made more enjoyable by social contact. But laziness and gregariousness do not satisfactorily explain all aspects of the problem. The crux of the problem is still to decide whether people crowd together in national parks because they want to or because they have no option. Lack of data makes discussion speculative, but some possibilities should be examined. Many people presumably visit national parks because they wish to have some contact with the natural environment but use patterns suggest that such contact is reduced because people are crowded together in campgrounds near highways. It therefore seems that visitors crowd together in national parks not so much because they want to but because there is little opportunity for them to do anything else.[2]

It is important to realise how limited the range of possibilities is for many park visitors. Obviously there is a physical limitation, for extensive hiking and camping expeditions into the back areas of national parks require physical fitness experience and expertise in travel techniques. Another factor is the limited mobility of families with young children. These limitations may well combine to restrict the visitor to the vicinity of highways. A residual fear of direct contact with a natural environment, which appears to be a fundamental atavistic component of human character may also be involved.[3]

Two types of action can be taken to alter the pattern of use in national parks. The first—extension of the highway system—has been discussed. This would spread park use, but is would not solve the problem of lack of contact with nature, in addition to other objections already raised. The second possibility is that the limitations which restrict visitors might be partly eliminated and that foot travel into back areas might be increased. Obviously the National Parks Branch cannot do much above physical limitations, but carefully planned instructional programs could greatly increase the number of visitors who are competent to travel in back areas. The provision of day care centres for young children could also prove effective.

Instructional programmes would have two main objectives: (1) to attract visitors to back areas by lectures on the park environment, and (2) to train visitors in the techniques and use of equipment necessary to travel in back areas. Such skills as map-reading, elementary rock climbing, canoeing, and camping could be taught. Nash has proposed field training centres called "wilderness stations," where visitors could be given practical advice on wilderness travel. Although this is a new approach in North America, similar centres such as Glenmore Lodge in Scotland, have been run for years in other countries. Field training schemes such as the Outward Bound and Duke of Edinburgh Award schemes are based on the same principles. To some extent the object is popularisation of wilderness areas, and no change could hold more hope for eventual widespread support for the aims and sympathy for the problems of national parks.

Incompatibility of National Park Functions

The four major functions indentified at the beginning of the chapter are all to some extent incompatible, which results not in a total failure to perform the functions but failure to perform them well. Any attempt to combine them is a compromise, but an unequal one, for the most clearly identified and most rapidly expanding function, outdoor recreation, will eventually drive the others out. Even so, this function is hindered by the others. To achieve maximum success in the outdoor recreation function, national parks should cater to all types and quantities of recreational demand within their physical capacity. Every facility should be provided to this end, regardless of its effect on, for example, wildlife populations.

To function successfully as wildlife sanctuaries, national parks should be operated to one end—the maintenance of wildlife at the highest levels of population and quality possible. Essentially this entails running the national parks as extensive, unenclosed, open-air zoos, in which animals would be fed if necessary, weaklings would be culled, and inoculation and planned breeding programmes would be carried out with the sole purpose of maintaining high-quality stock to ensure each species' survival. The wildlife populations which would result from such management might well be of superior quality, but they would be hardly more natural than a herd of prize Friesian cattle.

Maintaining a park to preserve a particular part of the natural heritage simply involves setting aside an area to develop in an entirely natural way without interference. To be successful the area must be large enough to be ecologically independent. The area will not be managed in any way. Forest fires will be allowed to burn unchecked, disease to affect overmature trees, wildlife to pass through population fluctuations and possibly to disappear. The reserve would be invaluable for research or as a living museum of a heritage but a poor wildlife sanctuary and obviously a poor recreational area, lacking facilities and hampered by forests jammed with windblown and burned trees.

The requirements of the fourth function, wilderness preservation, are more difficult to identify, for wilderness is a subjective concept that depends on individual perception, as shown both in Thorsell's study on trail use and in Lucas's study [5] of canoeists in the Boundary Waters Canoe Area in the Quetico–Lake Superior area. In both studies it is clear that some people do not believe in wilderness, whereas others would probably regard Central Park, New

York, as a wilderness! Space does not permit a thorough review of the development of the wilderness concept, but this has been reviewed in a number of books, in particular, R. Nash , *Wilderness and the American Mind,* (New Haven: Yale University Press, 1967).

The recognition that wilderness is a subjectively defined feeling rather than a physical entity departs from the most widely held view of a wilderness described by Aldo Leopold as "a wild, roadless area where those who are so inclined may enjoy primitive modes of travel and subsistence, such as exploration trips by pack train and canoe."[5] This is also basically the definition recognised in the 1964 United States Wilderness Law.[6] Wilderness may also be regarded in a biblical role, identified by Nash,[7] as a place of sanctuary and solitary thought. The main difference between these two concepts is that one is basically physical whereas the other is essentially a state of mind. One is demanding in terms of space; the other may be found in small areas not necessarily remote from large urban settlements. The practical application of what may appear to be a semantic distinction is that we should not ignore the potential which small and perhaps not completely undisturbed natural areas offer for the realisation of wilderness experience. Recognition of the variability of the wilderness also means that, depending on a person's wilderness perception, it may be a function which is compatible with all, or none, of the other functions.

Attempts to Reconcile Activities in National Parks

If the major functions are recognised as incompatible, two choices are available if we wish the parks to fulfill any function successfully. The first choice is to abandon all functions except the one given priority. This choice is unacceptable, for all the functions are legitimate and should be served. The second is to separate the functions, to zone areas for different functions. The National Parks Branch has adopted this policy and has applied it in the provisional master plans for Jasper, Banff, Yoho, and Kootenay national parks.[8]

Provisional master plans

In the zoning plans five classes of area are recognised:

1. *Special Areas.*
Special areas are those which have unique or otherwise valuable qualities to be preserved and strictly protected. There are two general types: special ecological areas containing major plant types, animal habitats or research areas, and special historical or cultural features.

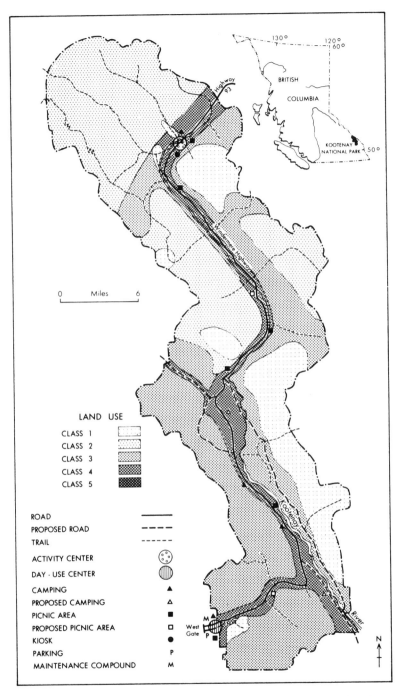

Figure 16.1. Provisional master plan for Kootenay National Park.
(Source: National and Historic Parks Branch).

2. *Wilderness Recreation Areas.*
Areas where the primary aim is the preservation of a wilderness recreation environment in contrast to a modern urban environment. Typical features include riding and hiking trails, primitive campgrounds, and wildlife habitat. Access by any type of motor vehicle is prohibited.

3. *Natural Environment Areas.*
Areas to act as buffers between wild terrain and more developed areas, presenting a natural background to developed facilities. The permissible uses are the same as in class 2 areas, but higher intensities are allowed.

4. *General Outdoor Recreation Areas.*
Defined as areas within the limits of existing and potential development including highway corridors, roads, campgrounds, viewpoints and other outdoor activity areas. They will be intensive use areas, which may require trails, paths, campsites, roads, parking lots and draining systems.

5. *Intensive Use Areas.*
Essentially urban areas which would serve as visitor service centres. Development would be controlled by urban planning and zoning, including aesthetic criteria.

The principle of zoning—the separation of mutually incompatible functions into separate areas—is sound, but its application in the provisional master plans is faulty, both generally and in detail. The provisional master plans fail to recognise that some of the areas provided for special functions are totally inadequate. This applies particularly to provision for wildlife, which require large areas free from disturbance and also protection of both winter and summer ranges.

The exact areal requirements of many species are not fully known, but it is believed that only the largest national parks are sufficient in area to ensure the survival of wolves. Unless the protected area is large enough to provide for all components of park ecosystems, a natural wildlife population will not survive, and wildlife management will be necessary. The application of the provisional master plans would create areas which are too small to be viable as wildlife preserves. The only two zones which can be regarded as potential wildlife preserves are zones 1 and 2. In Banff National Park, for example, these include 55.3 percent of the park area, or 1,419 square miles, and in Kootenay National Park they include 47.6 percent, or 258.3 square miles. Nature preservation is receiving at least its fair share of the total area; however, the area is too small for some species. This would be true even if the area was in one block, whereas it is usually divided into a series of isolated units.

The second problem is that even if the space provided is sufficient, unless it includes the necessary range areas many species will not survive. As already mentioned, in the western mountains many of the valley bottoms are important winter ranges, but most of these have been placed in zones 3, 4, and 5 in the provisional master plans. In the Banff plan no river valley of any size is included in zones 1 and 2, and the plan is in fact proposing a further major encroachment on winter range land with the Cascade Pipestone Road. (As a result of public hearings during 1971 this was removed from the plan.) The same is true of the proposed Ottertail Valley and Amiscwi Valley roads in Yoho National Park and the proposed Fortress Lake Road in Jasper National Park. The net result is that although nature preservation appears to have been generously treated in the provisional master plans, in fact, in the areas where it really matters, other park functions have been given complete priority.

It may seem an error not to include zone 3 lands, the natural environment areas, with nature preserves. This was intentional, for some of these areas cannot act as nature preserves. In Banff National Park, for example, Lake Minnewanka is classed as zone 3, an area where powerboats would be permitted. The same applies to Maligne Lake in Jasper National Park.

The fundamental fault with the application of zoning in the provisional master plans is the assumption that the zone boundaries can provide protection against excessive development. At the present the major demand among visitors is for land in zones 3, 4, or 5. If visitation to parks continues to grow at the rate experienced in the past decade, strong pressure will develop to extend the areas allotted to these zones. Such expansion would be at the expense of areas zoned as 1 and 2, which, as shown above, are already inadequate for their intended functions. The National Parks Branch believes that this pressure can be resisted, and states, for example, that "it is unlikely that any portions (of class 3 lands) would be reclassified to class 4."

This opinion does not appear to have adequate grounds. Several provisions in the plans already yield to developing pressures, such as the proposed Maligne-Poboktan Road in Jasper National Park, which would change an existing wilderness area into a zone 3 area. Likewise, the National Parks Branch has already shown its willingness to compromise zone boundaries by permitting satellite urbanisation to develop. Lake Louise in Banff National Park and Pocahontas and Sunwapta in Jasper National Park for examples. It seems probable that the zones established in the provisional master plans will be allowed to change in the future and that such change will be to the detriment of wilderness and nature preservation. It is also probable that the changes will be in response to visitor pressure and demands. To plan in response to such pressure is inappropriate, for, as pointed out in chapter 15, the wishes of visitors to parks do not necessarily represent the wishes of the whole Canadian population, to whom the parks belong.

Even if demands for the expansion of zone 3, 4, and 5 lands represent the wishes of Canadian people at present, there is no guarantee that they will do so in the future. The primary mandate of the National Parks Branch is to preserve the parks in an unimpaired condition for "the enjoyment of future generations." To fulfill this mandate the branch must consider not only present demands but must forecast future needs. Any areas allowed to develop into zone 4 or zone 5 lands cannot be reclassified as zone 1 for generations. A major demand for wilderness areas may well occur within a much shorter period; in the United States, for example, hiking is the most rapidly growing form of outdoor recreation.

All the functions of national parks are necessary and should be fulfilled. Their mutual incompatibility demands zoning separation, but such zoning cannot operate successfully within any one park. If we wish our national parks to continue to serve all functions, the only alternative is to develop a system whereby different parks are zoned for different functions.

A diversified national park system

A diversified park system was suggested in the 1964 statement on parks policy from the Department of Northern Affairs and Natural Resources, was discussed by Tyrrell,[9] and was clearly stated as a need by Chretien.[10] The current statement of national parks policy for the first time clearly recognises that the national park system is diversified in fact and function, although it is forced to conform to a universal policy. It states that "many . . . difficulties would be resolved if there were a more extensive classification of the areas which are now or which may be comprehended in the system,[11] and goes on to suggest four or five possible types of parks.

It is possible to conjure up a wide variety of diversified park systems, but a viable one must be based on two principles: (1) it must recognise the basic conflict between some functions and zone different parks accordingly, and (2) it must recognise that the national parks system cannot be expected to satisfy the complete recreational and preservational needs of our society. It is not appropriate that national parks be called upon to satisfy a demand which can be satisfied equally well by parks of provincial or local status, for this would be a wasteful use of a unique resource. A hierarchy of parks is needed for each major function.

The basically incompatible functions of national parks could be catered to by two types of national parks in addition to national historic parks. National wilderness parks could fulfill the triple role of wilderness preservation, national heritage preservation, and maintenance of wildlife species, albeit with some compromise; national recreation parks could serve the remaining function. In a completely integrated park system each of the national park types could be matched by equivalent provincial and local parks catering to local needs and preserving features of primarily local importance or interest.

Even if the basic concept of a diversified national park system is approved, it will take careful planning to develop a system that is widely acceptable. Not only must detailed regulations for each type and level of park be established but all existing parks must be examined to determine in which category and at which level they would best fit into the system. Some national parks which currently serve a primarily local function might have to be reclassified to provincial level and vice versa.

It is obviously impossible at this stage to suggest detailed regulations for various park categories. The outline of one possible type of differentiated park system is suggested below only as an example and a basis for discussion.

Wilderness parks. The basic purpose of wilderness parks would be to preserve natural areas free from exploitation or development. To fullfill this function they should be in as close to natural condition as possible. At a national level wilderness parks would be in areas remote from extensive urban, industrial, or agricultural development and from major transportation networks. Ideally they would be large enough to encompass all ecosystems characteristic of the landscape they are designed to preserve and to provide for the range requirements of all resident species.

Complete fulfillment of the functions outlined would require that roads and trails be absent and that travel be restricted to horse, foot, dog sled, or unpowered boats. It would require bans on all-terrain vehicles, snowmobiles, hovercraft, aircraft, powerboats, and all wheeled vehicles and would also require that no provision be made to accommodate visitors and that the parks be completely unmanaged. Fire control, predator control, planting of alien fish species (which has occurred in some national parks), and control and development of waterways would all be absent.

These requirements are suggested as an ideal for wilderness parks, but it is unlikely that a park system meeting these requirements could or would be set up in Canada. Areas which meet the criteria or sufficient areas to provide adequate representation of the national heritage would be difficult to find. For example, it would be virtually impossible to find any large area of prairie completely unaffected by man. To set up any wilderness park system would obviously require some modification of the stringent criteria outlined. With such modification some existing national parks, such as Wood Buffalo and perhaps Gros Morne and Kouchibouguac, could be incorporated. The Baffin Island, Nahanni and Kluane national parks would all be wilderness parks. Because most areas that meet the criteria of wilderness parks are in the north, the system might become unbalanced. To counteract this it would be necessary to establish parks in the prairies, in the southern part of the Western Cordillera, in the aspen poplar parkland, and in the boreal and eastern forests.

Some of the needs for wilderness parks can be met only by the creation of new national parks, but others could be met by the reclassification of land areas currently designated as provincial parks, provincial wilderness areas, or fish and game reserves. Although the possibilities are numerous, many would not meet wilderness requirements. In British Columbia, for example, Tweeds-muir Provincial Park has suffered considerably from hydroelectric power development and from lumbering. Ontario Quetico Provincial Park, classed as a zone 3 park in the Ontario classification system, has undergone some lumbering exploitation. This is not extensive, however, and lumbering has now been stopped by action of the Ontario government. The other great Ontario park, Algonquin (2,910 sq. mi.), which is also a zone 3 park, has suffered much greater alternation; over 75 percent of the park area is now held under timber licences.[12] To include this park in a wilderness system would involve a great relaxation of requirements. This is particularly sad, for the park was originally established in 1893 to be part of the fledgling national park system, but it was never ratified as a national park. This was also true of two of the large Quebec provincial parks, Mont Tremblant and Laurentide, which were established in 1894 and 1895 respectively. A number of the parks in Quebec have also been greatly changed by lumbering or by hydroelectric development.

Although both Newfoundland and Alberta have designated wilder-ness areas, in practise the degree of protection afforded is slight. In Newfound-land the wilderness areas are virtually unprotected, and extensive alteration by water management has taken place.[13] In Alberta the practical value of the three wilderness areas is limited by the belief of the Albertan government that resource exploitation and wilderness preservation are compatible land uses. Wilmore Wilderness Area in particular has been damaged by strip and pit coal mining at Grande Cache by the McIntyre Porcupine Company.

Provincial wilderness parks could be much smaller than the national parks, and they could duplicate exactly the type of landscape and wildlife preserved by a provincial park in another province. (At the national level, each wilderness park should be unique.) Ideally the provincial wilderness park would be protected as rigidly as the national ones, but realistically this would be unlikely. In fact, appreciably greater development could be permitted as the parks would not be expected to function as national heritage preserves. The other functions, wildlife preservation and provision of wilderness experience, can be carried out in the presence of some development, provided that it is carefully controlled.

The concept of a wilderness park at a local or municipal level would obviously be very different from that at the national or provincial level, and would provide wilderness experience only for those who can find it in small areas (this idea is not absurd; Thoreau's Walden Pond was only three miles from Concord). Obviously it could not serve as a wildlife sanctuary for large mammals, but it could provide a valuable refuge for small mammals such as rabbits and squirrels and for a wide variety of birds. Many cities in Canada have such natural areas, particularly along river valleys, which could be set aside as municipal wilderness or natural areas. They would serve a valuable pur-pose, for their accessibility would make them readily available as an antidote to the pressures of urban life in a way that would be impossible for national and provincial wilderness parks.

Recreation parks. The primary function of recreation parks would be to preserve areas of outstanding natural scenery for the use and enjoyment of outdoor recreationists. This implies that recreational use has priority, so that preservation would have to be compatible with recreational use. If, for example, conflicts were to arise between recreationists and animals, then the animals would have to be controlled and perhaps removed. It also implies that there would still be strict control over the type of recreation permitted. Ideally only recreation which is of necessity based on natural scenery would be permitted.

Concentration on recreation would infer that increasing demands for roads and facilities among tourist should be met as far as possible. At the same time careful attention should be paid to carrying capacities for each activity to ensure that overcrowding would not cause reduced enjoyment for participants. Toward the same end attempts could be made to spread recreational use through the parks as uniformly as possible. This could be done partly by some increases in roads, but visitors should also be encouraged to sample activities that would bring them into back areas. One important function would therefore be to inform visitors of the range of recreational possibilities available and to provide qualified instruction, as in Nash's suggestion for 'wilderness stations."

Diversification of visitor activities and more uniform distribution of use throughout park areas should reduce overcrowding problems for a period. Nevertheless, the whole question of carrying capacities for various activities in relation to user satisfaction would require careful consideration at an early stage of planning. To be successful, national recreation parks would have to be planned as part of a complete recreational system involving provincial and municipal recreation parks and recreational facilities operated by private enterprise.

Recreational parks would also differ from wilderness parks in that management would be a definite part of park policy, including forest fire control, clearing of dead and windblown trees, and the reduction of fire hazards by fuel clearance. To carry out such management effectively it might be necessary to permit some lumbering by selective cutting, preferably on short-term, nonrenewable leases. Likewise, some wildlife management, particularly of large predators, would probably be necessary.

It should be appreciably easier to set up a system of recreational parks than one of wilderness parks, as many suitable parks already exist. Obviously more parks would be needed, but provincial agreement would probably be more easily obtainable, as indicated by the case of Gros Morne and the former Newfoundland government. Administrative guidelines would require careful consideration, particularly with regard to the status of parks and the degree of resource exploitation permitted in them. At the national level resource exploitation would probably be excluded completely, apart from the forest management practises outlined. However, the prior existence of resource exploitation within a park should not exclude it from the system and parks such as Algonquin would be valuable despite lumbering activity.

Most existing national parks would be ideally suited as national recreation parks. Hopefully it would also be possible to include all the larger provincial parks except those suitable as wilderness parks. Parks such as Algonquin in Ontario (2,900 square miles), White Shell and Grass River in Manitoba (1,060 and 880 square miles respectively), and Garibaldi and Mount Robson in British Columbia (950 and 800 square miles respectively) would all be well-suited. Parks extending across provincial borders, such as the Cypress Hills parks in Alberta and Saskatchewan, would be of particular interest.

The last example raises the question of agriculture, for both of the Cypress Hills parks are extensively used for grazing. There could be positive advantages in allowing a certain amount of agricultural activity in recreational parks at all levels. Although agriculture is not strictly part of the natural scene, it need not detract from the landscape and may, in fact, add both interest and hospitality, as in British national parks where agriculture and recreation have been successfully integrated.

The inclusion of agriculture in national recreational parks would recognise that man is a part of the natural scene. This is true only if man does not disturb natural balances either by his presence or by his activities. The same principle applies to other species. Obviously man's activities do cause disturbance, as do a beaver's, yet they can be regarded as natural if they do not assume a disproportionate influence. In practical terms, people may be regarded as part of the natural scene only if they are not too numerous and if their activities do not cause sufficient disturbance to cause species imbalance. The same principle can be applied to landscapes; man's activities may be regarded as natural if they are integrated in such a way that they do not destroy the balance of the landscape.

Successful integration of man's activities into a natural landscape requires a degree of empathy with nature, and perhaps this can be developed only over a long period of time. Some successful integration has taken place in Canada, particularly in Quebec, but in general we have perhaps tended to superimpose our activities on the natural scene to a much greater degree than in countries like Denmark or Austria. The empathy with nature required for integration has been termed a "land ethic" by Aldo Leopold.[14] The development and extension of such a land ethic may be the most important function of national parks in our society and one which may have profound effects in alleviating some of our urban problems.

The successful implementation of a diversified park system would require setting aside considerable acreage for new parks. One advantage of the twofold system is that it would allow more flexible regulations over land use in recreation parks, and the possible inclusion of such uses as agriculture within national recreation parks might reduce the opposition of provincial governments to the creation of new parks. At the same time, two obstacles—loss of provincial control in perpetuity and the necessity for the provincial government to deliver land "free of all encumbrances"—would remain.

A new approach might help to overcome the reluctance of provincial governments to lose control over almost any land area in perpetuity. Control over lands allocated to the national recreation park system could pass to the federal government only for twenty-five years (or some other agreed-upon span), after which the provincial government would have the right to reclaim the land for resource exploration. If the right were unclaimed the land would continue in federal control for an additional twenty-five-year period. This system should not apply to national wilderness parks, which would of necessity be placed under federal control in perpetuity.

The second problem, the requirement for provincial governments to purchase back leases and to deliver land to the federal government without encumbrance, should be easier to overcome. A precedent has been established for the direct purchase of provincial land by federal government agencies, as the Canadian Wildlife Service has for a number of years carried out such purchases for wildlife preserves and wildfowl breeding grounds. There is no reason, other than budget deficiencies, why this policy should not be instituted. (The present national parks budget of approximately $35 million per year is clearly inadequate for many expensive land purchases in addition to park administrative expenses.)

Although expansion and rationalisation of the national park system is of paramount importance, the opportunities for making substantial amounts of recreational land available to the public by other means should not be overlooked. One possibility is to encourage the development of commercial recreation on private land. This policy is already well established in the United States but has just started in Canada. Another possibility is the negotiation of access agreements which would permit the development of long-distance hiking trails. In Britain the National Parks Commission is specifically charged with the responsibility for setting up such trails; the 250-mile Pennine Way is the first opened. In Sweden a similar trail called Kungsleden leads southward for 300 miles across the mountains from Abisko in Norrland. Perhaps the best-known trail is the 2,000-mile Appalachian Trail in the United States, which leads from Maine to Georgia, while the John Muir Trail in California and the 3,000-mile Continental Divide Trail in the western mountains, which ends at Waterton Lakes are also well-known. One major trail already exists in Canada— the 470-mile Bruce Trail, which runs along the Niagara Escarpment. Access negotiations are currently in progress for a 160-mile trail around Edmonton, the Waskehegan Trail, which will link sections of Elk Island National Park. The great merit of trails such as this is that they do not require capital or allocation of rights in perpetuity. Further, they do not require major reserves of land and can be set up successfully in small parcels of land that are of little use for other purposes, such as ridge tops and narrow river valleys. Pruitt[8] has proposed a Long Range Trail in the mountains of western Newfoundland, which would lie partly within Gros Morne National Park. One other proposal has been made, for a 300-mile Great Divide Trail to lead through Banff and Jasper national parks to other reserves, from Palliser Pass in Banff National Park to Mount Robson on the Yellowhead Highway,[15] with eventual extension to join the United States trail system.

Inventory for Park Development

One practical problem which will be encountered in attempting to develop and rationalise the Canadian national park system in the future will be attempts to identify areas where national parks should be located. In the past national parks have been developed largely by chance and expedience, at least in local siting. The result has been a system overweighted in area in favour of western Canada. The system also pays too much attention to natural peculiarities, like the hot springs at Banff and Miette, and not enough attention to typically Canadian landscapes, and it is therefore an inadequate representation of Canada's natural heritage.

It is also inadequate for some other functions. If the system had been planned by a perverse and malevolent genius, he could hardly have established a park system that could be guaranteed in have greater problems in wilderness preservation. Six of the most important national parks in area straddle the major essential road and rail links across the country. Inevitably such a conflict of interest has produced problems. We should not let our planning principles for the complete national park system be dictated by the measures essential in the western mountain parks because of their location.

It is unlikely that parks will ever be established in Canada as rapidly as would be desirable. It is therefore important that we select areas carefully so that the maximum needs can be fulfilled. Extensive work has already been carried out on land classification for recreational purposes, resulting from the 1961 Resources for Tomorrow Conference and carried out by the Canada Land Inventory, established under the Agricultural Rehabilitation Development Act of June, 1961.

An important criticism of the Canada Land Inventory classification is that it is preoccupied with the physical basis of recreation and pays little attention to the aesthetic impact of natural areas or exactly how this is created. The difficulty with attempts to classify these aspects is that they are usually subjective. L. B. Leopold has attempted to avoid this by developing a system whereby the scenic appeal of an area can be estimated by objective measurements.[16] Specifically, an objective criterion of exactly what makes a natural area unique and therefore worthy of preservation was advanced. Such methods are in their infancy in both the United States and Canada, and much development remains before they can be used as a tool to assess potential national park areas.

Another criticism of the Canada Land Inventory is that it covers only the rural settled parts of Canada and leaves vast areas of the country uncovered, particularly in the north. A vital planning need for inventory information from the complete country remains, including physical recreational data, wildlife information, and aesthetic landscape information. However, we probably will not obtain such comprehensive information in time to affect park development in this century. Our park system will probably continue to grow where growth is possible due to amenable provincial governments. Hopefully, in the future more attention will be paid to the needs of wilderness parks for inaccessibility and of recreation parks for accessibility.

Conclusion to Part Five

The Canadian national park system as it has developed is not adequate to serve the variety of functions expected of it in our society. This stems partly from an unclear concept of the nature of these functions and the conditions required for their successful fulfillment. The situation has also been confused by a changing government concept of park functions and is currently confused by indecision about how the parks should cater to increasing visitor demands, particularly as these will probably change in the future. Generally the National Parks Branch has carried out its confused mandate well and has retained in Canada an outstanding selection of basically unspoilt areas for the use of the Canadian public. The branch has perhaps been too willing to react to simple visitor demands and too reluctant to lead public opinion to develop a clear concept of the function and purpose of national parks in society. The future of the national parks system rests ultimately on public opinion. Its functions are diverse, but perhaps the most important is to develop in the people of Canada a "land ethic" and to provide a criterion against which they can judge their everyday environment and measure its change in quality. As Aldo Leopold wrote in 1941, "Wild places reveal what land was, what it is, and what it ought to be."[17]

References

1. J. W. Thorsell, *A Trail Use Survey, Banff and Yoho National Parks, 1967,* Recreational Research Report, 33, National Park Service Planning, National and Historic Parks Branch, Department of Indian Affairs and Northern Development, 1968.

2. R. Nash, "Wilderness and Man in North America," in *The Canadian National Parks: To-day and To-morrow*, edited by J. G. Nelson and R. C. Scace, pp. 66–93, Studies in Land Use and Landscape Change, National Park Series, No. 3, University of Calgary, 1969.

3. I. McT. Cowan, "Wilderness Concept, Function and Management," *8th H. M. Albright Conservation Lectureship*, pp. 1–34, (Berkeley: University of California, School of Forestry, 1968).

4. R. C. Lucas, "Wilderness Perception and Use: The Example of the Boundary Waters Canoe Area," *Natural Resources Journal* III (3) (1964): 363–378.

5. Aldo Leopold, "Wilderness as a Form of Land Use," *Journal of Land and Public Utility Economics* 1 (1925): 398–404.

6. S. Brandborg, "The Wilderness Law and the National Park System of the United States," in *The Canadian National Parks: To-day and To-morrow*, edited by J. G. Nelson and R. C. Scace, pp. 633–645, Studies in Land Use and Landscape Change, National Park Series, No. 3, University of Calgary, 1969.

7. R. Nash, 1969, *op. cit.*

8. Department of Indian Affairs and Northern Development, *Provisional master plans for Jasper, Banff, Yoho and Kootenay National Parks* (Ottawa: Queen's Printer, 1970).

9. J. M. Tyrrell, "Pressures on our National and Provincial Parks — Some Causes and Remedies," *Canadian Audubon* 28(4) (1966): 115–121.

10. J. Chretien, "Our Evolving National Parks System," in *The Canadian National Parks: To-day and To-morrow*, edited by J. G. Nelson and R. C. Scace, pp. 7–14, Studies in Land Use and Landscape Change, National Park Series No. 3, University of Calgary, 1969.

11. National and Historic Parks Branch, *National Parks Policy*, Department of Indian Affairs and Northern Development (Ottawa: Queen's Printer, 1969).

12. D. M. Pimlott, "The Struggle to Save a Park," *Canadian Audubon* 31(3) (1969): 73–81.

13. W. O. Pruitt, "The Newfoundland National Park Potential," *The Canadian Field-Naturalist* 84(2) (1970): 99–115.

14. Aldo Leopold, *A Sand County Almanac and Sketches Here and There* (New York: Oxford University Press, 1948).

15. J. Thorsell, "Proposal for a Great Divide Trail," *Canadian Audubon* 39(3) (1968): 70–77.

16. L. B. Leopold, "Quantitative Comparison of Some Aesthetic Factors among Rivers," *United States Geological Survey Circular 620*, United States Department of Interior (Washington: U. S. Government Printing Office, 1969).

17. Aldo Leopold, "Wilderness as a Land Laboratory," *The Living Wilderness* 6 (1941): 3.

Part 6

Conclusion

Chapter 17

Conclusion

All the issues discussed in preceding chapters are important in Canadian society, but inevitably many other significant environmental issues have been partially or totally ignored because of space limitations. At best it can be claimed that the issues discussed are representative of those which will govern the future pattern and quality of the Canadian environment. Whether they are necessarily the most important issues is debatable, for this depends on the nature of the society and environment we wish would exist in Canada. The choice of environmental objectives must be essentially a personal matter for each individual, because the nature of a preferred environment is dictated largely by personal taste and experience. The ideal environment for one person may be the epitome of discomfort for another.

The elusive and personal nature of ideals of environmental quality has undoubtedly contributed to environmental decline or at least has blunted the effectiveness of attempts to halt such decline. Nevertheless, it would be a mistake to suggest that all environmental issues can be judged only in a subjective manner. Certainly some issues can be judged objectively. If a pollutant is demonstrably injurious to health, it will cause a decline in environmental quality regardless of variations in definitions. The subjective element reappears, however, when one attempts to decide the relative importance of various pollutants. Some pollutants, such as 2,4,5-T, cadmium, or mercury, appear to be sufficiently hazardous to justify immediate control action and probably outright bans. Others, such as phosphates and nitrates, are more controversial. It will eventually be possible to objectively establish a priority listing for pollution control, but scientific and medical data are now still inadequate and are liable to remain so for many years. In the meantime we are forced into a subjective assessment of priorities more or less by guesswork.

A qualitative assessment of priorities among environmental issues is difficult, and it becomes infinitely more so when such issues are viewed in relation to other major issues confronting Canadian society. How important is control of pollution in relation to unemployment? In the ideal society we would undoubtedly have no pollution and no unemployment, but in our present imperfect world we have both. Should we stiffen antipollution legislation in full realisation that some industrial plants may be forced to close, or should we turn a blind eye to pollution in the hope that this may encourage industrial expansion and the provision of new employment opportunities?

The essential involvement of personal judgement in assessing many aspects of environmental quality has been stressed because it is of practical significance. The decisions on environmental issues that are taken by governments at all levels will affect the majority of the Canadian people. These decisions can be partly guided by experts from various disciplines on the basis of research data, but broad environmental objectives can only be decided by the personal evaluation of the Canadian public. It is therefore very important that we begin to consider the nature of the environment we would like to see in Canada. Which aspects of the Canadian environment are worth preserving or restoring? Attempts have been made in recent years to involve the Canadian public in debate on the nature of national social objectives. Such debate is equally desirable for environmental objectives. In our environment, as in our society, we can choose between unrestricted development and planned progression toward a preferred objective. It is safe to assume from the example of other countries and from parts of Canada that the product of unrestricted development would not be tolerable. What is the nature of the preferred environmental objective and what sort of positive action or guidance is necessary for its achievement?

Positive guidance on environmental matters has taken place in Canada in the past and at an increasing rate in recent years, with measures such as the Canada Water Act, the Clean Air Act and the establishment of a federal Department of the Environment. Such action has been piecemeal, however, and is oriented toward restricted objectives. We still lack a comprehensive picture of the environment we are trying to achieve. Is the present Canadian environment basically what we want or would we be happy to see a change to, for example, the type of environment which exists in Denmark or Holland. These countries are pleasant and certainly tolerable, but high population densities and a long history of settlement have created landscapes entirely dominated by man.

If spaciousness, low population density, and wild areas are among the preferred aspects of the Canadian environment, definite action must be taken to preserve them.

In deciding the nature of our environmental objectives we must remember that our physical environment is less forgiving than in many countries. In a moist and temperate country like Ireland vegetation can obliterate an environmental blunder in a few years; in dry areas like the prairies or the Yukon or the harsh cold areas of the Canadian north the consequences of mistakes may be with us for generations. It is therefore appropriate that we exercise great care in deciding our environmental objectives.

The achievement of a consensus of opinion on the manner in which the Canadian environment should develop is important, but it is only the first stage. The measures and methods required to implement environmental objectives must also be considered. What forms of action are necessary and effective? Can environmental objectives be achieved by educational changes alone or will new political initiatives be necessary? If so, should such initiatives be within existing party structures or will new alignments be necessary? How can environmental objectives be most effectively realised in the context of the existing federal-provincial division of jurisdiction? All these questions are important and urgently need discussion. The most important task, however, is still to make the Canadian public aware of environmental issues and to generate public discussion of alternative environmental objectives. Such discussion is urgently needed now, for the range of possibilities in environmental planning is diminishing rapidly. If this book helps to generate such discussion, it will have achieved its most important objective.

Index

Acts, legislative:
  Agricultural Rehabilitation Development Act
    (1961), 292
  Arctic Waters Pollution Prevention Act (1970), 15,
    103
  British North America Act (1867), 12
  Canada Shipping Act, 95
Canada Water Act (1970), 15, 20, 32, 35
  Canadian Food and Drugs Act, 61
  Clean Air Act (1971), 15
  Dominion Forests and Parks Act (1911), 247, 253
  International River Improvements Act (1955), 14
  Lands and Forests Act, 233
  Migratory Birds Convention Act, 233, 234
  National Parks Act (1930), 254–255
  Northern Inland Waters Act (1970), 15
  Ontario Game and Fisheries Act, 213
  Rocky Mountains Park Act (1887), 254, 273
Administration of Canadian wildlife, 234
Aerobic vs. anaerobic decay, 28
Aesthetics, environmental, 128, 156, 180, 189, 191
Agent Orange, 83, 85
Agriculture:
  environmental effect of, 7
  irrigation for, 132–134, 138–140, 154
  land lost for, 155–156
  water for, 142
  in national parks, 290
Air pollution, 15, 39, 43, 114
Antelope, 192
Arctic:
  development of, 111–113
  oil discoveries in, 95–96
Arsenic, 37
Atmosphere, insecticide residues in, 64–65
Attitudes, 236
  toward conservation, 232
  toward environment, 5–6, 9, 10
  toward nature, 243–244
  toward wildlife, 187–189
Auk, 209
Authority:
  fragmentation of, 14–15, 114
  for protection, 236

Bans, 298
  dairy products, 70
  DDT, 73, 75
  dumping, 53
  effects of, 76
  fishing, 56
  fungicides, 47, 51
  hunting, 51, 227
  insecticides, 73, 75
  killing, 223
  oil exploration, 95
  polluting agents, 31, 32
  2,4,5-t, 85
  in wilderness parks, 287
Bass, 174
Bears, 64, 68, 99, 173, 199, 204, 209, 213, 217,
    220–224, 228–232, 250, 269, 270
Beaver, 165, 177, 178, 191, 192, 193, 195–196,
    207, 235
Biochemical oxygen demand (BOD), 29, 33, 41
Biodegradability, 24, 30
Biomass production, 178
Biosphere, mercury in, 50
Bird watchers, 203
Birds, 47, 50–51, 63, 64, 67
  breeding grounds, 94, 129, 135, 177, 179
  contamination of, 54, 67
  effects of insecticides on, 67–68, 77
  poisoning of, 50–51, 236
  pollution induced mortality of, 67
  population declines, 178, 179
  predation by, 213, 235–236
Bison, 178, 192, 206, 207–208, 211, 217, 218, 224
Bloater (fish), 57
Bounty system, 213

Cadmium, 31, 57
Campgrounds, 264, 270
Canada:
  economic development, 6–11
  settlement, 6–7
Canals, 139, 142, 154, 160, 162–163, 164
  linings for, 140
Capital, for resource development, 10
Carbamates, 78

Carcinogens, 31, 72
Caribou, 97, 98, 107, 173, 192, 211, 212, 214, 217,
    218-220
Carrying capacity, 265-266, 277, 278, 289
Catfish, 29
Census taking (wildlife), 235
Central North America Water Project (CeNAWP),
    160-162
Char, 41
Chlor-alkali industry, pollution by, 47, 49, 52, 53
Chlorine, 43, 49
Cholinesterase, 76, 78
Climate:
  effects of, 5
  effects on, 174-175
Cloud seeding, 145
Coastal waters, pollution of, 53
Cobalt, 8
Coliform count, 28
Columbia River Treaty, 121
Concentration of pollutants:
  allowable, 55, see also Tolerance levels
  in birds, 54, 63, 64, 67
  cadmium, 56
  copper, 57
  DDT, 63, 64, 69
  in fish, 47, 52-53, 57, 66
  in foodstuffs, 56, 76
  in humans, 55, 69, 70
  insecticides, 63, 64, 66, 67, 69, 70, 76, 78
  in lakes, 52-53
  mercury, 47, 52-55
  in mothers's milk
  in plants, 76
  residual, 66, 67, 70, 76
  in seawater, 78
  in soil, 64-65
Conservation:
  beaver, 165, 195-196
  constraints on, 5-6, 10, 12
  first movement for, 9, 253
  fur animals, 196-199
  legislation, see Acts
  principle of, 11
  in national parks, 254
Contamination:
  defined, 45
  of fish, 52
  sources of mercury, 47-51, 53-54, 62
Continentality, 175
Control:
  detergents, 30-31
  effects of, 56, 73
  environmental, 14-15
  hunting, 223
  insecticides, 73-75
  international, 75
  land, 291
  legislation for, 14-15, 233-234;
    see also Acts
  oil pollution, 102-103
  pipelines, 111
  predator, 212-215

water pollution, 35, 141
  wildlife, 233-234
Copper, 8, 25, 57
Cormorants, 67, 68
Cosmetics, 69
Costs:
  pollution controls, 104-106, 113, 114
  resource waste, 53
  water, 144, 146-148, 155-156, 158-160, 170
  wildlife use, 190-191
Cougars, 213, 217
Coyote, 209, 213, 214
Cranes, 217, 218
Crows, 213
Cruelty in trapping, 199
Curlew, 217

Dairy products, contamination of, 70
Damming, 13, 153, 162-163, 165
  costs of, 13-14
  effects of, 157, 163-164, 165, 171, 173-174
Dams, 128, 131, 145, 156, 164, 171, 173, 176-178
  in national parks, 253
  proposed, 144, 157, 158
DDE, see DDT
DDT, 24, 62-79
  residues of, 65, 67
  resistance, 73-74
  toxicity, 63, 71
Decision-making processes, 4
Deer, 68, 191, 192, 206, 210, 236, 270
Defoliants, 83-84
Deoxygenation of water, 29, 41, 42
Depredation (wildlife), 99, 190, 209, 235-236
Desalination, 146
Detergents, 30-31
Development, ecological effects of, 21-22, 209-211
Dichlorodiphenyltrichloroethane, see DDT
Dilution, 20-22, 24, 32-33, 39, 41, 127
Diseases caused by pollutants, 28, 31, 34, 47, 57, 83
Diversion (river), 162-163, 167
  ecological effects of, 172-179
  Magnum scheme for, 164-165
  results of, 144, 157
Dogfish, 53
Domestication of wildlife, 228, 237
Drainage, 129, 141
Dry-weather flow (DWF) of sewage, 34
Ducks, 177, 179, 209

Eagle, 217, 250
Economy, Canadian, 6-12, 195, 259
Ecosystems:
  balance of, 190, 209, 271-273
  criterion of benefit or loss to, 178
  in national parks, 281
  rivers in, 128
Effluents, polluting effects of, 41-43
Elk, 68
Employment, 11, 44, 171, 199
Enforcement of pollution control, 44
Endangered species, 164, 178, 207-209, 217-231,
    236

Environment:
  constraints on control of, 4, 5-6, 10
  decisions affecting, 122
  defined, 3
  deleterious influences on, 11
  effects of herbicides on, 80-85
  effects of oil exploration on, 96-98
  effects of pipelines on, 106-109
  effects of recreational activity on, 268
  legislation concerned with, 14-15
  planned, 112
  priorities for, 122
  public awareness of, 262
Erosion:
  bank, 157, 160, 173, 179
  causes, 190
  shore, 156
  thermal, 156
  thermokarst, 97-98, 106
Eutrophication, 29-31, 41, 134, 178
Evaporation, 139, 144, 175
Evapotranspiration, 126, 140
Exploitation (resource), 6, 9
  barriers to, 9-10
  destructive, 195
  leases for, 248-249, 253, 255, 273-274, 289
  in national parks, 252
  phased, 112
  wildlife, 207
Extinction of wildlife species, 67, 178, 180, 193,
    204, 206, 207, 208-209, 217, 218, 225

Falcons, 67, 217, 236
Ferret, 217, 218
Fires (forest), ecological role of, 211-212, 220, 272,
    281
Fish:
  concentrations of pollutants in, 47, 52-53, 57, 66
  contamination of, 47
  effects of damming on, 174
  effects of pollution on, 41-42, 66, 78
  endangered, 217
  mortality, 66
  oxygen requirements, 29, 41
  population, 177
  tainting, 42
Fish kills, 25, 94, 173
Fishing:
  effects of pollution on, 41, 93, 94
  recreational, 56, 201
Fishing industry, effects of polution control on, 56,
    174, 202
Flood control, 135
Flooding:
  authority for, 14
  results of, 155-156, 171-173
Foam, pollution by, 30
Food, wildlife as, 55, 192-193, 207, 226
Foodstuffs:
  cadmium in, 57
  insectide residues in, 65, 76
  mercury in, 55

monitoring, 69
  pesticides in, 61-62
  pollution criteria for, 114
Forestry practises, 6-7
Fox, 98, 99, 196, 217
Fuel burning, mercury emission by, 50
Fungicides, 47, 49, 50, 51, 81
Fur trade, 6, 10, 191-196, 220, 226

Gannets, 67
Geese, 177-178, 179, 217
Godwit, 217
Gold, 11, 25
Goldeye, 52
Goshawks, 213
GRAND Canal, 165-167
Grebes, 63, 177, 179
Grizzly bears, 99, 199, 204, 209, 217, 228-232, 250,
    269
Grouse, 210
Growth (population):
  control of, 22-23, 85
  policy for, 148

Habitat(s) (wildlife):
  adaptability to changes in, 208
  damage to, 172-174, 177-179, 209-212
  management, 79
  manipulation, 197
  modification, 235
  nesting, 164
  requirements, 190
Hare, Arctic, 217
Hawk, 217
Health, hazards to, 27-28, 45, 54-56, 71-72
Herbicides, 80-85
Herring, 57
Hexadecanol, 141
Hibernation, 230
Hiking, long distance trails for, 291-292
Honeybees, 78
Hunting:
  control of, 51, 223-224, 227
  in national parks, 272
  recreational, 189, 199-203, 227
  results of, 220, 222, 230-231
  social benefits of, 201-202
  wasteful, 207
Hydrocarbons, 35
Hydroelectric power, 13, 121, 131, 134, 154

Ice, mercury content of, 54
Incinerators, mercury emission by, 50
Indian rights, 234
Industry, water pollution by, 37-56
"Integrated control" of pests, 79
International cooperation, 13
Insectides, 61-79
  alternative, 79
  toxicity, 63, 66-68, 71, 72, 77, 78
    See also DDT; Organochlorines; Pesticides;
      Residues
Insurance bonds, antipollution, 103-104

Investment, foreign, 10–11
Iron, 8
Irrigation, 132–134, 138–142, 154

Jurisdiction:
  public lands, 12, 247
  resources, 12, 247
  waters, 13
  wildlife, 233

Killing, defensive, 224
Kraft process, 40, 41, 43
Kuiper diversion plan, 158–160, 169, 170

Labrador duck, 209
Lakes:
  fluctuation of, 160, 161, 165, 172, 179
  loss of, 172, 175–178
  mercury concentrations in, 52–53
  park reserves for, 251
  pollution of, 65, 134, 141
  stabilisation of, 155, 158
  types of, 29–30
  water levels of, 141, 155
  water storage in, 125, 160–161, 164
Land, control of, 12, 247, 250
Land ethic, 290, 293
Landslipping, 156
Lead, 8, 25
Leases, in national parks, 248–249, 253, 255, 273–
    274, 289
Legislation (Canadian), 14–15
  protective, 207
  pollution control, 114
  relevant to control and conservation, *see* Acts
  wildlife control, 233–234
Losses:
  of agricultural land, 80, 148, 155–156, 171
  caused by pollution, 51
  caused by weeds, 80
  See also Wastage
Lumber industry, 6–8
Lumbering in national parks, 252–253, 288, 289

Magnum scheme, 164–165, 178
Magpies, 213
Man:
  -animal interaction, 99, 190, 224, 269, 270
  as part of the natural scene, 290
  wildlife threat to, 224, 228, 232, 269, 270–271
Marshes, *see* Wetlands
Martens, 210, 217
Mercury, 25, 31, 45–56
  contamination by, 54–56, 62
  as a pollutant, 45–56
Migration, 97, 107, 219, 221, 226
Mining, 8
  in national parks, 245, 252–253, 288
Mink, 68
Monitoring programs, 28, 69–70
Monomolecular films, effects of, 141
Moose, 97, 178, 191, 206, 210, 214
Mother's milk (human), organochlorine
    residues in, 70–71

Motor vehicles, 259, 264
  damage to vegetation by, 97–98, 106
  threat to wildlife, 269
Musk-oxen, 99, 217, 224–228, 236
Muskrat, 161, 177, 178, 196, 199, 235

Narwhal, 250
National parks:
  appropriate areas for, 292–293
  area of, 247, 250, 277, 290
  budget, 291
  Canadian development of, 247–256
  classification of, 286
  concept of, 244, 245
  first, 244–245
  functions of, 276–286
  legislation for, 254–255
  need for, 112
  obstacles to development of, 12, 248–249, 291
  opposition to, 250, 251
  overcrowding, 262, 268, 289
  overpopulation of, 272–273
  policy, 252, 253, 254–256, 265, 282, 286
  purposes, 244–245, 255, 263
  restriction of entry to, 279–280
  roads and traffic in, 264–265
  use patterns, 280
  value of, 254
  visitors to, 254, 262–263, 277–278
  zoning plans for, 282–286
Natural gas,
  deposits, 96
  pipelines, 111
Natural resources:
  in national parks, 248–250
  wildlife as, 189–204
    See also Exploitation; Resources
Nickel, 8
Nicotine, 79
Nitrates, 31, 33
North American Water and Power Alliance
    (NAWAPA), 152–158, 171–173

Oil:
  Arctic reserves of, 96
  industry, 8
  effects of drilling and wells, 98–99
  exploration and drilling, 95–98
  leases, 249
  spillage, 13, 93–95, 98, 107, 109, 110
  transportation, 99–111
Organochlorine insectides, 63–76
  poisoning of birds by, 236
  resistance to, 73–74
  toxicity, 72
Organomercurials, 43, 46
Organophosphorus insectides, 76–77
Osprey, 217
Overhunting, 207, 208, 214

Passenger pigeons, 206, 207, 209–210
Pathogens, 27–28
Pelicans, 67, 177, 179

Penguins, 64
Perch, 57
Permafrost, 97, 106, 125, 156
Pesticides:
   benefits vs. risks of, 61-62, 85-86
   control of, 114
   residues of, *see* Residues
   teratogenicity of, 84
   use of, 20
      See also Insectides
Pheasant, 47
Phenols, 43
Phosphamidon, 66, 77
Phosphates, 30-32, 33, 35
Phosphorus:
   essential, 32
   pollution by, 25
Pickerel, 177
Pike, 52, 177
Pipelines:
   oil, 106-109
   hazards of, 211
   natural gas, 111
Placental barrier, 46, 71
Planning:
   environmental, 112
   national parks, 282-286
   water sypply systems, 129-132, 144-145, 152-167
Plants, insectide residues in, 65-66
Platinum, 25
Poisoning:
   birds, 47, 77, 236
   honeybees, 78
   human, 46, 47, 55, 57, 69, 71, 77, 82
   for predator control, 214, 215
   shellfish, 78
   wildlife, 218, 235, 236
Polar bears, 64, 68, 99, 199, 217, 220-224
Pollutants, 30-32
   accumulation of, 24
   biodegradable, 24
   organic, 28
   phasing out, 50
   tolerance levels for, 21
   visual, 267
Pollution, 13
   abatement, *see* Pollution control
   aesthetic elements of, 28, 39, 156, 180, 189, 191
   defined, 19-20
   effects of, 27-32, 41
   legislation, *see* Acts
   malodorous, 33, 39
   measurement of, 28, 29
   oil spillage, 13, 93-95, 98, 107, 109, 110
   sources, 21-22, 26, 30-31, 137
   thermal, 30
      See also Contamination; Water pollution
Pollution control, 43-44, 141, 298
   cost of, 43, 113-114
   legislation, 15, *See also* Acts
   means of, 20-31, 134
   responsibility for, 15, 44, 57
   safety of, 57
Population:

Canadian, 7, 9
   control of, 22-23, 85
   growth, 138, 142-143
   and pollution, 21-22
Prairie dog, 217, 218
Prairie Rivers Improvement Management and
      Evaluation (PRIME), 129-131, 134, 178
Prairie Water Exchange Concept, 162
Predators, 190, 209, 220, 229
   control of, 212-215
   role of, 271, 272
   use of, 79
Preservation:
   national parks for, 253-255
   wilderness, 281
Preserves, 244
Protection (wildlife), 189, 250, 276
   authority for, 236-237
   bison, 207-208
   grizzly bear, 229, 231
   legislation for, 207
   musk-oxen, 226
   parks for, 250
   polar bear, 223
      See also Conservation, Preservation
Public, environmental desires of, 5, *see also* Attitudes
Public hearings, 5, 122, 131
Pulp and paper industries, 8, 29, 38-44
   pollution by, 47, 50
Pumpkinseed (fish), 53
Pyrethrum, 79

Radioactive waste, 24, 37
Recreation, 112, 156, 171, 181, 189, 199-203, 244,
      245, 291
   effects of pollution on, 41
   lakes for, 29
   loss to, 155
   national parks for, 253-254, 276, 281, 289-292
   in national parks, 255, 267, 284, 286
   planning for, 131, 135
   as resource use, 245
Recycling, 25, 32
Religion, 23
Reptiles, endangered, 217
Research, on wildlife, 204, 235
Reserves (wildlife), 197, 207, 244, 247, 254
   need for, 112
Reservoirs:
   as breeding grounds, 135
   capacity of, 153
   problems of creating, 156
   proposed, 158, 162
   recreational potential of, 131, 135, 155
Residues:
   concentrations of, 65, 76
   herbicide, 82
   in humans, 69
   insectide, 61-62, 64-72, 76
Resistance to insectides, 73-74, 78
Resources (natural):
   capital for development of, 10
   exploitation of, *see* Exploitation
   jurisdiction over, 12, 247

mismanagement of, 141-142
moratorium on development of, 112-113
supply of, 9, 25
waste of, 32, 53, 207
River basins, 125, 127
Rivers:
  diversion from, 144, 153, 158-160, 164, 165, *see also* Diversion
  flow volume of, 144, *see also* Streamflow
  fluctuating level of, 175
  length of, 125
  park reserve of, 250
  reduced flow of, 38, 157, 161, 165
  reversal, 175-176, 178
  total discharge, 126
Roads, 162-264
  damage caused by, 94, 271, 273
Ross' goose, 177-178, 217

Salinity:
  effects of increasing, 174
  of sea water, 175
Salinisation, 139-140
Salmon, 29, 41, 42, 66, 164, 174
Sanctuaries, 189, 196, 226, 234, 235, 237, 250, 276, 281
  damage to, 178
  reaction of wildlife to, 269
Sanitary land fill, 33
Saskatchewan-Nelson Basin Board, 131-132
Sea otter, 217
Sea water:
  desalination of, 146
  pollutants in, 78
  salinity, 175
Seals, 64, 68, 98, 192, 199, 217, 250
Seismic trails, 97-98
Septic tanks, 32
Settling lagoon, 32
Sewage:
  cost of treating, 35
  plants for industrial, 37-38
  pollution by, 27-32
  treatment and disposal of, 13, 32-34
Sewerage systems, 33-35
Shad, 174
Sheep, 173, 217, 250
Shellfish:
  concentration of mercury in, 47
  contamination of, 28, 47
  kills, 93
  poisoning of, 78
  salinity on, 174
Shrimp, 78
Siltation, 160, 179, 190
Silver, 8, 25
Skiing, 275
  environmental effects of, 266-267
Skuas, 64
Slimicides, pollution by, 42-43, 47, 50
Smog, 148
Sodium nitriloacetate (NTA), 31
Sodium tripolyphosphate, 30, 31

Soil:
  insecticide residues in, 64-65
  salinisation of, 139-140
Sovereignty, 102, 172
Sparrow, 217
Sterilisation, insect, 79
Streamflow:
  effects of diversion on, 173-174
  effects of reducing, 128
  estimation of, 126
  measurement of, 125
  reduction of, 172, 173-174
Submarine tankers, 105-106
Suckers (fish), 29, 52
Sulphates, 42
Sulphides, 42, 43
Swans, 164, 177, 179, 217
Swordfish, 53, 56
Synergism, 62, 72, 78, 84

Tankers (oil), 99-106
  submarine, 105-106
Teratogens, 31, 46, 71, 77, 78, 84
Terns, 68
Territoriality, 190-191
Thermokarst erosion, 97-98, 106
Timber:
  clearance, 135
  jurisdiction over, 12
  loss of, 173
Tin, 25
Tolerance levels, 69-70
  aresenic, 37
  coliform counts, 28
  detergents, 30
  for pollutants, 21
  provisions for, 61-62
Tourism, 252-254
Toxicity, 41
  cadmium, 57
  DDT, 63, 71
  herbicides, 80, 83, 84
  insectides, 63, 66-68, 71-72, 77, 78
  of pollutants, 31, 42, 43, 45-47
  selective, 77
  teratogenic, 31, 46, 71, 77, 78, 84
Traffic in national parks, 264, 269
Trans Alaska Pipeline System (TAPS), 109-110
Trapping, 98, 161, 178, 180, 190
Trophies, 22, 272
Trout, 29, 41, 53, 57, 66
Trumpeter swan, 164, 179, 217
Tuna, 53, 54

Uranium, 8, 11, 25
Urbanisation:
  around national parks, 264, 274
  results of, 148
  water for, 134
United States water supply, 137-149
United States Wilderness Law, 282

Vermin, 213

Visual pollution, 99, 267

Walleye, 52, 53
Walrus, 192, 250
Wapiti, 190, 214, 271
Warblers, 77
Waste:
 of natural resources, 8, 32, 43, 192
 of water, 139-141
 of wildlife resources, 207
Waste materials:
 industrial, 37-43
 pollution by, 20-24
 recycling, 25
 transportation of, 33-35, 127
Water:
 available, 126
 BOD in, 29, 33, 41
 deficit, 126
 demand for, 138-140, 142, 167
 effects of fluctuating levels of, 179
 forms of, 123
 loss, 139, 144
 per capita demand for, 138
 price of, 146-148, 158-160, 170
 shortage of, 137-138, 141, 147-148
 supplementing supply of, 145-146
 supply, see Water transfer
 surpluses of, 123, 126
 uses of, 127-128, 138-140
Water export, 13
 effects of, 169-180
 profitability of, 170-171
 proposals for, 151-165
Water pollution:
 control of, 15, 114
 defined, 20
 by domestic sewage, 27-35
 effects of, 41
 by industry, 37-56
 residue concentrations in, 65
Water transfer:
 benefits of, 128-129, 131, 132-135, 154, 170-171
 costs, 13, 14, 122, 128-129, 142, 144, 160-162, 170-171
 defined, 128
 feasibility studies for, 129-132
 means of, 142-144
 problems, 157
 projects for, 144-145, 160-162

small-scale, 167, 170
 social effects of, 180
Weather modification, 145
Weeds, loss due to, 80
Western States Water Augmentation Concept, 162-164, 172
Wetlands:
 drainage of, 129
 drying up of, 75-78, 172
Whale, 53, 192, 250
Whitefish, 174
Whooping crane, 218
Wilderness:
 concept of, 281-282
 parks, 287-288
 preservation of, 276
Wilderness stations, 280, 289
Wildlife:
 attitudes toward, 187-189
 current status of, 236-237
 damage by, 99, 190, 209, 235-236
 danger from 224, 228, 232, 269, 270-271
 decline in, 67, 177, 178, 179, 206-212, 218, 220
 depletion of, 90, 192
 disturbance of, 97-99, 107, 156, 164, 227, 266
 domestication of, 228
 elimination of, 165, see also Extinction
 as food, 55, 192-193, 207, 226
 -human interaction, 99, 190, 224, 269, 270
 impact of park visitors on, 266
 increases in, 210, 211, 226
 jurisdiction over, 12, 233
 management, 271-273
 in national parks, 269
 protection of, 189, 207-208, 223, 226, 236-237, 250, 276
 reasons for maintenance of, 204
 research on, 68-69, 235
 uses of, 189, 191-204
 value of, 202, 204
 See also Habitats
Wolf, 190, 209, 217, 220, 271
Wolverines, 210
Wolves, 210, 213, 214, 284
Woodcock, 67, 68

Zinc, 8, 25, 42
"Zoo" mentality of public, 270
Zoos, wildlife reduction by, 222, 226, 227
Zoning, national parks, 282-286